James Gibbons Huneker

James Gibbons Huneker in 1912

JAMES GIBBONS HUNEKER

Critic of the Seven Arts

ARNOLD T. SCHWAB

STANFORD UNIVERSITY PRESS

Stanford, California

1963

STANFORD UNIVERSITY PRESS
STANFORD, CALIFORNIA

© 1963 by the Board of Trustees of the
Leland Stanford Junior University

All rights reserved

Library of Congress Catalog Card Number: 63-14131

PRINTED IN THE UNITED STATES OF AMERICA

Published with the assistance of
the Ford Foundation

To my mother and father

PREFACE

Although James Gibbons Huneker, the most versatile and one of the most entertaining and influential of American critics, died more than forty years ago, no biography of him has heretofore been written, mainly because of the reluctance of his widow—who survived him by almost three decades—to have certain embarrassing aspects of his life revealed during her lifetime. Another reason, perhaps, was that his autobiography *Steeplejack* (upon which, I should state, I have had to rely for particulars unavailable elsewhere—not always comfortably, because of Huneker's reticence on private matters and his extravagant Celtic imagination and sense of the dramatic) may have given naïve potential biographers the impression that nearly everything important had been told. Then, too, Huneker's remarkable versatility may have scared off those more prudent persons who were not equally at home in the seven arts—as indeed I am not—and who declined to rush in where even specialists have only tiptoed.

For, surprisingly enough, no thorough study has appeared of Huneker's work in any *one* of the arts, despite his stature as the pre-eminent aesthetic explorer of his generation. Unlike most academic critics, he was willing to commit himself on living artists. Indeed, he sought them out: Ibsen, Shaw, and Strindberg; Strauss, Debussy, and Schönberg; Cézanne and Matisse—these were only a few of Huneker's prize foreign catches. "Almost singlehanded," says Alfred Kazin, "he brought the new currents of European art and thought to America and made them fashionable." The first effective opponent of the "genteel tradition," he also encouraged the most daring and enduring *American* writers, composers, and painters of his day—a contribution that has never been adequately acknowledged. If, indeed, a critic's competence could be judged by the present reputation of those whom he discovered or "boomed," Huneker might even be considered America's ablest critic.

Influence is difficult to measure, of course, but every person in this country who has any traffic with the arts might well be indebted in some way to Huneker for his incessant ridicule of the shoddy American fiction and drama of the 1890's and afterward; for his championing of adventuresome Continental novelists, dramatists, and poets; and for his support of neglected painters and composers. Later critics, carrying on what he began, may be deeper and more accurate in their individual fields, but no critic has done so much in so many arts to catch the interest and refine the taste of his countrymen.

To be forgotten is, I suppose, the destiny of every critic who is not also an outstanding creative writer or an original aesthetician; no matter how much he has educated his own generation or the next, the third one inevitably worships new gods and takes for granted the achievements of its grandfathers. Thus Huneker, a legend in his own era, is today a name known to relatively few, a name vaguely associated with H. L. Mencken, possibly, or Union Square bohemianism.

Yet he deserves a kinder fate, for he was not only an acute critic of music, drama, literature, and painting, one still quoted respectfully even though almost all of his own books are out of print; and he was far more than the torrential, Rabelaisian raconteur portrayed by his awe-struck cronies. To his "disciples"—Mencken, George Jean Nathan, Benjamin De Casseres, Carl Van Vechten, Lawrence Gilman, Paul Rosenfeld—and to the alert and literate members of at least one generation, he was the brightest symbol of a civilized way of living based on sophistication, gusto, curiosity, tolerance, wit—and art. A man admired by many of the most distinguished artists and critics of our day surely ought to be better known.

If Huneker's reputation has suffered since his death, his life, at least, was full and satisfying. Though he really wanted to be a concert pianist or, as second choice, a writer of fiction, he settled for criticism because, after all, he enjoyed art and enjoyed expressing the thoughts and emotion it aroused in him. He may have loved life more than art, as he claimed, yet life without art would certainly have been intolerable to him, for he was, I believe, more at ease inside his study with his books and piano than in the noisy world. He had his share of diffidence and disappointment, to be sure, and often groaned at the insatiable demands of daily journalism, but few men have come so close to making a vocation of their avocation.

Though his biography may, in passing, provide a commentary on the vicissitudes of the professional critic in America, I have not tried to "prove" anything with evidence derived from a study of one man's life. This, I think, would please Huneker, who was suspicious of facile generalizations and wary of biographers, and it may help to placate his no doubt curious, perhaps blushing, but I hope undismayed, ghost.

ARNOLD T. SCHWAB

Los Angeles, California
June 1, 1963

ACKNOWLEDGMENTS

For many services I am especially indebted to Miss Hazel E. Joslyn, Marcus A. McCorison, and Mrs. Elizabeth M. Sherrard of the Dartmouth College Library. I would also like to thank the library staffs of the following universities and colleges: Amherst, Buffalo, California (Los Angeles and Berkeley campuses), Chestnut Hill, Colby, Columbia, Cornell, Harvard, Haverford, Illinois, Indiana, Judson, Loyola (Chicago), Michigan, New York, Ohio State, Pennsylvania, Princeton, St. John's Seminary (Camarillo, California), St. Joseph's College (Philadelphia), Smith, Southern California, Stanford, Texas, Virginia, Wagner, and Yale. The New York Public Library's Newspaper Annex and Reference Department and Robert W. Hill, its Keeper of Manuscripts, assisted me, as did the following other institutions: the American Academy of Arts and Letters, the American Antiquarian Society, the Archives of American Art (Detroit), the Atlanta Public Library, the Boston Public Library, the Free Library of Philadelphia, the Historical Society of Pennsylvania, the Huntington Library, the Library of Congress, the Los Angeles Public Library, the Michigan State Library, the Missouri Historical Society, the Museum of the City of New York, the National Archives, the Newberry Library, the New Hampshire Historical Society, the Philadelphia Museum of Art, the Enoch Pratt Free Library of Baltimore, the Royal Library at Copenhagen, and the Wisconsin Historical Society.

The publishers and staff of *Etude*, the Philadelphia *Evening Bulletin, Musical Courier, The New York Times,* and *Town and Country* kindly allowed me access to their office files.

For special assistance I am grateful to Arthur M. Abell, "Lydia Barrington," Gustave L. Becker, Monsignor Cletus J. Benjamin, Mrs. Georgiana Carhart, Sister Miriam Gallagher, Ira Glackens, Mrs. Ruth Goldstein, Rupert Hughes, Mrs. Vera Kasow, Mrs. John J. Lonergan,

Richard H. Mandel, H. L. Mencken, George Jean Nathan, Francis Neilson, Arthur Pell, Miss Yvette Pinsker, Harrison Hale Schaff, Dr. Sigmund Spaeth, Raymond A. Speiser, Miss Emma T. Spitzmueller, and John Hall Wheelock.

For other aid I am obliged to Mrs. Richard Aldrich, Norman T. Byrne, Herman Cohen, Dr. James Francis Cooke, John Corbin, John Cullen, Arthur Farwell, Paolo Gallico, Mary Garden, Charles L. Lagen, Samuel Loveman, William D. Luks, Henry McBride, Robert G. MacIntyre, Neil MacNeil, Isidore Philipp, James Shields, Nathan Straus, Gertrude Traubel, Carl Van Vechten, and Thomas R. Ybarra.

I should also like to thank the following persons, who permitted me to examine Huneker correspondence in their possession or under their control: Clifton Waller Barrett, Mrs. Richard J. Beamish, Martin Birnbaum, Mrs. William C. Brownell, Barrett H. Clark, H. T. Craven, Miss Beatrice Fenton, Waldo Frank, Mrs. Philip Hale, Miss Edith C. Heinrich, B. W. Huebsch, S. Jay Kaufman, Alfred A. Knopf, Mrs. Alden March, George Middleton, Mrs. Edward P. Mitchell, Philip Moeller, Albert Mordell, Miss Harriet B. Prescott, Burton Rascoe, F. L. Rodgers, Dr. Herbert B. Satcher, Leonard S. Saxe, Vincent Starrett, G. A. Van Nosdall, George Sylvester Viereck, Dr. Davenport West, and Mrs. Sigmund Zeisler.

Permission to quote letters written to Huneker has been granted by the Trustees of the Joseph Conrad Estate; Eugene J. McGuinness, Bishop of Oklahoma (executor of Bishop Francis C. Kelley); Charles D. Medley (executor of George Moore); Mrs. Edith Brandes Philipp (executor of Georg Brandes); the Society of Authors, acting for the Public Trustee (executor of George Bernard Shaw); and O. L. Zangwill (executor of Israel Zangwill).

Mrs. Josephine Huneker's attorney and executor, Alfred Rice, has patiently responded to inquiries both in interviews and in correspondence, and has permitted me to quote from Huneker's published and unpublished writings.

Charles Scribner's Sons and the Liveright Publishing Corporation have kindly allowed me to quote from the Huneker books they published.

B. W. Huebsch kindly gave me the benefit of his close reading of the manuscript, helping me to avoid a number of slips.

I wish to express my gratitude to Mrs. Elizabeth Spurr and J. G. Bell of Stanford University Press for editorial services performed not only with patience and skill but also with what was almost as helpful—a sense of humor.

I am happy, too, to acknowledge the cordial, enthusiastic, and painstaking assistance of Erik H. Huneker. A thick file of letters from him, a mass of notes taken at several interviews, family documents and photographs which he sent me from time to time, and the results of research undertaken for me at the Library of Congress and the New York Public Library amply testify to his active and continued interest in his father's biography.

I am indebted to Erik Huneker for family photographs, Nos. 1, 2, 3, 4, 8, 12, 13, 14, and to the Dartmouth College Library for Nos. 5, 6, 9, 11, 17, 18, and 21; to Mrs. Vera Kasow for the frontispiece and for No. 20; to Charles E. Feinberg (who owns the original document) for No. 7; to Mrs. Edward Cushing for No. 15; to Mrs. Georgiana Carhart for No. 16; to the Archives of American Art for Nos. 19 and 23; to Mrs. John J. Lonergan for No. 22; and to Mrs. Richard J. Beamish for No. 24. No. 10 is supplied by and reprinted through the courtesy of The Presser Foundation, Philadelphia, Pa.

Profound is my debt to Professor Howard Mumford Jones of Harvard University, who read several versions of the manuscript and made many valuable suggestions. Through his recommendation, moreover, I received a Harvard Sheldon Fellowship in 1951–52, which enabled me to devote full time to research and writing. I am grateful to Harvard for this help; to the University of California at Los Angeles and the Horace H. Rackham School of Graduate Studies at the University of Michigan for research grants in 1952–54 and 1954–55, respectively; and to the James D. Phelan Awards in Literature for an encouraging prize in 1954.

I could not end without a word of thanks to Marg and the late Sid Heywood of Lexington, Massachusetts, at whose hospitable home much of this book was written and rewritten; with Professor Jones and Professor Bradford A. Booth of the University of California at Los Angeles, Marg will recognize this first biography of James Huneker as a more than twice-told tale.

CONTENTS

James Gibbons
Huneker

❧ One

A PHILADELPHIA CHILDHOOD

James Gibbons Huneker was born on January 31, 1857,[1] in Philadelphia, where his father, John Joseph Huneker, a prosperous house painter, lived with his wife, two other children, and his wife's sister. Although it is not clear whether the Hunekers who settled in Philadelphia at the beginning of the eighteenth century were Germans or Magyars,[2] or which pronunciation of the name most of their descendants adopted (the "hu" was usually pronounced "huh" in Philadelphia, "hue" in New York, and "who" in Europe, so that even James Huneker's friends were not sure, later, which form *he* preferred),[3] there was no doubt whatsoever about John Joseph's Catholicism or his love of music. His father, also named John (1783–1836), was a professional musician, organist at St. Mary's Church, and a charter member of the Musical Fund Society, and John Joseph himself, for decades an active member of a group of music patrons known as the Philharmonic Society,[4] was prominent in the city's music circles. He enjoyed mixing with actors, painters, and writers as well as musicians, and among his friends were Edwin Booth and Edgar Allan Poe, who for six years lived within walking distance of the Huneker home.

James Huneker's mother, born Mary Gibbons in Philadelphia in 1825,[5] was the second daughter of James Gibbons, a printer who had immigrated to America from County Donegal in 1820. A passionate Irish patriot who poured the profits of his printing business into the cause of Irish independence, Gibbons served as vice-president of the American branch of the Fenian brotherhood, and was eventually involved in the group's abortive invasion of Canada. He was also a temperance advocate—much to the annoyance of his convivial son-in-law, John Huneker—and the author of *Miscellaneous and Patriotic Poems*, privately printed in 1870, three years before his death.[6]

Mary Gibbons Huneker inherited or absorbed many of the qualities of her father, for whom she wrote Fenian "state papers." Remarkably intellectual for a woman of her day, she had taught school[7] for five years before her marriage in 1849, and throughout her lifetime was exceedingly well read. "Mother, a second Mme de Staël," recalled her daughter, herself a writer and actress who remained vivacious and *au courant* in her nineties, "could have dominated an 18th century salon if she so desired."[8] Theology, probably the subject of her later correspondence with Henry James, Sr., a friend of the family,[9] was one of her main interests, and she was an extremely devout Catholic; yet she was tolerant toward non-Catholics. If there was anything lacking in her character, it was a sense of humor.

By 1857 the Hunekers had two children: a son named John, born in 1850, and a daughter, Mary Julia, two years younger; another daughter died in infancy in July 1856. The mother was still grieving over this loss when James (named, of course, after her father) was born two months prematurely, and, without neglecting her other children, she naturally lavished attention upon the child who had replaced her lost daughter and who was so frail that for weeks his bed was a wool-padded box placed on a broad mantelpiece over a blazing fire. As a result, he was somewhat spoiled. Though the birth of Paul Eugene in 1859 restored the psychological balance, Jim's attachment to his mother was to remain exceptionally strong, and he never fully outgrew the shyness, morbid sensitivity, and physical cowardice encouraged by the conditions of his childhood.

It was from his mother, he felt later, that he had inherited his "centrifugal" Celtic temperament, his tendency toward picturesque exaggeration, a quick temper, and a flashing mode of thought, more sensual than logical. From the paternal side of the family, apparently, came his musical talent, his distrust of fanaticism, his wit, his convivial proclivities, and his fondness for frank speech.

About a year after Jim's birth the Hunekers moved into a narrow three-story brick house at 1434 North Seventh Street, where they lived for the next sixteen years. At the family's parish church, fashionable and wealthy St. Malachi's on Eleventh Street near Jefferson, Jim studied his catechism under a terrifyingly harsh instructor. Far pleasanter were Sunday afternoon visits to the Sisters of Mercy Convent, where the nuns made a fuss over the boy who promised to become a priest like his distant relative James (later Cardinal) Gibbons. This was his mother's fondest dream and his early education was built around it.

He hated the Irish toughs who considered everyone with a clean collar a sissy and made his walk to St. Malachi's miserable. Much more congenial were his Jewish playmates, who also took piano lessons and loved to read. Because Mrs. Huneker thought that a priest should know Hebrew, Jim studied with the rabbi teaching the sons of the next-door neighbors, the Eisners;[10] long afterward he could still make out the headlines in Yiddish newspapers and use Yiddish words and expressions, which always surprised his Jewish friends. And he even tagged along to the synagogue and learned Jewish ritual.

In the fall of 1865,[11] Jim enrolled in the Preparatory Department of the Broad Street Academy, where his brother John was an upperclassman. Founded in 1863 by Edward Roth, an Irish-born classical scholar who had taught for fifteen years at St. Mary's College in Wilmington, Delaware,[12] the Academy was modeled on excellent German schools and soon became the best one in Philadelphia.[13] Roth apparently believed in militant Christianity, for, in addition to the regular subjects, his "cadets"—mostly Catholics—were required to study Christian doctrine and also to wear uniforms and follow a modified military discipline.[14]

In his first year, Jim ranked eighth in a class of fifteen, winning first-place honors in spelling and reading in the semiannual examinations, even though he was out of school more than a third of the year because of illness. Nothing is known of his second year, but during his third he wrote on Academy stationery—it was apparently a school exercise—a letter to his parents. Dated December 25, 1867, it reads as follows:

My Dear Parents

Again I am called upon to perform the pleasing task of writing you a Christmas letter which although not all my own composition still will afford you a specimen of my writing among the many offering made you to day. I well know that will be more acceptable than these few lines with all [crossed out] their imperfection. I need not tell you how I am gitting along in school as you are already aware by our little monthly paper of the rank I hold in class I sometimes think I might have done better yet I am pretty sure you have noticed an improvement. I like to go to school very well but am very glad Christmas has come as it is a season of much enjoyment, then too it is pleasant to throw off the anxiety of trying to be perfect which to me as well as the rest of my composition [class?] is rather a hard task. I hope Kriss Kingle will not forget me in his visitations. He has always been very generous and I flatter myself that this year I have tried to deserve a continuance of his fovors. My dear Parents how can I thank or repay you for all your loving kindness. How many blessings I enjoy both at home and in school. God has been very good indeed to me. I trust that my future life will prove my gratitude to all   With many loving wishes for a merry Christmas and a happy New year I remain

Affectionately
your son
JAMES[15]

By 1869 or 1870 he had, by passing an examination, graduated to the Academic section. During 1869–70 he distinguished himself chiefly by the number of his absences and by his ability to elude the final examinations. His academic showing in 1870–71 is unknown, but in the following year his mark in Christian Doctrine was 100, and an essay on that subject which he submitted in a competition received special mention in the annual catalogue. In French his grade was almost as high, and he also excelled in physics, history, music, and spelling. His record shows no grades for drilling or gymnastics,[16] and one surmises that the boy who preferred reading to games—though he enjoyed swimming and was good at it—had no great physical skill or stamina and avoided the gymnasium as often as he dared. ("In my veins flows sporting blood," he remarked long afterward, "but only in the Darwinian sense am I a 'sport,' a deviation from the normal history of my family, which has always been devoted to athletic pleasures.")[17] He certainly could not hope to rival his brother John, an outstanding oarsman and sailor, for he lacked competitive spirit and quickly became flustered under pressure.

The thing he disliked most at the Academy was the regimentation. The uniform made him a trembling target for gangs of less-privileged boys who waylaid him as he hurried home from school, hurled names and stones at him, and snatched his books. Sometimes, too, when Jim tangled with Lewis Baker, his deskmate, for stealing his lunch, Professor Roth rapped his knuckles with a ruler—the injustice of which led the boy to play hooky or deliberately misbehave. (Long afterward, he said, he got even with Baker, who had become an actor, by criticizing the cut of his coat or his trousers.)[18] In Huneker's early rebellion against school authority, indeed, may lie the roots of his lifelong championship of extreme individualism.

Roth emphasized Latin so much that he may have neglected the fundamentals of English composition. Huneker's punctuation, at any rate, always remained shaky. But he liked and respected the professor, who exerted a real influence upon him. Roth loved French culture almost as much as the classics, and during the Franco-Prussian War he and his pupils donated five hundred francs toward the liberation of France,[19] an act that Mrs. Huneker heartily approved. When he translated for his classes an exciting story by Jules Verne, Roth had little trouble holding Jim's attention, and at the same time he instilled in the boy a persisting taste for science fiction. Jim may have learned some French from his mother before he started school, but his interest in French literature probably dates from his Academy days. For the rest of his life his admiration for Roth's erudition and his impatience with the professor's inflexible teaching methods colored Huneker's attitude toward the academic world.

He took part in the Commencement play in 1872[20]—"I then and there made a blighting failure as an incipient elocutionist and a budding actor," he recalled almost fifty years later[21]—a trying experience for a shy boy, which may help to account for his later aversion to public speaking. If he had to perform, he preferred to have in his hands the paraphernalia of a new love, magic, kindled about this time by his reading of the memoirs of the famous French conjurer Robert-Houdin. Jim had previously attended performances by "Robert Heller" (William Henry Palmer), an English imitator of Robert-Houdin, who combined feats of magic and "second sight" with piano virtuosity,[22] linking the two arts in the boy's mind. ("Magician of the Keyboard" became a favorite phrase of the mature critic.) Excited now by Houdin, he tried to master the art of prestidigitation, spending much of his time—including school hours—and most of his allowance at a magic shop to acquire apparatus and skills with which to dazzle his family and young friends. This new passion, however, proved too much for his father, who decided that it was a waste of money to keep in school a truant son more interested in magic than mathematics, and withdrew him from the Academy in September 1872. Thus ended his formal education.

Jim's education, of course, had not been confined to the classroom. Ever since he had attended his first play at the age of ten, he had been fascinated by the footlights. Sitting in a twenty-five-cent seat in the "family circle" at the Arch Street Theater, in the gallery at the Walnut Street Theater, or at Wood's Museum, he applauded productions of

Shakespeare, Restoration and eighteenth-century comedy classics, and mid-Victorian pieces, starring Edwin Booth, Ada Rehan, and other leading actors and actresses of the period. He had often heard his father's account of the celebrated Forrest-Macready row, and he himself had had the honor of being chased off the brownstone steps of Forrest's North Broad Street home by the angry actor. Though Jim had not witnessed the eccentric (and no doubt intoxicated) Junius Brutus Booth riding backwards on a horse, precariously hanging on to the animal's tail, he never forgot his father's description of the hilarious scene.

He was also developing a taste for painting, encouraged by his father, who owned a choice collection of mezzotints, etchings, and lithographs,[23] and by his mother, who knew enough about art to publish a review of a book on engraving in 1872.[24] The walls of the Huneker home were hung with fine pictures, one of which, John Martin's mezzotint "The Fall of Nineveh," Jim faced every time he ate at the family table. John Huneker forgot about punishing his truant son when the boy slyly switched the subject to art, and the two of them spent many happy hours over the prints.

Magazines such as *Godey's Lady's Book* and the *Saturday Evening Post* made Philadelphia a focal point for engravers, etchers, and illustrators, a number of whom were regular visitors to the Huneker home on Sunday nights. The oil paintings John Huneker possessed, indeed, were limited to the American school, Philadelphians preferred. Jim heard his parents' friends talk about chiaroscuro, disposition of the model, complementary colors, and the arrangement of the palette. He heard them praise Raphael, Correggio, Murillo, Peale, Gilbert Stuart, and Meissonier, and click their tongues over the vogue of Bouguereau, Cabanel, and Lefebvre, all of whom glorified the nude body. The Philadelphia artists knew little of Vermeer and Velásquez, and they abhorred realism. No one mentioned the names of the newfangled "Impressionists," but the opening of the Paris "Salon of the Refused" in 1867 had not escaped them, and the boy listened carefully as the local painters damned the new theories in the Huneker parlor. And he did not forget his father's faith in American painting.

After moving to 1711 Race Street in 1874, the Hunekers lived only a short distance from one of the major showplaces of Philadelphia, the Claghorn Galleries, located at Logan Square. James L. Claghorn, a merchant prince and the city's chief art connoisseur, owned what Huneker later described as the only collection of black-and-white larger than John Huneker's—over forty thousand etchings and engravings of all periods, including many rare specimens.[25] Jim Huneker eagerly cultivated Claghorn's friendship and for years used to help him display the prints to art lovers. Nearby, too, was the Pennsylvania Academy of the Fine Arts, the first and probably the best American art school, which moved into its new building on North Broad Street in the spring of 1876.[26] Here Jim heard lectures on painting and sculpture and studied Benjamin West's famous "Death on the Pale Horse" and many other pictures.

Music, too, had been an integral part of the Huneker household. Though relatively few pianos were then to be found in homes,[27] the Hunekers owned one, and Jim's sister, "Maim" to the family, could wheedle anything out of her father by playing Beethoven on it. "A fine musician but no perseverance" was Jim's comment on his sister's playing in 1879.[28] (She became a capable accompanist, and her interest in the arts brought her closer to Jim than to her other brothers.) He himself began to take lessons at the age of eight, but what he later recognized as faulty instruction stiffened his wrists and fingers, and he gave up temporarily. At Roth's Academy, however, he learned much about music from Leopold Engelke, a talented pianist, organist, and cellist. And from an early age he went to concerts and operas with his father, who, in addition, often entertained the musical great at his home.[29]

Science, too, attracted Jim in the early 1870's. At the Academy of Natural Sciences, which moved in 1876 to a new building within two blocks of the Huneker home, the witty, cultured young librarian, Edward J. Nolan, showed Jim paleontological exhibits and discussed science with him as well as painting, music, and modern literature.[30] Nolan, indeed, did much to form Huneker's taste.[31]

The bookish mama's boy obviously hero-worshiped the dashing, well dressed young-men-about-town. "The blond magnificence of Montezuma Rogers made my heart beat," he recalled more than forty years later.[32] Of one obscure friend the twenty-two-year-old Huneker wrote: "He is a goodlooking flippant clever society man, and he is very selfish. I will always be intimate with him but never congenial."[33] One suspects that Jim not only did not bypass the homosexual phase of adolescence but may even have unconsciously prolonged it. And his own susceptibilities to masculine beauty and charm may have made him sensitive, if not sympathetic, to the sexual variation he was to encounter among artists of all kinds.

He managed to find a few companions of his own age who shared his interests. He and his friends often walked to Fairmount Park, ate catfish and waffles on the picturesque banks of Wissahickon Creek, and gorged on shad at Gloucester. Jim never missed the annual Schuylkill regattas in which his brother John, a member of the Schuylkill Navy Athletic Club, either rowed or officiated. Jim himself hoped that his close friend John Boyd, an intelligent mechanic who liked music,[34] would teach him how to "pull" during their summer vacation in 1874,[35] but nothing may have come of this. He spent other vacations in Maryland, where he mixed happily with Negroes, and at Atlantic City, then a modest fishing resort. But even as a lad Jim was restless; no matter where he was, he always wanted to be somewhere else. The trait became even more marked when he reached the difficult years of adolescence.

LAW, LADIES, AND LISZT

Not diversions but an occupation was the pressing problem facing Jim in 1872. He had displayed little taste for systematic study, and college was apparently out of the question. His disappointed mother realized that he had no call for the priesthood, though the beauty of the Catholic service would always appeal to his senses and he would never forget the writings of the Church fathers. Then one day Jim made the surprising announcement that he intended to become a railroad engineer. John Huneker must have sensed that his son was not cut out for such a career, but thinking, probably, that physical labor would be good for him, accompanied him to a machine shop of the Baldwin Locomotive Works (one of whose executives was related by marriage to the Hunekers), where a foreman whom his father knew took Jim under his wing. Early the next morning—the date was September 18, 1872—a scared youth dressed in outsize overalls and a laborer's cap and carrying a lunch pail was introduced to the working world.

The fingers that were deft with coins were not so skillful at first with hammer and chisel, but he had been promoted to drill-press operator, two months later, when his sleeves were caught in the drill and he was nearly killed. Several weeks afterward he left the factory. The job had toughened him and made him less shy with strangers, and he acquired something of the easy camaraderie that he was to find useful with bartenders, policemen, and taxi drivers.

Chastened by his experience, Jim made no protest when his father suggested that he study law. On January 13, 1873, a skeptical but resigned adolescent, almost sixteen, was led to the Walnut Street office-home of Elwood Wilson, Jr., the lawyer son of the Huneker family doctor. About this time Jim's friend Maurice Egan, a staunch, bookish Catholic, also started to read Blackstone. Since there were no law schools, a young man who wanted to enter the legal profession usually paid a lawyer for instruction or received it in return for doing odd jobs about the office, without pay.[1] In three months at Baldwin's Jim earned more than he was to earn in five years of legal apprenticeship.

His remarkable memory made it easy for him to retain whole pages of opinions and terminology, but when he had to rely on his own understanding and interpretation of the law he was hopelessly lost. Conventional usage and musty precedent soon disgusted him. Instead of reading law, he would look out of the windows in Wilson's office and compare the eccentric lawyers who passed by with characters in Dickens and Thackeray. Fortunately, Mr. Wilson also possessed an excellent collection of fiction, and Jim eagerly plunged into Defoe, Smollett, Richardson, and Fielding.

The one law book he read willingly was Wharton and Stillé's authoritative *Medical Jurisprudence*, which had gone through three editions by 1873. Its chapters on mental unsoundness—and, even better, on sexual deviation—contained bizarre and lurid case histories, many of them dealing with persons and places in Philadelphia, where the book was published. "I invariably deserted [Blackstone] for *Medical Jurisprudence*," he recalled. "There was metal more attractive. The horrors of criminology had never been set down so attractively since I had devoured Eugene Sue's *Mysteries of Paris*."[2] The book undoubtedly stimulated, if, indeed, it did not initiate, Huneker's interest in abnormal psychology, which was to become one of his chief trademarks as a critic.

Since Wilson was a notary public and conveyancer, his student spent many hours searching titles and copying wills, leases, mortgages, and deeds. Occasionally Jim stepped inside a courtroom and in a trembling voice asked the judge for a delay. His most memorable legal maneuver was delivering a subpoena to Jay Cooke and Co., an act that he later whimsically associated with that firm's failure and the resulting financial panic of 1873.

But Huneker was far less interested in law than in girls and clothes. One of the two or three surviving photographs of him taken during his young manhood probably dates from the mid-1870's, when he was going through an attack of exaggerated dandyism. In this photograph[3] the face that, by 1890, at least, tended to be heavy and round, is long, thin, and angular; the brown hair, afterwards loose and wavy, is plastered down, a jagged part in the center revealing a scar received from diving into shallow water at a swimming pool. The eyes have a slightly un-

natural cast, suggesting that they were usually covered by glasses, which
he wore from about the age of fifteen,[4] when he was not sporting the
monocle he sometimes affected during this period.[5] The long, well-
shaped nose is the strongest feature, while the weakest is the taut,
slightly twisted, almost cruel mouth. The shoulders seem surprisingly
broad, the chest deep, for a bookworm—they were never meant by nature to be wasted at a writer's desk, a friend later remarked[6]—suggesting that he had inherited an athletic build despite his lack of interest
in sports. Posing in front of a camera apparently intensified his self-
consciousness, for all the extant photographs of him are somber, hiding
his more characteristic light side. Perhaps this is why he disliked being
photographed, especially in later years when he grew gray, jowly, and
paunchy.

In the spring of 1875 Jim moved to the office of Daniel M. Fox, a
former mayor of Philadelphia and a distant relation of the Hunekers
by marriage. Conveyancing kept Jim busy, but his heart was not in
the law and he made little progress in it. He felt more and more that
he was a square peg in a round hole. His worried mother even took
him to a phrenologist, the pre-Freudian psychiatrist and vocational
counselor, who solemnly assured her that even though the young man's
temperament was centrifugal rather than centripetal, he could do anything he set his mind to, if only he applied himself seriously.

While going through the motions of learning law, Jim gradually
discovered that his real love was music, just as Maurice Egan decided
that he liked Shakespeare better than Blackstone.[7] The large German
population had helped to make Philadelphia's musical life full and
varied. Michael H. Cross and Charles H. Jarvis, the city's leading musical figures at this time, had educated their townsmen in the classical
repertory before the Theodore Thomas Orchestra introduced modern
works at the summer night concerts held during the Centennial Exposition of 1876. (Twenty years later Huneker remarked that Thomas—
whose grimness and rudeness he disliked—had done more for musical
culture in America than any other man.)[8] It was at Jarvis's series of
Classical Soirées, begun in 1862 and continued for more than thirty
years,[9] that Huneker learned to love the literature of the piano.[10]

On Saturday nights, released from the monotony of the law, Jim
went to the string quartet parties held in Cross's home, two doors away
from the Hunekers', which usually ended with a feast of oysters and

beer,[11] good eating and drinking being as important to these musicians as music. He also attended the concerts of the vain, violent-tempered violinist Carl Gaertner in the foyer of the Academy of Music. (For a short time Jim himself studied the violin.) In 1873 he heard the great Anton Rubinstein, and though he was too young to fully appreciate Rubinstein's playing, he treasured the memory of it.

In 1875 Jim became friendly with Max Heinrich, a twenty-three-year-old German Jew who had escaped military duty in Saxony and settled in Philadelphia in the early 1870's as a singer and voice teacher. For some time Heinrich entertained in a German beer hall, but aided by a good word from Huneker's mother, he was appointed soloist at the Cathedral on Sundays, while on Saturdays he performed at a synagogue.[12] Heinrich's violin-playing brother-in-law, Franz Schubert, the talented son of the late first violinist of the Germania Orchestra, eventually became Jim's closest friend.

Heinrich's bohemian zest for life appealed greatly to Jim. When he was not singing, teaching, or playing pinochle, Heinrich joyously painted landscapes and animals, surrounded by his own children (he had seven), his wife's four orphaned sisters and brothers, who lived with the Heinrichs, uncaged birds, puppies of various breeds, and a huge Russian mastiff named "Sedan" whose favorite trick was jumping after cats from a second-story window.[13] Heinrich amused himself by trying to teach the rather priggish Huneker to live like an artist—and drink like a man. Mrs. Huneker did not approve of Heinrich's irregular hours, his drinking, or his influence on Jim, and felt relieved when he took a teaching job at Judson Female Institute in Marion, Alabama, in 1877.[14] But the baritone's "wickedness" made him even more engaging in the eyes of Jim, who described him in 1879 as "one of the most talented and brilliant men I have ever met."[15]

Huneker's renewed interest in the piano was also stimulated by Aubertine Woodward, who lived opposite the Hunekers with her father and nephew, Samuel George Woodward Wickersham. Almost fifty years later, she remembered Jim as a "handsome attractive lad, with the eyes and general expression . . . of one who sees visions and dreams dreams." She was so accomplished a pianist herself that when Rubinstein had come to Philadelphia, Carl Gaertner, her teacher, had selected her to play for the great virtuoso to illustrate how Gaertner taught Bach.[16] She probably introduced Jim to the *Well-Tempered Clavichord.*

Once, after playing Bach, she happened to go to her front door and found Jim on the steps, where he had been listening.[17] They became good friends, and she discussed his talent with John Huneker, who, foreseeing loose company, irregular hours, and the drudgery of teaching, frowned upon a musical career for his son.

Mrs. Huneker decided that if Jim could not be a priest, perhaps he could do the next best thing by becoming a church organist, which would at least ensure his frequent attendance at mass. In September 1875, therefore, with his mother's connivance, Jim began to study piano secretly with Michael Cross, promising to pay him later for the lessons. During the next three years, he would sneak out in the morning, music hidden under his coat, walk to the Cross house, begin a lesson by six o'clock, and reach his law office about three hours later. Cross, who spoke several languages fluently, loved engravings, and possessed a fine library in which Jim browsed for years, warned him that the musician's life was a dog's life and advised him to stick to the law, but to no avail.

The record of Huneker's study with Cross is preserved in a torn, faded notebook.[18] He took two lessons a week the first year and practiced an average of two hours a day. Though he received only one lesson a week in the second year, he increased his daily practice to three hours. In the third year, he took lessons less regularly, but practiced four hours a day. Sometimes he studied in the long, narrow drawing room of an elderly maiden aunt:

A hair-cloth sofa of uncompromising rectitude [he recalled] was pushed so close to the wall that the imprints of two generations of heads might be discerned upon the wallpaper—a pattern of flowers and grapes of gigantic size. A massive mahogany sideboard stood at the upper end of the room; in one window hung a cage containing a stuffed canary—a souvenir of still living affection. Under a conical glass was an ornamental wax fruit piece. Antimacassars were abundant. Cowper's poems, Beecher's sermons, and the bible (unrevised version) were always to be found on the table. On the marble mantelpiece, scrupulously cleaned weekly, was a large mezzotint depicting some biblical event, a dramatic massing of darks and lights. Here I once spent happy hours trying to extract music from a toneless square pianoforte, built by Jonas Chickering, the keys of which were mother-of-pearl.[19]

One Christmas morning, at his mother's urging, he reluctantly agreed to substitute at short notice for the regular organist at the Annunciation Church, a block from Moyamensing Prison.[20] He almost managed to get through early mass without disgracing himself, but when the priest started to sing the "Pater Noster" a half-tone flat, Huneker, frantically trying to transpose, produced "a series of dissonances that would have made Richard Strauss or Stravinsky envious." The indignant priest gave him a dirty look—"If he had shot me," Huneker remarked, "I should have died with a martyr's aureole and a heavenly smile on my lips"—and the sweating neophyte fled as soon as he finished "Adeste Fideles." As a public speaker, pianist, or organist, he suffered acutely from stage fright, and this was probably why he gave up playing the organ in church—and not, as he jokingly told a friend, because the footwork was too strenuous.[21] Mrs. Huneker's hopes were doomed.

In 1877 Jim met Alfredo Barili, son of the original "Rigoletto" and nephew of the Patti sisters. Born in Florence in 1854 but brought to America as a child, Barili had studied piano under Ferdinand Hiller in Cologne and Theodore Ritter in Paris, and, after concertizing in Europe and America, had settled in Philadelphia as a teacher in the late 1870's.[22] He may have given Jim lessons at this time, and a close friendship developed between them. When he first heard Barili play Chopin, Jim was so moved that he rolled over and over on the floor, sheepishly explaining that he felt like a cat with catnip.[23] Though Barili could offer him little encouragement—he probably recognized Huneker's intrinsic limitations—Jim persisted at the piano.

During the mid-1870's the piano did not take up all of Huneker's spare time. Since childhood he had read omnivorously, guided by his mother, who sometimes excused mediocrity on the grounds of piety but did not slight the classics. At Roth's, Jim had struggled through Latin literature in the original and Greek in translation,[24] and had read Shakespeare, Dante, Cervantes, Bunyan, Bossuet, and Lacordaire. In his late teens Ouida, George A. Lawrence's *Guy Livingstone,* and the heavy swells in *Punch* gripped his imagination, and for a while he devoured English fiction. He had also discovered the contemporary English poets, especially the daringly sensual Swinburne and Rossetti, the painter in verse. Among prose writers he most admired Pater for writing criticism as if it were a fine art and for his famous conclusion to *Studies in the History of the Renaissance,* which crystallized Huneker's worship of the present.

His father's friendship with Poe, whose former cottage Jim used to pass daily on his way to school, had helped lead him to Poe's work. Huneker's first short story[25] was largely an imitation of Poe, and Huneker's later tales show traces of the same influence. Eventually, some of Huneker's prejudices and mannerisms as a critic, too, resembled Poe's: his antididacticism, political conservatism, and allusiveness, and his habit of republishing old materials. And Poe remained for Huneker the apotheosis of the romantic type, the American equivalent of Chopin.

Jim thought that Walt Whitman, who had moved to nearby Camden in 1873 and had become a familiar figure on the streets of Philadelphia, was the most imposing-looking man he had ever seen, but it was not until he had read an essay by Moncure D. Conway[26] urging a fair hearing for the poet that he discovered *Leaves of Grass*. Aubertine Woodward, who had met Whitman in the spring of 1874 and played the piano for him at her home,[27] may have aroused Jim's interest in him. At any rate, in the spring of 1878—"ab[ou]t April 18th," Whitman recorded in his notebook—Huneker visited him in Camden. The youth began by telling Whitman how much *Leaves of Grass* meant to him, but soon switched to the story of his life, showing the poet a photograph of the hefty miss with whom he was then in love. Whitman remarked that she would be "the mother of ten, at least." Jim's generally amiable father, aware of Whitman's unsavory reputation, was furious when he heard about the visit, and put his foot down on any further intimacy.[28]

By this time Huneker was also absorbed in French literature. It was *St. Martin's Summer* (1866), written by Annie Hampton Brewster, Paris and later Rome correspondent of the Philadelphia *Evening Bulletin,* that introduced him to Stendhal, Chateaubriand, and other French writers. A series of travel sketches, mainly of Italy, *St. Martin's Summer* contained perceptive and well-phrased, if somewhat sentimental, criticism of music, painting, sculpture, architecture, and literature. Among other things, Miss Brewster pleaded for greater catholicity of taste and noted how difficult it was to criticize music or painting without borrowing technical terms from one art to characterize the other— ideas that apparently made a deep impression on Huneker.

Mrs. Huneker's ecclesiastical friends shook their heads when they saw books by Whitman, Baudelaire, Gautier, and Flaubert on her son's table. "What can you expect in the future if you turn your mind into a sewer for all those vile poets and infidels?" she once asked him, but he continued to read whatever interested him. When George Wickersham—who became a leading corporation lawyer and, eventually, Attorney General under President Taft—would come over to Jim's place to read law with him, he found that his young host preferred to discuss Baudelaire on the back porch.²⁹ Jim's uncle, James S. Gibbons, was a director of the Mercantile Library,³⁰ which had an excellent collection of volumes in French,³¹ and Jim browsed there almost daily. Maurice Egan, a better Catholic than Huneker, recalled that by 1878 Huneker was "quoting from recondite books which were looked upon by our friends as almost diabolical . . . and was already dominated by French literature."³²

Another activity Jim undertook to compensate for the boredom of "studying" law was music criticism. Encouraged by a friend of the family who was one of the publishers of the city's leading newspaper, the *Evening Bulletin*, Huneker made his debut in journalism in 1875 with an article on a Jarvis Soirée.³³ These concerts invariably took place on Saturday nights; Huneker wrote his notice on Sunday, submitted it to his mother for revision, and then brought it to the *Bulletin*'s office. The two paragraphs appeared on the following Monday.³⁴ His only reward was the thrill of seeing his unsigned work in print. He continued to write these critiques from time to time during four concert seasons.³⁵ Rereading them after thirty years as a music critic, he was embarrassed by the excess adjectives, the amateurish reminiscence, and the disproportionate amount of space given to mediocre composers. Though it is almost impossible to identify his contributions, he also tried his hand at reporting lectures and séances, one of which ended in the ex-magician's being thrown out for holding the medium's wrist until the lights went on.

The great event of 1876, the Centennial Exposition, brought on Huneker's first severe attack of wanderlust. Although there was an impressive display of contemporary French art, never before seen in America,³⁶ it was chiefly the concerts brought by the Centennial that stimulated Huneker's interest in European culture. He heard the "corked champagne" music of Jacques Offenbach,³⁷ who had come from France to conduct his popular compositions, and the "Centennial March" by Wagner,³⁸ whose first Festival at Bayreuth, then under way, Huneker eagerly read about in the newspapers. He mentally compared the celebrated Hans von Bülow, whom he had recently heard in an all-Chopin program,³⁹ with Frédéric Boscovitz, a pupil of Liszt and a cousin of the pianist Rafael Joseffy, who gave recitals at the Exposition and urged the young student to try for admission to the piano classes at the Paris Conservatoire.[40] Huneker's desire to go to Paris was surely whetted, moreover, by a visit to the spectacular Colosseum, erected in Philadelphia for the Centennial, where looking down from a height of fifty feet one could see painted on more than an acre of canvas spread on the walls of the circular structure a magnificent panorama of "Paris by Night," which included every street and prominent building in a seven-square-mile area.[41] Colorful sights and exciting sounds pervaded the Quaker City—and the law seemed drearier than ever.

Besides, it was summer and the nights were warm and the park benches inviting. Like most young men, Jim carried a whole harem in his head, and though they were not as captivating, perhaps, as the gorgeous actresses of the day—especially Adelaide Neilson and Mary Scott-Siddons—whom he idolized, or as lovely and talented as Teresita Carreño, whom he heard during the Centennial shortly after she abandoned singing for the piano, and who seemed to him the most beautiful woman he had ever seen,[42] pretty Philadelphia girls were enticing—and more accessible. To attract them he dressed carefully and watched his figure, envying the handsome dandies who could dance, since his own sense of rhythm never reached his feet. But he had little to offer a girl on the lookout for a substantial provider.

At the beginning of 1878, Jim, still receiving no salary, changed law preceptors again, moving to the office of William Ernst. The practical John Huneker was bewildered by the inability of his twenty-one-year-old son to establish himself in a money-making vocation, and used to declare that if Jim saw a ten-dollar bill coming to greet him, he would run the other way. Nor was the elder Huneker pleased when he finally discovered that Jim owed Michael Cross a sizable sum for three years of piano lessons—a bill that he himself paid.

The situation was not in the least improved when, on May 9, 1878, Jim quietly (perhaps secretly) married Elizabeth Holmes at old Saint Joseph's Church in Willing's Alley, Philadelphia. Since the marriage took place only three weeks after Huneker had visited Whitman, it may have been Elizabeth's photograph he showed him. But tantalizingly little is known about her. Born in Philadelphia in 1851,[43] "Lizzie" came from a middle-class Irish Catholic family. She and her younger sister, Margaret (who was to marry Franz Schubert in 1885),[44] both working girls, lived in the Cathedral area with their mother. According to one tradition Lizzie was a seamstress or cook in the Huneker household.[45] Rupert Hughes, the writer, who met Huneker almost twenty years afterward, recalled a story in which Lizzie was portrayed as a large and nearly illiterate woman,[46] but a person who knew her in her later years pictured her as tall, stately, and intellectual.[47] Jim, at any rate, considered her cultivated and generous—the words he used to describe her in 1879[48]—and fell in love with her. After their marriage they moved directly to the home of Lizzie's mother, where they lived until the following September.[49]

Ten days after the ceremony, Huneker obtained a clerking job at Dutton's Chickering piano agency,[50] abandoning law, finally, with a sense of relief. But he did not give up music. Arriving at the store at six in the morning, he practiced in the basement for two hours before going to work, pursuing, throughout the summer, a two-year course of study probably outlined by Cross.[51] He needed money for two reasons: to support his wife, presumably, and to get to the Paris Conservatoire, as Boscovitz had suggested. Still remembering the excitement of the Centennial, he longingly read the newspaper reports of the International Exposition, which had opened in Paris on May 1. Imagine getting a glimpse there of the legendary Franz Liszt, the honorary director of the Exposition's Austro-Hungarian section! And a trip abroad might ease the uncomfortable situation created, one guesses, by the precipitate marriage for which he was obviously not ready, financially at least. At best, the visit to Paris could be a delayed, extended honeymoon, even if he could hardly afford such a luxury.

Soon nothing seemed so important to him as going to Paris. He sold his books and pictures, saved his small salary with unusual thrift, and somehow scraped together or borrowed enough money to buy fourth-class tickets and to support himself (and Lizzie?) for a little while, though it is unlikely he accumulated the $600 in gold that the hero of his fictionalized version of his Paris adventure takes with him.[52] According to the account of the episode in his autobiography—which, however, is to be taken with a large supply of salt because he nowhere mentions his marriage to Lizzie but, instead, poses as a footloose bachelor—he did not tell his parents about the trip until the night before the ship was scheduled to depart; with so little time to object they reluctantly consented. Alfredo Barili and a few other friends saw Jim, Lizzie, and his brother John off to New York, where John made sure the couple boarded the *Canada,* which sailed for Europe on September 25, 1878.[53] A day later, Jim's marriage, heretofore divulged only to the families and to close friends, was "published" in Philadelphia.[54] Lizzie was already expecting a child.

℈ *Three*

PARIS AND THE DARK INTERVAL

Huneker and his wife survived the voyage despite bedbugs, poor food, and heavy storms. The dirt and odors of the steerage repelled him, but when he sought relief on the upper-class decks he was chased off—his first encounter with social and economic discrimination. Though he soon discovered that his French was shaky, he could make out the general meaning of a phrase and listened closely to Gallic passengers to train his ear and improve his accent. On October 6 the *Canada* docked in Le Havre, and the next day Huneker arrived in Paris.

The tenements banking the railroad yards made his first view of the city disappointing. Besides, he was exhausted from the voyage and worried about finding quarters he could afford. He almost wished he was back in Philadelphia. But he felt better after reading reassuring letters from home and learning that his mother had arranged to send him a small allowance. Having read Murger's *Scènes de la Vie de Bohème* and determined not to be taken for a bourgeois tourist, he soon donned a Scotch cap, velveteen coat, flaring necktie, low collar, and baggy breeches, and set out to explore the fabulous city.

A friend of his parents, M. Lefevre, a fashionable dressmaker who had once lived in Philadelphia, showed him the sights and insisted that he speak only French. Madame Lefevre had evidently promised Jim's mother to keep an eye on the condition of his soul, for she took him to church so often that he was glad when the Lefevres moved to the village of Villiers-le-Bel, ten miles away, and left him on his own. Lizzie may have gone with them during her pregnancy, for if we take Huneker at his word—a risky procedure, but there is no other evidence—he lived alone in Paris.

The solicitous Lefevre obtained lodgings for him on the top floor of an old, damp building on the Rue Puteaux. A bed, washstand, armoire,

stove, and tiny upright piano filled his sunless room so full that he had
to dress in the hall outside. The only window overlooked a garden, five
stories below, and an array of chimney pots. For these quarters (hardly
the proper place for an expectant mother) he paid fifteen francs a week,
which left him only twenty francs a week to live on. By careful management he could eat one full meal a day at cheap restaurants frequented
by workmen or at wine houses where, for a single franc, one could get
bouillon, boiled beef, carrots, a potato, and a large bottle of wine. With
only a bowl of chocolate and a dry roll to keep him going before dinner,
he spent many an afternoon reading in bed, a large volume of Chopin
perched on his stomach to lessen the hunger pains.[1] He ate so much
bread at the wine house that the proprietress archly asked if he suffered
from tapeworms. After one rent-day he had so little money that in order
to eat he took part in a grim game of chance held in the central market
district of Paris, in which for one centime a try the hungry participants
could jab with a long wooden fork at a whirling cauldron filled with
meat and vegetables, eating whatever they speared.[2]

In his tiny room Huneker practiced the piano from six to ten hours
a day and sometimes longer, despite the complaints of neighbors. He
had applied for an audition at the Conservatoire, declaring that he was
eighteen years old, thus starting, in all likelihood, the lifelong lie about
the date of his birth.[3] He was told that sixteen was the age limit for
entering students, and that there were far more applicants than openings. (One of the few American students at the Conservatoire was Edward MacDowell, who had enrolled in 1876 at the age of fifteen.) But
with the help of Lucy Hamilton Hooper, onetime Paris correspondent
of the Philadelphia *Evening Bulletin* and wife of the American vice-
consul at Paris, Huneker received a letter of special recommendation
from the consul, which got him the audition.

He went to church every day during the week before his tryout,
which took place on November 1, 1878. When the big moment came
and he approached the piano, he was asked how old he was. "Eighteen,"
he lied, whereupon a woman in the examining group laughed. Nearing
his twenty-second birthday, the gawky Huneker, nursing a little beard,
looked more like twenty-five than eighteen. Upset by the laugh, perhaps, he did not play well,[4] and his application for regular instruction
was denied, though he was permitted to audit the piano class of Georges
Mathias, Chopin's greatest pupil. (Among the students at the Conser-

vatoire was young Claude Debussy, who had won second prize in piano in 1877.)[5] Huneker was disappointed but he still had confidence in himself, and there were good private teachers in Paris. He played for Theodore Ritter, one of Europe's outstanding pianists and pedagogues, who sent him to the rather obscure Léopold Doutreleau,[6] from whom Huneker proceeded to take semiweekly lessons in piano and harmony.[7]

Shortly after his audition, he started contributing to the *Evening Bulletin* a series of articles about Paris, still in the limelight because of the great Exposition, the first public expression of French liberation since the Franco-Prussian War. "Paris! Beautiful Paris!" began his first letter, which was dated November 14, 1878, and appeared in the newspaper on November 20. For the next five months he sent his mother, who edited them before they were published, weekly accounts of Paris' churches, lotteries, political changes, concerts, art salons, and plays. When an American, or, better yet, a Philadelphia, musician or painter performed or exhibited in Paris, Huneker proudly reported the event. He informed his townspeople that it was cheaper to live in Paris than in America if one knew how to manage properly,[8] and that the stately buildings, spacious avenues, monuments, and art galleries were more than adequate compensation for such inconveniences as the lack of water.[9] After one of his numerous visits to the Louvre, he made probably his first public reference to the critic from whom he was to learn so much when he remarked that "not even the pen of such a word-painter as Gautier can give an idea of the overwhelming revelation of beauty in all its forms, from the lovely to the sublime, that is found here in such profusion."[10] He even went to the atelier of M. Worth, the famous dress designer, whose creations for the trousseau of the Grand Duchess Anastasia of Russia Huneker described for Philadelphia readers. "It was fair reporting," Huneker recalled with tongue in cheek, "and served to train my eye for the operatic stage, where costume counts more than singing."[11]

Though Huneker, rereading these letters after forty years, detected the "same preoccupation with the arts . . . the same speed, vocabulary, and lack of sequence,"[12] they contain, perhaps as a result of his mother's editing, few traces of the color, wit, and colloquial ease of his mature style. The best thing about them to the young man skimping in a garret was the five dollars each one brought. Yet he usually preferred to squander this small fortune on one royal spree rather than save part of it for the lean last week of the month, by which time he had usually spent his allowance.

After a long day at the piano, he was glad to leave his room and roam over Paris, guided at first by M. Grandjean, a retired functionary who lived in the same building. No doubt the seamier sides of the city attracted him, but he could not afford much dissipation. If the amusing story related in his autobiography is true, he fell in love (?) with a French girl who lived on the floor below his, and wooed her with beefsteaks until he discovered that she was a coachman's mistress.

Paris was exciting in other ways, too. Its historical and literary shrines kindled Huneker's vivid imagination. When his monthly check arrived, he often went to drink, smoke, and look for celebrities at the Café Guerbois, once the rendezvous for the Impressionist painters already notorious in Paris; it was here that he saw Manet and Degas and heard some of the bizarre and beautiful stories improvised so charmingly by the eccentric Villiers de l'Isle-Adam.[13] Elsewhere he saw Victor Hugo, Turgenev, Guy de Maupassant, Mallarmé, Zola, Daudet, and—his most cherished recollection—Gustave Flaubert. He liked to believe that the old man sitting in the carriage that he pursued down the Rue de Rivoli was Franz Liszt, but he was never sure, and one of his biggest disappointments was that he never heard Liszt play.

During its closing weeks he attended the Exposition, which had attracted many American tourists including Brander Matthews, son of a New York millionaire, who was collecting material for articles on the French stage,[14] and John Drew and his friend Lewis Baker—Huneker's hungry deskmate at Roth's—who took time off from sightseeing to see the incomparable Sarah Bernhardt at the Comédie Française.[15] The painting, sculpture, music, and architecture shown at the Paris fair were far superior, Huneker found, to that displayed at Philadelphia's two years earlier. Any attempt, indeed, to compare the two events was discouraged by the touchy Philadelphia press, which admitted that the Paris Exposition was the greatest the world had ever known.[16]

In the huge building on the Champ de Mars, the site of the fair, Huneker haunted the art salons filled with large, highly finished canvases on historical and allegorical subjects by the most popular French painters of the day, among them the portrait painter Bonnat; Meissonier, a specialist in depicting the battles of Napoleon; and Carolus-Duran, teacher of John Singer Sargent. These were the artists who im-

pressed the twenty-one-year-old Huneker and the American painters and
art students he met at the hospitable Paris studio of Milne Ramsey, a
young Philadelphian who had married a friend of the Huneker family.[17]
Although his recollections, set down almost forty years later, of the
pictures he saw in Paris were not entirely trustworthy[18]—he probably
attended the official Salon and the Exposition des Indépendants, the
fourth exhibition by the Impressionists, both in the spring of 1879,[19]
and may have confused the two shows—he and his friends derided the
glaring, striped brushwork and "ugly" subjects of Manet, Monet, Renoir,
Pissarro, and Sisley. Not one word about the struggling insurrectionists,
some of whom were so desperate in 1878 that they were exchanging
pictures for meals[20] (just as Ernest Lawson and other young American
painters did in New York twenty-five years later),[21] appeared in Huneker's letters in the *Evening Bulletin*. After three decades of battling for
little-known artists, writers, and composers in America, he confessed
that he simply had not known enough in 1878 or 1879 to feel the "current of fresh air that swept through Parisian ateliers."[22]

The music in Paris, of course, constantly lured the young pianist.
He heard Nicholas Rubinstein play Tchaikovsky's *Piano Concerto in
B Flat Minor*, as did Edward MacDowell—who was so impressed by
Rubinstein's torrential style that he became dissatisfied with the standards at the Conservatoire and went to study in Stuttgart.[23] Huneker
also fought to get a front-row gallery seat in the Cirque d'Hiver for the
popular Sunday afternoon concerts led by courageous Jacques Pasdeloup, who had caused an uproar by playing Wagner's music after the
Franco-Prussian War. ("Music has no fatherland," the small, stocky
conductor had shouted at the audience.)[24] At one of these concerts,
early in December 1878, Huneker heard for the first time the name of
Moussorgsky and the music of Rimsky-Korsakov, whose symphonic
poem *Sadko* produced a riot in the audience.[25] Huneker frequently
mentioned the Pasdeloup concerts in the *Bulletin* correspondence; in the
spring of 1879, for example, he reported singer Emma Thursby's sensational triumph as a soloist with the orchestra.[26] He attended a piano
recital by Saint-Saëns, and at the debut of the French pianist Clotilde
Kleeberg saw the celebrated composer Charles Gounod. Though he preferred instrumental music, in one week Huneker went to four operas.
To be successful in Paris, he remarked, music had to be embellished
with scenery, ballet, and costumes, while the Germans, on the other
hand, liked music for its own sake.[27]

Richard Wagner, however, was not now one of Huneker's favorites. "Paris, when I lived there," he wrote fourteen years later, "had but one Wagner, a monstrous creature with an enormous head, a mouthful of cruel teeth, perpetually crunching the melodic bones of Bellini, Donizetti and Rossini. A squat figure, eyes weary, insolent and compelling, he seemed a sort of musical ogre, killing all the valiant young knights of harmony. How I hated that picture, and my hate extended to Wagner's music."[28] In 1879 Huneker protested that the human voice was not made of sheet iron and could never have the endurance of an instrument.[29] But his opinion of Wagner was to change radically in the next decade.

Huneker also went to the theater and read the latest French fiction and poetry. Though he was hardly an expert in the field, he hazarded the opinion that the ultramodern school in literature, music, and painting was sacrificing content for virtuosity. "I have seen lately some new productions of a new French poet, little known outside," he reported, "and I could find nothing to admire except the ingenious mechanism of the words."[30] He was clearly not yet a wholehearted apostle of modernism.

Time passed quickly in Paris. After a winter in the house on the Rue Puteaux, Huneker shipped his piano and moved to Villiers-le-Bel, motivated, one suspects, less by his fear of a jealous coachman than by Lizzie's approaching accouchement. The couple took a large room in an inn, a long, low building of flagstone floors and whitewashed walls. Here he practiced and read, commuting to Paris twice a week for his piano lessons and a philosophy course at the Sorbonne, which he soon dropped because the professor was dull. Shortly before the death of Thomas Couture, the teacher of Manet and William Morris Hunt, Huneker visited the painter, the most distinguished resident of Villiers-le-Bel. A pupil of Couture's, John Dusmore, who became a leading painter of historical subjects in America, invited Huneker to accompany him on sketching tours in the area. Nearby, too, was the villa of his friends the Lefevres. He spent several happy months in this village, where, in all likelihood, his first child, a daughter named Marie, was born on March 6, 1879.[31]

His parents, who may well have feared that Jim was wasting his time with a bohemian crowd, must have wanted him to come home. They could probably spare the money they were sending him, but they were anxious to see their first granddaughter. Jim himself was undoubtedly homesick, despite his recollections to the contrary.[32] Whatever the reason, he left Paris after only nine months (instead of the two or three years he later liked to imply he had spent there), and on July 20, 1879,[33] sailed on the *Vaderland* from Antwerp with his wife and daughter.

On August 5, two days after their return to Philadelphia,[34] the following announcement appeared in the *Evening Bulletin*:

James Huneker, the young Philadelphian whose recent letters published in the *Bulletin* attracted such general attention in musical circles, has arrived home from the French capital. While in Paris Mr. Huneker's time was devoted to the study of music, being the pupil of the ablest French professors, and he comes home a thorough musician. He will settle in his native city and adopt the profession of music teaching.[35]

Relatively little, however, is known about his activities during the next six years, the "dark interval" in his life.[36] He and Lizzie moved into a boardinghouse at 1715 Spruce Street, where he gave piano lessons for some months, beginning in mid-October.[37] At this time, or perhaps a little later, he taught two days a week in nearby Riverton, New Jersey. Though he probably exaggerated, afterward, the extent of his "homesickness" for Paris, his "patrie physique," he missed the excitement and freedom he had found there; he sensed that the Paris adventure was to be an important milestone in his experience, for when it occurred to him, less than two months after he had come home, to record in his notebook significant facts of his life, it was surely no coincidence that he began writing on September 25, exactly one year since his departure for Paris. (Even this early, he revealed a disturbing tendency to decorate the truth for romantic or dramatic effect: his parents, he noted, "celebrated their Nuptials on the 21st of Oct. 1849, the day of Chopin's & Poe's death," Poe's name, it seems, having been inserted later;[38] the plain truth, however, is that the Hunekers were married on October 18,[39] Chopin died on October 17, and Poe on October 7.) Huneker kept busy teaching, reading, and studying piano, taking lessons from Alfredo Barili from September 1879 until Barili moved to Atlanta a year later.[40] In October 1880 he resumed his studies with Cross,[41] and later he worked with two other prominent Philadelphia musicians, Samuel L. Herrmann, organist at the Cathedral for sixteen years and at a synagogue for thirty,[42] and Anthony Stankowitch, pupil of Anton Bruckner and a talented pianist four years younger than Huneker.[43]

He continued the old music-making with Franz Schubert, who became a fresco painter but played the violin in public as late as 1886,[44] and saw much of Max Heinrich, who returned to Philadelphia in 1879 or 1880[45] and in 1882 and 1883 lived opposite the Race Street residence of Huneker's parents. And a few other cultured families opened their doors to the young piano teacher, who was already known locally as a wit and raconteur.

In November 1879 he probably attended the first annual exhibition of the Philadelphia Society of Artists, for he had friends among the members, one of them being Herman N. Hynemann, whom he had met in Paris and whose "Desdemona" was the hit of the show.[46] Another exhibitor was Thomas P. Anschutz, who helped to inspire the realistic painting that emerged in America shortly after the turn of the century,[47] the style that Huneker made his chief "cause" as an art critic. Huneker undoubtedly admired Thomas Eakins, a professor at the Pennsylvania Academy in 1879, who defied the taboo against painting from the nude in his life-drawing classes, and must have sympathized with Eakins when the latter resigned in 1886 over the hullabaloo caused when he removed the loincloth from a male model while pointing out the details of the pelvis to a class of women.[48] Huneker himself surely frowned upon the heritage of Quaker modesty which forced Academy officials to clothe their statues in muslin on ladies' days,[49] and was later to protest vehemently against all such signs of prudery.

The most picturesque man Huneker ever saw, apart from Walt Whitman—whom Huneker sometimes encountered in 1879–80 at the Carl Gaertner Quintette Club Concerts held at the Academy of Music and escorted afterward to the Camden ferry streetcar[50]—was Ole Bull, whom he heard during the violinist's last American tour in 1880. "The grand old fellow bewitched you," he recalled. "He was a handsome Merlin, with a touch of the charlatan and a touch of Liszt in his tall, willowy figure, small waist, and heavy head of hair." Though he indulged in the rubato and abused the portamento, Bull nevertheless pleased the masses with his simple melodies, and only the most confirmed musical snob, Huneker felt, would sniff at his playing.[51]

In the early 1880's an even greater violinist, Eduard Remenyi, who had caused a sensation at the Paris Exposition in 1878[52] and was now performing at Philadelphia's Männerchor Garden, used to visit the elder Hunekers on Sunday nights.[53] From this cosmopolitan musician Huneker learned much about Liszt and Wagner.

On January 31, 1880, Huneker's infant daughter died.[54] ("The death of a child is like the death of a tiny tender flower," he remarked long afterward.)[55] He and Lizzie moved from one boardinghouse to another; by the following summer, when he had acquired more pupils and was cheerful about his prospects, they had lived in at least three, and in the next six years they stayed in three others.[56] The birth of a second daughter, named Frances Edna, on December 16, 1880,[57] may account for the fact that the couple lived with his parents for a short period thereafter and then kept house with her mother.[58] Versatile as he proved to be, Huneker had little talent for domesticity and was hard-pressed, or even unable, during most of this period, to earn a living.

Meanwhile, attempting to fill the gaps in his desultory education, he outlined for himself a gigantic five-year reading course including at least five hundred authors of major works in history, art, music, painting, and sculpture as well as belles-lettres. He also listed textbooks on astronomy, poetry, chemistry, natural philosophy, mythology, and modern languages.[59] He managed to read almost every book on his long list—though it took him fifty years instead of five. And with his remarkable memory he retained most of what he read.

He kept abreast of modern European culture by scanning the many international publications available in Philadelphia libraries, the Mercantile alone subscribing to more than a dozen foreign newspapers.[60] The *Evening Bulletin* printed news items about popular English writers, often quoting London newspapers and magazines, and occasionally referred to lesser-known Continental figures such as Ibsen and Strindberg.[61] It also publicized stage appearances of Henry Irving, Tommaso Salvini, the great Italian actor, and Sarah Bernhardt (who made her American debut in 1880). Huneker's claim that he himself wrote for the newspaper at this time cannot be proved or disproved on available evidence.[62] If he did, it may have been about the stage, for he once stated that he began writing drama criticism in 1881.[63] During 1881, at any rate, he was keeping a scrapbook of newspaper and magazine clippings—many of them from the New York *Dramatic Mirror*—about the theater in Philadelphia and New York.[64] None of the articles can be positively identified as his work, but the racy stories and bits of theatrical gossip anticipate the frothier material that was to appear in his later writings.

In 1880, he recorded, he "went to Kennett June 19th but didn't like it. Read and saw many books & memorials by Bayard Taylor."[65] This cryptic entry in his notebook suggests two possibilities: either he found an opening for a music teacher at Kennett Square, some forty miles southwest of Philadelphia, considered moving or actually moved there, was unimpressed or dissatisfied, and returned home; or else he simply made a pilgrimage to the estate of the late Taylor, whose cosmopolitanism, knowledge of German literature, and exotic travel sketches had made him an idol of Huneker's, and was disappointed that the village was not like the place Taylor had romanticized in his novel *The Story of Kennett* (1866). The first hypothesis seems more probable, since Huneker would hardly be concerned about liking or disliking Kennett if he merely went on a literary pilgrimage, but no proof that he ever lived in Kennett has turned up.

He was present at Philadelphia's Horticultural Hall on January 17, 1882, when Oscar Wilde, the talk of London drawing rooms, butt of Du Maurier's caricatures in *Punch*, and target of the new, sensationally successful Gilbert and Sullivan opera *Patience*, softly urged Americans to create a distinctive, indigenous art. "Let the Greek carve his lions and the Goth his dragons," said Wilde, lecturing across the country on a lucrative tour arranged by D'Oyly Carte, producer of *Patience*, "buffalo and wild deer are the animals for you." Huneker himself would not have chosen such Western symbols, but he undoubtedly agreed with Wilde. The visitor's attacks on American materialism—"America's gold should be used for the goldsmith's art, not merely for barren speculation. There should be some better record of it left in your history than the merchant's panic and the ruined home"—may not have stirred most of his audience,[66] but it must have pleased the aesthetic music teacher struggling so ineffectively to get his hands on a little of that gold and despising the money standards by which Americans were measured and by which he was, so far, a failure. One surmises that without approving such trappings of Wilde's posing as the famous sunflowers and knee breeches, Huneker was already sophisticated enough to sympathize with Wilde's condemnation of the efforts of American newspapers to "induce the public to judge a sculptor, for instance, never by his statues but by the way he treats his wife; a painter by the amount of his income; and a poet by the color of his necktie."[67] Though there is no supporting evidence, Huneker claimed that he managed to meet

Wilde somehow[68]—either at Horticultural Hall after the lecture or at one of the Philadelphia receptions held for the visitor.

This lecture must have provided a lively topic of conversation for a well-informed group consisting of Huneker, Professor Roth, Dr. Nolan, and another friend, Frank Cunningham.[69] On Saturday afternoons, especially in the summer, this quartet would walk from the Academy of Natural Sciences to Fairmount Park. At the park café Huneker and Cunningham would drink beer and listen while Roth, the humanist and classical scholar, argued fiercely with Nolan, the scientist with a bias toward modern literature and one of the wittiest men in town.[70] Then, as later, Huneker found men more stimulating, intellectually, than women.

At the end of 1883 the local appearance of two distinguished Englishmen gave his circle something else to talk about. On December 4, 1883, Huneker and his father saw Henry Irving's first American production of *Hamlet* at the Chestnut Street Theater. "As cold as Macready, without the elocution," whispered John Huneker after Irving's first speech. Jim was to see Irving many times and was never to admire him as much as did William Winter, then the leading American drama critic. Huneker, indeed, found Irving's style too cerebral and his gait and speech mannerisms distracting, and remembered him, long afterward, as "that worst of great actors."[71]

On the next day, December 5, Huneker went to New York to attend the American première of Boito's *Mefistofele* at the Metropolitan Opera,[72] which had just begun its first season, but on the 28th he was back home to hear a lecture on Emerson by the other English visitor, Matthew Arnold. Apart from their high regard for certain French writers, the famous critic and the much younger Huneker had little in common. Huneker, for instance, was already an idolater of the "goddess lubricity," who, Arnold lamented, was worshiped in France;[73] moreover, Arnold had a low opinion of Whitman. Shaking Arnold's chilly hand in Association Hall[74] after a poorly delivered and ill-received lecture (the *Evening Bulletin* editorially reprimanded Arnold for declaring that Longfellow's poem "The Bridge" was worth all of Emerson's poetry),[75] Huneker sensed Arnold's coolness toward Americans in general. He probably would have agreed with the Philadelphia writer Charles Godfrey Leland, better known as "Hans Breitmann," whom Arnold impressed as the "prince of prigs."[76]

Actually, Huneker could not have been in the most receptive mood for "culture," for on November 12, 1883, occurred one of the few events in his personal life that can be dated precisely during this period, the death of his second daughter, not quite three years old.[77] Lizzie bore no more children, and the couple's childlessness further weakened Huneker's thin sense of family responsibility.

About this time Huneker met Theodore Presser, who was to have a great influence upon his future career. Presser had attended the Leipzig Conservatory (where Samuel L. Herrmann, later Huneker's teacher, was also studying),[78] returning to teach at Hollins Institute in Virginia. There, in October 1883, he started *Etude*, a monthly magazine for pianists and piano teachers, which he soon moved to Philadelphia.[79]

Huneker's opposite in most ways, Presser, too, was something of a dreamer, though a more practical one: he had visions of establishing a music-publishing business as well as a magazine—a dream that eventually materialized into the Presser Company, the world's largest music publisher. Nourishing this business, *Etude* was to last for seventy-four years (until June 1957),[80] but in the 1880's Presser frequently had to pawn his watch to keep it and himself alive.[81]

By the spring of 1885, if not earlier,[82] Huneker was writing for *Etude*; his first signed contribution, a letter to the editor on "The Modern School of Piano Playing," appeared in the April issue. During the rest of 1885 articles by him were printed almost every month, though he signed none of them after May. In that month emerged "Old Fogy," the fictitious character—he may have been modeled in part on Charles Jarvis[83]—through whom Huneker in a series of humorous essays contrasted his own classical and romantic musical tastes and made fun of bigoted antimodernism. To liven up the somewhat Teutonic magazine, he even composed and printed indignant letters to the editor, signed "Old Maid" or "One of the Girls," attacking his own articles. These were the first indications in print of the lightness of touch which was to distinguish much of his work. He also displayed his love of the bizarre tale in "A Fantasy After Chopin: An Intense Romance After Poe," which foreshadowed the stories that became his trademark in fiction.

In early July 1885, he and Lizzie were in New York to cover for *Etude* the annual meeting of the Music Teachers' National Association, which had been founded by Presser. (One wonders whether Huneker still wore the whiskers, mustache, and goatee he was wearing three months earlier—and had perhaps cultivated ever since his visit to Paris —when his photograph, the only extant one revealing any such adornment, had been taken with Franz Schubert and another friend.)[84] The couple stayed at the home of Rudolph Garrigue, president of an insurance company and the head of a cultured family; his eldest daughter married Thomas Masaryk, first president of Czechoslovakia, and another daughter, Eleanor, the wife of Henry Ferguson, a landscape painter, was an excellent pianist and piano teacher, who convinced Huneker that to become a pianist it was not necessary to master *all* the studies written for that instrument, as he had been trying to do.[85] Located in the heart of New York's concert-hall district, the Garrigue home was frequented by world-famous musicians. From here Huneker sent the only letter addressed to his mother alone which seems to have survived:

MY DEAR MOTHER,

I refrained from writing until after the convention had ended as I was not only busy but had nothing in particular to say, except to remark the agreeable coolness of the weather at this season usually so oppressive. The days have gone by so rapidly & have been such a whirl of excitement as to leave very little time for reflection. I shirked all the work I could as it was at once onerous & unprofitable. I didn't come to New York to be a clerk & I told Presser so when he complained of my lack of enthusiasm. We are indeed in clover. A lovely large house, lovely people. Oh Mother what an ideal home. What courtesy & what respect & love to each other—no company manners, no airs. Everything runs on oiled wheels. Wealth of course facilitates matters but money would never give the beautiful atmosphere that bathes all. The Mother is all the word could possibly convey & the family adore her. I will tell you lots when we come back which is a hard matter at present even to think of. Mr. G. wants me to stay in N. Y. & try for something. He has influence both as a man of wealth & business but also as a public man in everything going & do you know I am almost tempted to think of it. The style of life & freedom suits me & is bound to develop individuality & independence of character—something I lack terribly. However time enough. The convention with a few exceptions it must be confessed was a bore & things were very crude. How could it be otherwise when you have such representatives. *Hoosiers* for the most part. You can tell Paul that there were few if any Germans & I saw no beer nor even heard of it. To tell the truth they were so slow a set of old dried up fogies as you could meet & it took all the young blood could do to hold their own. The music was fair until last night when I heard for the first time a genius *Fanny Bloomfield* play as I never expected to hear a woman play or to hear the much abused Piano sing. Oh it was superb, nothing superlative enough could describe it. It was *violin* playing on the Piano so intense, so electric, so sweet & so masterly. I met her & had a long talk, in fact I met everybody & was complimented for the *Etude* a hundred times. Brotherhood the Technicon [a silent keyboard for strengthening the fingers][86] man made very flattering offers to take the agency in Phila. The instrument carried all before it & was a great success. Good bye dear Mother & excuse the hurry of this letter. Will see you Tuesday probably. Love to all from both Lizzie and myself & also to you.

Love from your fond
JIM[87]

From Philadelphia, he mailed Miss Bloomfield a clipping from the August *Etude* of his enthusiastic notice of her playing, requesting her photograph,[88] which she sent. If she came to Philadelphia, he replied on September 18, "don't hesitate in asking me to do anything for you as I feel a little strongly on the subject. . . . I have your picture where I can always see it—opposite my grand—& a capital inspiration it is." A month later, he soon learned, she married Sigmund Zeisler, the distinguished Chicago lawyer, but they continued to correspond[89] and became good friends, though they seldom saw each other. (When he congratulated the couple on their silver wedding anniversary, Huneker remarked that he had not felt very kindly toward Zeisler twenty-five years earlier.)[90] Huneker called her his "representative musical woman" and praised her at every opportunity, while she apparently encouraged his writing. "I don't forget the good angel who first gave me confidence," he wrote her almost twenty years after their meeting.[91]

At the Novelties Exhibition, a display of new inventions which opened in Franklin Hall on September 15, 1885, Huneker demonstrated the pianos exhibited by his former employer, William Dutton, for whom he may have continued to work occasionally as a clerk. On October 31 both Presser and Huneker—who played at the Exhibition that night as usual[92]—had a surgeon cut the superciliary tendon between the ring and little fingers on the left hand to increase its stretching power, an operation "Old Fogy" had derided a few months earlier.[93] Instead of improving his playing, however, the operation probably hindered it.[94]

In January 1886, shortly after the Metropolitan Opera had concluded a two-week stay in Philadelphia, Huneker was restless and un-

happy.[95] He could not make a living by writing for the struggling *Etude*
or by teaching (if he had not given up this occupation entirely, he was
obviously losing interest in it), and the seemingly patient Lizzie had to
work at dressmaking to support both of them—which did not ease his
sense of failure or increase his fondness for Philadelphia. They were
now boarding across the street from his parents' home, and his father,
who aided the couple financially,[96] would have been a saint if he had
not reminded Jim that he had warned him against a career in music.
To make matters worse, Jim was all too aware of the success of his hard-
headed brother John, rapidly rising in the business world for which Jim
was temperamentally unsuited. Among the solid Hunekers, indeed, he
was already the gray sheep, and his hue appeared to be darkening. No
wonder he wanted to forget these painful years.

Jim had not forgotten his visit to New York or Garrigue's suggestion that he settle in the country's musical center, compared to which
Philadelphia seemed downright dull. "I quite agree with our friend of
the *Musical Courier* that the City of Brotherly Love is the most unmusical of any city in the Union," wrote *Etude*'s "News of the Month" columnist—probably Huneker—in the issue of February 1886.[97] Presser
had introduced him in the previous summer to Marc Blumenberg, co-
owner of the thriving young *Courier*, who might, perhaps, give him a
job on that magazine. In New York, moreover, he could take lessons
from the best piano teachers in America, for he still had hopes of becoming a concert pianist.

He must have thought the matter over carefully, and on Tuesday
afternoon, February 16, 1886, he told Lizzie that he was tired of the
responsibilities of marriage,[98] packed his bags, and went to New York
alone—"without a godspeed," he recalled, "save from one faithful
soul."[99] Was this "faithful soul" Lizzie? One wonders. He had left
behind him a board bill of $23, which his father had to pay for the
improvident and now footloose son just turned twenty-nine.[100]

NEW YORK: MUSICAL BOHEMIA

In 1886 New York was not yet a city of skyscrapers, the most prominent structures being the steeple of Trinity Church, the Produce Exchange Tower, and the Washington, Times, and Tribune buildings.
But stores, hotels, boardinghouses, and cafés had already invaded Union
Square, and fashionable people no longer lived around it. At the corner of Fourteenth Street and Irving Place was the Academy of Music,
the largest hall in the city. A little farther east were the white façade of
Steinway Hall and the piano showrooms of Steinway and Sons. Nearby
clustered English chophouses, German beer gardens, Italian restaurants,
and Jewish delicatessens.

The chief theaters—Wallack's (where Huneker saw his first New
York play on his first visit to Manhattan in May 1877),[1] Union Square,
Fifth Avenue, Daly's, Madison Square, Tony Pastor's—were located
south of Thirty-fourth Street. At the recently opened Lyceum, soon to
become one of society's favorite showhouses, Steele Mackaye had just
initiated a theatrical era by installing in a theater the first electric lights,
asbestos curtain, elevator-stage, folding seats, and air-conditioning system.[2] Lined with luxurious hotels and glittering bars, the "Rialto" ran
from Madison Square to Thirty-fourth Street, new incandescent lamps
brightly illuminating marquees and hotel lobbies. The gas-lit streets
were filled with horsecars, coupés, hansoms, victorias, carry-alls, surreys,
and elevated railways. The Metropolitan Opera House, not yet three
years old, had been built far uptown by Wall Street financiers who could
not obtain boxes at the Academy. Diagonally across from it on Broadway was the new Moorish Casino, already the Mecca of light opera and
beautiful showgirls.

Most of the art galleries were situated on Fifth Avenue below Thirty-
fourth Street. The Metropolitan Museum of Art in Central Park had
been opened in 1880, and the National Academy of Design occupied

a Venetian palace on the corner of Fourth Avenue and Twenty-third Street, much more opulent quarters than those of the Society of American Artists, formed nine years earlier in opposition to the powerful, conservative Academy. To this handsome building, three months after Huneker's arrival, was transferred from the American Art Galleries the striking exhibition of "Works in Oil and Pastel by the Impressionists of Paris," brought to New York for the first time that spring by the Paris art dealer Durand-Ruel—an epoch-making event marking the introduction of modern art to America at almost the precise time when Impressionism as a movement was ending in France. Though some critics found fault with the "new" style—the *Sun's*, for example, objected to Renoir's "lumpy and obnoxious creations," Degas' drawing, Sisley's "bad painting," and Seurat's "coarse, vulgar and commonplace mind"—the American response to the show was surprisingly favorable, giving Durand-Ruel high hopes for future sales.[3]

Starting a successful run in mid-February 1886, Johann Strauss's *The Gypsy Baron* included in its cast Francis Wilson of Philadelphia, three years older than Huneker, whose reputation in comic opera was shortly to be made by the smash hit *Erminie*. Veteran actors Edwin Booth, Lawrence Barrett, and James O'Neill were all appearing in the city, as was the famous Madame Modjeska. Before the end of the year, *Jim the Penman,* the source of Huneker's favorite private "alias," made its memorable Broadway debut. Theodore Thomas was conducting a series of popular concerts, while in lectures delivered in French, novelist "Henry Gréville" (Alice Durand) was maintaining that the French novel *could* safely be placed in the hands of American virgins.[4] And literary people were amused to read in the newspapers that Oscar Wilde, back in London, wished to outlaw "all books that try to prove anything."[5]

Determined to be on his own, Huneker had not informed his New York friends of his arrival. Once in Manhattan, he obtained a room at the Morton House, overlooking Union Square, and then headed straight for Lienau's Café on Fourteenth Street, opposite Steinway Hall, a gathering place for musical celebrities, its back room the scene of many impromptu concerts by Joseffy, Friedheim, Neupert, Rosenthal, and other great pianists. After dinner, Huneker walked a few doors down to Lüchow's, a German café established a few years earlier, where Hugh Craig of the *Musical Courier,* a cultivated Englishman whom Huneker had met in Philadelphia, introduced him to Otto Floersheim, the fat, pompous co-proprietor of the *Courier*. Wandering back to Lienau's, the three men joined Marc Blumenberg, a shrewd, piercing-eyed Jew, who, reminded that Huneker wrote about music, invited him to call at the East Fourteenth Street office of the weekly.

The next day, Jim rented (for eight dollars a week, with meals) a comfortable top-floor room in a boardinghouse at 40 Seventh Avenue, on the corner of Thirteenth Street. Then, thirsty, he went to Mould's, near Union Square, another rendezvous for musicians, actors, painters, poets, and newspapermen, where he met the café's most famous habitué, the extraordinary Francis Saltus.[6] A half-brother of Edgar Saltus, the novelist, and once a protégé of Théophile Gautier in Paris, this dissipated bohemian poet spoke thirteen and wrote twenty languages,[7] played the piano, was an expert on Donizetti, and coined more witty epigrams than any man Huneker ever heard except Oscar Wilde. At Mould's almost every day from noon until two in the morning, Saltus would drink, talk, and write articles and poems for the *Musical Courier, Town Topics*, and any other publication that would buy them. He and Huneker became friends, and over the next few years he must have told Huneker many intriguing stories about Gautier's circle.

During the rest of 1886 and throughout 1887 Huneker's activities are shadowy. These were seemingly lean days; the free bean soup and the possibility of getting writing commissions attracted him to Mould's even more than the presence of the exhilarating Saltus. Obviously untrue was his later claim that in Paris he attended Anton Rubinstein's Seven Historical Concerts, given in April 1886.[8] His steadiest job was with *Etude*, for which he wrote regularly until February 1888. Despite Mould's soup he was not able to live on what Presser could pay him, for he was also taking piano lessons from Edmund Neupert—the Norwegian to whom Edvard Grieg dedicated his *A Minor Concerto*—and later from Rafael Joseffy. When he could spare it, which was not often, he would also send Lizzie a few dollars. By the spring of 1887, he was playing the piano at private entertainments to make a little money.[9]

Huneker's mother had asked Maurice Egan, who had moved to New York in 1878 and gone into journalism, to see that Jim went to mass every Sunday, and he was often a guest at the Egans' home in Brooklyn,[10] though their strict Catholicism and ultraconservative literary tastes made him a little uneasy. (As editor of the Catholic *Freeman's*

Journal, Egan was warning young readers against "thoughtless and indiscriminate novel reading," condemning Balzac for teaching bad lessons, describing Dostoevski's *Crime and Punishment* as a book "no careful mother could give to her daughter, no prudent father advise his son to read," and chiding Tolstoy for not portraying as reprehensible the "premature lovemaking" of children in *War and Peace.*)[11] Huneker's favorite breakfast of beefsteak and claret (he may not have eaten much the night before) seemed strange to Egan's wife, but she served it unquestioningly after Huneker assured her that Parisian Catholics would consider it perfectly respectable.

Believing that the trouble between him and Lizzie was mainly economic, the Egans tried to unite the couple by getting him musical engagements in private homes, even telling their friends about Huneker's finger operation—which was considered so *dernier cri* that once or twice it enabled him to collect a fee of fifty dollars instead of the usual twenty-five. But he was not very tractable, refusing to play at a Washington Square mansion, for example, on the pretext that it lacked a Steinway grand, whereas the real reason was that he wanted to see an opera that afternoon. He turned down another good job to attend the American première of *Tristan und Isolde* on December 1, 1886, even though he had to pawn his overcoat to buy a top gallery seat at the Metropolitan. ("People don't do such things," Egan expostulated with Huneker, "even for art.")[12]

Jim's spicy stories shocked Mrs. Egan, but they brightened the bachelor parties that Egan gave during her absence. "His curiosity was illimitable," Egan recalled, "and it seemed to me his power of expressing what he had seen and heard was beyond that of anybody who ever spoke in English."[13] Other testimony of Huneker's astonishing conversational pyrotechnics, the release in company of a mind loaded to overflowing in lonely, ravenous reading, comes from Charles J. Rosebault, a *Sun* reporter (as a twenty-year-old cub he had scored a memorable scoop by confirming the rumor that ex-President Grant was suffering from cancer),[14] who met Huneker a few years later and was eventually one of his closest friends. Rosebault depicted the Huneker of the early 1890's:

Imagine the *Encyclopædia Britannica* suddenly becoming vocal and giving tongue with all its potential eloquence; skipping from A to L and thence to G and on to Z, selecting topics helter-skelter, so that the pattern on the whole, if reduced to design and color, would be very like a crazy quilt of many hues.

Have the speed of speech equal to that of the motor of a twin-six at an exhibition tryout. Lend to it the fire and enthusiasm of a young Sicilian at the climax of his first love avowal.[15]

Another friend, Walter Damrosch, the eminent conductor, never forgot Huneker's "torrents of seething aphorisms and witticisms."[16] Skeptical acquaintances could scarcely believe that any human being—let alone a pianist *manqué*—could be such a virtuoso of language and have so much curious lore at his fingertips.

There was a rumor that after James Gibbons had been made a Cardinal in 1886, Huneker had wired him: "Dear Uncle,[17] where did you get that hat? Love, Jimmy." Though it sounded like something a playful Huneker might have done, what really happened was that he jokingly remarked in the *Musical Courier* three years after Gibbons' elevation that there was "absolutely no truth in the report that the organist of the Baltimore Cathedral, while suffering from emotional insanity, played 'Where Did You Get That Hat?' [the hit song of 1888] just as Cardinal Gibbons entered the church last week during the Catholic Council."[18]

If Huneker went to mass, it was mainly to please his mother or to enjoy the beauty of the ritual, for art was his chief god, as Alfredo Barili's wife had discovered in the late 1870's when she once found him kneeling in front of a bust of Beethoven in her parlor and praying, "O Divine Creator of the Ninth . . ."[19] The story he told in *Etude* of a dying pianist who, when asked by a priest if he was Catholic or Protestant, replied "Father, I am a pianist,"[20] illustrates his own attitude toward religion. Like Gautier, Huneker was a man for whom the visible world existed, though in certain moods he liked to speculate about the eternal mysteries.

Indeed, the former amateur magician was soon to be, if not already, engrossed in the literature of theosophy, a fashionable movement of the time. Too close to the earthly plane to be a real believer, Huneker was intrigued more by the personality of the cult's leaders than by their esoteric outpourings. His recollection of the exotic founder of the Theosophical Society, Helena Blavatsky, seems strong and vivid—"Whenever I smell a Russian cigarette I recall her eyes," he wrote—but the episode may be another creation of his lively imagination.[21] Yet his intense intellectual curiosity and his spiritual restlessness, spurred by his growing estrangement from the Catholic Church, led him to examine the bible of theosophy as well as the Koran, the Mormon revelations, and

Science and Health. The result of this study was one of the earliest non-musical sketches he produced in New York, a humorous satire entitled "The Occult Fly," written in August 1889 and printed two months later in the New York *Home Journal.*[22]

The plain fact, nevertheless, was that Huneker preferred Pilsner to a church pew or mystic philosophy. He was far more comfortable at a café with his cronies than at a dinner party with dull people, for he was used to speaking his mind and could not always hide his boredom. At one such affair the hostess, a celebrated beauty, said to him: "If I lost my looks, my husband would cease to love me and I would commit suicide." "Don't let that trouble you," said Huneker. "If you've been married two years, he probably doesn't know whether you're a Venus or a Hottentot."[23] Yet Huneker himself had a keen eye for a pretty face and figure, and he took full advantage of his freedom. In corresponding with Jim's mother, Egan had to suppress some details which would have pained her, but Huneker's witty and worldly brother Paul could read much between the lines.[24]

When Matthew Arnold made his second visit to America early in 1886, Egan wanted Huneker to try to thaw out and impress the icy Englishman. According to one dubious report, however, Jim refused to talk to Arnold because at a party Huneker had heard him whisper to his wife in the middle of a Chopin Etude, "I think, my dear, we ought to get out of this hole tomorrow on the nine o'clock train."[25] (It is more likely that Huneker was too shy or too much awed by Arnold to have wanted to talk with him.) At the Garrigues' Huneker encountered friendlier, more musical people than Arnold—among them Theodore Thomas, who lived across the street; William Mason, the pianist and teacher who had studied with Liszt and knew dozens of stories about him; and Victor Herbert, a young cellist who had come to New York in 1886 when the Metropolitan Opera had engaged his wife.

On March 7, 1887, Huneker wrote Alfredo Barili:

I am in musical journalism. I write for a half dozen papers. Do you like my work in the *Etude*? I do all the work signed "Old Fogy" and "J.H." I will give you a notice in March—news of the month—look out for it. . . . I am studying with Neupert—I play the Chopin Etudes and the Chopin E Minor Concerto. Just think of Huneker ever getting tone & technic. But I have and can prove it although I am only a salon pianiste. . . . I am crazy to tell you about the season. I am Wagner mad. I know all the *leit motiven.*[26]

He was special correspondent for North's *Philadelphia Musical Journal,* published by that city's largest sheet-music and piano firm,[27] but the other "papers" remain unidentified. One of them may have been the *American Art Journal,* which used two of his pieces in July 1887 and in the following October printed his "Wagner and Swinburne," the "first article" he had written in New York.[28] Here he emphasized the treatment of passion by these two men—his habit of comparing artists in different fields began early—whose sexual proclivities, one suspects, piqued his curiosity almost as much as their work. As his friends soon discovered, indeed, Huneker's talk was already loaded with succulent tidbits on the sexual vagaries of artists. "A streak of strange morbidity ran through [his] wildest sallies," Charles Henry Meltzer, the drama critic, remembered. "His mind was in turn attuned to harmony and psychopathy . . . a craving for the rare and dark and curious."[29] (Huneker eventually hinted publicly that Wagner had a strong homosexual component, and declared privately, with more confidence than later and more thorough students of the poet's life have been able to muster up, that Swinburne was *not* homosexual.)[30] None of these remarks, to be sure, got into this early essay; Huneker clearly revealed that although he had read widely and could move easily from one art to another, he had not yet renounced the standards of "genteel" moralistic criticism:

Shakespeare with his types of humanity and Beethoven with his ever fresh themes, never hysterical, never morbid, are after all the truer and greater artists. . . . To them then must we look for the highest or best spiritual nourishment. Wagner has left the world an imperishable legacy of art but heaven forbid that we should allow the spirit of his music to guide our moralities. . . . Swinburne has drawn from the English language some of the loveliest music it is capable of giving; but where would we be if we followed him as a guide and teacher? . . . It is the duty and the gift of every great artist to instruct in some latent way, for in the beautiful can be found the best and most genuine lessons.

This sounds much more like his mother than the James Huneker who emerged in the 1890's as the apostle of nondidactic, amoral art—and, indeed, she may well have had a hand in polishing the essay.

By the middle of 1887 Huneker was contributing meatier articles to *Etude.* Taking a long look at American composers in the June issue, for example, he ascribed the backwardness of our music to American materialism and also to the fact that no indigenous type had evolved out of the enormous amalgam created by foreign immigration. The true American of the future would be "a product of all nations, the most cosmopolitan, and let us hope the most original, man on the globe." Meanwhile, the recent development of a leisure class had resulted in the construction of conservatories, opera houses, and concert halls as well as museums, libraries, and theaters. Americans could proudly claim several of the world's finest orchestras; capable singers, musicians, and composers; and an opera house in New York which, in the past season, had artistically produced Wagner's demanding masterpieces before appreciative audiences.[31] Shortly afterward, Huneker reported that the work of the young American composer Edward MacDowell possessed "extreme finish, originality, and a certain something that augurs well for his future," and at the end of the year he commended Frank Van der Stucken for conducting the compositions of American composers in a series of New York concerts.[32]

In July 1887 Huneker talked to Marc Blumenberg at the Music Teachers' meeting in Indianapolis, which he covered for *Etude*,[33] and in August he joined the staff of the *Musical Courier* on a trial basis, receiving no salary until the beginning of 1888. (As his father had often remarked, Jim's specialty was working for others at reduced rates.)[34] The *Courier* had begun in 1880 as a magazine for the piano, organ, and sewing-machine trade, but Blumenberg and Otto Floersheim, who had bought it early in 1883, had turned it into a music journal exclusively.[35] Well-versed in history, philosophy, literature, and art in addition to music, Blumenberg had a phenomenal memory on which he could rely instead of reference books,[36] and a head for business which might have made him a multimillionaire like his famous cousin Otto Kahn if he had gone into finance.[37] He was egotistic, aggressive, and, his enemies claimed, unethical.[38] Some musicians who did not advertise in the *Courier* complained that they were given poorer critical notices than those who did, and others protested that they had been charged for advertisements which they had not ordered and had been forced to pay for them to avoid unfavorable criticism.[39] Rival editors, jealous of the magazine's success, may have exaggerated its unsavoriness, which was better publicized than Blumenberg's generosity to needy music teachers. At any rate, his agile intellect and cheerfulness appealed to Huneker, who had little to do with the business side of the *Courier*. "If there were 'ill-gotten gains,' " he recalled, "they were scrupulously concealed from me."[40]

Musical journalism in the 1880's was not, to be sure, a pretty business. Rival piano manufacturers supported the various publications and used them for advertising. When newspaper critics thumbed down artists who happened to prefer a certain make of piano, they were denounced by journals in which the manufacturer of that piano advertised. Sometimes the critics were blasted by the same journal for which, at other times, they wrote feature articles. Ugly language and libel actions were profuse.[41]

In 1887 the chief music critics of New York newspapers—all quartered on or near Park Row, a short street in lower Manhattan—were Henry E. Krehbiel of the *Tribune*, the rather conservative dean of the group, an authority on folk music, opera, and Beethoven, and the type of critic whom Huneker (who nevertheless respected him) labeled a "datehound";[42] the *Evening Post*'s Henry T. Finck, a strong supporter of Wagner, Liszt, Chopin, and Grieg (his special favorite), author of books on anthropology and food, and a lecturer on music history at the National Conservatory in New York, whose faculty Huneker was to join soon; William J. Henderson of the *Times*, an expert on singing, whose tastes were as conservative as Krehbiel's but whose witty, epigrammatic style, much livelier than Krehbiel's, Huneker greatly admired;[43] and Albert Steinberg of the *Herald*, a brilliant young stylist whose ugly sarcasm, however, made him unpopular with his colleagues, and whose career was cut short by ill-health and a mania for gambling.[44] (Huneker, who was probably closer, personally, to Steinberg than to any of the other critics, later portrayed him as "Alfred Stone" in *Painted Veils*.) Shortly afterward, Richard Aldrich, a competent and scholarly if not too entertaining writer, became Krehbiel's assistant—he shared many of his mentor's prejudices—and he took over as the *Times*'s critic when Henderson shifted to the *Sun* in 1902.[45]

For more than three decades these men were to be Huneker's coworkers and friends, with whom he sometimes disagreed but seldom, if ever, quarreled. Believing that good music would survive *all* criticism, aware of the critic's drudgery, and placing high value on camaraderie, he kept his friendships in good repair and was always quick to praise the work of his associates.[46] Consequently, he was generally liked in New York from the first, even if jealousy of him sometimes came close to the surface or actually erupted because "his mistake in the eyes of his colleagues"—as Huneker later remarked of Baudelaire—"was to write so well about the seven arts."[47]

Although Huneker worked on the *Musical Courier* during 1887, his name did not appear there until the following year. He must have attended dozens of concerts and operas in the season of 1887–88, and his criticisms of them, together with the news items he collected, were probably incorporated into unsigned columns difficult now to detect as his. Perhaps his earliest recognizable contribution, a delightful take-off on the public craze for and the managerial exploitation of infant prodigies, appeared in the issue of February 22, 1888, the portrait of a piano virtuoso making his debut on his hundredth birthday being in Huneker's lightest vein.[48] Almost every day, at any rate, he would encounter Krehbiel, Steinberg, and the rest of what he liked to call the "critical chain gang,"[49] exchange intermission pleasantries with them, and, after they had all turned in their copy, join them at Lienau's, Mould's, or any one of a dozen cafés, where they would talk far into the night, drinking beer and eating the free lunches that helped sustain Huneker.

He drank a good deal during these years, indeed, as did most journalists who constantly faced deadlines and the grim demand for copy. Staggering out of Mould's one night, he planted himself on a chair at "Dead Man's Curve," Fourteenth Street and Broadway, and defied the cable cars to push him off the track.[50] At Hubel's, a favorite haunt on Third Avenue near Seventeenth Street, he was probably the thirstiest and wittiest member of a group that included John P. Jackson, music critic of the *World*; Frank Van der Stucken; Joseffy; Albert Steinberg; and Charles Henry Meltzer, the early supporter of Ibsen and the modern Continental drama, who had won renown among his colleagues of the press by ignoring the order of his capricious boss, James Gordon Bennett, Jr., to change the way he wore his hair, and collecting damages after Bennett fired him.[51] When Huneker once described Jackson as "portly" at Hubel's, he was challenged to a race around Union Square and lost, even though he was not as heavy then as later.[52] Here, too, he quipped merrily and told stories later printed in his columns—and many that could not be.[53]

In December 1887 Huneker went to Philadelphia,[54] probably to spend the Christmas holidays with his family. There is no way of knowing whether this was the first time he had been back since he had left, twenty-two months earlier, or whether he and Lizzie were on friendly terms. Even if he had not tired of her, however, he was still unable to support a wife, and he was too fond of his new freedom to resume the irksome responsibilities of marriage. Lizzie could have sued for divorce on the grounds of desertion as early as February 1888, but she either hoped for a reconciliation or, more likely, hesitated because of her religion, while Huneker, considerate of his mother's feelings, if not Lizzie's, was equally reluctant to get a divorce. This impasse was to last four more years.

Back in New York at the beginning of 1888, he worked hard at his unsigned contributions to the *Musical Courier*. Since Huneker had clerked in a piano agency, Blumenberg thought that he might help out in the journal's trade department, and for months took him along on visits to piano manufacturers and dealers.[55] But Huneker had trouble taking seriously what he later described as "that great neurosis, called Commerce."[56] When he was introduced to the head of the Ernest Gabler piano house, for example, he said: "Mr. Gabler, you make me think of an aunt of mine we always called an earnest gabbler." Blumenberg was more amused by the remark than the manufacturer,[57] but eventually realized that Huneker was no businessman and put him back in the editorial department permanently.

From this sanctuary, however, the irrepressible Huneker occasionally satirized the piano trade in amusing burlesques aimed at the exaggerated claims of competing manufacturers and dealers. Recurring characters in these unsigned pieces, which appeared irregularly in the *Courier* for several years beginning at least as early as January 1889,[58] were Harvey Hayseed and Jared (or Peleg) Diggs, portrayed as rival dealers. In creating Diggs, Huneker may have been having fun with Spencer T. Driggs, the *Courier*'s shrewd business manager, who, unlike Blumenberg, had no interest in music and objected to Huneker's cavalier attitude toward the business that brought him his bread.[59] As playful as the "Old Fogy" stories in *Etude* but sometimes more obscure in their topical satire, these hastily written sketches not only reveal Huneker's keen sense of the ridiculous in advertising but also constitute his mild revenge on the materialistic civilization with which he had had so much difficulty coping.

Upon his return to New York from Chicago, where he went to the Music Teachers' convention in the summer of 1888, Huneker received his big chance on the *Musical Courier* when he was allowed to review at length the newly published Wagner-Liszt letters. Anton Seidl's magnifi-

cent conducting of Wagnerian opera at the Metropolitan had partially
converted Huneker, though he still found the librettos long-winded and
often undramatic, and urged that they be severely cut. ("I can see Harry
Finck's hair turning black at the horrid idea," he remarked in 1895.)[60]
Liszt, of course, was one of the century's most romantic figures and, like
Wagner—the century's most controversial composer—was enormously
interesting to music lovers. Printed in late August and early September, the unsigned review of their correspondence was extremely lively
and comprehensive, and so many people inquired who had written it
that on September 12, 1888, the *Courier* credited it to Huneker.[61] His
career in New York journalism was now officially launched.

Another intimation of things to come was published in October:
his unsigned but recognizable notice of *With the Innocents,* a novel by
F. Marion Crawford, whom Huneker described as "one of the few
novelists of the age who can write sensibly and coherently on the subject of music."[62] By January 1889 Huneker's name was listed on the
editorial page of the magazine under Blumenberg's and Floersheim's.
A month later, in the issue of February 6, readers of the *Courier* noticed a new column whose heading, "The Raconteur," was decorated
with a picture of a bee with a human head sporting pince-nez, top hat,
and mustache, the insect zooming among flowers labeled "spice," "gossip," "chitchat," and "tittletat." For almost fifteen years Huneker was
to fill this weekly *olla-podrida* with countless critiques, short stories,
fantasies, parodies, news items, anecdotes, and puns. Here one can best
trace the evolution of his witty, colorful, conversational prose style.
Although the column seldom bore his name, everyone in the music
world soon knew that Jim Huneker was the whimsical, genial "Raconteur" and eagerly awaited his finely phrased judgments and delicious
quips.

In 1887 or 1888[63] he moved from the Seventh Avenue boardinghouse into a small family hotel, run by a couple named Werle, at the
northeast corner of Irving Place and Seventeenth Street, diagonally
across from the old Washington Irving residence. Directly opposite the
hotel stood Victor Herbert's home, and nearby, too, were the Garrigues
and the National Conservatory. A favorite abode among musicians, who
were permitted to play their instruments there until midnight, Werle's
also boasted excellent table d'hôte dinners served in the basement dining
room.

While dining here one night, Huneker was introduced to a woman who, much to his surprise and delight, turned out to be the celebrated Helene von Schewitsch, the aristocratic lover of Ferdinand Lassalle, the Jewish Socialist leader killed in 1864 in a sensational duel over her with Prince Racowitza, whom she proceeded to marry. After the Prince's early death, she had married and divorced an actor, and then in 1877 had come to New York with her third husband, Count Serge von Schewitsch, a radical forced to leave Russia following a revolutionary enterprise and now editing a labor newspaper and engaging in political demonstrations, while she played on the German-speaking stage, criticized drama and art for German newspapers, and wrote fiction about the East Side proletariat.[64] If Huneker was not familiar with her memories of Lassalle, published in German in 1879, he had read George Meredith's *The Tragic Comedians* (1880), a fictionalized version of the romance, and this unexpected encounter sent him scurrying back to the novel.

The fat and fortyish "Red Countess" possessed only remnants of the beauty that had dazzled Liszt, Dickens, and other celebrities she had known, and her former affluence had also disappeared, but her scintillating, multilingual comments on art, philosophy, drama, and politics charmed Huneker, and he listened sympathetically to her account of the Lassalle affair—which Meredith, she protested, had misinterpreted. Two decades later, a few years before Helene and von Schewitsch ended the tragicomedy by committing suicide in 1911, Huneker described her as a maligned woman, though he eventually concluded that Meredith had been right in portraying her as insincere and cowardly, and that he himself had been naïve in believing her.[65]

His small, ground-floor room at Werle's had a convenient private entrance, but, annoyingly, his tipsy friends could knock on the windows and serenade him at times when he wanted privacy and quiet. To escape these intrusions, he sometimes spent the night at various hideaways, seldom unaccompanied or unrefreshed by beer. He liked to explore the picturesque parts of Manhattan which were providing H. C. Bunner, Henry Harland, and other writers with material for novels and short stories and young newspapermen with human interest yarns. (Afterward, Huneker met O. Henry, who "never had the leisure to polish his anecdotes," Huneker wrote. ". . . When he is called the American De Maupassant . . . then criticism should go hide its head.")[66] Huneker took his chances slumming among the hoodlums, thieves, and derelicts of the Bowery and the Tenderloin, though he was too fastidious to feel comfortable in such surroundings. Far more interesting to him was the noisy, colorful heart of New York's foreign colony—of which Helene von Schewitsch was the most famous member—in the lower East Side between the Bowery and the East River, whose inhabitants clung desperately to the customs, dress, and tongue of the old country. As he walked through the crowded streets, he could hear almost every major language but English, and see cafés not unlike the "poor men's clubs" of Europe, where oldsters with heavy beards played pinochle and shook their heads over the injustices of life, while young radicals spouted Proudhon and Marx over seidels of imported beer.

At Justus Schwab's greasy saloon near the German neighborhood of Tompkins Square, Huneker hobnobbed with French communards, Spanish and Italian refugees, German socialists, and Russian politicals. On one occasion he was playing the "Marseillaise" and the "Internationale" on a battered piano there when the place was suddenly raided, and he was carted off to the police station with the others.[67] Here, too, in the early 1890's he and his friends heard fierce defenses of anarchism by a short, plain woman named Emma Goldman, egged on by the huge, red-bearded Schwab.[68] (Huneker was to use his experience at Schwab's and his acquaintance with the energetic Emma in a short story called "A Sentimental Rebellion," published in 1905, which contains a vivid portrait of her, a satirical study of the millionaire "do-gooder" she and Huneker both disliked, and an evocative glimpse of East Side anarchists.)[69] Huneker was so impressed that he began collecting books on philosophical anarchism, which struck his fancy because it defied convention, including conventional art forms, and supported his growing admiration for individualism.[70] When Prince Kropotkin, the great Russian student of anarchism, was lecturing in America some years later, Huneker called him "one of the biggest-brained, biggest-souled men of two continents."[71] Huneker's interest in the subject may account in part for his enjoyment and high opinion of Henry James's novel *The Princess Casamassima*, a study of the anarchist movement.[72]

The novelists, poets, and dramatists of the East Side found outlets in the city's foreign-language newspapers and theaters, and they eagerly discussed "new" writers such as Dostoevski, whose work many of them had read in the original before most educated Americans had even heard of him. They were familiar with the thought of Schopenhauer and Von

Hartmann popularized in 1885 by Edgar Saltus in *The Philosophy of Disenchantment*,[73] which had helped to create a fad that Huneker, with his sense of humor and nose for the new, satirized in a fantasy called "Suicide of the World," printed in the New York *Home Journal* on September 4, 1889. (Too much addicted to worldly pleasures to be a "no-sayer" himself, Huneker, whose own style was not yet fully developed, was so fond of Saltus's rich, epigrammatic prose[74]—which made even pessimism enjoyable—that he may have emulated it.) Nor would the East Side intellectuals cringe at the name of that "mad atheist" Friedrich Nietzsche, whom most readers of the *Musical Courier* would have known mainly as Wagner's apostate friend whose about-face *The Case of Wagner*, published a year before Nietzsche's mental breakdown in 1889, had caused a sensation. The arguments Huneker heard in the East Side on the relative merits of Schopenhauer and Nietzsche, on ascetic renunciation versus joyous, passionate acceptance of life (his own philosophy), may well have led him to read Nietzsche's other books in German.[75] All these attractions—the languages and costumes of the old world, the nonconformity, tolerance, and sense of the past coupled with an awareness of literature that had hardly reached America—made this area the most charming and stimulating part of New York to Huneker. Before it was "improved" by the settlement-house workers and reformers who prowled about, he said, "in search of sociological prey,"[76] he felt more at home here among these poor, artistic immigrants than among the well-fed, well-bred, but often boring members of the uptown club world.[77] For years the East Side was as close as he could get to Paris—and it was probably as close as he ever got to bohemia.

❧ *Five*

PIANIST, PEDAGOGUE, AND PLAYBOY

The difference between musical participation and musical appreciation," Huneker once said, "is similar to that of kissing a pretty girl and watching someone else kiss her."[1] He still longed to be a concert pianist, but his last hopes were killed when his friend and idol, Rafael Joseffy, with whom he studied in the late 1880's, finally gave him the sad news that he lacked the ability to be a top-rate performer.[2] Measured by ordinary standards, to be sure, he was more than competent at the piano, the great Paderewski himself remarking that Huneker was "an excellent musician . . . and used to play well."[3] Arthur Farwell, the well-known American composer, who during 1900 and 1901 occasionally worked in a friend's apartment adjacent to Huneker's,[4] liked to place his ear against the wall and listen to Huneker play, with a "very beautiful tone and . . . a very considerable technique," a "series of rushing tonal gleams, of ecstatic moments, snatched from Chopin, Liszt, or perhaps Wagner—one burst flashing out for a moment until it dissolved unexpectedly into nothingness, to reappear clad in the shimmering vestments of the imagination of some other composer."[5] Huneker had a real gift for expressing nuance and color, but lacked the patience necessary to master detail, and his muscular reaction was slow.[6] He had probably begun serious study too late to acquire certain crucial elements of technique.

Failing to come up to his own high expectations, Huneker at last abandoned his dream of half a lifetime, disappointed and, at first, a little bitter.[7] In 1889 he told the story of an unidentified young man, obviously himself, who had studied all kinds of piano techniques since childhood, only to become a pianist whose playing reminded one of a "mosaic table fractured by lightning, or of a crazy quilt into which were woven the most heterogeneous colors." The moral was: "Do not play the piano unless you have talent, and do not mistake a fondness for

music as a sign positive that you possess the gift divine, for . . . 'Many
are called, but few are chosen.' "⁸ In the same year he also noted in the
Musical Courier that upon being told that Huneker was studying the
Grieg concerto, Joseffy had replied: "Isn't it funny that everybody who
can't play the piano studies the Grieg concerto?" "I assented with a
sad suffering smile," Huneker commented, "and went home immediately and fell to studying the Dussek *A Flat Concerto*, which, while it
is not as difficult as the Grieg, is a good cure for insomnia, conceit, and
besides, prepares the hand for Czerny's velocity studies."⁹ Almost two
years later, he reported the remark made to him by "a little pianist, a
friend of mine" (Pachmann?): "For a man that can't play, you are
one of the best pianists I know."¹⁰

His sensitivity on the subject can be gauged by his reaction in 1892,
after he had given up serious study, when someone sent him a postcard
with the words "disappointed pianist" written below Huneker's name.
"In the inscription there lurks some truth," Huneker admitted in the
Courier. "It is no crime to confess that one's ambitions were piano-
ward. Better, far better, to be a failure as a pianist than a failure as a
villain, as the sneak is who sent me the card . . . too cowardly to sign
his name."¹¹ By 1896, however, Huneker could smile at his disappointment, even if it still hurt. Shortly after another journalist-pianist played,
with unhappy results, under Seidl's baton, Huneker met the conductor.
"Now, when do *you* play with me?" asked Seidl. Telling this story on
himself, Huneker added that "anyone who has heard of my pianistic
aspirations would have appreciated the glint in Anton's left eye."¹²

But if Huneker could not be a great pianist himself, he could still
help others, for, as Joseffy discovered, he had a knack for teaching,¹³
together with a vast knowledge of piano literature—so vast, indeed, that
Isidore Philipp, a successor of Georges Mathias at the Paris Conservatoire and one of the world's leading piano pedagogues (he dedicated
at least one volume of technical studies to Huneker),¹⁴ later asserted
that Huneker "knew more about the literature of piano than many great
pianists."¹⁵ In October 1888¹⁶ he was hired, through Joseffy's recommendation, as a member of the six-man piano department, headed by
Joseffy, of the National Conservatory of Music, an excellent school
founded in 1885 by Jeannette M. Thurber, who eventually spent a million dollars on it.¹⁷ The public-spirited wife of a wealthy merchant, Mrs.
Thurber had recently led the abortive attempt to establish opera in Eng-

lish as manager of New York's American (later the National) Opera Company, and was now determined to assist American performers and composers. Modeled on the Paris Conservatoire, the nonprofit institution flourished for years, and in 1891, when Mrs. Thurber obtained a charter of incorporation from Congress, even seemed on the verge of becoming truly national in scope, with a central school in Washington, though the expansion failed to materialize.[18] It already boasted a brilliant faculty, which was to include, in addition to Joseffy, such world-renowned musicians as Seidl, Emil Paur, Victor Herbert, and Anton Dvorak. Huneker was proud to be associated with it.

Twice weekly for the next ten years he taught at the Conservatory, then located on Seventeenth Street east of Irving Place, and during 1889–91 (and perhaps later) he also took private pupils.[19] Irma Hinton Le Gallienne, who studied with Huneker at the Conservatory, recalled that in the classroom

he was unique and most sympathetic. He had a way of bringing the best out of his pupils. If there was a spark of talent he discovered it, but he had no patience with too much conceit, in fact was almost ruthless, being so very modest himself about his own gifts. He, unlike many teachers, did not watch you while you played, but often walked about the room and made one feel at home and at ease. One of his great features was teaching one how to listen and to love the sound, and never to be mechanical and prosaic even in playing scales. He was never unkind but truthful. He played a great deal during these lessons to illustrate his meaning, often too nervous but always inspiring.[20]

(He was so self-conscious in playing before knowledgeable listeners that he backed out of one public performance at the last minute, even though he had been announced as soloist with orchestra.)[21] He gave special attention to an all-Negro class, two members of which, Paul Bolin and Henry Guy, were especially talented, if never as well known as Harry T. Burleigh, the Negro composer of "Deep River," a singer and student of composition at the Conservatory during this period.[22] Yet despite his fine qualities as a teacher—and he considered himself a much better teacher than pianist—none of Huneker's pupils ever reached great eminence.[23]

Apart from his earlier writings in *Etude*, he seldom printed his ideas on pedagogy. He used to complain that the teaching vocabularies of too many music instructors were piteously weak because they did not read enough in a variety of fields, and he advocated the study of foreign languages as another means of acquiring new tools of expression.[24] In a pamphlet on the study and profession of music, signed by Mrs. Thurber but elsewhere identified by her as Huneker's work (though undated, it was probably written while he was associated with the Conservatory), he struck a rare didactic note:

The first quality necessary for a musical career is, of course, marked talent. . . . The next quality—a most needful one—is perseverance in the face of obstacles. . . . There is but one course to pursue to obtain the highest honors in musical art—the course of undaunted industry. Sound musical training, backed up by talent and energy, will practically accomplish anything. There is no royal road to success, artistic or pecuniary. . . . The main quality besides musical talent that is most contributory to success is sound common-sense, in other words, a clear head which is not confused by either failure or success, the latter usually being the most unsettling. A good head is generally the result of a good heart, a clear conscience. Without principle one may become an artist, but a great artist never.[25]

Virtuosity on the piano was "a thing apart" and had nothing to do with musicianship, Huneker told Arthur M. Abell, Berlin correspondent of the *Musical Courier*, in 1893, citing two of the "greatest musical geniuses who ever lived," Robert Schumann and Richard Wagner, who could never master the keyboard. "What, then, is the secret of virtuosity on an instrument?" asked Abell. Huneker replied:

I wish I knew. Analysis does not seem to reveal it and yet there is a potent something there that baffles description. I myself had to work very hard for the little technique I possess, and in trying to master difficult passages I have always been conscious of formidable inhibitions but I never knew just what they were. I have often observed that some of Joseffy's pupils, although of very inferior mentality, acquired technique with comparative ease, while others who were far superior to them intellectually could not get it no matter how hard they practiced.

But if a Schumann or Wagner could not solve this knotty problem, Huneker concluded, how could *he* be expected to?[26]

He had nothing but contempt for the charlatans among voice teachers, whom he satirized entertainingly in 1897 in a sketch called "Cast Upon the Water." Here a Midwestern girl comes to New York and goes from one money-minded coach to another, each one expounding a "method" based on some ridiculous *idée fixe* such as singing soundlessly or developing the knees to place the voice properly. One "teacher" formulates a list of rules in a booklet distributed to his students. "Wear corsets," one rule reads, "the tighter laced the better. The pressure makes the voice easier to escape from the throat." Another rule goes: "Don't drink beer for breakfast; whiskey is better . . ." The disillusioned girl soon goes back home, gets married, and forgets about a singing career.[27] The story illustrates the answer Huneker gave, years later, when a friend asked him to recommend a good voice teacher for a young woman:

New York is the last place for a girl with a voice—good, bad or indifferent— and if she happens to be pretty, then all the *worse*. If, however, she has relatives, plenty of money, patience—then, perhaps, she might make the experiment without the inevitable disillusionments, bitter deceptions, sad endings. I say "perhaps," for heart burnings are sure to result in this hell's kitchen of music. . . . A beautiful voice is no guarantee of success—and as for teachers—phew![28]

His own criticism of female singers, indeed, was sometimes tempered by pity. "If a girl sings badly," he once remarked, "but is pretty, then, like a polite coward, I praise her pulchritude. If she is both plain . . . and voiceless, then I am forced to admire the fortitude that prompts her to make a howling show of herself in public."[29]

In addition to teaching at the National Conservatory, in the early 1890's Huneker acted as the school's press representative and as private secretary to Edmund G. Stanton, who became (in June 1892) Secretary of the Conservatory, a position once held by Edward MacDowell's mother.[30] Notwithstanding his complete lack of managerial and musical experience, this distinguished-looking clubman had been appointed manager of the Metropolitan Opera in 1885 following Leopold Damrosch's sudden death.[31] Stanton himself died shortly after fire gutted the stage of the Metropolitan in August 1892—the work of Loki, the fire god, wrote Huneker, in revenge for the banishment of Wagner in favor of Italian and French opera[32]—and Huneker succeeded him as Secretary of the Conservatory. His duties, he recalled, were to come daily to the home of the rather vain Mrs. Thurber, speak French with her, and admire her good looks. (In 1890, when someone described her as "not pretty," Huneker wrote: "Mrs. Thurber *is* pretty, take my word for it, and girls, *you know* I am a recognized authority.")[33]

He received his most memorable assignment as Secretary in late September 1892, when Anton Dvorak, the newly appointed musical director of the Conservatory, was entrusted to him upon the composer's arrival in New York. Conversing with him in German (which Huneker had learned somehow and which Dvorak apparently preferred to English, a language he could also speak), Huneker found a Bohemian Roman Catholic church for the fierce-looking but mild-mannered Dvorak and introduced him to some of the city's special attractions, including the whiskey cocktail—to which he took so readily that even Huneker, trying to keep up on beer, finally had to call a halt and take his protesting companion home.

Huneker later helped introduce Dvorak to something more substantial and, consequently, played a part in the composition of the *New World Symphony*, the most celebrated artistic result of his stay in America. When Dvorak was planning a cantata based on *Hiawatha*, Huneker acted as go-between and interpreter for him and Huneker's friend Francis Neilson, a young English actor, playwright, and librettist, who was to prepare the book. Neilson eventually decided that Longfellow's poem was unsuitable,[34] and the idea was dropped, but Dvorak, whose attention had been called to Negro spirituals by Huneker and Harry T. Burleigh,[35] incorporated into his famous symphony some of the sketches originally intended for the cantata. Opposing the theory that purely American music had its origin either in Negro melodies or in Indian chants, and denying that the use of such themes would prove to be the panacea for American music, Huneker observed that the most original "Negro" melodies were written by Stephen Foster, a white man, and maintained that "American music must be white man's music or it will be naught."[36] Huneker used to joke that from the very beginning Dvorak had mistaken Negro for Indian themes.[37]

After the highly publicized première of the "American" symphony at Carnegie Hall on December 16, 1893, it was probably Huneker who wrote the unusually restrained, unsigned review of the work in the *Musical Courier* (was he trying to be especially dignified and tactful because of his connection with the composer at the Conservatory?), in which he called it an "exceedingly beautiful symphony . . . perilously near being a great work," and predicted that it would be an enormous favorite with the public all over the world. But it was not "American," he insisted, unless to be American was to be composite, for, thematically considered, the symphony was composite, sounding Irish, Slavic, Scandinavian, Scotch, Negro, and German themes. If there could be such a thing as a symphony "racy of the soil" of America, it, like the American novel, was yet to be written, and it would be written by an American. More in Huneker's customary vein was the squib appended to the review: "Dvorak's is an American symphony: is it? Themes from Negro melodies; composed by a Bohemian; conducted by a Hungarian and played by Germans in a hall built by a Scotchman. About one-third of the audience were Americans and so were the critics. All the rest of it was anything but American. . . ."[38] He may have been referring, in this last phrase, to the quotations from Schubert and Wagner he detected in the score,[39] which, indeed, he came to dislike, perhaps because he heard it so often. Its "essential shallowness," he wrote in 1920, "its lack of personal profile, its insincerity . . . show plainer at every performance." He remained fonder of some of Dvorak's other compositions—especially the *Husitzka* overture, *Scherzo a Capriccioso,* and the Slavic dances and songs—and admired him as a born Impressionist with a happy color sense in his orchestration, though finding him inferior to his countryman Smetana.[40]

In late April, in early July (for the meeting of the Music Teachers' Association), and again in November 1889 Huneker visited Philadelphia,[41] its "dull apathy," he reported, acting as a "wet blanket on all the high enthusiasms of one's aspirations"—which probably reflects his family's disapproval of his way of life. The list of musicians who had fled the city and become famous was, indeed, gratifyingly impressive: Barili, embarked on a brilliant career in Atlanta; John Rhodes, a talented violinist; Max Heinrich, now a leading singer in London and professor of singing at the Royal Academy; and Max Bendix, concertmaster of the Thomas Orchestra.[42] (Two names could be added, before long, to the roll of distinguished departees: David Bispham, the singer,[43] and Huneker himself.)

The growing irksomeness of the impasse with Lizzie may have dampened his mood, for by now another woman loomed large in his life. Not long after his arrival in New York, he had met Mrs. Josephine Ahrensdorf Laski, a fair, green-eyed, auburn-haired[44] painter of miniatures and a student of William Wallace Scott,[45] a prominent American artist. On February 10, 1886, at the age of twenty-one she had married Maksymilian J. Laski, a Polish-born merchant in his middle twenties,[46] with whom she moved, sometime in 1886, into the Seventh Avenue boardinghouse where Huneker lived.[47] The marriage was unhappy, Laski, according to one account, being an onanist.[48] (This might have given Huneker the idea for a rather clinical story he wrote, probably in the early 1890's,[49] called "The V-Shaped Corsage," in which a man discovers that his inamorata is kept by an elderly lecher, who completely satisfies his passion by gazing raptly at her as she sits before him, her partially exposed bosom adorned with a V-shaped corsage. Is it more than a coincidence that a photograph of the youthful Josephine shows her in a low-cut dress holding a small bouquet at her bosom?)[50] Huneker, a sympathetic neighbor at first, proceeded to become Josephine's lover. One story has it that the real reason he climbed naked one night from the second-floor piazza to the third—an escapade that won him an invitation to live elsewhere and resulted in his moving to Werle's— was that Max Laski had surprised him with Josephine.[51] Their relationship was a serious one, however, and, in all likelihood, it caused Josephine to leave her husband.

No one knows how much he was motivated by this situation, but on December 8, 1890, Laski shot himself through the head in Central Park, an act that his employer, a worsted goods manufacturer, attributed to overwork. A veiled woman (Josephine?) went to the morgue on the following night and declared that she recognized the suicide but refused to give either her name or his. The body was finally identified by a friend of Laski's the next morning as it lay on the dissecting table in a medical school amphitheater, and it was removed for burial.[52] Two months later Josephine filed a petition to administer Laski's "estate"— which, she alleged, did not exceed $25.[53]

But even illegal monogamy seemed dull to Huneker, who once declared that a man should have seven wives at a time, each one adept at satisfying a special need.[54] Believing that a woman could experience only one real love and that she had found hers, the childless Josephine catered to him, often overlooking his philandering because she knew that he was usually more chased after than chasing.[55] The better known he became as a critic, the more frequently female singers and pianists, not averse to furthering their careers by what Huneker called "approved horizontal methods," sent him flowers, gifts, and invitations difficult to decline, no matter how hard he tried not to get involved with those he had to criticize. Josephine thought that despite his occasional excursions the affection and care she lavished on him (among her ac-

complishments was a talent for preparing the Jewish dishes he relished)
gave her a secure hold, but she would have needed the patience and
serenity of an angel to have shut her eyes when Huneker began to focus
his almost exclusively on a woman prettier and far more talented as an
artist than Josephine—and four years younger.

Among his acquaintances was Howard Hinton of the New York
Home Journal, a distinguished weekly that published work by the French
symbolists, English Pre-Raphaelites, and respectable American bohemians.[56] "H.H.," the signature Hinton used for political articles and
occasional reviews of books by modern Continental authors, was a
prominent journalist.[57] A supporter of Henry George, William Jen-
nings Bryan, and Women's Suffrage, and an opponent of formalized
religion, Hinton, who drank a quart of wine a day and climbed the
Alps in his seventies, was a free-thinking, idealistic nonconformist.[58]
George Ripley once described him as one who professed none of the
Christian virtues but possessed them all. How or when Huneker met
him is uncertain—it may have been in connection with the publication,
in September and October 1889, of sketches by Huneker in the *Home
Journal,* which Hinton sometimes edited—but by February 1890 Huneker was referring to him as "my very good friend."[59]

Hinton was then living with his family on East Fourteenth Street
in the midst of Huneker's happy hunting grounds. His wife, Lucy, a
student of the distinguished sculptor Launt Thompson, had been one
of America's earliest sculptresses.[60] (A lively bohemian who even in
her eighties delighted in shocking her prim New England relatives, she
later figured in Huneker's novel *Painted Veils,* as did her husband.)
Sculpture seems to have been a family talent, two of her three children
—Erwald, the eldest, and Clio, the older of two exceptionally attractive
girls—having taken up the art, and their first cousin, Roland Hinton
Perry, the most gifted of the three, eventually becoming a noted sculptor. The other daughter, Irma, was musical, studying piano with Huneker at the National Conservatory while still in her teens.[61]

The story goes that Irma, smitten with Huneker, introduced him to
the even lovelier Clio, with whom he promptly fell in love. Born in
1869 in Rhinebeck, New York, a village on the Hudson sixteen miles
north of Poughkeepsie, Clio had learned the rudiments of sculpture
from her mother and had come to New York City in the late 1880's
with the rest of her family to join Hinton (who, for some years previously, had apparently resided with his wife and children only during

the summer, except for week-end visits). When Huneker met her about the beginning of 1891, Clio was living at home and sculpting in a Ninth Street studio she shared with Perry. Beautiful and vivacious as well as talented, she dazzled Huneker with her lovely figure and her fine, slightly irregular features, gray-blue eyes, smooth complexion, and copper-colored hair. Though an expert horsewoman and a good rifle shot, she was nevertheless exquisitely feminine, as Huneker liked his women to be.[62]

By May 1891, when he praised her portrait bust of Anton Seidl in the *Musical Courier*,[63] Huneker must have been a frequent visitor at the cultivated Hinton home, where he enjoyed long talks on classical literature and politics with the dreamy, scholarly Hinton. Clio, however, was certainly the main attraction there—so much so that he began to think of marrying her. There were, of course, two obstacles: Lizzie and Josephine. If he had not legally ended his first marriage because of his reluctance to hurt his pious mother, who strongly disapproved of divorce, this could not be a bar much longer, for he knew she was now dying of tuberculosis. Though he probably said nothing of his intentions to his mother, he finally told Lizzie of his love for Clio and even brought Clio to Philadelphia to meet her. (Josephine, getting wind of this plan, somehow followed them and managed to spend the night with him.)[64] Lizzie liked Clio, and on March 4, 1891, she finally brought suit for divorce, charging desertion. The proceedings had obviously been arranged, for Huneker, supposedly living in New York at the time, was personally served with papers in Philadelphia the day after they were issued. On April 29 Huneker's mother died at the age of sixty-five[65]— possibly without having learned about the divorce action. The case was heard on September 25, and the divorce became final on November 7, 1891.[66]

Little is known about Lizzie's activities thereafter, and nothing about her relations, if any, with Huneker. The divorce records do not indicate that she was one of the recipients of the alimony he used to joke about paying. (Standing in the *Sun*'s counting room after being paid, some years afterward, Huneker placed three groups of bills between the fingers of one hand and showed them to Walter Prichard Eaton, his colleague. "Alimony, alimony, alimony," he muttered. And then displaying a bill or two in the other hand, he added: "This is for me.")[67] Neither does it seem likely that she was present at a luncheon party he reportedly once gave for his three wives[68] (or, in view of the strong antipathy between Clio and Josephine, which only intense curiosity could have temporarily overcome, that any such party occurred at all). Adopting the name of "Mrs. Holmes" and pretending to be a widow, Lizzie became a practical nurse. In 1907 the death of her brother-in-law, Franz Schubert,[69] whom Huneker occasionally visited, probably broke her last link with Jim. Afterward, she lived with her widowed sister, who ran a boardinghouse, and they were still living together at 15th and Race Streets—two blocks from the old Huneker home—when Lizzie died of pneumonia on April 17, 1916, in her sixty-fifth year.[70] A High Requiem Mass was sung for her at the Cathedral, and she was buried in the Holmes plot in the old Cathedral Cemetery, the resting place (in a different section) of her two infant daughters.[71]

As for Huneker, he preferred, understandably, to conceal this marriage, never referring to it in any of his published writings and alluding to it only once, it seems, in the letters that have survived (practically all of which, to be sure, were written after the divorce). " 'Lizzie' (as you will call Jozie) sends her regards," he wrote his brother John in 1909. "We shudder at the ghosts you evoke."[72]

Though Josephine hovered in the background, Jim courted Clio after his divorce in much the same way that Ulick Invern woos Mona Milton in Huneker's novel *Painted Veils*. On January 20, 1892, they were married at her father's house,[73] Mr. Hinton conducting the service which he himself wrote, no minister officiating because a Catholic priest could not perform the ceremony and a Protestant clergyman was unacceptable to Huneker.[74] After staying in at least two other boardinghouses,[75] the couple moved into the Maison Félix, a brownstone building in the heart of the theater district on West Twenty-fifth Street near Sixth Avenue. The lively, unconventional guests, mostly theater folk—David Belasco, then stage producer for the Frohmans, lived with his family on Huneker's floor, and on the midnight walks the two men took together urged Huneker to write plays if he wanted to make money—sometimes engaged in intramural affairs which were smiled upon by the proprietors as long as they did not interrupt their own poker games.[76] The place was appropriately bohemian for a musician and a sculptor, but the boardinghouse pattern was ominously familiar. Yet now, at least, Huneker had a job.

❧ Six

THE PRACTICE YEARS

The early 1890's were the crucial years of Huneker's apprenticeship as a critic of music, drama, and literature. "I'm glad, as a rule, to forget what I wrote during the practice years," he told Aubertine Woodward Moore in 1911,[1] but actually he need not have been ashamed of that work. By 1895, at any rate, his prose style was formed and the main interests and attitudes of his maturity were evident.

Shortly after the New York *Recorder* made its debut in February 1891, Huneker was engaged as its music critic. Backed in part by the Duke tobacco people, the *Recorder* began as a politically independent newspaper but soon turned Republican. It accented sensational local news and introduced such features as special pages for women and children and a daily department of theatrical and musical news. Two of its best-known columns were "Cholly Knickerbocker," society items written by John W. Keller, the managing editor, and Joe Howard's entertaining miscellany of gossip and comment.[2]

An unsigned article on Vladimir de Pachmann, which Josephine brought to the newspaper's office[3] and which was printed on April 26, may have been Huneker's first work on the *Recorder*. Seemingly his was an unsigned department entitled "Here and There in Music," which, beginning in October 1891, appeared every Sunday and sometimes on a weekday, and by November 1 of that year he was also contributing an occasional Sunday feature article.[4] Until September 1895, when he left the *Recorder* (it ceased publication in the following year), he covered the chief musical events for both the newspaper and the *Musical Courier*, though most of his serious essays on music were published in the *Courier*.

During his apprenticeship Huneker frequently changed his mind, flexibility being one of his outstanding traits as a critic. In 1891, for example, Liszt's music struck him as pompous, empty, and artificial;

covering the American debut of Arthur Friedheim, Liszt's prize pupil in his last years and his leading interpreter, Huneker admitted that he considered it so foolish to call Liszt a great composer that he could not write an unbiased criticism of anyone announced as a "great Liszt player," and his account of the recital was less than lukewarm. (Friedheim, who became one of the critic's friends and favorite pianists— many years later they worked together on fingering pieces collected in *Romantic Preludes and Studies for Piano* edited by Huneker for Schirmer—never quite forgave Huneker for this early critique, which, he recalled, did him "great harm" in musical America.) Eventually, however, influenced at least partly by Friedheim's masterly playing, Huneker completely reversed his position and warmly defended Liszt against the very charges he himself had once made.[5]

His attitude toward Tchaikovsky also changed, though perhaps not so drastically. In May 1891, shortly after Tchaikovsky arrived in New York to take part in the heralded opening of Carnegie Hall, Huneker described him glowingly to an indifferent public[6] as the greatest man then in America. Six years later, he felt that Tchaikovsky's "masterly manipulation of mediocre thematic material often leads us astray; yet, at his best, when idea and execution are firmly welded, this man is a great man." By 1891 Huneker had probably heard rumors of Tchaikovsky's homosexuality, a subject that fascinated him more and more as he became better acquainted, through reading and personal encounters, with artists of all kinds, but he remarked only that Tchaikovsky had "tasted at the acrid spring of sorrow." In 1897, after the Russian's death, supposedly from cholera, Huneker maintained that it had really been suicide, and that Tchaikovsky had possessed an "unfortunate and undoubted psychopathic temperament." "Women delighted him not," Huneker explained, "and so he solaced himself with herculean labors— labors that made him the most interesting, but not the greatest, composer of his day."[7] (Fifteen years later, Huneker edited a collection of Tchaikovsky's songs, which was published by Ditson's in 1912.)

Another important musical event in 1891 was the American debut of Ignace Jan Paderewski as soloist with the New York Symphony Orchestra at Carnegie Hall. This Polish student of the famous Theodor Leschetizky had been wildly acclaimed in Europe, where George Bernard Shaw, music critic of the London *Star*, had described him as "an immensely spirited, young, harmonious blacksmith, who puts a concerto on the piano as upon an anvil and hammers it out with an exuberant

enjoyment of the swing and strength of the proceedings."⁸ Hailing him
after the concert in a brilliantly prescient review as "a Rubinstein tech-
nically infallible . . . a new personality in music that will bear curious
and close study," Huneker was one of the few New York critics to recognize Paderewski's greatness immediately, and his enthusiastic notice
won him the pianist's lasting friendship and gratitude.⁹ If, as Huneker
claimed,¹⁰ he actually wrote the appreciative article on Paderewski
signed by William Mason and published—with a footnoted acknowledgment to Huneker—in the *Century* in March 1892, it marked his own
debut in a first-class American magazine.

In a piece on "Music Criticism, Past and Present," printed in the
Home Journal in the spring of 1892, Huneker pointed out that for too
long the criticism of music had floundered between the Scylla of absurd
rhapsody and the Charybdis of dull, didactic, and technical analysis so
far above the layman's head that city editors tended to settle for semi-
humorous accounts of the performer's appearance or peculiarities.¹¹
True, it was difficult to write well about music, for without using its
technical terms—which ranged through several languages and were not
pretty when translated into English—the critic was reduced to mere reporting, while attempts at description frequently produced bad Ruskin.
"I have wrestled with the 'purple phrase,' " Huneker later admitted,
"and have been thrown every time. . . . How often have I envied men
the gift of simple, strong Saxon, *with a subject to match it.*"¹² The writing on music in the American press was improving, he felt, but a fuller,
more competent coverage of musical activities was needed, together
with a style that would be readable as well as informative.

No one in America was doing more to make music criticism lively
than Huneker, who tried to combine the pertinent comment with the
light touch. Shortly after Paderewski's memorable concert, for example,
the "Raconteur," in a rare outburst of doggerel, laughed at reporters
(including himself) for paying so much attention to the Pole's striking
hair:

THE HAIR IS NOT PIANO

What's the useki,
Paderewski,
Of your phalangial skill,
When your playing
Goes sasshaying
With your frontal hirsute frill?

> You're not so-so
> Virtuoso
> But a reg'lar, 'way up player;
> Still your phrasing
> 'S not amazing
> As your perturbating hair.
>
> You can churn the
> Sweet nocturne,
> Of th' andante you've the hang;
> But your pounding
> Lacks the sounding
> Timbre of your towzled bang.[13]

In the season of 1892–93, when Henri Marteau, a handsome, nineteen-year-old French violinist, made a big hit in Boston (where Paderewski played to packed halls during the same season),[14] Huneker indulged in another bit of versification:

> Hey diddle diddle, Marteau with his fiddle
> Has conquered the belles of the Hub;
> When next year comes in the fun will begin
> For he'll give Paddyroosky a rub![15]

Marteau's manager used this poem to good advantage in advertising the artist.[16]

The opening sentence of Huneker's review of the icy Emma Eames's unimpassioned performance in *Aida*—"There was skating on the Nile last night"[17]—may not have pleased the prima donna (though she always had great respect for his judgment),[18] but he tickled his readers, and the criticism was sound. Even the pianist must have smiled when she read that "at her first concert Mme Carreño played the second concerto of her third husband."[19] Instead of castigating the company for a poorly rehearsed *Don Giovanni*, Huneker praised its "fine impromptu air," adding: "If there had been a rehearsal it did not reveal itself in any particular part of the score—except that Scotti, the Don Giovanni, sang the drinking song at a *presto* pace that would have made the piano virtuoso Rosenthal envious. And he only left the orchestra behind him twice."[20] Of another production Huneker remarked that even the prompter was in good voice, as everybody could clearly hear.[21] Recognizably his, too, was the succinct subtitle of a much later review of a performance of Wolf-Ferrari's opera *The Jewels of the Madonna*: "Paste Jewels."[22]

He soon found out that a smile scarified a mediocrity more effectively than a snarl. ("How often," he declared after a lifetime of listening to music, "have we felt like crying aloud: 'Hats on, gentlemen, this
is not a genius!' " reversing Robert Schumann's historic recognition of
Chopin.)[23] Criticizing, for example, the recital of a woman pianist-
medium who had announced that she would play "under the guidance of
some deceased composers," he wrote: "Beethoven, Schumann, Chopin
and a few other immortal shades were to have been present, of course
in the spirit, but pressing engagements elsewhere prevented their par-
ticipating. . . ."[24]

Those who were not musicians or even music lovers were hugely
entertained by the "Raconteur's" puns (he referred to the standees at
the opera, for example, as "railbirds");[25] his penchant for using unusual words such as "gracile," "lilal," and "phylloxera";[26] his gems
of humorous description (of the famous strong man Sandow he wrote:
"[His] chest inflated to the extent of fourteen inches as his stomach retired respectfully to the vicinity of his backbone");[27] his gossip about
the foibles of celebrities; his short stories, fantasies, and humorous
sketches; and the select passages he quoted from his vast and continual
reading of contemporary novels, plays, and criticism.

He liked musicians to look and act "normal"—on stage, at least—
fearing that a careless, affected, or queer member of the tribe would
damn all the others in the public's mind.[28] For this reason, apparently,
though he seldom engaged in offensive personalities, Vladimir de Pachmann seemed to bring out the worst in him. Ultimately, a series of
brilliant gibes by Huneker resulted in a feud with the eccentric pianist.
Even before Pachmann made his American debut in April 1890, Huneker, following his recitals in London, questioned whether he could be
successful here. "He is too effeminate and his style is stilted," the
"Raconteur" wrote. "His wife . . . is in reality a better pianist than
her husband, who is as mad as a March hare when it is chased by the
shadow of the festive ground hog."[29] It must have been about the time
of Pachmann's first New York concert, in the spring of 1890, that the
pianist, having had an argument with his manager, pretended that he
wanted to make up with a kiss—and proceeded, instead, to bite him
viciously in the neck. "His Bach," Huneker reportedly commented,
"was worse than his bite."[30] A year later, an even more inspired
Huneker publicly dubbed the small, bearded, grimacing, gesturing,

mumbling, unmasculine Chopin specialist "The Chopinzee"[31]—a triple-barreled pun that titillated musical New York and pursued its victim to the grave. At the end of 1891 Huneker relentlessly described the delicate-touched Pachmann as the "fairy of the piano" and added another jab by confessing that "I fancy after all that I prefer morbidity, diseased chords of the thirty-ninth and Vladimir de Pachmann to healthy C-major piano players and Kalkbrenner rondos."[32]

Not long afterward, one surmises, Huneker's celebrated encounter with Pachmann at Lüchow's took place. Accounts of it differ,[33] but according to the famous pianist Arthur Friedheim—who was not present but heard the story from others who were—the long-suffering Pachmann stepped up to Huneker, started calling him vile names, and became so insufferable that Huneker picked up a stein of beer and calmly dumped its contents on Pachmann's shirt front. The furious Pachmann made such a commotion that the manager of the restaurant intervened, told him that he had been in the wrong, and that unless he apologized to Huneker immediately he would be asked to leave and not to return. Agreeing, reluctantly, Pachmann returned to Huneker's table and at the top of his voice shouted: "Skunk! I apologize, Skunk!"[34] Huneker may have been thinking of this same episode when he recalled that he once threw a glass of beer at Pachmann when the latter insulted Joseffy —only to be reprimanded by Joseffy for wasting good beer.[35]

Still another tale that Huneker liked to tell was that once, as he was about to begin a recital, Pachmann, looking at the audience and waiting for complete silence, spied Huneker slipping into his seat. "Ah," he said gleefully, "I see you, Huneker. Now I play this just for you." The Chopin he played was beautiful—but rather unfamiliar. When he finished he looked at Huneker and said, "How do you like, Huneker?" "I never like any composition played backwards, especially Chopin," the critic replied, refusing to be caught in the trap. "Now stop fooling and let's have it as it was written." Pachmann laughed and clapped his hands. "You are very bright man, Huneker," he said. "Now I play it right for you." And he played it exquisitely.[36]

The two men eventually ended their feud, as Huneker grew less critical of Pachmann's personal idiosyncrasies and more appreciative of his artistry. Some years afterward Huneker even invited the pianist for dinner at his apartment, where Pachmann played superbly for five hours —until three in the morning.[37]

The psychology of artists, especially those who had failed, was a favorite theme in the curious tales Huneker wrote for the *Musical Courier*. Failure seemed to interest him even more than success, which, he believed, was often achieved at the expense of a well-rounded personality; perhaps, too, he agreed with Henry James that only so long as he was a failure was the artist a person, for when he succeeded he disappeared into his work.[38] Too many musicians, at any rate, were personally obnoxious. "Must hatred and jealousy preside at even this seemingly happy musicale?" inquired the narrator in a sketch written by Huneker in 1891. "Hush," was the reply, "they are only amateurs."[39] Five years later, he observed that "art needs good, warm, rich blood in its veins, and if it does not get it becomes pallid and artificial. . . . Beethoven was a greater man than artist. That is why he holds us forever in thrall."[40] He cautioned artists to remember that "no matter how finely attuned are your sensibilities there are other persons footing the globe, persons who love, hate, work, struggle, battle and weep, while you but give a feeble representation, a dream picture, a sound pantomime of their motives and motions. In a word, O musician, get not the swelled head."[41] He considered himself one of the failures, of course. "I have met them, known them, lived with them, 'Les Miserables,' " he rhapsodized in June 1892, "these toilers of the sea of art, and I fain would be a Hugo to write of their sad, noble, bitter, unheroic, degraded, miserably happy lives."[42] "To have dared the impossible," he wrote in 1896, "to have tried to fly to the sun, to have wooed the moon, to have burned your boats behind you and resolutely entered that trackless region of art where the soul must be its own compass, its own rudder, its own captain, is to have done something. . . . Better a million times to have failed than the success of the sleek, smug philistine who counts his coupons and his steps."[43]

If he needed any doctrine to bolster his boundless curiosity about the vagaries and weaknesses of other men, which perhaps consoled him for his own, Huneker would have claimed that music, like all the arts, was an expression of human emotion and experience, and that criticism, therefore, must be partly biographical. Gorging himself on memoirs—"I have read everything from Apuleius to Pepys, from Boswell to Amiel," he remarked in March 1892[44]—he tirelessly examined countless intimate details in the lives of Chopin, Liszt, Wagner, and other composers. Yet he did not overemphasize the literary content in music by attempting, for example, to establish programs in symphonic pieces. Music, the least specific and most subjective of the arts, should be enjoyed as pure sound, he maintained, and its emotional overtones communicated directly, without the aid of an intervening medium. And because censors of the sensuous found its speech less clear than the written or spoken word, music "the most immoral and dangerous of the arts," could speak more freely and impart more ecstasy than any of them.[45]

Huneker argued that a critic should state his prejudices to help the reader evaluate his criticism,[46] and he honestly admitted his. He preferred the symphony to opera, declaring that "music, pure and simple, for itself and undefiled by costumes, scenery, limelights and vocal virtuosi, is the greatest and noblest music."[47] By the end of the decade, his favorite composers among the symphonists were Liszt (the symphonic poems especially), Brahms, and Richard Strauss, though none of these quite reached the pedestal occupied in Huneker's affections by Chopin. At the opera, he wanted to enjoy first the voices (he received much technical information on singing from one of his closest friends, Frida Ashforth, a former singer and a capable voice teacher),[48] then the score, and finally the acting.[49] He liked to hear opera in the original language rather than in English, which, he felt, lacked euphony.[50] The oratorio as an art form left him cold.[51] Piano music, of course, was his specialty, and, as the distinguished Boston critic Philip Hale remarked in 1897, after a series of articles by Huneker on piano studies had appeared in the *Musical Courier*, there was probably no other man living who wrote about the piano with such "rare critical acumen, felicity of expression, practical knowledge, dazzling phraseology, and high imagination."[52]

Huneker believed, moreover, that there was a time and place for all kinds of music, and instead of sniffing at a Reginald De Koven operetta, for example, he welcomed it as a happy change from a steady diet of heavy fare; yet at the same time, he did not hesitate to point out weaknesses in De Koven's popular success *Robin Hood*, and was pleased that the composer avoided similar lapses in his later work *Rob Roy*.[53] And the musical comedy clown Francis Wilson eventually became one of Huneker's favorite entertainers.[54]

The relentless repetition of the day's hit songs, to be sure, irritated his sensitive ears. Gustave L. Becker, the New York composer and piano teacher who also studied with Joseffy and taught at the National Conservatory, relates an amusing incident which probably occurred in the fall of 1890.[55] One night, when Becker was going to a concert with Huneker, he arrived at the latter's room a little early. "Becker," said Huneker, "play me something new and interesting while I finish dressing." Recalling that Huneker had recently protested against the inescapable epidemic of "Little Annie Rooney"—it was most likely Huneker who had commented in the *Musical Courier* that the popular tune would be greatly improved in the form of a Bach fugue[56]—Becker improvised a piece using the melody of "Annie" disguised by radical changes in harmony and rhythm. "Say, that's nice," Huneker called out. "Is it one of your own compositions?" When Becker finally explained what he had done, Huneker was momentarily deflated. "For God's sake," he said, "don't tell anyone you inveigled me into admiring that nauseating tune!" And Becker kept his promise for sixty years.[57]

By 1892, if not before, the "Raconteur" had become the *Musical Courier*'s most eagerly read column, and Huneker New York's wittiest and most colorful critic. In June 1891, a colleague suggested in the *Evening World* that Huneker try writing for the magazines, for he could "discount Scheherazade as a teller of tales," and if he let himself be as brilliant as he could be he would "probably die of spontaneous combustion."[58] Six months later, when the prosperous Blumenberg-Floersheim partnership had expanded into a corporation, Huneker not only had been "promoted" to the board of directors but also had been editorially praised by Blumenberg:

Let it be understood that the work he has performed during nearly five years has found no deeper recognition than among his immediate associates in this office, who have learned to esteem him not only for his many and magnetic qualities, but also and chiefly because of his intellectual attainments, the general bent of his acquisitive mind and the character and texture of the work he has performed in these columns, which for originality and breadth of conception remains unexcelled in contemporaneous musical literature.[59]

At the end of 1892, Floersheim left the *Courier*'s New York office to live in Germany, and Huneker succeeded him as musical editor of the magazine, though Blumenberg remained editor in chief.[60]

Other music journalists went out of their way to compliment Huneker. "Perhaps those sparkling paragraphs are as easy to do as 'rolling off a log,'" wrote G. H. Wilson in the *Boston Musical Herald* of February 1892, "and on the other hand, perhaps only the genius which comes with persistent energy is behind [Huneker's] facile pen."[61] In the following July, W. S. B. Matthews, editor of *Music*, another Boston magazine, referred to Huneker as "a brilliant and versatile writer, of wide journalistic experience," and also described him a month later as a distinguished teacher of piano.[62] His reputation in music circles was clearly rising.

During his early years on the *Recorder*, Huneker grew friendly with Harry Neagle, the newspaper's drama editor, and was soon acting as his unpaid assistant. At times Huneker was so satiated with music that a chance at any other topic, as he confessed in 1894, made him feel like "a boy playing truant on a glorious, sunshiny day."[63] Moreover, he could make good use of his stage gleanings in his *Musical Courier* column. Gradually, Huneker did more and more of the writing of Neagle's department, his unsigned drama criticism usually appearing in a long Sunday article headed "The Prompter."

The city's playhouses were now moving northward, as indicated by the portentous opening, in January 1893, of Charles Frohman's beautiful new Fortieth Street showplace, the Empire. Several other significant events that affected the American theater occurred in 1893: the death of Edwin Booth, last of the grand tragedians, whose $700,000 estate gave practical Americans new respect for the profession of acting; the invitation extended to leading actresses to address the international Congress of Women at the Columbian Exposition in Chicago, an honor that also helped to dignify the stage; the American debut of Eleonora Duse, who introduced, or at least popularized, the natural style of acting destined to become the standard of the modern theater;[64] and the successful production of Pinero's *The Second Mrs. Tanqueray*, a play about a kept woman, which reflected the toehold gained on Broadway by the realistic sex drama.

In 1887 Daniel Frohman had assumed control of the Lyceum Theater, dedicated to the production of modern drama, and had secured David Belasco, formerly stage manager at the Madison Square Theater, to produce his plays. And under the management of Charles Frohman, who organized a company in 1890, Maude Adams, Ethel Barrymore, Otis Skinner, and Margaret Anglin were to become stars before the end of the decade. Also emerging in the eighties were Richard Mansfield, who introduced Shaw to the American stage with *Arms and the Man* in 1894; Minnie Maddern Fiske, the best American actress of Ibsen roles; Julia Marlowe, famous for her portrayal of Shakespearean heroines; and the luscious, much-married Lillian Russell (whose favorite composer, Huneker once declared, was "Divorceshak").[65]

Since happy-ending adaptations of Continental plays—especially French—were safer commercial risks, native dramatists had struggled for years to get a hearing. Mansfield, Skinner, and E. H. Sothern were either reviving the older heroic vehicles, which had it all over realistic plays such as James Herne's *Margaret Fleming*, or commissioning new ones. Mansfield, for example, hired young Clyde Fitch to write *Beau Brummel*, which became a smash hit. Best-selling historical novels like *Ben Hur*, adapted for these actors, were tremendous money-winners, as were several Civil War plays which followed close on the heels of Bronson Howard's *Shenandoah* and gave American playwrights a chance to demonstrate their ability.

A few performances of Ibsen were given in New York in the 1890's, notably those starring Mrs. Fiske. *Ghosts* was produced for the first time in America in 1891, ten years after it had been written; a cut version of *A Doll's House* with Mrs. Fiske was performed at a single, historical matinee on February 15, 1894; and the world première of *John Gabriel Borkman* in English took place in 1897. In addition, Hauptmann's *Hannele* had been performed in 1894, the author coming to America to supervise Harrison Grey Fiske's production of the play—and being threatened with mobbing and arrest for "blasphemy." Hauptmann's *The Weavers* and *The Sunken Bell* were also staged in New York during the decade, as were Sudermann's *Magda* and Maeterlinck's *Les Aveugles*. But experimental European dramatists were shunned as morbid, if not immoral, by most Americans, and their effect on the American theater was not felt until after the turn of the century.

The chief drama critics of the nineties were William Winter of the *Tribune*, John Ranken Towse of the *Evening Post*, Edward A. Dithmar of the *Times*, "Nym Crinkle" (Andrew C. Wheeler) of the *World*, Franklin Fyles of the *Sun*, and "Alan Dale" (Alfred Cohen) of the *Evening World* and *Morning Journal*. Winter, who had joined the *Tribune* in 1865, was the dean of the group and the best-known drama critic in the country. Erudite, opinionated, and conservative, he labeled Ibsen a menace and Shaw a degenerate, and lambasted any drama that touched upon social or economic questions or smacked of sex.[66] ("What an arrant damned fool he is!" Walt Whitman—whom Winter disliked— remarked in 1888. "[He] knows nothing beyond traditions, customs, habits, stage conventions.")[67] He favored American and English stars and invariably attacked European "hussies" such as Bernhardt, Duse, and Réjane. Huneker admired Winter's knowledge of the technique of acting, his graceful, polished style, and the experience that allowed him to write most of a long criticism of a classic play even before the per- formance began. Huneker's tastes, however, differed radically from those of "Weeping Willie," the nickname given Winter because of his lachrymose poetic tributes to deceased friends. During the nineties, the veteran critic was still a power in the theater, though his influence was rapidly diminishing.

Next in seniority was Towse, also a conservative but less bigoted and probably a better judge of plays than Winter.[68] Like Huneker, and un- like Winter, he had little personal association with stage celebrities.[69] Dithmar, probably Huneker's closest friend among this group—he was never as chummy with them as he was with his fellow music critics— liked serious plays with literary overtones (he was to leave drama criti- cism to become the *Times*'s literary editor).[70] Versatile "Nym Crinkle," a student of law, medicine, and theology as well as the drama,[71] wrote criticism that Huneker found more brilliant than reliable. Co-author— with David Belasco—of *The Girl I Left Behind Me*, Fyles was the *Sun*'s competent critic for over fifteen years.[72] "Alan Dale," who has been called the literary progenitor of George Jean Nathan, practically founded a new school of drama criticism, the school of the flippant remark.[73]

As a newcomer to the field, Huneker realized that he did not have the experience to compete with Winter and Towse, no matter how hard he studied the classic English dramatists. But ransacking foreign jour- nals for material to use in his various columns, he had followed the emergence of a new kind of drama which did not require expeditions of literary archaeology to be fully understood. "The last play of a Hauptmann or a Maeterlinck," he remarked later, "gives me more of a thrill than all the musty memories of the days that are no more."[74] Modern drama was his proper province, and he soon spoke out on its behalf.

Ibsen's name, for example, began to appear frequently in his columns. Huneker had felt at first that the preacher in Ibsen constantly interfered with the artist,[75] but comparing the Norwegian's seldom-performed plays with the mediocre offerings of the New York stage, he began to appreciate their quality. "Admit that you do not like [Ibsen]," he wrote in 1894, "admit that you believe he is all wrong about the mission of the drama . . . but if you are curious, if you are critical, why not study this new and rare theatrical flower, or weed, if you will? . . . If the stage is to be the vehicle of mere eye and ear tickling, why, let us part company at once. . . . He is the product of his times, and, if his scalpel digs down deep and jars some hidden and diseased nerves, what shall we say?"[76] In mid-February of the same year, Huneker enjoyed Mrs. Fiske's performance in *A Doll's House*, though he disapproved of the editing because it changed Ibsen's meaning.[77]

By 1892 Huneker was already discussing the ethereal, antinaturalistic plays of Maurice Maeterlinck[78] and becoming increasingly familiar with the strong dramas of Hauptmann,[79] Sudermann,[80] and Schnitzler, which he saw at the Irving Place Theater, the German-language playhouse managed by Heinrich Conried. And as early as 1893 the "Prompter" remarked that *The Father* by the Swedish dramatist August Strindberg—whose strange, violent works had not yet been translated into English—had caused the London papers to predict that Ibsen would soon be passé.[81]

While he agreed that Oscar Wilde was one of the cleverest men in England, Huneker was plainly skeptical of Wilde's dramatic genius. He had become acquainted with Oscar's journalist brother, Willie, who had settled in New York in the fall of 1891, married the notorious Mrs. Frank Leslie (for a bedroom, Huneker reported him as saying),[82] and spent most of his time in bed or at bars, where he told stories about London society, recited parodies of Oscar's poems, or wrote articles, several of which appeared in the *Recorder* in the early spring of 1892.[83] Whether he told tales about his brother's private life is uncertain, but some months, at least, before the scandal broke, Huneker had heard of Oscar's sexual proclivities. "It is an age of inversion," wrote the "Raconteur" in August 1894. "Everybody is trying to invert thought and art, and Oscar Wilde manufactures an epigram by turning it topsyturvy, 'soixante-neuf' fashion."[84]

When the Wilde affair was reaching its sensational climax in the

spring of 1895 during the London run of Oscar's ironically titled play
An Ideal Husband, the "Prompter" described him as a "clever confec-
tioner whose tarts, jellies, souffles and ices are ingeniously turned out
from other men's moulds." "I salute you, Oscar," he added, "not as
the coming dramatist, but as the *chef de cuisine* who deserves the *cor-
don bleu.* Perhaps the Marquis of Queensberry will decorate you." Yet
Huneker had the courage to recommend the play.[85] After Wilde had
lost his foolish libel case against Queensberry, the "Prompter" took a
less frivolous view of the matter, protesting that Wilde's name should
not be taken off the housebills of the Haymarket Theater in London,
that even if he were the biggest scoundrel on earth the play was still his.
"I suppose the virtuous British public will have one of its huge moral
spasms," he remarked, "and kill Wilde socially, after lionizing him for
years." Three days later he observed that "all Paris is laughing at the
moral sensitivity displayed by John Bull. . . . If [Wilde] is a degenerate and a victim of some form of sexual mania, why, in heaven's
name, lock the poor wretch up and hand him over to the alienist."
Shortly afterward he applauded Charles Frohman's brave if shrewd de-
cision to produce *The Importance of Being Earnest* at the Empire Theater, and some weeks following Wilde's conviction and imprisonment,
he noted that "London seems at last to realize that Oscar Wilde the
dramatist has nothing to do with Oscar Wilde the convict, for *The Ideal
Husband* is being played with the author's name boldly displayed."[86]

Thus spoke a sophisticated, heterosexual American on *the* great
scandal of the "decadent" nineties. Huneker was not so shocked by
Wilde's deviation that he refused to acknowledge his artistic achievements, even though he eventually concluded that Wilde lacked originality as a poet, that his plays were "fascinating as fireworks, and as
remote from human interest," and that his most individual contribution was his perishable conversation.[87]

He kept posted on the sad anticlimax of Wilde's life. In November
1897, after Oscar had been released from prison, it was probably Huneker who observed in the *Musical Courier* how completely he had been
forgotten, and in the following May the "Raconteur" headed his column
with an unsigned excerpt from Wilde's newly printed poem, "The Bal-
lad of Reading Gaol."[88] If, as Huneker claimed, he talked with Wilde
once again after their meeting in 1882[89] (was this another imaginary
episode?), it could not have been before the summer of 1899, as Wilde

made only the one trip to America, and Huneker did not revisit Europe before 1896, when Wilde was still in jail. In 1909 he described this rather dubious meeting to the Wilde enthusiast George Sylvester Viereck:

He was simply huge. Better 1,000 times than his books or plays. He said some pleasant things to me, I remember, also several cutting. He looked like a vile Adonis, a beast with swollen lips and heavy jaw, the eyes dull until the man was aroused and then they became phosphorescent. It was a clear case of booze; he drank early and often, champagne, brandy, absinthe. Huysmans he adored.[90]

If this meeting took place and if Wilde and Huneker were at their best, it must have been one of the most scintillating conversations of the century.

Huneker also kept an eye on the relatively tame and unexciting American drama. In 1893 he applauded Herne's realistic *Shore Acres*, declaring that in Nathaniel Berry, Herne had created "one of the sweetest, sanest and most compelling characters in American dramatic literature."[91] Augustus Thomas's *The Capitol* dealt with "things which are left unsaid by the everyday dramatist," Huneker remarked in 1895, and Thomas was "one of the few men we may look to for something distinctively American."[92] Yet Huneker bristled patriotically when British critics spoke contemptuously of our better playwrights. Americans, he boasted in 1895, could furnish London—which he called artistically backward compared to New York—with a large number of new plays that would cause the British to open their eyes in amazement.[93] In the same year, Huneker dismissed the respected, conservative English drama critic Clement Scott as a "prince of Philistines and mouthpiece of middle-class morality."[94]

Huneker's criteria for judging a play were simple: Were the characters convincing and placed in essentially dramatic situations? Was the play original, firmly constructed, logically motivated? Was its theme believable? He did not watch the stage with the eyes of a playwright, an actor, or a spectator who looked for nothing more than the exercise of his emotions; he observed as a cultivated student of books and human nature who instinctively recognized the literary values of drama and yet realized that it should be criticized according to the effect produced in the theater.[95] He objected to comic relief, incidental music, "asides," distracting mannerisms in actors, limitation of the dramatist's subject, and censorship on prudish grounds. And again, as in his criticism of music, his personal, witty style often made his criticism exceedingly entertaining.

The step to literary criticism was short and inevitable for the "Raconteur," as the restless desire for variety led him from the musical associations of Baudelaire, Gautier, Huysmans, George Moore, and others to their nonmusical books. Though conscious of his faulty accent and shaky grammar in speaking French and German (little is known about his ability in Italian), Huneker read these languages easily.[96] By the mid-nineties he knew the work of the leading modern novelists and poets of France and Germany as well as England and America, and had mentioned many of them in the *Musical Courier*. The writers he quoted or criticized were usually contemporary, for Huneker, believing that the art of his own day expressed the thoughts and emotions that he (and his readers) could best understand, and that living artists were more interesting to study than dead ones, was trying to make his column a kind of critical, if casual, review of the latest music, drama, fiction, and poetry.

He ventured into literary criticism with the self-educated man's almost excessive respect for sources and authorities and something of the scholar's bent for accuracy and thoroughness which the exigencies of journalism often frustrated. His tendency to dart from topic to topic, idea to idea, name to name, paying little attention to connecting links and logical development, sometimes made him seem superficial to those who valued clear, sustained reasoning above the picturesque phrase and the evocative association. But the staccato manner and the incessant allusions sprang from a mind richly loaded with gleanings from life and literature and quick with intuitive perception and sympathy. To literary criticism Huneker also brought a powerful curiosity about the writer as a human being and as the product of his age; a taste for both the poetically romantic and the psychologically realistic; an ear for musical verse and subtle prose rhythms; and a sensibility not easily shocked by the sensuous treatment of sex. He had, by this time, none of the "genteel" critic's limiting notions that art should reflect only the ideal, and no fixed attitude on the function of criticism other than the belief that art was a significant human activity which should be encouraged because of the pleasure and understanding it produced.

It is not surprising that as a supporter of modern music and drama, both of which had originated in Europe, Huneker should have become especially interested in Continental literature. What is surprising is that in his search for the most exciting in contemporary letters, he did not ignore the comparatively dull American literature of the nineties. Actually, however, he was thoroughly aware of the literary situation here, responded generously to the best fiction and poetry produced in America during this period, and constantly urged native writers to improve their work by becoming more daring and cosmopolitan.

Opposed to reformers of all kinds, Huneker did not consciously set out to reform American literary taste. "If I was among the first to import 'poisonous honey' from Europe," he later declared, "it was never with the idea that all those foreign writers were to be swallowed whole. I wrote of them because their art appealed to me."[97] Nor was he, of course, the first in this country to criticize modern European literature. But his ingratiating personality and style captivated so many readers for so long that he was able to acquaint more Americans with European literature than any other critic of his time. In addition, he was to found a "school" of critics whose most distinguished members were H. L. Mencken and George Jean Nathan—still youngsters when Huneker was writing for the *Musical Courier* and the *Recorder*.

The writer who probably exerted the most noticeable effect upon Huneker in the 1890's was J.-K. Huysmans, the littérateur par excellence of *fin de siècle* "decadence," whose championship of the symbolists and revolt against the naturalistic novel in favor of the *roman de la vie cérébrale* had preceded and influenced Huneker's similar course. A capable critic of literature and art—he was one of the first admirers of the Impressionists—Huysmans had expressed, in his notorious novel *A Rebours*, ideas that later formed the nucleus of Huneker's critical creed. There were "no such things as schools," wrote the Frenchman; "only the writer's temperament matters, only the working of the creator's brain." Critical impartiality was impossible, he added, "for the simple reason that, while desiring to be rid of prejudice, to refrain from all passion, every man goes for choice to those works which correspond most intimately with his own temperament, and he ends by relegating all the rest to the background."[98]

The cynical, blasphemous author of *Là-bas*, which gratified Huneker's taste for the occult, the fantastic, and the spine-tingling (the novel would "melt your teeth and grizzle your hair with horror," he remarked in 1894),[99] intrigued him more than the "amateur monk" miraculously won back to Catholicism in the era's most dramatic reconversion.[100] Yet Huneker, seeing in satanism only a daring and unconventional, if somewhat repelling and melodramatic, literary subject, was not taken in by the Parisian fad for the pseudo-mystic reflected in the novel.[101] What most impressed him, however, was Huysmans' extraordinarily vivid style, with its enormous vocabulary and complex, carefully varied sentence structure used so effectively to describe and evoke sensations, particularly unpleasant ones. In Huneker's estimate, Huysmans was by 1894 the "master in French prose since poor Maupassant went to Hell's Foundry."[102]

No writer of the decade irritated Huneker more than Max Nordau (the pen name of Max Simon Sudfeld), the Hungarian-Jewish physician and author, who in 1892–93 published in German his sensational *Degeneration,* a sweeping, "scientific" denunciation of later nineteenth-century literature and art as the product of degenerates. Fascinated by the psychology of the artist-genius—"I have an aching nerve," he once wrote, "called by the psychiatrists 'a craving for psychical insight' "[103]— Huneker had read a good deal of the new literature of pre-Freudian psychiatry. All men of genius, he observed in January 1892, were deflections from the normal man, "who lives for the hour, and [whose] natural motto reads 'Carpe Boodle.' "[104] Afterward he described genius as the "sacrificial goat of humanity," the man of genius as one "afflicted by the burden of the flesh intensified many times, burdened with the affliction of the spirit, raised to a pitch abnormal," who is "stoned because he staggers beneath the load of his sensitive temperament or wavers from the straight and narrow path usually blocked by bores too thick-headed and too obese to realize the flower-fringed abysses on either side of the road."[105]

Though he conceded, in March 1894, that there was some truth in Nordau's attack on Wagner and Ibsen, even if the case was overstated,[106] Huneker soon decided that the falsehood in *Degeneration* greatly outweighed the truth. In early July 1895, at the height of the lively international controversy that followed the publication, three months earlier, of the English translation of the book,[107] and almost a month before the appearance of George Bernard Shaw's devastating reply to Nordau, Huneker issued a rejoinder as savage as Shaw's:

Nordau has, despite his varied reading and experience, a petty, provincial, even parochial mind; his soul lives up an alley, he is utterly without imagination. It is his priggish insolence, his filthy insults, leveled at men, living men, whose shoestrings he is not worthy to unlatch that I resent. This contemptible specimen has failed in everything he has undertaken. . . . This old woman scold . . . is absolutely without the saving grace of humor. . . . Nordau reminds me of those wicked little boys who scribble words on walls. . . . He always praises what is dead and what the world has stamped with the seal of approval. . . . Ah! Nordau, Nordau, *du Schlemihl!* You are very human after all; you only quote favorable authorities. . . . Nordau is a poser. . . . His pose is not the pose for beauty, but the pose for rottenness. He is a literary slop jar.[108]

Huneker denied here an implication made by a Nordau sympathizer, Dr. Oscar Panizza, that Wagner was an active homosexual, despite the fact that he himself later detected invert symbolism in *Parsifal*. (He was interested enough in Panizza's argument, at any rate, to write out a thirteen-page translation of it—presumably his own—from the original German.)[109] Even after the furor over *Degeneration* had died down, Huneker continued to pursue its author, whom he eventually termed the "Comstock of Europe . . . plus intellect," though he was not too prejudiced against Nordau to praise his philanthropy and Zionism.[110]

Huneker's anti-British bias did not prevent him from keeping himself and his readers informed on the latest artistic trends and gossip in England by scanning London periodicals and reprinting excerpts. He repeated, for example, the rumor that Robert Louis Stevenson, whose prose he admired, had been an opium eater in San Francisco—which, Huneker commented, would account for much that was uncanny in the Scot's work.[111] But as the posthumous vogue of Stevenson—a healthy foil to Oscar Wilde, whose imprisonment followed R.L.S.'s death by six months—began to reach fantastic proportions, Huneker refused to join the bandwagon, concluding, eventually, that Stevenson wrote "superlatively well" but had little to say that was original or significant.[112] Nor did Huneker's dislike of the poseurs among the aesthetes in England prevent him from advertising the *Yellow Book*, in August 1894, as "one of the few things out of England that are clever and entertaining."[113]

Meanwhile, he was also criticizing American literature. Whitman and the old guard of New England were now dead or dying, and Mark Twain, Howells, and Henry James were the most esteemed home-grown authors, though James's early popularity had practically disappeared. Lafcadio Hearn was writing impressions of his adopted Japan, and some of Emily Dickinson's poetry had been published posthumously. (When the "Raconteur" reprinted, in 1891, her poem "I'm Nobody! Who Are You?" he compared her to Sappho.)[114] Local color fiction was still in demand, and if there were signs of a more somber realism in the grim stories of Hamlin Garland, those of Zola, Huysmans, and other modern French novelists were considered pornographic and unpleasant. Editors scrutinized their magazines for indelicate allusions to sex, for none dared to offend the all-powerful woman reader, watchdog over the moral welfare of the "young person." The "gay nineties" did not seem so gay to those who felt the pinch of the financial panic of 1893, worked in the sweatshops, or sickened in the military camps of Cuba. Conditions in America warranted a literature of tragic realism, and Huneker not only lamented its absence but also lambasted the hypocrisy and vague idealism of the "genteel tradition" and the mild mouthings of such ultra-respectable critics as Hamilton Wright Mabie and Maurice Thompson.[115]

Walt Whitman, at least, was frank about his sensuousness, and that is probably why Huneker admired him enough to write the long, complimentary article about him printed in the *Recorder* on November 1, 1891. Huneker deprecated America's neglect of the bard and the "violently unfair" attacks made against him, praised his "peculiar magnetic qualities," and discussed his poetry. Whitman might or might not be one of the world's great poets, Huneker concluded, but in an age of "hyper refinement" his figure loomed out large and distinct, and he was certainly "one of the greatest forces in American literature."[116]

Gradually, however, Huneker began to find Whitman distasteful, partly because of the homosexual connotations he discovered in *Leaves of Grass*, which he later dubbed the "bible of the third sex."[117] Not so naïve, presumably, as he had been as a youth in Philadelphia (he had been awed by Whitman's "Greek manner," he wrote in 1892),[118] annoyed by eccentric, noisy "Whitmaniacs," and influenced, in all likelihood, by Swinburne's famous recantation,[119] Havelock Ellis's remarks in *Sexual Inversion*,[120] and John Jay Chapman's condemnation of Whitman,[121] Huneker, less charitable to the poet than to Tchaikovsky, seemingly allowed his repulsion for homosexuality to color his judgment of Whitman. In 1898, shortly after attending a Whitman Fellowship dinner at which Walt's now middle-aged friend, Peter Doyle, was the guest of honor,[122] Huneker complained that the "slush,[123] hash, obscurity, morbid eroticism, vulgarity and preposterous mouthings well nigh spoil one's taste for what is really great in *Leaves of Grass*. . . . Don't believe the absurd lies told by his silly disciples. He was no man of the people. . . . Besides, he had a streak of the effeminate in him. All who knew his intimate side were aware of this."[124] This was probably the first *explicit* public reference by an American critic—or, at least, by one who had known him personally—to Whitman's homosexual leaning.[125]

Huneker's early admiration for Poe, on the other hand, never weakened. At the end of 1892, in an extended comparison of Poe and Chopin which was one of the most sustained essays he wrote during his apprenticeship and also, judging by the number of times he reprinted it (with minor variations), one of his favorite pieces, Huneker proclaimed Poe a genius and defended him against Griswold's distortions.[126] "Oh, if we but appreciated Poe as do our Gallic neighbors!" he exclaimed in 1893, five months after the results of a poll on great American books conducted by the *Critic* revealed that no work by Poe had appeared among the thirty-nine receiving the highest number of votes.[127]

Though he reproached the younger men for finding no beauty or interest in American life, by 1895 Huneker believed that a few writers were pointing the way to "one of the richest literary fields in the world," the undiscovered United States.[128] Impressed in 1891 by Henry B. Fuller's first book, *The Chevalier of Pensieri-Vani*, a sensitive study of the arts in Italy reflecting, with deft touches of irony, the aesthetic limitations of America (it probably reminded Huneker of Miss Brewster's less artistic *St. Martin's Summer*), Huneker reviewed the Chicagoan's early novels and even predicted that he would produce the American novel so long prayed for[129]—before he decided that the country was too large, its people and localities too varied, to be represented adequately by any single novel, no matter how great.[130] He also liked the earlier, sensuous fiction of Edgar Saltus, whose lush style Huneker (and others) overrated.[131]

In Huneker's estimation, however, an older American novelist remained unsurpassed. In 1895, a little over a year after Theodore Roosevelt in a letter to Brander Matthews had derided Henry James's snob-bishness and his "polished, pointless stories [in the *Yellow Book*] about the upper social classes of England,"[132] Huneker wrote: "Our greatest artist lives in London. When he publishes we poke fun at his exquisite style and cadenced prose. I mean, of course, Henry James."[133] He was to mention James more frequently than any other American author.

❧ *Seven*

THE CONJUGAL COMEDY

Meanwhile, Huneker was again having domestic difficulties, he and Clio becoming increasingly incompatible. It was hard for him to adjust to the rigors of marriage after so many years of freedom, nor was he willing to detach himself completely from Josephine, who refused even to admit, later, that Clio had ever been legally married to Huneker—either because of the ministerless ceremony or because she considered herself his common-law wife. (Long afterward, on a clipping of Huneker's obituary which contained the remark that his widow was his third wife, Clio being the first, Josephine crossed out the word "third" and the entire reference to Clio, writing in the margin: 1st wife dead. Mrs. J. is 2nd wife.")[1] "I couldn't marry more than one woman at a time because of certain social prejudices," he once joked. "And sometimes a man's wife won't let him marry the girl he likes (women are so unreasonable)."[2]

He would stay away from home for several days at a time, or, occasionally, would bring friends in at midnight without warning, and Clio would have to stay up until three or four in the morning.[3] To put the "buzz" into his pen, as he used to say,[4] or to relax afterward, he drank twelve or fifteen bottles of beer daily,[5] often spending half the night drinking at a café with his colleagues and cronies. To make matters worse, he was a poor provider. As Clio began serious study under Saint-Gaudens at the Art Students' League in 1893, she and "Jamie" (her pet name for him) clashed more frequently. "When artist mates with artist then comes the tug of tongues," he once remarked, thinking, surely, of his own marriage. "No family can harbour two prima donnas —that is, not without fur flying."[6]

Early in 1894 she went to the new home of her parents in Piermont, New York,[7] where on February 15 she gave birth to a son named Erik. Huneker did not arrive there until a week later, explaining to his outraged in-laws that he had not come sooner because he could not stand to see anyone in pain.[8] During most of 1895 he, Clio, and Erik lived in a Carnegie Hall studio apartment,[9] where their troubles continued. Once, while riding with her and the baby, he suddenly decided to escape an out-of-town excursion by jumping from the cab; she tried to hold him back, and in the scuffle he struck her and slammed the door on Erik's head.[10] Since she wanted further training, though her busts of Seidl, Paderewski, Fanny Bloomfield-Zeisler, and Emma Eames had already attracted considerable attention,[11] the best solution for her domestic and professional problems seemed to be a trip abroad. Accordingly, in November 1895[12]—about the time that Huneker published a short story about a gentile and his nonreligious Jewish wife, which may reflect his continuing relationship with Josephine[13]—Clio left for Paris to study with MacMonnies and Louis Oury, taking Erik with her. (Huneker sent her money regularly, at least during 1897 and the first half of 1898.)[14] "She'll be better off," Jim sadly told Joseph I. C. Clarke, the writer and editor, who went with Huneker to see Clio off. "And you?" asked Clarke. "I have my work," he replied.[15]

Before the end of May 1896, Huneker, en route to his first Wagner festival in Bayreuth, arrived in Paris after an absence of seventeen years. One of the first places he visited was the Rue Puteaux to see if the dingy building in which he had lived was still standing. It was, and the same proprietor stood at the doorway, but he did not recognize Huneker, now fat and almost forty. In early June he attended the glittering concert celebrating the fiftieth anniversary of the debut of Saint-Saëns, probably telling the composer, when he was presented to him afterward, that he had heard him play in Paris in 1878. The "Raconteur" reported that Saint-Saëns did much of his composing away from Paris, the "greatest show town on earth and perhaps the loveliest" and a "wonderful place for the painter, sculptor, and literary man," but "too modern, too shallow and artificial" for the creative musician.[16]

Though the erstwhile bohemian was disturbed by the scarcity of bathtubs, even in the city's better hotels, he again reveled in the glorious architecture, picture galleries, bookshops, and outdoor cafés. "You can eat your dinner in the cool of the evening," he wrote, "surrounded by gaily dressed, well-bred people, a world about you instinct with color, grace, movement and a certain Greek-like gaiety."[17] He conceded, however, that it would be dangerous for a critic like himself to live and study here because "I might become a lotus eater, and dream my life away under rhythmic winged cathedrals and palaces of marble."[18] Yet the most delightful thing about Paris was the presence of Clio, for if everyone there, as Huneker told his readers, was humming a song called "Cléo"—a tribute to the popular dancer Cléo de Mérode—the name on *his* mind was spelled a little differently.[19]

In mid-June (not on July 4, the more colorful date he chose when he published several versions of the story years later), he spent a rollicking bachelor's night in Paris. At a performance of *Die Walküre*, he met Wallace Goodrich, a student of organ and composition who afterward became director of the New England Conservatory. When the opera was over, they went to the Café Monferino, drinking Pilsner and discussing Wagner until midnight, when they moved to Maxim's, joining a group of young Americans including poets Joseph Trumbull Stickney and George Cabot Lodge.[20] Bored with the gypsy band, they all gathered around a shabby piano in an upstairs room, sang the Negro and Irish songs played by Goodrich, danced, recited Racine, and improvised tugs of war with a richly brocaded tablecloth. Finally Goodrich relinquished the piano to Huneker, who started to play Chopin, only to be lassoed with the tablecloth and dragged over the floor. As dawn approached, Goodrich regained the piano and played the prelude to *Tristan und Isolde*, which made everyone melancholy. Leaving Maxim's, finally, the group dropped in at a coachman's haunt to drink beer. Huneker staggered back to his lodgings to lie down for a brief nap before meeting Goodrich to hear Widor play the organ at St. Sulpice—and slept for twelve hours, long past the recital.[21]

On another visit to the Café Monferino, Huneker had the unique experience of "interviewing" a king, the notorious, pleasure-loving ex-King Milan of Serbia—and had to pay for the drinks when His Majesty skipped out while Huneker was briefly out of the room. "Alas, kings are but human," he wrote, "especially Slavic kings with fantastic kingdoms!" Anyhow, it was worth something to be able to say that one had treated a king.[22] A soberer Huneker visited the Louvre and two salons, where he admired Dagnan-Bouveret's "Last Supper," pictures by the American painter Alexander Harrison, and especially the "morbid and masterful marbles" of Rodin, whom he called the "one genius of whom France can boast to-day . . . the only successor to Michel Angelo, a morbid, unhealthy, paroxysmal Angelo, a man given to strange visions, but whose technique is supreme as his touch is often harsh, angular and unpleasant."[23]

In late June, Huneker went to London, crossing the Channel in the company of Heinrich Conried and reporting—probably mistakenly—that on the ship he had seen the aging Swinburne.[24] During the four or five days he spent in London, he attended concerts and at least two operas at Covent Garden, including *Tristan* with Jean de Reszke (the tenor's first appearance in the role), and also was present at the burial of the famous English impresario Sir Augustus Harris. Back in Paris by July 4, the "Raconteur" stated that at the café frequented by both Huysmans and Nordau he had seen the former, who, it was said, had not spoken to the author of *Degeneration* since the book had come out; Huneker explained afterward that the humorless Nordau had not realized that Huysmans was caricaturing the decadents in *A Rebours* and did not expect its hero to be taken seriously.[25] (Much later, Huneker recalled that he went to the funeral of Edmond de Goncourt,[26] which took place in Auteuil on July 20, but this, too, is unlikely, for, as he himself recorded at the time, he reached Bayreuth on July 19 and remained there until July 30.)[27]

In Bayreuth someone else temporarily took his mind off Clio. Singing minor roles in the *Ring* was Olive Fremstad, a strikingly beautiful woman with a chiseled, piquantly tilted nose, deep-set blue eyes, high eyebrows, and brown-gold hair. Born in Stockholm (in 1868) but reared in Oslo, she had been brought to America at the age of twelve by her father, who gradually gave up his medical practice to become a Methodist missionary among the Scandinavian immigrants in Minnesota. While still in her teens, Anna Olivia taught piano and played the organ at her father's revival meetings. Then she had come to New York to study voice with the well-known teacher Frederick E. Bristol, playing accompaniments in exchange for her own lessons.[28] On November 8, 1891, she had made her New York debut at a concert conducted by Anton Seidl at the Lenox Lyceum,[29] and had also sung in various churches before going to Germany in 1892 to study with the great Lilli Lehmann. Though a natural soprano, she joined the Cologne Opera as the leading contralto three years later because there was no opening for a soprano,[30] and she was now making her first appearance in Bayreuth.

It is not certain whether Huneker already knew her. Francis Neilson, who heard her Lyceum performance and was so struck by her beauty that he wrote a sonnet about her the same night, thinks that Huneker was seeing her shortly afterward, though Huneker himself claimed that he did not meet her until the summer of 1896.[31] The "Raconteur" did not mention her debut in 1891, but he must have seen—if, indeed, he did not write—the brief, unsigned criticism, printed elsewhere in the *Musical Courier*, praising her "remarkable" voice and recommending practice to make her singing "artistically acceptable."[32] Two months later he had married Clio, and then Olive had gone to Europe, while he remained in New York.

The Rhinedaughters in Bayreuth's *Das Rheingold* were not as seductive as they might have been, Huneker felt—"they swam well for graduates of a natatorium," he wrote, "but they were not voluptuous in their pose nor winning in movement"—but he observed that the auburn hair of one of them, Olive Fremstadt [*sic*], "dyed the River Rhine with its warm color." A week later he remarked that in *Siegfried* she was "miles away" from the other two Rhinedaughters in "beauty of voice, plasticity of pose and artistic singing."[33] Personally, he found her so seductive that he decided to stay in Bayreuth for the second cycle of the *Ring*. "Is it Bayreuth, Wagner, the *Rhine Daughters* or the *Valkyrie*," he wrote on July 27, "that makes me anchor here, despite the fair blandishments of Paris?" Three days later he reluctantly left[34] a budding prima donna understandably attracted by his intellect and charm, and flattered by the attentions (and favorable notices) of a famous critic. From Paris he sent her passionate letters, hinting that he was not free, apparently, but not actually telling her that he was married. In early August she playfully replied that they had been impetuous and rash, and that if he were serious about any other woman, she wanted to have no more to do with him. Why had he run off again to Paris just when they were getting to know each other better? ("I have left my heart in Bayreuth," wrote the "Raconteur"[35]—and only Olive knew what he really meant.) She wished that he had never looked at her, and yet she wanted to hold him and kiss him, without having to keep one eye on the door. How the sparks flew that first evening they had been together! Resigned, finally, to his departure, she wished him a good voyage home and begged him to destroy her letters if he had already forgotten her.

He had not forgotten her, nor did he destroy the letters.[36] The first thing he sent to the *Musical Courier* after he left Bayreuth at the end of

July was a short story called "The Last of the Valkyries," in which Olive and himself were patently portrayed as Rue Towne and Paul Goddard. In the story, Goddard falls in love in Bayreuth with both Rue, an American contralto singing in the *Ring,* and Helena, a Roumanian beauty (whose background resembled that of Helene von Schewitsch, but whose prototype—if there was one—is unknown); he becomes engaged to Rue, but she breaks off with him when she learns about Helena, who also drops him, and he finally goes back to his "steady" girl friend, Edith Vicker, in Paris.[37] Pleading for an answer, Huneker sent Olive the story along with a notice he had previously written about her good looks.[38] The story was very good, she replied, though he had drawn her too plainly, and it made her jealous to learn of her rival. Had he come to her in Bayreuth only after he had been discarded by someone else, and was he still corresponding with this Roumanian? If so, Olive would drop him like a hot coal. He was the wittiest person she knew, but if she were with him, she would know a good way to keep him quiet!

She remained in Europe during the next three years, however, while Huneker stayed in America, and the short-lived romance never had a chance to develop. They continued to correspond, Olive advising him to be more sensible and not to fall in love so often because it diminished his individuality, and wondering how he found time to think of her, when he was so busy with his writing and teaching. Huneker wanted her to come home, but Lilli Lehmann had warned her that if she did, family troubles would hinder her progress and she had worked too hard to let anything interfere with her career. "A serious artist can't have lovers and still *think,*" Olive once remarked, maintaining that even marriage was wrong for such persons—an opinion eventually confirmed by her two marital experiences.[39] But she was lonely and moody, now, and wished that Jim would come to her, a tempting invitation which, alas, he could not afford to accept. When she wrote him again, a few months afterward, she had recovered her equilibrium and the "affair" was over. They remained good friends and mutual admirers,[40] and he occasionally saw her years later, when she had become the world's greatest Wagnerian soprano. Yet, as an old, sick woman whose glorious singing had ended thirty years earlier, she had "forgotten" this brief Bayreuth episode, perhaps out of consideration for her friend Josephine, then still alive.[41] But Jim (and Josephine) saved the letters that tell the story.

In Paris Huneker tried to persuade Clio to return with him to America, but she refused, and he came back alone. Still in love with her, he asked his friend Vance Thompson, who visited Paris in January 1897, to see if he could persuade her to rejoin her husband, but he, too, had no luck. (Thompson found Clio so attractive, indeed, that after his mission failed, he wooed her himself, again without success.)[42] Huneker sought solace with Josephine, but his weakness for pretty singers soon involved him with another woman, almost as attractive as Fremstad and, more important, closer at hand.

One of the leading roles in the operetta *La Falote*, which opened at the Casino on March 1, 1897, was taken by a statuesque beauty in her early thirties making her professional stage debut under the name of Georgia Powers. Her real name was Georgiana Powers Carhart, and she was married to Carrington E. Carhart, a Kansas City educator and newspaperman, whom she had left when she came to New York to study voice in 1893.[43] Her performance in the operetta delighted Huneker, who publicly applauded her "natural mimetic gifts" and "fine natural voice," suggested that her part be built up, and predicted a bright future for this "handsome" artist.[44] He soon decided that this future should include him, and by September 1, 1897, when "Georgie" had taken a room at the Maison Félix, where Huneker was living again, the chambermaids noticed that she seemed to prefer Huneker's quarters to her own.[45] Not deeply in love with him, she nevertheless admired his intellect and, like Fremstad, was grateful for the attentions of such an influential critic.

On Georgie's birthday in May 1897, he invited her to a concert, but shortly before he was supposed to call for her, she received a telegram saying that he could not keep the appointment because he had to go to the "Offenheim Institute." Suspecting that he was up to no good, she managed somehow to trace the wire to Josephine's apartment at the Carrollton (Madison and Seventy-sixth Street)—always *"offen heim"* or "open house" to Jim—and went there. As Josephine admitted her into the room, Georgie saw Huneker sitting on the edge of the bed with a blanket wrapped around him. "Well," he exclaimed, "thank God you two have met at last!" Georgie stayed for dinner, and the three of them talked till morning and then took a long walk to the Everett House, where they had breakfast.[46]

For two years Jim was intimate with both Josephine and Georgie. Late in 1898 Clio finally returned to New York, leaving a handsome young French nobleman, Vicomte Raoul de L'Estrange, disconsolate in Paris.[47] Her sister and brother-in-law, who had lived at the Maison Félix from December 1897 to June 1898 and had seen Huneker and Georgie together in his room, probably told Clio about his girl friend. In the spring of 1899, at any rate, Clio filed suit for divorce, Irma personally serving the summons and complaint on Huneker, who was charged with committing adultery with Georgie, Josephine, and other women (though only the liaison with Georgie is described in the records). Huneker gallantly denied the charges, but Clio obtained the divorce on May 1, 1899, the court ordering him to pay ten dollars a week for the support of Erik and notifying him that under New York law he could not remarry there during Clio's lifetime.[48]

After the divorce, Huneker remarked to Georgie: "I don't see why we can't get married and have Jo live with us," a suggestion that neither woman jumped at. Once, indeed, Josephine told Georgie in dead earnest that she carried poison in the gold locket she wore around her neck and would kill herself if she ever lost Jim.

She never did—for long. Approaching middle age, he felt that it was time to settle down into a comfortable, if not sober, married life with a practical, "feather-bed" kind of woman to take care of him. (In this respect he was not unlike Goethe, whom he once called the "perfect type of the inconstant lover who in middle life married some one to look after his material comfort: a Don Juan on the retired list.")[49] On June 18, 1899, he informed Krehbiel, who had evidently heard a rumor that Huneker had married again: "My withers are yet unwrung by any matrimonial foolishness. Never fear, Uncle Krehbiel, your fat nephew has had enough of the noose, hence a violent separation of certain persons."[50] He had probably broken with Georgie, but if the date engraved on Josephine's wedding ring[51] is to be trusted, he had either married her on May 15, 1899—though an extensive search has failed to produce any record of the marriage[52]—or accepted her as his common-law wife from that date. "Since I remarried, 1899, my Jewish wife," Huneker wrote Israel Zangwill long afterward, "I have had peace, happiness."[53]

At the turn of the century—probably in 1899 and not later than August 1900[54]—the couple moved into a top-floor suite of the ten-story Carrollton, one of the first tall hotels in the area. High windows and a

skylight made their apartment (and the larger one on the same floor
into which they moved in December 1904)[55] bright and airy, which
compensated for the noise of the rain striking the skylight and the eery,
startling effects of lightning flashing through the glass and emblazoning
the studio. From the second apartment especially, they had a breath-
taking view of the East and Hudson rivers, the harbor, the Statue of
Liberty, and Central Park. The chief furnishings in the rather bare
studio of his "dream barn" were the low bookcases, a Steinway grand
piano, and a few original pictures: a head by George Luks, a study
by Thomas Sully, and, eventually, several Ernest Lawson landscapes.
Perched atop a desk once owned by Thaddeus Stevens was a group of
little ivory skeletons, which Huneker often fondled as he wrote, and
one of the desk drawers contained a collection of engravings, some of
them more than slightly pornographic, which he brought out, now and
then, to amuse himself or his close friends.[56] In this comfortable setting, he and Josephine were to lead an increasingly sedate and bourgeois life for the next dozen years.

In 1900 Georgie went to Germany to study voice, and during the
following decade she sang Wagnerian roles (Elsa, Elizabeth, Sieglinde)
in Dresden. She could compare notes on Huneker with her friend Olive
Fremstad, who remained in Germany until she joined the Metropolitan
in 1903. Long afterward, curiously enough, Georgie became an intimate friend of Huneker's sister, who once told Mencken that of all her
brother's women friends (apart from Josephine?), Georgie was the one
to whom he was probably "most attached."[57] After almost forty years
of retirement from the stage, Georgie returned to the entertainment
world in 1947 as the star panelist on the radio and television program
"Life Begins at Eighty." For nine years the irrepressible oldster
bubbled over with humorous philosophical quips and stories that often
had to be interrupted because they were too risqué. Though she protested that her role on the panel was that of a "fat foolish woman, very
undignified," she loved this twilight adulation, which was far greater
than any she had ever received as a singer. Sometimes after the show
was over, she would sing for an enthusiastic audience, with more show-
manship than voice, before ensconcing herself at her favorite bar. In
1956, when "Life Begins at Eighty" went off the air, she became a convert to Catholicism and spent her last years in a Catholic rest home in
Manhattan, where she died in 1959 at the age of ninety-three.[58]

In 1898 or 1899, meanwhile, Clio and Roland Hinton Perry opened a studio in the West 10th Street building long occupied by William M. Chase, the noted artist, and made it a popular gathering place for New York bohemians.[59] She was living here in the spring of 1900 when Huneker's conjugal comedy ended in a burst of front-page publicity: at the last minute, it seems, the rector of the New York church in which Clio was scheduled to be married to William B. Bracken (a fifty-year-old New York bachelor lawyer, stock promoter, and man-about-town, whom Clio had met late in 1898 or early in 1899) refused to officiate when he learned that she was a divorcée instead of a widow, and the ceremony finally had to be held in Delmonico's.[60] The editor of *Town Topics,* of which Huneker was then music critic, laughed at the incident in a humorous poem and commented that some people had concluded from the proceedings that Clio's ex-husband was dead. "I can only say that in the music centers of the world he is regarded as a lively corpse," he added, "and that with characteristic good taste he played a silent part in the comedy or tragedy, whichever one chooses to call it."[61] Josephine must have enjoyed Clio's discomfiture, especially since her own name was not mentioned, while Huneker, of course, could well afford to remain silent on matters matrimonial.

His relations, afterward, with his son, who used to visit him occasionally, were always awkward, though he apparently liked children and went out of his way to amuse them. Mrs. Vera Kasow, the daughter of Josephine's youngest sister, recalls that in her uncle's last years, when she and her sister were old enough to visit him, he was "very pleasant and charming," and would tell them lovely stories as he played the piano. From Europe, about 1913, he sent his little nieces whimsical postcards signed "Gollygubs," and in Vera's autograph book he wrote a "love letter" and a poem.[62] Raymond A. Speiser, son of Huneker's Philadelphia friends the Maurice Speisers (Mrs. Speiser was the sister of Benjamin F. Glazer, Huneker's colleague on the Philadelphia *Press* in 1917–18), never forgot how kind and companionable Huneker was to him when as a boy of eight or nine—in 1917 or 1918—he went crab fishing with the vacationing critic at Atlantic City.[63] But his ludicrous paternal gestures indicated that he was more at ease with someone else's child than with his own. When Erik was fourteen, for example, his father offered him a cigar, which the startled boy declined. "You don't smoke?" was the incredulous reply. "*I've* smoked since I was eleven!"

Two years later, when asked if he had any girl friends, Erik told his father that he was more interested in sports than in girls. "What will *running* do for you?" snorted Huneker. "The only time *I* ever ran in my life was from a policeman." The most fatherly thing he ever said to his son, then in his twenties, was: "I have a little money put away; any time you have a girl in trouble and you have to do something about it, come and see me; we don't have to tell the women in the family."[64]

ᴊᴘ *Eight*

'M'LLE NEW YORK'

In 1893 Huneker met Vance Thompson, his closest friend during the rest of the decade.[1] The son of a Presbyterian minister, Thompson had graduated from Princeton in 1883, and after studying in Heidelberg and Jena, had returned to America with a Ph.D., yellow gloves, long paddock coats, the most English Lincoln and Bennet toppers, and a monocle.[2] In 1890 he had married Lillian Spencer, an actress whose professional name was Madame Severine,[3] and later had become the drama, music, and literary critic of the New York *Commercial Advertiser*. An insatiably curious student of eccentricities and a practitioner of gorgeous prose, the versatile Thompson had much in common with Huneker, including a tremendous capacity for beer.[4] They sometimes argued long and ferociously and reviled each other lovingly,[5] but on one subject they were in complete agreement: American periodicals were much too circumspect and tame. What could two cosmopolitan journalists do about this situation?

Why not start a magazine, thought Thompson, a fortnightly modeled on lively Parisian weeklies? In 1895 two such magazines, neither of them published in New York, were creating a stir: the *Chap-Book*, founded a year earlier by two Harvard students and now issuing from Chicago, and San Francisco's *The Lark*, which had just begun its merry two-year career. The serious *Chap-Book* could boast among its contributors Henry James, Hamlin Garland, H. G. Wells, Max Beerbohm, Robert Louis Stevenson, and W. B. Yeats. Edited by Gelett Burgess and a group of literary aesthetes known as "Les Jeunes," *The Lark* had disarmingly announced in May 1895 that its sole intention was to be gay, and was proceeding to carry out this program by printing, among other entertaining pieces, the drawings and nonsense verse of Burgess, including his immortal "Purple Cow." Deciding that New York had room for a similar enterprise, Thompson enlisted the aid of Huneker and two talented illustrators, Thomas Fleming and Thomas Powers.

Early in August 1895, regular newsstand browsers noticed the attractive cover of a new magazine: on a pink, buff, and black background was the picture of a woman with elaborate headgear, smiling seductively near a group of beer drinkers watching a café entertainment. In thin, black, angular letters were the words "M'lle New York" (the un-French apostrophe inserted and the French hyphen in the place-name missing), the "M'lle" superimposed on the decorative face. The browsers who thumbed through the six unnumbered pages probably noticed first of all the delicate drawings, both black-and-white and colored, of lightly dressed women and leering men. Unless they were unusually sophisticated, those who skimmed over Thompson's brash preface must have been more irritated than amused by its tone:

The public . . . corrupts the language it has inherited from the mob and the poets; it has debauched the stage to the level of Mr. Richard Watson Gilder's poetry and looks upon the drama merely as a help to digestion, a peptic or aperitive; not content with having vulgarized literature and art, it has begun to "popularize" science—your bootmaker has theories of the creation and your tailor argues the existence of God; counter-jumpers play at atheism; lawyers and pedagogues are flattered at reading in the Astor Library that Moses was only a "medicine man" and Christ a politician. . . .

This grotesque aggregation of foolish individuals pretends to literary taste; it has its painters, its playwrights, its authors; that part of it which reads the male blue-stocking, William Dean Howells, looks down upon that part of it which reads the female blue-stocking, Richard Harding Davis; that part which reads Richard Harding Davis looks down upon the part which reads Laura Jean Libbey (why, in Heaven's name?), and the readers of Miss Libbey look down in turn upon the readers of the *Police Gazette*.

M'LLE NEW YORK is not concerned with the public. Her only ambition is to disintegrate some small portion of the public into its original component parts—the aristocracies of birth, wit, learning and art and the joyously vulgar mob.

Huneker made no signed contribution to the first issue of *M'lle New York*, which, however, he enthusiastically welcomed in the *Recorder* and *Musical Courier*. "The new color process, the cleverness of the drawings of Fleming and Powers, and the dash and lightness of touch, are positively refreshing," he wrote. "*M'lle New York* is a free lance, and even in this first number draws blood. Such a publication that neither fears nor favors, is sure to win recognition, enemies and friends."[6] But beginning with the second issue, which he also recommended,[7] he became a regular contributor, writing as many as three pieces a number, and by the fifth issue his name appeared on the cover as the magazine's associate editor.

Though he was to do a little music and literary criticism for *M'lle New York*—in a more highly colored style than usual, to blend with its preciosity—Huneker looked on the magazine as a more appropriate outlet for the whimsical, fantastic sketches and short stories he had been printing in the *Musical Courier* since 1889. He had a deep-seated feeling, indeed, that criticizing other men's music, plays, novels, poems, and pictures was a poor substitute for creating them oneself, and at times he even doubted that criticism did much to improve art or public taste.[8] "That it is better to create than to criticize everyone must admit," he wrote in 1891, adding, long afterward, that "at best the critic sits down to a Barmecide's feast, to see, to smell, but not to taste the celestial manna vouchsafed by the gods. We are only contemporaries of genius."[9] But in the mid-nineties he still had hopes of leaving criticism for fiction, and he jumped at the chance of enlarging his audience, especially since he could use practically all of the same material in both the *Musical Courier* and *M'lle New York*.

In the new magazine, he continued to publish his experiments with various kinds of imaginative prose. Satirical fantasies like "The Dream of a Decadent" and "Nosophilia: A Nordau Heroine" were in the "Raconteur's" customary spoofing vein. But his serious short stories, the prose poems inspired by Baudelaire, Mallarmé, and Huysmans, and the prose episode "Venus Victrix"—which suggests a Remy de Gourmont idea handled in the manner of Jules Laforgue[10]—were so largely derivative that one is reminded of a passage in *Painted Veils* (whose time scheme begins in the year *M'lle New York* was founded), in which the writer-hero, Huneker's *alter ego,* ponders the problem of how to achieve originality, how to escape the influence of Flaubert, the Goncourts, and "above all, Huysmans."[11] The Huysmans touch is especially evident in Huneker's story "Where the Black Mass Was Heard"—published in late November 1898[12]—which the Catholic clergy condemned as blasphemy. (Was Huneker's unconscious at work when he placed his devil in the crypt of St. Joseph's Church in Willing's Alley, where he and Lizzie had been married?) In 1899 Remy de Gourmont, the greatest living French critic, Huneker believed, and one of his idols—he shared so many of the Frenchman's interests and tastes that in *Painted Veils* he has Gourmont advise the hero to be more original[13]—sent Huneker a card of thanks for this story.[14]

In 1895 Huneker imitated Israel Zangwill in a story called "The Shofar Blew at Sunset," a denunciation of Jewish materialism, which brought a pleasant letter from Zangwill and some complaints from Jews that Huneker had maligned them,[15] though his other writings were so outspokenly pro-Semitic that for years he was thought to be Jewish himself.[16] The protests against the story were understandable, in a way, for in previous issues of *M'lle New York* Thompson had printed Fleming's caricatures of the Jewish physiognomy and had made derogatory remarks about Jewish artists, all of whom, he declared, were "without genius or originality."[17] Huneker's position was equally extreme: he maintained that *all* of the great artists were Jews, and he and Thompson had long arguments on the subject.[18]

Meanwhile, Thompson, whose criticism in the magazine was actually more substantial and significant than Huneker's, discussed modern European authors and painters—Knut Hamsun, Stanislaw Przybyszewski, Maeterlinck, Ibsen, Verlaine, Verhaeren, and some younger poets completely unknown in America. His essays were collected in *French Portraits* (1900), which borrowed heavily for text and illustrations from Gourmont's *Le Livre des masques* (1896),[19] and which was dedicated to someone Huneker described in his favorable review as "a personal enemy of mine"—himself.[20] Among the many poems reprinted in *M'lle New York*, in French or in translation, were some by the symbolists, including Laforgue,[21] also little known in this country. To show up the naïveté of so-called critics, Thompson, class poet at Princeton, wrote "symbolistic" poems solemnly attributed to one Lingwood Evans, Australian "anarchist, libertine, mystic," and was bombarded with letters requesting more information about this exciting new author.[22]

The editors of *M'lle New York* were aided by their friend Philip Hale, whose humorous story about Jack the Ripper was one of the best things they printed.[23] "We had a Philip Hale cult then," Huneker recalled. "No wonder. An artist in prose, he literally educated Boston in the gentle art of paganism."[24] Born in Vermont in 1854, Hale had graduated from Yale in 1876, passed the bar in Albany, where he held a job as church organist, and studied music on the Continent. Settling in

Boston as a music critic and organist, he began to write for magazines and newspapers there a few years after Huneker joined the *Musical Courier*, and eventually served as the Boston *Herald*'s music and
drama critic for thirty years (1903–33). During the 1890's he regularly contributed sprightly letters to the *Musical Courier* on musical
events in Boston, and this association led to his friendship with Huneker. Astonishingly erudite in many fields, a witty and entertaining
writer, Hale was probably the American journalistic critic Huneker admired most.[25] His translations of modern French literature[26] and his
support of the symbolists—in November 1893, when the "Raconteur"
reversed himself by defending the symbolists he had belittled a year
earlier, Hale thanked him publicly[27]—undoubtedly stimulated Huneker's interest in the "decadents."

More Parisian than either the *Chap-Book* or *The Lark*,[28] *M'lle New
York* was advanced and daring for its time. The colored illustrations,
wide margins, tiny pictures across the letterpress, and impertinent mar-
ginal comments widened the eyes of editors and layout men, while Powers' mildly bawdy, Beardsleyan drawings might have offended Anthony Comstock if the "precious" prose surrounding them had not
given the magazine a certain highbrow dignity. Its editors were also
sex-conscious in another sense, for in the midst of the "new woman"
movement, Thompson raged against the American worship of what
Huneker elsewhere called the "unfair sex," while Huneker, with tongue
in cheek, gaily took the other side. Those who knew the two men well
found this exchange even funnier, for Thompson happened to be a hen-
pecked husband, while Huneker was rather roosterish in his relations
with women. "It isn't true that I beat my wives," Huneker once told Rupert Hughes. "I could never treat a woman roughly. But when they grew
hysterical, I would put them on the floor and sit on them so that they
wouldn't hurt themselves!"[29] (Twenty years later, ironically enough,
Thompson's most successful book, *Eat and Grow Thin* [1914], a man-
ual on dieting actually compiled by his wife,[30] was succeeded by *Woman*,
a defense of the female.)[31] In the nineties Thompson's other social ideas
were equally iconoclastic. He derided the "fatuous phrases that the
makers of the American constitution filched from soppy sentimentalists
like Rousseau and Mirabeau," and laughed at the notion that all men
were born free and equal. "This so-called Christian organization of society," he added, "is as base and vicious a one as ever existed. . . . It

is not a democracy. It is not even a tolerable aristocracy. It is the rule of the dollar."[32] Reading *M'lle New York* as a youth in Baltimore, Mencken remembered, he got a "special thrill" from Huneker's "illumination, sophistication and colorful, rapid style";[33] he must also have been impressed by Thompson's lively diatribes.

As issue succeeded issue, many readers wondered how such an *outré* publication could survive. Asked how much was required to get out a number of *M'lle New York*, Elbert Hubbard, editor of another new magazine, *The Philistine*, estimated that it took "three pipefuls" of opium.[34] Fortunately the staff members had other jobs (Powers, at this time, was happily under contract to both Pulitzer and Hearst and had been legally enjoined from working for either, though permitted to receive a salary from both!)[35] and paid for their fun, Thompson bearing the financial brunt,[36] until January 1896, when the magazine was suspended. It was published again in the following April but only for a short time, and two years passed before it made a sudden and short-lived reappearance.

The first eleven numbers were eagerly read by the literati and editors of little magazines. In November 1896, Walter Blackburn Harte, the Boston essayist and editor of *Lotus*, called the series "one of the most bizarre . . . literary curiosities" in English, "certainly unique in American literature." The "knowledge of life and literature and music it contained was unusually extensive, varied, and peculiar," Harte observed, "and the style and habits of thought . . . were imported into imaginative literature bodily from the laboratory of the experimenter in psychic and physiological psychology." Though the magazine had gone too far, he thought, "imprisoning the imagination in the stews, and banishing the mind and spirit out of life in a poetic mist of purely sensual existence," it had nevertheless provided "glimpses of the play of free minds in other literatures where Mrs. Grundy does not rule as in the American domestic periodical and story-book," and that, Harte admitted, was salutary.[37]

With the aim of making the *Musical Courier* a weekly review of the arts, Marc Blumenberg engaged Vance Thompson in 1897 to write a drama, literary, and art section, and also added "The Tattler," an unsigned column occasionally written by Huneker and devoted mainly to literature and drama. Before it was well launched, however, the drama department ran afoul of the Puritans. "It is only necessary to say that it is on a level with the stage," sniffed the Springfield *Republican* on

September 12, 1897. "Its chief writers, Vance Thompson and James Huneker, were the leading spirits of the defunct *Mademoiselle New York*, a vile and sensual sheet, whose career was none too short for the good of the community."[38] "How disrespectful to speak of a dead girl," replied the "Raconteur," "a young thing snatched away from the Philistines by the gods at the age of eleven months, or was it weeks. Bah, what stupidity! What provincialism!"[39] A year later Blumenberg decided to confine the *Courier* to music (except for Huneker's usual digressions), but he agreed to publish a new series of *M'lle New York* on the Blumenberg Press.

On October 26, 1898, Huneker plugged the revived magazine by announcing that it contained a shocking story written by Marmaduke Humphrey, "a genius discovered by *M'lle New York*."[40] "Marmaduke Humphrey"—a name coined from the Elizabethan phrase, "I dined with Duke Humphrey today," meaning "I did not eat today"—was young Rupert Hughes, an ex-graduate student at Yale who had turned to journalism and free-lance writing. The pseudonym was appropriate since *M'lle New York* paid its contributors nothing except the compliment of allowing their work to be seen in sophisticated company. In 1895 Hughes had submitted a story about a worn-out prostitute, "When Badger Meets Con," which appeared in the fifth issue of the first series (October 1895), and soon Huneker, Thompson, and Hughes became such good friends and constant companions that they were known as the "Three Musketeers." Hughes made the editors promise not to reveal the real identity of Marmaduke Humphrey, two of whose humorously racy stories were published in the second series, for he feared that conventional magazines would reject his other work if it were known that he had written "off-color" tales;[41] as late as 1914, indeed, he protested when Huneker inadvertently disclosed the secret.[42] (Huneker did not include, in his two volumes of short stories, a more somber, probably autobiographical story about a pianist and a music-loving courtesan set in a genteel bordello, which appeared in the second series of *M'lle New York*, though he reprinted it, under a different title, in *Smart Set* in 1913 and eventually placed it in one of his last books.)[43]

Huneker, meanwhile, contributed fiction, prose poems, and critical essays to the new series, three separate pieces by him appearing in each of the first three numbers. But neither he nor Marmaduke Humphrey could keep the magazine afloat, and after four issues it died.

Though its appeal was limited and its material more historically important than intrinsically distinguished, *M'lle New York* made a distinct impression on the American press, as one of its contributors, George Henry Payne,[44] discovered; touring the United States some years after the magazine had folded, he found the scrapbooks of local newspapermen filled with bits from it.[45] At a time when English opinion dominated American periodicals, *M'lle New York* was symptomatic of a healthy tendency to bring ideas directly from France without first putting them through the sieve of English judgment. It printed far more works by modern French authors than any other American publication of its time, and not until the period of Amy Lowell and the Imagists was this high point of American criticism of French symbolism reached again.[46] Helping to pave the way for the host of little magazines that sprang up in New York a decade or so later, *M'lle New York* gave impetus to the undercurrent of revolt in America against the moralistic conception of literature, art, and life, and it spread Nietzsche's ideas among the intellectuals who later emerged as the exponents of artistic (and sexual) freedom.[47] And in their critical attitude toward sacrosanct American institutions, Thompson and Huneker anticipated more powerful iconoclasts, the most famous of whom was H. L. Mencken.

The availability of *M'lle New York* as an outlet for Huneker's noncritical writings (and, even more perhaps, his association with Thompson and Hughes) undoubtedly spurred his imagination, for during the magazine's span, from 1895 through 1898, he produced at least twenty-six short stories or sketches, many more than his output in any other four-year period, before or after. The best of these, however, including most of those he chose to reprint, appeared in the *Musical Courier* rather than in *M'lle New York,* probably because he had more space and was less self-conscious in the former. The notoriety he achieved through *M'lle New York* may have helped him sell stories later to advanced magazines such as *Reedy's Mirror* and *Smart Set,* but it must have made editors of conservative ones arch an eyebrow when they saw Huneker's name on a manuscript. Yet it cannot be said that by the end of 1898 he was noticeably closer to his secret goal of being a full-time "creator" rather than a critic. Criticism, after all, was to be his métier, fight as he would against his fate.

𝕴 *Nine*

CRITIC-ABOUT-TOWN

From 1895 to 1900 the mature Huneker steadily developed his style, method, and personality as a critic. During this period, he changed newspaper jobs and joined the staff of a magazine more prominent and longer-lived than *M'lle New York*, thus reaching more American readers. By the turn of the century, when he published his first book, he was known as a music critic not only at home but also in England, for starting in 1895 and continuing through most of 1900, the London *Musical Courier*, established as a weekly affiliate of the New York journal, reprinted Huneker's more serious articles (to match the more stolid character of British musical journalism).[1]

Unhappy with the salary paid him by the *Recorder* and nettled at not receiving credit for his time-consuming drama criticism, Huneker left the newspaper in the late summer of 1895 to become drama and music critic of its competitor, the *Morning Advertiser*, formerly Frank Munsey's first venture in daily journalism but now the morning edition of Vance Thompson's newspaper the *Commercial Advertiser*.[2] Huneker's signed Sunday department, "The Play's the Thing," began on September 1, and a few days later he started another signed column, first headed "Touch and Go" but soon changed to "The Players" and finally to "Plays and Players," which usually came out on Wednesdays and Fridays. The columns were popular and widely quoted. Two months after he had initiated them *Current Literature* announced with satisfaction that Huneker was now rightly getting recognition for the work that had "attracted tremendous interest among lovers of good literature" during the past two years, and with his lavish experience and rich powers of temperament was "fast making himself felt."[3]

The new job was easier than the old one, and $75 a week—considerably more than top reporters were then paid[4]—plus his salary from the *Musical Courier* seemed a small fortune to Huneker, even if his living expenses and those of Clio and Erik in Paris ate up a good part of his income, which came almost entirely from his pen. (Though his father, who died in 1893, had left an estate valued at $55,000, including proceeds from the sale of his cherished engravings, it was years before Huneker received his full share—and it amounted, finally, to only $6,600.)[5] He remained with the *Morning Advertiser* until April 1, 1897, when Hearst bought it for its Associated Press franchise and merged it with the New York *Journal.*

Emboldened perhaps by his association with *M'lle New York,* Huneker grew more and more impatient with the finicky Philistines he derided as "morality yowlers." In October 1896, two weeks after the Boston Art Commission, supported by church and other groups, had rejected a gift of MacMonnies' graceful, airy Bacchante on the grounds that the courtyard of the beautiful new Public Library was no place for the statue of a naked, drunken woman (and fifteen months before young Theodore Dreiser scoffed at the Commission's action),[6] Huneker wrote:

The burghers of bean fed Boston should wear fig leaves on their imaginations and forbid marrying and giving in marriage within the city limits. Considering that the State of Massachusetts shows such a lively list of births outside wedlock, I think that the obscene minded old men of Boston might have accepted MacMonnies' lovely Bacchante and held their peace about suggestive art. The rotten puritanism of a city that is notoriously immoral, a city that is notoriously hypocritical, is very disheartening.[7]

(Though the Bacchante was quickly accepted by New York's Metropolitan Museum, Boston's turn to gloat came eight months later when complaints against a statute of the nude Discobolus presented to the Art Department of the YWCA in Manhattan caused it to be replaced by a figure of Minerva, heavily draped.)[8]

In March 1897, Huneker exploded at the seizure of D'Annunzio's sensual novel *The Triumph of Death* by "Saint" Anthony Comstock, whose vigorous campaign against bare limbs Huneker had ridiculed in the previous year. Huneker cared little for D'Annunzio (two years later he changed his mind), but he insisted that a novelist should be permitted any theme, as long as the language he used was decorous. "It is a subject for national laughter," he commented, "to think of this morbid minded fellow nosing among the masterpieces and setting up a cry of 'obscenity' in a city where the foulest newspapers in the world print prose and pictures of unmentionable kinds. . . . We allow a man . . . who has grown gray in the pursuit of the nasty to dictate to us our reading matter."[9]

Huneker had little sympathy with reformers, evangelists, or do-gooders of any kind. As an artist, Tolstoy, for example, delighted him, but as a Christian-Socialist who attacked the giants of modern literature in *What Is Art?* and thereby rekindled the embers of the Nordau controversy, Tolstoy reminded Huneker of a man who had forsworn drink and loose living for the Salvation Army.[10] The America of 1897, he complained, was the country of the "wild-eyed crank, the ignorant tramp, the off-scouring from Europe . . . the humbugging, thieving, lying politician."[11] This outburst again antagonized the Springfield *Republican,* which observed later in 1897 that although he usually had something interesting to say about music, Huneker's comments on literature had the "yellow unwholesome character which is one of the worst traits of the *Courier.* It needs a censor. There have been copies which ought not to go into any decent house."[12] Ten days afterward, however, Huneker showed no signs of intimidation in answering a charge that Wagner's music was indecently sensual:

What is life itself, my virtuous master? Isn't it gross? Isn't love itself something shocking in its manifestations? Oh, you people who are so nasty nice that Goethe is coarse, Shakespeare shocking and Wagner sensual. . . . The man whose pulses do not quiver during the second act of *Tristan* is as bloodless as a turnip, and we'll have none of him.[13]

Were actors immoral? Nonsense, Huneker replied, they were no different from other men. "If every merchant, every lawyer, who dies, had the respective history of his life exposed in public print, wouldn't there be a rustling of the old bones of scandal and also a rustling of skirts?"[14] He laughed at the controversy provoked in 1897 by Clement Scott's remark that few actresses could remain "pure"; even if the English critic were right, Huneker maintained, a little impurity might well improve an actress.[15]

His tastes in drama were veering further toward the ultra-modern. Already an Ibsenite, he was predicting in 1897 that the Ibsen play and its imitations were the "plays of the future,"[16] though he continued to dislike such "preachers" as the popular Henry Arthur Jones—whose true vocation, Huneker remarked in 1896, was the pulpit.[17] Arthur Wing Pinero was, in his opinion, the peer of all living English dramatists. "Not so radical as Mr. Shaw," he elaborated in 1903, Pinero was the "superior artist; not so fantastic as Mr. Barrie, he knows humanity better, and he makes a better play than either of the two."[18] (Considering Pinero's present oblivion, this was not one of Huneker's most prescient judgments, sound as it may have seemed at the time.) American playwrights could scarcely compete with Ibsen and Pinero, but Huneker believed some of them were certainly worth watching. Preferring modern problem plays to the Civil War melodramas in vogue in the nineties,[19] he still considered William Gillette's *Secret Service* a "remarkable contribution to the stage of any land."[20] It was not the "great American play," to be sure, for the country was too vast and its people still too heterogeneous to be captured in any single drama. But when the "big blending" was completed, Huneker declared in 1896, a native dramatist would arise in all his might and write a play "gloriously and cohesively American."[21]

In October 1897, Huneker, continuing as the "Raconteur," also became music critic of *Town Topics,* a position he held for the next five years.[22] This weekly magazine was owned by Colonel William D'Alton Mann, inventor of numerous military accoutrements and railway appliances, the former head of the Mann Boudoir Car Company (which was absorbed by Pullman), and the founder and publisher of the monthly *Smart Set.* One of New York's most colorful figures, the white-bearded Colonel usually wore a bow tie, a fancy waistcoat, a clerical coat, and a black slouch hat, and always carried lumps of sugar for the horses he encountered on his strolls. He was less solicitous toward members of high society, who, he had discovered, loved to read gossip about each other in *Town Topics* and were often willing to supply it themselves, though sometimes he had to send disguised snoopers or bribe servants to get his information. He also made the discovery that he could collect hush money for *not* printing the juiciest bits of scandal, and it was rumored that this was actually Mann's most lucrative business.[23]

"Saunterings," the main section of *Town Topics,* consisted of news of the Four Hundred's parties, engagements, marriages, divorces, and amorous escapades, while the back pages were devoted to music, drama, and literature. Huneker's "Crotchets and Quivers" was signed "The Melomaniac," the drama criticism of Charles Frederic Nirdlinger (George Jean Nathan's uncle) was headed "Masques and Mummers" and signed "The All-Nighter," and the book reviews in Percival Pollard's "The Literary Show" were signed "The Ringmaster." The magazine also contained poems, short stories, satirical sketches, art criticism, and feature articles on sports, fashions, and finance. Charles Bohm, the small, bald, pale-eyed, long-nosed editor, saw to it that blackmail never interfered with culture, and Huneker, Nirdlinger, and Pollard had no inkling of Mann's extracurricular shenanigans.[24]

For both *Town Topics* and the *Musical Courier*, Huneker wrote countless reviews of performances by local and visiting orchestras, leading instrumental soloists, and the great singers of the "golden age" of opera. Considering the reputation they eventually acquired here, his judgment of composers then little known in America was remarkably acute. Thanks to the proselytizing of probably the two foremost Brahms exponents in this country, Rafael Joseffy and Ferdinand Sinzig,[25] a bohemian German pianist and New York piano teacher,[26] Huneker became a supporter of Brahms when his music was by no means popular here, later editing a collection of his songs and writing a preface to Joseffy's edition of Brahms's piano compositions.[27] While Brahms's warmest advocate, Dr. Eduard Hanslick of Vienna, was scarifying an even more controversial figure, Richard Strauss, Huneker was vehemently defending the young composer. In August 1897 he printed "as a matter of record" a list of Strauss's works, and four months later, after hearing *Also Sprach Zarathustra*, he observed that though this daring attempt to inject definite meaning into tone without the aid of words had failed, it was a failure "so glorious that it will blind a generation before its glory is apprehended; so glorious that it blazes a new turn in the path made straight by Beethoven, Berlioz, Liszt and Wagner." Huneker declared that Strauss was Liszt's "natural musical son, and the son has quite as much to say thematically as the father, while in the matter of brush, brilliancy, massing of color, startling figure drawing . . . and swift thinking, Strauss is easily the superior."[28] Pleased by these remarks, Edward MacDowell wrote Huneker that they could not "fail to have a great effect on the art of criticism, and must set a standard that will help the whole country. It's enough to make the direst pessimist have faith in America's musical future."[29]

Try to enjoy modern music, Huneker urged his fellow critics, for who knew which composers time would immortalize? The critics' grandchildren would inevitably mock their taste and call them old-fashioned. Why dislike Brahms and Strauss simply because they were not Wagner or Beethoven?[30]

Huneker also encouraged American composers struggling to get their music played by European-oriented conductors, boosting the work of MacDowell, Charles Martin Loeffler, George Chadwick, H. W. Parker, and others.[31] In 1898, for example, he reproached the New York Philharmonic Society for not performing the compositions of these men more often—not on all-American programs, for he felt that native composers should not be segregated as a special breed, but in conjunction with classical and modern European music.[32] He took special delight, moreover, in praising American artists such as Olive Fremstad, Fanny Bloomfield-Zeisler,[33] Wallace Goodrich,[34] and David Bispham, the Metropolitan's only American male singer in 1896.[35] "It will be a great day for this country," he wrote in that year, "when the abundance of the home product will warrant her in building a very high protective wall to keep out the influx of foreign artists."[36] American teachers of piano, he happily noted, were already so proficient that it was no longer necessary to go abroad to study.[37]

Meanwhile, immersed in contemporary literature, Huneker was now constantly defending the unconventional "decadent" writers. In 1896, for example, when Nietzsche was still anathematized here as a near relation of Satan himself—in the following year a Newark lecture on the philosopher by George Henry Payne ended in angry recriminations between the speaker and audience[38]—Huneker courageously denied Nordau's charge that Nietzsche was the philosopher of degeneracy, maintaining that Nietzsche merely preached "egoism, individualism, personal freedom, and selfhood." In 1898 Huneker went even further, stating that "all men of liberated intellects" were Nietzscheans.[39]

As he studied Nietzsche, indeed, Huneker had found in him certain affinities with his own temperament. Subordinating metaphysics to psychology, Nietzsche was, of course, the great philosophical exponent of the egoism characteristic of some of the greatest artists of the nineteenth century, especially Ibsen and Baudelaire. His skeptical attitude toward conventional morality and his belief that nothing should stand in the way of the highest spiritual development of the individual personality clearly helped to form Huneker's basic attitude toward art and life. Nietzsche's defense of inconsistency and his faith in an intellectual aristocracy gratified a none-too-consistent Huneker, who sympathized with the poor and oppressed but had no illusions about their taste. Both Huneker and Nietzsche had turned away from formal religion (Huneker less drastically perhaps, for he always retained a vague religious feeling and believed, he said, in a personal god and a personal devil),[40] Huneker attempting to find in art the substitute for religion that Nietzsche had sought in philosophy. Most important, Huneker's hedonism, conditioned by the vagaries of his temperament and private life, was strongly bolstered by Nietzsche's doctrine of full, joyous living. For all these reasons, and because he greatly admired the philosopher's witty, poetic prose, Huneker became one of the earliest and most persistent champions of Nietzsche in America.

Often mentioned in his columns were Arthur Symons—whom Huneker probably quoted more frequently than any other critic[41]—and Havelock Ellis, who, together with Georg Brandes and Remy de Gourmont, were the cosmopolitan critics Huneker most respected. Symons was not an expert musician, and his style was more subdued than Huneker's, but in versatility, subject matter, and critical method the two men were much alike, as reviewers often noted.[42] Huneker also had a good deal in common with Symons' intimate friend Ellis, whose writings on modern writers[43] and on abnormal psychology deeply impressed Huneker.[44] As early as 1885, furthermore, Ellis had agreed with certain French critics that criticism could never be purely objective, that the individuality of the critic must always be weighed in assessing his work. The critic's business was not to say beautiful things, Ellis wrote, but "to take hold of his subject with the largest and firmest grasp, to express from it its most characteristic essence"; yet a "piercing and apparently instantaneous insight into the heart of his subject . . . frequently marks the discursive and catholic critic."[45] This was the kind of critic Symons, Ellis, and Huneker preferred to a pedantic, dogmatic academician such as Ferdinand Brunetière, whom Huneker denounced in 1900 as the author, with Nordau, of the "most solemnly absurd criticism of the century."[46] ("Academic criticism," Huneker later quipped, "may be loosely defined as the expression of another's opinion. . . . [Impressionistic criticism] tells how much *you* enjoyed a work of art . . . [academic criticism] what some other fellow liked.")[47]

In 1899, at the height of Rudyard Kipling's tremendous American vogue, Huneker pooh-poohed most of the Englishman's verse as mere "banjo strumming" and placed his fiction "miles beneath" Meredith and Hardy.[48] One wonders whether Kipling saw this criticism and remembered it when Huneker encountered him at Rouen in 1901. As

Huneker tells the story, he saw the Kiplings in a railroad dining car as he passed by after getting off the train. "Mr. Kipling," he said through the open window, "you should have stopped at Rouen and made a pro-pitiatory pilgrimage to the tomb of Flaubert in the Monumental Ceme-tery, if for nothing else but to expiate your literary sins." Mrs. Kipling smiled (Huneker knew her brother, Wolcott Balestier, a newspaper-man), but Kipling preserved a stony mask. "No doubt he took me for a harmless lunatic," Huneker recalled, "and perhaps he was right. I tried to stir his artistic conscience, and I knew of nothing more effi-cacious."[49] (If Huneker had actually been so impudent, one can only admire Kipling's self-restraint.)

Though he believed that English fiction was generally inferior to French or Russian—since the death of Balzac and Flaubert, he remarked in 1900, no novelist could approach Turgenev, Tolstoy, Dostoevski, and Gogol[50]—the contemporary English novelist who, beginning in the nine-ties, most attracted Huneker was George Moore.[51] The Paris-nurtured Moore, too, had little use for prudes, especially those who had been hor-rified by his naturalistic novels *A Modern Lover* (1883) and *A Mum-mer's Wife* (1885), whom he continued to defy by writing books con-sidered too wicked for general circulation in American public libraries,[52] and "confessions" less true than artfully erotic. (He was, someone quipped, a lover who "tells but doesn't kiss.")[53] Repelled, at first, by the lack of sympathy, humor, and sincerity in Moore's fiction, Huneker was won over by *Mike Fletcher*, whose author he applauded in 1901 as the only writer in English since Fielding to draw a "virile, naked man."[54] A few years later, when he praised Moore for never calling a leg a limb, for not being afraid to remind us that the "facts of sex, of birth, of death, are gross" or to declare that the "love-passion is a blessing, good wine a boon, art alone enduring,"[55] Huneker had become Moore's most fer-vent supporter. Not only was he Ireland's greatest novelist, Huneker maintained in 1918, but "no man of his time in or out of England has written with such imaginative sympathy in his fiction."[56]

Corresponding with Huneker during the first decade of the twen-tieth century, Moore often thanked him for enthusiastic reviews. "I hope it never occurs to you to think I do not appreciate your kindness in writing about my books and persuading the American public to read them," he assured him in October 1906.[57] Fifteen years later, Barrett H. Clark, the American author and drama expert, asked Moore what he thought about Huneker. "I never knew anyone with such literary facility," he replied, "and since he spoke highly of my work why should I not feel well-disposed toward him? I am almost embarrassed when I recall all the pleasant things he wrote about me."[58]

In the late 1890's, however, no living writer, foreign or American, pleased Huneker more than Henry James, to whom, throughout his own career, he devoted more space than to any other American writer.[59] More than forty years before the "rediscovery" of James ("Nothing succeeds like the success which follows death," Huneker once remarked),[60] he was proclaiming him America's greatest contemporary novelist. In 1896, for example, he asserted that the very qualities that made James's work so distinguished, "fineness of analysis and supreme finish," were derided by many critics. "Oh, Lord," he exclaimed, "how long?"[61] When the expatriated novelist was charged with being un-American, Huneker quickly came to his defense:

What American writer has given us such absolutely tempting and truthful national types? . . . The master of living American novelists, I am tempted to say the greatest of American fictionists until I remember Hawthorne, sits serenely at his desk in London and carves for us the Americans at home and abroad. I know that he does not indulge in the melodramatic type of American, the sort that talks dialect, chews tobacco and swears in Church, the sort that Mr. Garland[62] and his group believe to represent these States. . . . Henry James is sneered at by the press here because his artistic ideals are high.[63]

Huneker also admired, and often quoted, the criticism written by James —who had once declared, incidentally, that "the critic is simply a reader like all the others—a reader who prints his impressions."[64]

Reviewing William Dean Howells' *The Story of a Play*, Huneker observed in 1898 that the art of Howells, toward whose fiction he had previously been lukewarm,[65] was growing "finer and more veristic in every new work. The characters are very American and the conduct of the tale is at once a model and a reproach to those writers here who pitch their style too high and draw their characters after the manner of the yellow journalists."[66] Thereafter Huneker always spoke highly of Howells' novels.

Nor did he neglect the younger American writers. In 1897 and 1898 he recommended Agnes Repplier, Henry B. Fuller, and John Jay Chapman, and reprinted a poem—"Luke Havergal"—by Edwin Arlington Robinson.[67] Not long after its publication, Huneker declared that though Edith Wharton's first book, *The Greater Inclination,* a collection of short stories, showed signs of Henry James's influence, it had charm, power, humor, and a "neat, telling style," and he predicted that Mrs. Wharton would eventually produce a "strong novel."[68] Even more to his liking was Frank Norris' naturalistic novel *McTeague,* whose protagonist was so primitive and brutal that even the usually unsqueamish Percival Pollard consigned it to the gutter.[69] But Huneker believed that its coarseness was redeemed by its grim, hearty, Rabelaisian humor, and that Norris, gifted with the keenest vision of all the young American writers and a powerful, natural style, would outgrow the "note-taking bird's-eye-view school" of Zola and "touch the hem of higher issues."[70]

The virility of Norris' work gave Huneker hope for the future of American fiction. "After the simpering attenuations and Miss Nancy reticences" of our novelists, he wrote in 1900, "the presence of a real, vital man would set the crowd giggling and screaming. In the devil's name . . . throw up the window and give us air, light, nature; not sawdust, sentimentality, and bad history."[71] This was the year in which Doubleday, Page, acting on the advice of Norris, their reader, signed a contract with a young newspaperman named Theodore Dreiser to publish his *Sister Carrie*—and then "buried" a small edition of the book when they decided that a novel about a kept woman was too raw. (Huneker recalled that Norris sent him a copy and that he reviewed it favorably, but the review has not been found.)[72]

Huneker's personal circle now included composers, musicians, singers, writers, painters, and newspapermen, with whom he often gathered, after he and his colleagues had turned in their copy, for midnight festivities.[73] He was a popular figure at the Sunday afternoon parties given by William Henderson, where he would meet Marcella Sembrich, Josef Hofmann, the De Reszke brothers, and other musical celebrities.[74] At one of his favorite haunts, the Hotel St. James bar, he would pick up the latest operatic news from his friend Maurice Grau, the Metropolitan's general manager from 1896 to 1902.[75] With Victor Herbert, who had just started to write the operettas that made him rich and famous, Huneker often swapped stories and matched drinks. (Instead of punching an unfriendly critic, Huneker suggested, a crafty artist would buy him a drink each time he met him—and eventually ruin the critic's stomach and brains.)[76] Huneker and Herbert admired each other's work, however, and seldom disagreed—though one night at Lüchow's, when Huneker declared that only a Jew could have written Herbert's beautiful melodies, Herbert vehemently pointed out that his grandfather was Samuel Lover, the *Irish* author. "Lover?" repeated Huneker, his eyes twinkling. "*Samuel* Lover? Now I believe more than ever that the Irish were one of the lost tribes of Israel!"[77]

At Mouquin's, the red-plush French restaurant under the Sixth Avenue elevated railway near Twenty-eighth Street, Huneker engaged in bouts of self-expression with George Luks, a former prizefighter and professional football player (so he claimed, at least, but he could lie even more magnificently than Huneker—and in language as colorful as his palette),[78] staff artist for various Philadelphia newspapers (including the *Evening Bulletin,* for which he also doubled as reporter), and correspondent in Cuba, whose caricatures on the Spanish-American War had got him a job as an artist on the New York *World.*[79] In 1898 he was drawing the "Hogan's Alley" comic strip originated by R. F. Outcault, who continued to do the same strip for Hearst's *Journal,* thus fanning a circulation war which produced the famous term "yellow journalism" (one of the strip's characters always wearing yellow clothes).[80] Outside of Huneker, no better judge of beer was to be found in New York than Luks, who learned, however, that he could not match his friend's capacity. "It's not fair," he once protested after Huneker downed twenty-two seidels in a drinking contest with him, "you have a false stomach!"[81] (Thirty years later, Luks, who had done far more than his share to keep bootleggers alive during Prohibition, was beaten to death by a fellow customer in a speakeasy, though it was romantically reported in the newspapers, after his body was found in a doorway, that he had gone out to paint the dawn as it filtered through the elevated railway tracks.)[82] Drunk or sober, the Falstaffian Luks loved to talk about "punks and phonies and lice and swine and chiselers and mugs and tramps"[83]—the human types he was already painting with sympathy and magnificent gusto—and he was always ready to pour out his sharp opinions on art. Still a student of pictures, which he sometimes discussed in the *Musical Courier,*[84] Huneker relaxed in the leather-padded seats of the "art corner" at Mouquin's and listened to Luks argue that it was more important to support modern American art than the old masters.[85] During the first decade of the new century, Ernest

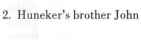
2. Huneker's brother John

Huneker's mother, Mary Gibbons Huneker
portrait by William K. Hewitt, about 1860)

4. Huneker's father, John Huneker
(portrait by William K. Hewitt, about 1862)

3. James Huneker, age 12 (1869)

12. Erik Huneker about 1905

13. Clio Hinton Huneker and Erik
about 1898

14. Clio Hinton about 1890

16. Georgiana Carhart in 1900

15. Olive Fremstad as Waltraute, 1896

18. Mary Garden as Mélisande

17. Mary Garden as Salome

24. James Huneker, age 61 (1918)

Lawson, William Glackens, John Sloan, Everett Shinn, James Earle Fraser, Jo Davidson, and the other young American painters and sculptors who occasionally joined Huneker and Luks were happy to let them monopolize the conversation, while newspapermen, poets, actors, and musicians, sitting nearby, strained to catch the *bons mots* and stories that caused such hilarity. With Julian Hawthorne, Brander Matthews, and others, Huneker and Luks were also charter members of an informal group called "The Friendly Sons of Saint Bacchus," who met in the nineties at Maria's, a bohemian basement café located on Greenwich Village's MacDougal Street (later on West Twelfth Street), and entertained each other with songs, poems, monologues, and jokes.[86]

At the turn of the century, Huneker belonged to a coterie associated with one of New York's liveliest magazines, the *Criterion*. Originating in St. Louis as a social weekly named *Life*, the *Criterion* had been brought to New York in 1897 by its owner, Mrs. Grace L. Davidson, a retired schoolteacher subsidized by the wealthy daughter of William McKee, founder of the St. Louis *Globe-Democrat*. Under the editorship of Henri Dumay, one-time instructor of French at Washington University, it acquired the tone of a French review of 1880, attracting contributions from such popular, "advanced" poets as Ella Wheeler Wilcox, Richard Hovey, and Bliss Carman, and such clever young versifiers as Gelett Burgess, Carolyn Wells, and Arthur Guiterman. After Joseph I. C. Clarke became editor in March 1898, almost every member of the staff was a friend of Huneker's—Clarke; Rupert Hughes, assistant editor and music critic; Charles Henry Meltzer, drama editor; and Vance Thompson, art editor[87]—and five months later an article by Huneker on Flaubert was printed in the magazine.[88] Despite the ultra-respectability, even prudishness, of its owner, this cosmopolitan group made the *Criterion* hospitable to ideas and writers that conservative editors shied from; as William Marion Reedy, editor of *Reedy's Mirror*, remarked in 1900, the *Criterion* stood for "Ibsenism, Hauptmannism, Huysmansism, Verlaineism, George Bernard Shawism, and George Mooreism."[89] Some librarians found it as malodorous as its predecessor, *M'lle New York*, and refused to subscribe to it. When Mrs. Davidson's backer became less generous, the magazine quickly declined, and though it managed to survive until 1905, it was already past its heyday in 1901, when Huneker was most closely associated with it (six articles by him appeared that year).

In 1897–98 the *Criterion* also sponsored the short-lived and somewhat obscure Criterion Independent Theater, which presented at mati-
nees at the Berkley Lyceum and the Madison Square Theater single
performances of a number of modern plays, including the American
première of Ibsen's *John Gabriel Borkman* and Echegaray's *El gran
Galeoto*.[90] Huneker must have been interested in this venture, but his
part in it, if he had any, is unknown. (Surely the unidentified columnist
who described him as the "business head" of the Theater was joking.)[91]
Most of the publicity for these productions was written by Huneker's
friend and colleague Percival Pollard, a frequent contributor to the
Criterion until 1899, when his divorce scandal made him *persona non
grata* with Mrs. Davidson.[92]

The son of a German opera singer and an English grain merchant,
Pollard, Huneker's junior by twelve years, had immigrated to America
in 1885 and had become a newspaper reporter in St. Joseph, Missouri.
Early in 1891 he went to Chicago, where he married his landlady's
daughter (who divorced him when she discovered his affair with the
woman he later married), wrote for little magazines, and tried unsuc-
cessfully to establish his own journal. Moving to New York, in the
autumn of 1896 he was for a short time press agent and writer for
Richard Mansfield, whom he later satirized in his novel *The Imitator*.
In March 1897, seven months before Huneker became *Town Topics'*
music critic, Pollard became its literary critic, and except for an absence
from 1902 to 1904, he held this post until his death in 1911. Between
1892 and 1911 he published—usually at his own expense—ten volumes
of fiction and criticism, but it was as "The Ringmaster" of *Town Topics*
that Pollard, the third member of the American "school" of impressionistic criticism which included Huneker and Thompson, made his
main impact upon American literature.[93] He, too, disliked English snob-
bishness toward American writers, the historical romance, the "he-man"
novel, socialism, and the puritanism in American literature,[94] and in
Masks and Minstrels of New Germany (1911) eventually attempted to
do for contemporary German writers what Thompson and Huneker had
done for French. But he was habitually far more belligerent and ill-
tempered than Huneker was even in his most exasperated moments.
They remained good friends for years—until Pollard suddenly turned
against Huneker with a vengeance.

In the last two months of 1898 Huneker saw much of Stephen

Crane,[95] whom he may have met in 1893 or 1894 when the struggling young author lived with friends in a studio on East Twenty-third Street. Huneker told the story that one night in the spring of 1894, while he and Crane were walking to the Everett House, they were accosted by a boy who was soliciting, though Crane did not realize it until he noticed the youth's painted face in the glare of the hotel-front. Curious, Crane took him into the hotel, fed him, listened to his story, and gave him fifty dollars. Shortly afterward, he supposedly began, but never finished, a novel about a boy prostitute to be called *Flowers of Asphalt*.[96] In 1896 after the publication of the best-selling book of that year, F. Hopkinson Smith's *Tom Grogan*, a novel about an Irishwoman, the now famous Crane (whose *The Red Badge of Courage* was also a best-seller) brought Huneker to a party given by a woman who admired Smith's book. During dinner both men derided Smith's stereotyped characterization of the Irish, Huneker maintaining that they were seldom as gay as they were pictured in literature, and Crane asserting that they were not always so brave, either, for he had known Irish cowards.[97] (Three years later Crane began *The O'Ruddy*, a satirical romance of old Ireland, which he did not live to complete.)

In 1897 Crane wrote Huneker at least one letter from England, where he was living after the end of the brief Greco-Turkish War he had covered for the New York *Journal*, informing Huneker that the English were not as polite or delicate as Huneker and other Americans had led him to expect.[98] It is not known whether they saw each other in July 1898, when Crane was in New York on a short respite from his duties as the New York *World*'s Cuban correspondent following the outbreak of the Spanish-American War. In August, however, the *Musical Courier* printed what seems to be Huneker's only public allusion to Crane's work during the latter's lifetime: a parody of Crane's often parodied,[99] highly colored war correspondence, which Huneker identified as a reprint but which he probably wrote himself, for it sounds like one of the "Raconteur's" playful excursions:

The American fleet came redly on like a bunch of waving bandana handkerchiefs. The air was full of prunes as a plum pudding. The whitish-green rattle of the rapid-fire guns was exacerbatingly shrill.

The Spanish met the onslaught with a mauve determination. Ecruly they stood at the post shepherds doggedly.

The two fleets hurtled in a magenta hurtle. They feinted and thrust with a deep canary-yellow vigor. The battle looked like two overturned garbage-cans on a hot night. The shells whistled seal-brownly. The death screams of the Spaniards were full of purplish pink despair. One Spaniard with a cerise voice like the aftermath of an aurora borealis screamed paintily his desire to kill the Americanos.

Then with a blackish white tremor, strong battleships sank greenly chromely black into the water. A gauntly greenish smell tore the air. The whole thing looked like a German pouring dark wine into a dingy funnel. Admiral Dewey had won.[100]

When Crane returned to New York for a month in the middle of November 1898, he and Huneker dined and drank together on several occasions. Huneker remembered that Crane's conversation at these long sessions was charming—full of adjectives and adverbs.[101] Both men, indeed, handled words as a painter handles color, delighting in unusual images, quaint similes, and sharp phrases.[102] They probably talked about the writers they both admired: Tolstoy, Emily Dickinson, Mark Twain, Flaubert, and Maupassant. At the Everett House one afternoon, Huneker first heard, from Crane, the name of Joseph Conrad, a former sea captain whom Crane had met a year earlier in England.[103] If they talked about Crane's writing ("I never encourage friends to read my work—they sometimes advise one," Crane once told a correspondent[104]), there is no evidence of it in Huneker's criticism, nor any sign, surprisingly, that he was greatly impressed by Crane's talent. Yet he surely did not subscribe to Vance Thompson's contemptuous description of Crane—published in the *Musical Courier* on September 21, 1898—as "an illiterate writer [who] describes illiterate people in their own and his own locutions."[105]

Huneker did not believe the exaggerated reports of Crane's dissoluteness. After the two of them had spent a relatively mild evening together, he recalled, men who had not even seen them would tell Huneker in the morning how drunk and disorderly Crane had been (though, to be sure, Huneker may not be the most reliable witness on these matters). Crane's imaginative contemporaries, Huneker later suggested, "turned a little Flaubert into a big Verlaine."[106] In early January 1899, Crane left for England, and a year and a half afterward he died. "He was a good fellow and a promising writer," Huneker wrote in June 1900. "Without the sustained power or formal gifts of Frank Norris, Crane would nevertheless have made a strong book some day." And he did

Crane a final service by recommending the accurate article about him
written by Crane's friend and fellow war correspondent, Acton Davies,
the *Evening Sun*'s dramatic critic.[107]

Ten months later, Huneker was more touched by the death of a
former colleague, the once-powerful *Herald* critic Albert Steinberg.
His few illusions concerning the gratitude of artists toward the critics
who sang their praises disappeared when he was the only member of
the music and theater world among the handful of persons attending
funeral services for Steinberg.[108] "It was the saddest thing I ever went
through," he wrote Frida Ashforth, who had been assisting the stricken
Steinberg with money. "Poor Al, not weighing 60 pounds, was put on
a platter like a duck to be roasted and pushed into the furnace. I waited
and saw the sheet catch fire. So ends a sad life! . . . I can't forget that
lonely little coffin!"[109] He could not help wondering whether he, too,
would be forgotten by ungrateful artists and the public,[110] especially if
he left no more permanent record of his work than ephemeral reviews
buried in magazines and newspapers.

❧ Ten

AUTHOR AND COSMOPOLITE

Have you ever thought how short your life is?" wrote the "Raconteur" in 1899. "I mean your conscious life. . . . Twenty active, working years and you have reached the grand climacteric. Before twenty-five or thirty you are mentally a pulp; after fifty begins the return to the traits of your individual tribe or family. . . . From thirty to fifty should be the harvest years."[1]

Forty-two himself, his mid-section expanding, making him look shorter than his actual height—5′9″—and his wavy brown hair rapidly graying, Huneker had decided that *his* harvest time was overdue. At last he felt ready to do what Vance Thompson, Philip Hale, and others had long urged: publish a book of critical essays.[2] Separating the wheat from the chaff, he put together studies of Brahms, Tchaikovsky, Richard Strauss and Nietzsche, Chopin, Liszt, and piano literature in a volume called *Mezzotints in Modern Music.* Published in March 1899 by Scribner's, then the leading American publisher of books on music,[3] it began an association that was to last for more than two decades.

He was afraid that the growing hostility between Marc Blumenberg and the music critics of the daily press—whom Blumenberg denounced for "booming" certain opera singers instead of promoting good music— would involve him and prejudice his friends against the book. In the same week in which *Mezzotints* came out, Huneker assured Krehbiel, to whom it was dedicated,[4] that he had not written, and indeed had protested against, a derogatory reference to the older critic which had appeared in the *Musical Courier* just when he needed and desired the amiability of his confreres more than ever.[5] But Finck, Henderson, Hale, Pollard, and Rupert Hughes all threw their critical hats into the air over *Mezzotints*[6] (Krehbiel apparently did not review it), Finck, for example, hailing it as "one of the most readable and at the same time useful books on music ever issued in this country."[7]

Though a few reviewers were annoyed by Huneker's flamboyance and carelessness—William F. Apthorp of the Boston *Evening Transcript* suggested that Huneker should "take more pains to make the most of his innate gift for clear and glowing prose,"[8] while the Chicago *Dial* felt that Huneker's reaction against academic criticism had gone too far[9]—most of the book's notices were highly favorable. Describing Huneker as a man of "large imagination, one of the genial, ever-fertile writers," *Music*'s critic was especially pleased with the chapter on Brahms, which constituted, he pointed out, what previously did not exist in English—a summarized treatment of Brahms's entire work.[10] Harry Thurston Peck, the earthy professor of Latin at Columbia University, editor of the influential *Bookman*, enthusiastically praised Huneker's style, vigor, and spontaneity.[11] Peck and Remy de Gourmont, who privately thanked Huneker for sending him the book (he, too, was particularly impressed by the essay on Brahms), both remarked that he displayed a real talent for explaining the mysteries of music to the layman.[12]

"What knowledge of the world and of modern thought are inwoven with your musical consciousness!" exclaimed Israel Zangwill from London in a note to Huneker about the book. "And there is always a gusto as if you enjoyed this humorous tragic life of ours!"[13] And John Runciman, the famous music critic of London's *Saturday Review*, gave *Mezzotints* as hearty and dramatic a welcome as any American book on music had ever received in a British magazine. Huneker's hasty writing and self-contradiction—which bothered other English reviewers[14]—did not prevent the book from being, in Runciman's estimation, an "original and very valuable contribution to the world's tiny musical literature." Whatever his subject, Runciman added, Huneker "always displays the same audacity, brains, emotional sensitiveness and—curious in a distinctly 'new' critic—knowledge." He was a tremendous personality— indeed, "almost too tremendous for England. His force and sincerity would make him feared and hated; his rashness would give his enemies endless opportunities to harass and even to destroy him." Like Runciman himself, whom Huneker had described in 1898 as the best-hated man in London next to George Bernard Shaw,[15] the author of *Mezzotints* was the kind of man this redoubtable Englishman liked best—one of those who "take up the work that is lying for them to do and go through with it, instead of wasting their lives by staying to count the possible cost."[16] This remarkable notice must have introduced Huneker to many English readers unfamiliar with the London *Musical Courier*.

In the summer of 1899 Huneker again went to Europe, spending most of July at Bayreuth. Nothing he wrote about the Wagner Festival amused London so much as his witty, if ungallant, quip—reprinted in the London *Daily News*—that at Bayreuth he saw Natalie Jonotha, the pianist, Mrs. Pearl Craigie ("John Oliver Hobbes"), the novelist, and Lady Randolph Churchill (Sir Winston Churchill's American mother), who brought with them "Bach's triple concerto for one pianist and two ladies of leisure."[17] (The trio had recently played Bach in public.)

By the fall of 1899, when he was back in New York after a vacation in New Hampshire—where, the hay-fever sufferer wrote, the "rag-weed does not incite the nose to rag-time"[18]—Huneker had become absorbed in a study of his favorite composer. He had decided that the standard biography of Chopin by Frederick Niecks, which he had reviewed at great length for the *Musical Courier* as early as 1889, left something to be desired,[19] and it probably occurred to him that the fiftieth anniversary of Chopin's death, in October 1899, would be an appropriate time to bring out a book about him. In the latter part of 1898, in any event, Huneker had begun to write a series of essays on Chopin which appeared in the New York and London *Musical Courier* during the next two years, and which were published by Scribner's as *Chopin: The Man and His Music* in April 1900.

Though he relied mainly on printed sources for biographical facts, Huneker's wide reading and his interpretative synthesis pleasantly surprised scholars, while his evocative description and technical analysis of Chopin's work delighted musicians. His comments on Chopin's life reveal a good deal of Huneker himself. He insisted—wrongly, it seems —that Chopin was born in 1809 rather than 1810, the date supported by a baptismal certificate. "Perhaps the composer was to blame," he wrote. "Artists, male as well as female, have been known to make themselves younger . . . by conveniently forgetting their birthdate, or by attributing the error to carelessness in the registry of dates."[20] (Critics, too, for Huneker had already deducted three years from his own age, as his baptismal certificate showed.) He defended Chopin against charges of effeminacy, maintaining that the relationship between him and George Sand was not only physical but also productive, providing both of them with excellent raw material for their respective talents. Their separation, however, was inevitable, for the "dynamics of free love have yet to be formulated"[21]—as Huneker well knew.

English and American reviewers generally agreed that the book was the most readable biography of Chopin written in English, and in 1904 one music historian, Louis C. Elson, even called it the best single volume on the subject in existence.[22] In Paris, Isidore Philipp read portions of the copy Huneker sent him to old Georges Mathias, who remembered the young American "auditeur"—and also pointed out some errors.[23] Pleased by his handling of the Chopin-Sand affair, Remy de Gourmont privately complimented Huneker and published in the distinguished *Mercure de France*, a month later, an article based on the book.[24] Still consulted by musicians and Chopin specialists, Huneker's *Chopin* remains one of his most solid accomplishments.[25]

Late in July 1901, Huneker and Josephine—who always accompanied him to Europe after 1899—embarked on a three-month visit to Continental art centers which he financed by writing travel articles for the *Musical Courier*. In Bayreuth he met and had a rather unsatisfying interview with George Moore. ("I can spill out my own soul on paper," Huneker admitted after this encounter, ". . . but to tap another's, to play the male midwife and deliver some poor struggling celebrity of a sentence—in that I am not successful.")[26] Moore would have been less reserved, he later confessed, if he had remembered that Huneker was the author of *Chopin*, in which he had discovered "a great many things which I felt in the music myself beautifully expressed in words."[27] Huneker complained that Bayreuth was peopled by "howling beer-vats for singers,"[28] though, of course, he would not have included in this category the lovely Olive Fremstad, singing Ortrud in *Lohengrin*, or Milka Ternina, whose Kundry struck him as a creation of rare imagination and technical skill. Otherwise, however, *Parsifal* left him cold. Portions of the opera constituted a "miracle of polyphonic architecture," he granted, but the libretto was a "farrago of odds and ends, the very dustbin of [Wagner's] philosophies, beliefs, vegetarianism, anti-vivisectionism, and other fads," and an undramatic "mish-mash of gospel narrative, mediaeval romance, and Teutonic philosophy." The opera was not sacrilegious but morbid: Amfortas and Parsifal symbolized Wagner and his homosexual benefactor, King Ludwig of Bavaria, respectively, and, as psychiatrists had pointed out, the relationship between them, colored by Wagner's gratitude to Ludwig, illuminated the "psychology of Kundry's kiss and its repelling effect and its arousing of pity for Amfortas in Parsifal."[29]

Huneker witnessed the opening of the new Prinz Regent's Opera House in Munich, informing a friend that Fremstad was the "best thing down here. She sings Mozart as well as Wagner. . . . A versatile girl!"[30] Here Huneker met his old friend Francis Neilson, now Charles Frohman's stage director at the Duke of York's Theatre in London, who joined the Hunekers and Fremstad one day on a picnic to Starnberg, an outing that Neilson vividly recalled long afterward:

[Huneker] was then writing something about Wagner and Ludwig and wanted to visit the castle at the lake. We started out early one morning, and Jim and Olive quarrelled like two Kilkenny cats the whole of the railway journey to the lake. . . . Some of Jim's bawdy stories about Wagner and Ludwig were too much for Olive. Josephine . . . whispered to me that Jim's breakfast had disagreed with him, but that he would be all right after a meal and some beer.

When we reached the spot, it was too early for lunch, and Huneker thought that if we went to the castle first, it would be rather late for déjeuner. Then there was another altercation. Olive said she did not care about eating, and Jim said that was all he cared about. It was put to a vote, and it was three to one against taking lunch. Then the impish mind of Huneker rose to the situation and Jim, with a guffaw, said, "I didn't want any lunch anyway, but I knew that Olive was dying to eat."

At length, we went off to the gimcrack palace that King Ludwig had built for Wagner. The guide who took us around, I feel sure, never forgot that day. Huneker was at his best; his sallies and quips came as if they had been fired from a machine gun. As we passed down the neglected statuary-halls, we laughed so heartily at Huneker's comments and chaff that even the solemn attendants were infected. "Caligula, Nero and Heliogabalus!—by thunder, if this isn't Götterdämmerung with a vengeance!" he cried, as he read the names of the busts and statues. The trick-table in the dining room, which sank into the kitchen after every course, was clear proof to Jim that Ludwig and Wagner were both teetotalers.

"You see," he said, "it's truly Wagnerian! The food comes up from Nibelheim and is consumed in Valhalla."

The sadness of the last days of Ludwig did not touch us for a moment, and we wondered afterwards what imp of mischief had prompted so much ribaldry. We took our evening meal near the edge of the lake and had a couple of gypsies to entertain us. The man played the fiddle fairly well, and the girl with him danced. But Huneker would have no dancing on the solid earth. He popped the girl up on a table and had the proprietor push the piano out on the terrace, where Jim played while the man fiddled and the girl danced.

The Austrian Alps were bathed in the light of the setting sun when we made our way to the station. Country life was not for Huneker, but something in that scene touched him deeply: "A beautiful, fragrant spot, and I don't mind the stillness"—a great concession for him to make.

We were a tired party when we reached Munich, but Huneker had not had enough, for he took me off to the Café Luitpold, a place he called the Holy Grail because of its likeness to the setting of the last scene in *Parsifal*. There we "beered" and "yarned" until four o'clock in the morning, when Jim said: "Friendship between man and woman, bah! See, we have been talking six hours on end. Now if you were a woman—well, what on earth should we have said, and how long should we have taken to say it?"[31]

Remaining in Munich for almost four weeks, Huneker spent his days at the art galleries and his nights at the opera.

At 9 o'clock [he wrote] I was in a gallery; at six I left it. . . . Finding after a few days of this galley slave toil that I was harvesting no permanent impressions, I reverted to my original scheme—a thorough study of certain masters [in] isolated groups. The scheme broke down after I had spent three hours in front of a Whistler, so I said to myself, "You can't hear *all* the music of the composers in a lifetime, nor do you dare to, therefore why attempt the impossibility with paintings?" Having said this I turned my back on acres of Rubens, passed the Raphaels at a military pace, and confined myself to the masters I most admired.

He also bought at least one picture, Edvard Munch's "Les Curieuses."[32]

On the way to Paris by a roundabout route, Huneker spent five days in Switzerland, making side trips, while "resting" in Geneva, to various shrines: Voltaire's house at Ferney; the villas of Byron, Napoleon's Josephine, and Lola Montez; Rousseau's birthplace; and the cathedral in which Calvin preached. There is no evidence, however, to support his later claim that he went to Aix in 1901 to meet Cézanne,[33] though if he actually did make such a visit, it would have been during, or shortly after, his stay in Geneva. At Auteuil, the Paris suburb, Vance Thompson, who now occupied a house that once belonged to Boileau, found lodgings for the Hunekers and took his friend on a de luxe tour of famous literary landmarks. The atmosphere at Auteuil was so inspiring that Huneker even wrote a short story there ("The Iron Virgin").[34] In Paris he saw for the first time Charpentier's new opera *Louise*, in which young Mary Garden had made her memorable debut a year earlier (she was not singing the title role when he attended), but he reported that all he could detect in the score was warmed-up Wagner.[35]

In London Neilson showed him the new stage at Covent Garden and got him seats for Beerbohm Tree's brilliant, elaborate production of *Twelfth Night*. At the performance Neilson saw to it that Huneker was seated next to an aging but alert woman who proudly pointed out her daughter in the play and seemed to be merely another stage mother. When he discovered later that she was none other than the famous Lydia Thompson, who in 1866 had introduced the leg show to America in *The Black Crook* and whom he had often mentioned glowingly to Neilson, Huneker felt like kicking himself for having missed the chance of telling her how grateful he was for her significant contribution to the American theater.[36] At a midnight supper Tree gave for Huneker a night or two afterward, the scintillating guest of honor completely charmed his host. "I should like a week off with Huneker," Tree told Neilson. "He has a splendid thrust. Didn't he sharpen me up a bit?"[37]

In November 1899, Huneker had told Richard Aldrich that he had written *Chopin* for Scribner's on condition that they publish his short stories.[38] "I want to write naturalistic prose," he had informed Ziegler on the same day, "but an unsympathetic public i.e. publishers want rhapsodies, dancing on the verbal tight rope."[39] Though Scribner's had seemed hesitant, early in 1900, to publish Huneker's fiction,[40] in February 1902 the firm issued his *Melomaniacs,* a collection of twenty-four short stories—hardly naturalistic—printed mainly in the *Musical Courier* during the previous ten years. Dedicated to Philip Hale, who had encouraged Huneker's creative work, the book could not claim any special purpose, but, as Huneker explained, it offered

a sort of carnival in prose—Wagner, Chopin, Ibsen, Nietzsche, Richard Strauss; their poetic, wild, dramatic and anarchic ideas are presented . . . in the form of fiction. . . . The obvious sentimental treatment of musicians . . . is avoided. I wish to show the true life of these people, their posing, their real joys and woes, their absolutely theatric attitude toward life. . . . The Bohemian, the mock-Bohemian and the silly, gruesome nightside of this seamy existence I have dwelt upon at length.

The pessimism in the book, he remarked, was the result of his profession, two decades of criticism being "enough to turn a saint skeptical."[41]

As the title suggests, *Melomaniacs* deals with musicians—pianists, composers, and singers—or music-listeners. Though they clearly reveal Huneker's absorption in Chopin, Wagner, Liszt, and Strauss, the stories are varied in subject, style, and tone. "Dusk of the Gods" and "Music the Conqueror" are entirely prose poems, while a third story, "The Corridor of Time," contains three such poems. Probably inspired by Vladimir de Pachmann's five-hour session of piano playing at Huneker's apartment, "Dusk of the Gods," which presents a vivid panorama of musical history, is, indeed, the volume's most brilliant tour de force. In the humorous-satirical, "Old Fogy" vein are five sketches in which Huneker pokes fun at the phonies and foibles of the music world: the pianists who falsely claim to be pupils—or even illegitimate children—of Liszt ("A Son of Liszt"); the naïveté of the untalented American girl studying abroad ("The Quest of the Elusive," in which the elderly, amorous piano teacher is a take-off on the much-married Theodor Leschetizky);[42] the influence of a critic's wife on his criticism ("Hunding's Wife"); the musical ignorance and posing of guests at private musicales ("The Wegstaffes Give a Musicale"); and Wagner's philosophy of renunciation as found in *Tannhäuser,* which Huneker reinterprets in modern terms, applauding Henry Tannhäuser's liaison with Mrs. Venus Holda, "of Berg Street, Piccadilly" ("Tannhäuser's Choice").

In many of the stories Huneker examines the emotional life of the musician, whom he frequently sees as the sick-souled victim of music. From the opening tale, "The Lord's Prayer in B," in which the musician-atheist is tortured to death by the repeated sound of one note (an idea that came to him, Huneker stated, during a neuralgic attack he suffered in 1896, when he himself kept hearing one note),[43] to the final piece, "Music the Conqueror," whose position in the book is no accident, music's "conquering power for evil" is a recurring theme. ("Why is it," he had complained in 1896, "when I fall to writing much about the ideal in art . . . I get congratulatory letters about the elevation of art and sentiment and rot of that sort? But let me . . . utter the awful truth that music is the most immoral and dangerous of the arts . . . and lo! I am besieged with letters, cries of 'Shame' and hints of my awful responsibility as a critic and writer.")[44] Music can hypnotize the masses ("The Piper of Dreams"), produce hallucinations ("The Disenchanted Symphony"), and evoke hatred against itself by its practitioner ("An Involuntary Insurgent"), and in mastering it the artist can maim himself psychologically, hurt his loved ones, wreck his marriage, sink into alcoholism, or become a raving maniac. Thus Huneker revenges himself, in his music-satiated moods, on the art that brought him pain and frustration as well as exquisite pleasure.

The problem in human relations that occupies him most, however, is the triangle, which figures, in one form or another, in ten of the stories—not surprising considering his own triangular, not to say quadrilateral, experience (with Lizzie, Josephine, Clio, and Georgie, in various combinations). Huneker does not use the triangle simply as a conventional plot device; the question he poses is not who will marry whom, but whether the artist should marry at all, whether a marriage can withstand the rigorous, selfish demands of art, which is sometimes the third side of the triangle. (In 1908 Huneker published an essay, "The Artist and His Wife," in which this same question is examined.)[45] Looming most prominently among the triangle tales are "The Rim of Finer Issues" and its sequel, "An Ibsen Girl" (first published as "A Zone of Silence"), both written in 1896 when Clio and Huneker were separated.[46] Here a strong-willed, literary "new woman" leaves her composer-husband and runs away to Philadelphia with a dilettante critic and boulevardier, regretting it when the husband's art flourishes and he becomes famous; after being desterted by the critic, she remains in Philadelphia under an assumed name (shades of Lizzie!). Though this is not, of course, an exact transcription from Huneker's life, the characters are so convincing (the most convincing in the book) that one is tempted to consider it a veiled reflection of his own feelings toward Clio, interpreting "An Ibsen Girl" as Huneker's "you'll-be-sorry-you-left-me" reproach to Clio. One also surmises that his interest in the American girl who goes abroad to study and becomes involved with European men was stimulated by Clio's going off to Paris.

More obvious traces of his personal experience crop up in the stories. His "Chopin of the Gutter" lives at 5 Rue Puteaux, Huneker's own address during his first stay in Paris. The composer Illowski of "The Piper of Dreams" knows anarchistic literature, haunts the Café Monferino, lives in a "dream barn," and is influenced by Lingwood Evans, Thompson's fictional poet. In "An Involuntary Insurgent," a young man becomes a pianist instead of a priest. "Not a drop," the critic's spouse in "Hunding's Wife" tells him as he goes off to work, but she leaves a case of imported beer for him to drink when he comes home. "Siegfried's Death" concerns a man married to two women at the same time (one of them a common-law wife). Probably the most subjective story in *Melomaniacs* is "The Corridor of Time," first published in 1898,[47] in which Huneker patently portrays himself as Cintras, the prose-mad author, who wants to become a great writer of fiction but lacks the leisure and the talent. "I swear that the most miserable men," says Cintras, "are those who have caught a glimpse of the eternal beauty of art, who pursue her ideal face, who have the vision but not the voice."[48]

Huneker's flair for the humorously bizarre is immediately evident in the plot situations in *Melomaniacs*. To give her son more confidence as a pianist, a mother persuades him that Liszt was his father, whereas his real father was Liszt's favorite piano tuner ("A Son of Liszt"). Chopin is reincarnated in the form of the valet of a leading concert pianist, a Chopin expert, who proceeds to deteriorate as an artist because of his fear that his servant is a better pianist than he ("Avatar"). A pianist marries a deaf woman so that she can never hear him practice ("A Spinner of Silence"). A tympani player expects to win immortality from a symphony he has written for tympani alone ("An Emotional Acrobat"). If Huneker's skill in execution—especially in characterization and dialogue—had matched his inventive facility, he might have become an outstanding writer of fiction.

Delightful touches of description and humor accompany his lively imagination. One character's nose "jutted well into the outer world," while another's mouth was "a trap filled with white blocks of polished bone."[49] A certain dilettante is "too much of a gentleman to make a good musician."[50] A woman tavern-keeper relates that her much younger husband had "run up such a big slate with me that he married me to sponge it out. *Schwamm d'rüber!*, you know."[51] "Take on courage," the mother of a pianist says to her disconsolate husband, who had wanted him to become a priest, "The boy plays badly—there is yet hope."[52] A composer-conductor whose orchestra returns after being cast into the fourth dimension of space while playing his "enchanted" symphony, breathlessly asks what happened in that mysterious region where no man had ever been before or lived to tell about it. "When the men weren't grumbling at having nothing to drink," comes the down-to-earth reply, "they were playing pinochle."[53] Describing, in a letter to her husband, their daughter's seduction by a married European, a distraught woman skirts around the important question until the pregnant postscript, which reads, in its entirety: "I don't know, William."[54]

In "Isolde's Mother" and "The Quest of the Elusive," his use of the theme of the naïve American versus the calculating European suggests the influence of Henry James. If, indeed, there is any underlying unity in *Melomaniacs*, it could perhaps be best expressed by an exclamation in "The Rim of Finer Issues": "What a menstruum is music—what curious trafficking it causes, what opposites it intertwines"—an echo of James's allusion to music as a solvent which Huneker refers to elsewhere in the book.[55] With their lack of depth, superficial development of character, and overliterary dialogue, however, the stories bear few other resemblances to James's, showing more clearly their derivation from the grotesques of Hoffmann and Poe. Yet if they are merely "lath and plaster held together not by the glue of humanity but by a few ideas," as he deprecatingly described them later to Joseph Conrad,[56] they surely illuminate Huneker's mind and temperament.

He thought enough of *Melomaniacs* to send copies to writers he admired. "You are to blame, partially, for its publication," he wrote Henry B. Fuller, then literary editor of the Chicago *Evening Post*. "Your letter in 1896 set me working."[57] (Praising it privately, Fuller apparently did not review it,[58] perhaps because it might have smacked too much of log-rolling, Huneker having publicly applauded every book Fuller had written.) Arthur Symons, who later used "A Spinner of Silence" from the collection to illustrate a criticism of Paderewski,[59] told Huneker that the book was "full of pungent, vivid things, nervous and subtle. You write about music as if it were alive and unhappy: strange after the kind of musical criticism one is used to here."[60] George Moore wrote Huneker that some of the stories were "quite as good as anything that has ever been done in that line."[61] And Frank Norris observed—without elaborating—that Huneker had attained the "most difficult of all achievements . . . originality without grotesqueness."[62]

Few *reviewers*, however, were as enthusiastic as Rupert Hughes, who declared that Huneker "played upon the language as if it were a concert grand piano and he an Abbé Liszt,"[63] and the lukewarm notices and the small sale of *Melomaniacs* disappointed Huneker, even though he had predicted that it would be a "vile failure."[64] In June 1902, he told Harry Thurston Peck (who, he hoped, would review the book in the *Bookman*, though he was disappointed again, for no review seems to have appeared there) that "Fellow-maniacs," as his irreverent newspaper colleagues (or Huneker himself) had christened it, had been misunderstood by most critics, who had said little about his handling of exotic subjects and had not pointed out that the stories were hoaxes; Huneker set this down to the misleading announcement on the cover of the book that he was satirizing figures such as Tolstoy and Wagner.[65] "I know of no other book of musical fiction, that is, music dealt with imaginatively, like *Melomaniacs*," he remarked long afterward, still wishing that he could have been more successful as a creative writer. "The trouble is that these stories demand both a trained musical reader and a lover of fiction—not a combination to be found growing on grapevines."[66] The real trouble, as "Cintras"-Huneker had realized, was that his ability to appreciate good fiction exceeded his talent for creating it.

Meanwhile, he continued to discuss other men's books. His most substantial essays on European literature during 1900–1902 were devoted to Turgenev, Balzac, and Alphonse Daudet, and were published in the *Criterion* in June, July, and August, 1901, respectively. As for American writers, he frequently quoted Finley Peter Dunne's "Dooley"[67] and the anecdotes of Mark Twain[68] (with whose belief that the "trade of critic in literature, music and the drama is the most degraded of all trades and . . . has no real value—certainly no large value"[69] Huneker in his most pessimistic moods would have agreed). "Mr. Clemens is one of the most original writers America has produced," he wrote in 1899, "and more of an artist than is generally believed. . . . I pin my faith to *Huckleberry Finn*. For me it is the great American novel, even if it is written for boys."[70] In 1901 he exulted that Poe, the "victim of Yankee college professors, who find him lacking the patriotism of Whittier, the humor of O. W. Holmes, the sanity of Lowell, and the human qualities of Longfellow," had become the best-known American author in Europe.[71] In 1901 Huneker also seconded Howells' plea for more fiction from the "natural school" and warmly welcomed Frank Norris' *The Octopus*, the "biggest novel of the purely American type since *Silas Lapham*," which "partially fulfilled" the promise of *McTeague*, he declared, and placed Norris in the front rank of fiction writers.[72] Norris' early death in 1902 struck Huneker as a great loss to American literature.[73]

He frequently complained that the English-speaking peoples considered fiction inferior to sculpture, music, painting, or poetry. "A good rattling story, not disfigured by style or ideas, preferably historical, is what the public wants," he asserted in 1902. "We admire the great gifts of Frank Norris, but we really read *Ben Hur*."[74] After a Presbyterian council met in New York in 1902 and approved certain changes in doctrine, Huneker, disgusted by the "preachiness" of popular American novels, wrote: "Now that the devil is decreed dead . . . and the Pope is no longer anti-Christ, may we not hope for more meat and drink in Dr. [Henry] van Dyke's fiction, a fiction hitherto fit for babes at the breast?" Reporting that one member of the council had cast a dissenting vote with the cry, "It is the beginning of the end!" Huneker commented that the phrase was "probably originated by Eve in Eden when she pulled the hairy tip of Adam's tail."[75]

The American novelist who measured up completely to Huneker's artistic standards was Henry James, whose technical accomplishments Huneker praised in a lengthy review of *The Wings of the Dove* in 1902:

All the old-time conventional chapter endings are dispensed with; many are suspended cadences. All barren modulations from event to event are swept away—unprepared dissonances are of continual occurrence. There is no descriptive padding—that bane of second-class writers; nor are we informed at every speech of a character's name. The elliptical method Mr. James has absorbed from Flaubert. . . . Nothing is forestalled, nothing is obvious and one is forever turning the curves of the unexpected; yet the story is trying in its bareness, the situation not abnormal. . . . Surely Milly Theale is the most exquisite portrait in his gallery of exquisite portraitures. . . . It is all art in the superlative, the art of Jane Austen raised to the Nth degree, superadded by Mr. James' implacable curiosity about causes final. . . . The style is crackjaw—a jungle of inversions, suspensions, elisions, repetitions, echoes, transpositions, transformations, neologisms, in which the heads of young adjectives gaze despairingly and from afar at verbs that come thundering in Teutonic fashion at the close of sentences leagues long. . . . It is fiction of the future; it is a precursor of the book our children and grandchildren will enjoy when all the hurly-burly of noisy adventure, of cheap historical tales and still cheaper drawing room struttings shall have vanished from fiction.[76]

✂ Eleven

SHINING ON THE 'SUN'

In the fall of 1900, after being out of daily journalism for three years, Huneker became music critic of the New York *Sun*. Under Charles A. Dana, who had died in 1897, this "newspaperman's newspaper" had been a brilliant, if sometimes perverse, organ of personal journalism, supporting few winning candidates or popular causes, and so independent that for years it did not even own an Associated Press franchise. H. L. Mencken called it the "grandest, gaudiest newspaper that ever went to press."[1] Dana taught young reporters to observe and depict vividly the life swarming about them, and thereby helped to shape the course of American literature, for one of these reporters, David Graham Phillips, and his emulators went on to produce some of the best muckraking and naturalistic fiction. No other American newspaper could match the *Sun*'s clear, leisurely, and lively style or its bold, sarcastic editorials, full of the unusual words and memorable phrases that revealed Dana's partiality for good prose.[2]

Dana had surrounded himself with able, college-educated aides, chief of whom was Edward Page Mitchell, who joined the *Sun* in 1875 and remained with it for over fifty years. A scholar with a penchant for the freakish and bizarre as well as a superlative journalist, Mitchell wrote witty, often whimsical, and always finished editorials.[3] Other *Sun* veterans were Chester S. Lord, managing editor; Carr V. Van Anda, night editor for eleven years before he left in 1904 to become the legendary managing editor of the *New York Times*; and William M. Laffan, who came to the newspaper in 1877 as drama critic and general writer on art subjects, and served successively as business adviser, publisher, general manager, and, beginning in 1902, nominal owner.[4] For more than three decades the leading article on the book review page and countless editorials on foreign affairs were written by Mayo William Hazeltine, a Harvard graduate and a trained lawyer, reputedly the most accomplished book reviewer in daily journalism.[5]

Edward E. Ziegler, whom Huneker had met in the late 1890's, was his assistant on the *Sun* (and perhaps also on *Town Topics*) and now his most intimate friend. "Don't, my boy, start in life quarreling with your own bread," Huneker advised Ziegler, thirteen years his junior, in 1900, when the latter had apparently attacked his colleagues. "It's bad form, besides it will prove a serious bar to your advancement. Remember that . . . we must hang together or else—hang altogether. . . . If you leave your books and theories and get to dealing with concrete facts your style will become more robust, more red-blooded, more readable." "Not too harsh, not so bitter; use the dagger not dynamite," Huneker suggested later. And he added, shortly afterward: "Don't write with grave pauses, profound smirks and all the pompous, silly amatory mean little reservations, attenuations, periphrases and involutions of your contemporaries. Far better an honest staccato phrase than a wilderness of sostenutos."[6] It was excellent advice and Ziegler profited from it.

As the *Sun*'s critic, Huneker followed the same tack he had taken on the *Musical Courier*. Probably his chief enthusiasm in 1900–1902 was Richard Strauss, whose early *Symphonic Fantasia*, called noisy and unmusical when it had last been performed in New York over a decade earlier (as Huneker pointed out to his readers in January 1901), now sounded as clear as a Mozart rondo. Here was a chance, he said, for the anti-Strauss contingent—which included Krehbiel, Finck, and Henderson—to wag wise heads and exclaim: "If Strauss had but adhered to this brilliant and comprehensible style!" In another ten years, Huneker predicted, "some of us may groan over the decadence of a Strauss whose *Don Quixote, Also Sprach Zarathustra* and *Ein Heldenleben* were miracles of music, pure and undefiled."[7] At the end of 1901 he described Strauss as the greatest living musician and the greatest master of orchestration in the history of music.[8]

During this period, two operas by Puccini received Metropolitan premières—*La Bohème* in 1900 and *Tosca* in 1901. Puccini's music was unknown in New York in 1896 when Huneker reviewed R. A. Streatfeild's *Masters of Italian Music* and reported that Puccini, with his melodic gifts, dramatic feeling, and fine sense of orchestral color, was considered the best equipped of the younger Italian composers.[9] Huneker found *La Bohème* intensely modern in that everything, including eu-

phony and form, was sacrificed to the dramatic situation. He felt that
Puccini's humorous vein was more sincere and better sustained than his
tragic, but that the score contained too many echoes of Mascagni, Gounod, Wagner, Meyerbeer, Leoncavallo, Ponchielli, and Verdi. Yet the
opera had color, movement, and rhythmic variety, and its *parlando* was
handled with "uncommon sympathy and technical address." *La Bohème*
greatly enhanced its composer's reputation, Huneker concluded, and
promised to be a pleasing addition to the Metropolitan's repertory.[10]
As for *Tosca,* Huneker called it an absorbing, enjoyable melodrama,
though Puccini's themes, he thought, were "neither original nor generally expressive," and his writing "all top and bottom," the inner
weaving being "puerile." Yet, Huneker declared, the second act—and
a Tosca like Ternina—would ensure the opera's popularity.[11] He never
became a strong supporter of Puccini.

Though his new job enhanced his own reputation—he was asked
to write articles on music for the *New International Encyclopedia* published later in 1902[12]—it complicated his relationship with Marc Blumenberg, who complained at the beginning of 1901 that Huneker was
"booming" in the *Sun* the *Musical Courier*'s enemies.[13] What Blumenberg feared most was that his own employee would make him look ridiculous by praising his own pet hate, Victor Herbert, whom Huneker had
touted for years in the *Courier.* The "Raconteur," for example, had
applauded Herbert's dramatic cantata *The Captive* in 1891, his *Irish
Rhapsody* in 1892, and his operetta *The Serenade* in 1897, and early in
1900 had even traveled to Pittsburgh to hear Herbert conduct his *Suite
Romantique,* which, Huneker predicted in the *Courier,* was "sure to
become a favorite in concert rooms, American and European."[14] Herbert's appointment as conductor of the Pittsburgh Orchestra in February 1898 had displeased Blumenberg, who in a series of unsigned editorials insisted that a former bandleader and a composer of operettas
was not the proper person to head a symphony orchestra. Perhaps, as
his latest biographer suggests, Herbert refused to advertise in the
Courier,[15] or perhaps Blumenberg was actually motivated by his highbrow standards and a sense of musical decorum. In any event, he was
annoyed at Huneker for having disagreed with him in his own journal,
and was afraid that Huneker would also speak up for Herbert in the
Sun. If this happened, Blumenberg declared, he would engage a "big

man (maybe Krehbiel)" to write editorials—thus winning over the
Tribune to his side in his war against Herbert—and allow Huneker to
do only his "Raconteur" column at a reduced salary.[16]

Huneker was in a dilemma: if he praised Herbert's next composition, his job on the *Musical Courier* would be jeopardized, while any
adverse comment (or silence) would probably endanger his friendship
with Herbert and with Huneker's colleagues, who disliked Blumenberg
and resented his nasty attacks on Herbert. Huneker followed his conscience, however, and on January 23, 1901, when the newspaper ver-
dicts came in on Herbert's new symphonic poem *Hero and Leander*,
none was more favorable than the *Sun*'s.[17] Blumenberg was furious, and
though he apparently did not carry out his threat to demote Huneker,
he never forgave him.

In July 1901, Blumenberg suddenly pounced on Herbert again, announcing in the *Musical Courier* that all of his "written to order" comic
operas were "pure and simple plagiarisms,"[18] and Herbert, his patience
finally exhausted, promptly filed suit for libel. Huneker publicly ignored
the issue while the case was pending but let it be known privately that
he had not approved of Blumenberg's remarks.[19] In the late summer of
1902, the simmering disagreement between Blumenberg and Huneker
erupted in a curious exchange of editorials in the *Courier*. Blaming
the press critics for the "discouraging condition of abstract music in this
city—the only kind of music requiring expert criticism"—Blumenberg
urged them to judge the music instead of the performer, and thus
elevate the dignity of the critical profession. Huneker replied that "objective" criticism was impossible, and Blumenberg, in turn, answered
that Huneker's argument was beside the point. The critics were artists
and deserved greater pay and prestige than they were getting for building up the reputations of others. "We can accomplish nothing for our
critics," he remarked, "if they will swing themselves, like Mr. Huneker
did . . . out of reach, living in a trance." Huneker then pointed out
that the public bought a newspaper to read of persons, not of things,
and that pure music criticism, accordingly, bore little weight in editorial councils. But if he had "boomed" artists it was simply because
their art excited his "too susceptible enthusiasms." He readily agreed
with Blumenberg that critics were underpaid. "I suspect that newspaper proprietors count on the love of critics for music and discount it
in their salaries," he wrote. "Mr. Huneker's sentimental discourse,"

responded Blumenberg, "is just one other evidence of the inability of the music critic to apprehend the economic principle at stake."[20]

Other persons sent in letters to the *Courier* on the subject, among them "A Daily Music Critic of New York," who did not help matters in the least. "It is well and good for James Huneker to sit back in his $10,000 a year *Musical Courier* editorial chair," he began, "and squint lazily through rosy glasses at the rest of us struggling along with cracked nerves and office boy salaries."[21] Though reputedly the most highly paid musical writer in the world at this time,[22] Huneker surely did not receive anything near $10,000 a year. Still, if people thought he did, maybe he *was* worth more, he felt, than the $100 a week or so he was getting.[23]

At this juncture, Franklin Fyles, drama critic of the *Sun*, resigned because of illness, and Huneker was offered the position. Tired of music criticism and Blumenberg's quarrelsomeness, he accepted, and on October 8, 1902, resigned from the *Musical Courier*,[24] ending an association that had lasted more than fifteen years. In his letter of resignation to Blumenberg, Huneker alluded to their recent editorial tiff:

I expect to earn more money elsewhere and not divide my energies as I have been doing for the past ten years. I have been grievously underpaid by the *Musical Courier* during the past five years. . . . The *Courier* should have claimed my entire time by paying me enough money. So you can't blame me for being practical at last, can you? For coming out of my idealistic "trance.". . . I am leaving music journalism for good. I need more leisure for my personal work and I am heartily weary of the atmosphere of petty intrigue, personalities, and futile bickering that disgrace the profession of weekly musical journalism. I know you will be surprised at this move and I hope you will be sorry, for personally I am sorry to leave you. . . . You cannot forget and I will not, that I helped to make the artistic end of the paper what it is. . . . *Auf wiedersehen* Marc, and don't forget the good, old times. I shall not.[25]

A notice in the magazine on October 15 announced Huneker's retirement from musical journalism:

Mr. Huneker has been a devoted member of the staff of the *Musical Courier*, and has impressed his strong personality with power and brilliancy upon the vast host of people who are readers of this paper; his articles, essays, reviews and criticism have established him as one of the foremost writers on the music subject, and his versatility, his wit and humor, as well as his authority have been a source of unending enjoyment and study to the world of music, for the world of music read him through these columns. It is the sincere hope of all those who are associated with this publication that his future pursuits will prove pleasant to him, and that his sunny nature will never be clouded by one unpropitious moment.[26]

Despite these gestures, however, there was ill feeling on both sides.[27] The magazine withheld his last week's salary, Huneker later complained, and he never received his shares of stock in the corporation.[28] "God help my successor," he wrote Krehbiel. "He will have to work like a slave and do dirty work without end."[29] Not long afterward, he was drinking beer at Lüchow's with Leonard Liebling, who announced that Blumenberg had offered him a job. "You have ability and promise as a musical writer," Huneker told him. "However, you are very young and there is still time for your salvation. Reflect before you hang yourself by the neck. But if nothing will stop you from undertaking the accursed career, you have my blessing and may God have mercy on your soul." Blumenberg hired Liebling and informed him that he was to take Huneker's place. "You mean *space*, don't you?" replied Liebling, who eventually became the magazine's editor in chief.[30] Huneker's departure from musical journalism caused a shift among his former colleagues, Henderson leaving the *Times* for the *Sun*, Aldrich going from the *Tribune* to the *Times*, and Ziegler succeeding Huneker on *Town Topics*.[31]

On October 22, 1902, Victor Herbert's libel suit came to trial. Although Blumenberg was defended by the cagey Abe Hummel, Walter Damrosch's convincing testimony helped win Herbert a verdict of $15,000 damages, later reduced to $5,000.[32] "Considering that he was the author of most of the complimentary comment upon Victor Herbert's musical achievements quoted from the *Courier* in contrast to Blumenberg's attack," the *Concert-Goer* editorialized, "Mr. James Huneker . . . must be glad that he was out of [the *Courier*] before the case came to trial. What a witness for the prosecution he would have made!"[33] On November 10 a gala banquet celebrating Herbert's victory was attended by many of New York's musical celebrities. Huneker was apparently not present.

In the five years since Huneker had left drama criticism in 1897, a number of changes had taken place in New York's theatrical life. The Syndicate had gained control of most of the theaters in America and could dictate terms to actors and rival managers. For over a decade this monopoly was bitterly fought by producers and stars. New theaters were springing up around Forty-second Street to house resident stock companies, still the chief training schools for actors. Though short films were often shown on variety programs, motion pictures were not yet a serious threat to vaudeville, burlesque, and the legitimate stage.

At the turn of the century, audiences applauded the spectacular dramatizations of *Ben Hur, Quo Vadis?, When Knighthood Was in Flower,* and other historical novels. In 1900, a year before his death, James A. Herne scored one of his infrequent successes with *Sag Harbor.* Another rural drama, adapted from Edward Westcott's celebrated novel *David Harum,* was even more popular. David Belasco's versions of French melodramas like *Zaza* and *Du Barry,* featuring Mrs. Leslie Carter, brought money into the till, as did various costume pieces which showed off the talents of Mansfield, Kyrle Bellew, E. H. Sothern, and Otis Skinner. The classic repertory, kept alive by Mme Modjeska, Sarah Bernhardt, and Coquelin, was amply balanced by the lighter entertainment of the record-breaking musical comedy *Florodora,* which won fame and fortune for half a dozen beautiful chorus girls. The "Four Cohans" emerged from vaudeville to appear in a Broadway musical farce written by the young George M. Cohan. Pacing American playwrights in quantity as well as quality, Clyde Fitch produced three successful plays during 1900–1901, one of them, *Captain Jinks of the Horse Marines,* providing Ethel Barrymore with her first starring role. Maude Adams, Broadway's greatest box-office attraction, received rave notices for her performances in Rostand's poetic historical drama *L'Aiglon,* and in James Barrie's charming comedy *Quality Street.*

The modern Continental drama was represented by the American première of Ibsen's *The Master Builder,* which closed after a single showing in 1900; E. H. Sothern's production of Hauptmann's *The Sunken Bell*; and Sudermann's *Magda,* Pinero's *The Second Mrs. Tanqueray* (which Huneker considered "easily the greatest play of latter-day British dramas"),[34] and Björnson's *Beyond Human Power,* all presented by Mrs. Patrick Campbell and her leading man George Arliss. But the public still saw the theater primarily as a means of escape from everyday life. William Winter and J. Ranken Towse continued to lead the conservative critics, but younger men like Walter Prichard Eaton and John Corbin were speaking out against Victorian prejudices.

Rusty at drama criticism, Huneker was uneasy over his debut as critic for a major newspaper. But his first assignment, fortunately, was congenial: a group of three experimental plays by D'Annunzio—*La Gioconda, Francesca da Rimini,* and *La Città Morta*—performed by the incomparable Duse, whose first American visit Huneker had discussed in the *Recorder* almost ten years earlier. The review printed in the *Sun* on November 9, 1902,[35] proved to be the first of a series of Sunday articles which constituted the most remarkable writings on the modern drama published in America. Week after week Huneker turned out illuminating essays on D'Annunzio, Ibsen, Hauptmann, Shaw, and other dramatists in addition to his almost daily reviews of New York's varied theatrical fare.

In 1902–4, when antagonism toward Ibsen had by no means disappeared—a London magazine described an Ibsen audience of 1903 as "pallid spinsters with uneasy eyes; sickly-looking youths with effeminate airs and affectations; strange hollow-eyed old men with a suggestion of depraved refinement; Socialists, vegetarians, pro-Boers, bromide drinkers, ego maniacs, solitaries and superfluous women"[36]—Mrs. Fiske's anti-Ibsen article in the Christmas issue of *Theatre* in 1902 inspired a reply by Huneker which was perhaps the best commentary on Ibsen written in America. It was sad that Mrs. Fiske had turned her shapely shoulders on the dramatist, he remarked, for with her "clear brain and powers of adaptability she would have been an ideal interpreter of the Scandinavian's feminine gallery."[37] (Mrs. Fiske, of course, went back to Ibsen with brilliant results.) Henry Irving's dislike of Ibsen's subjects because they smacked of the dissecting room struck Huneker as strange for one who had "spent his entire professional career in delineating melodramatic lunatics"; at least Ibsen's characters were real, if disagreeable, whereas those in Irving's repertory were "flimsy silhouettes."[38]

Beginning on April 12, 1903, the *Sun* ran a series of five articles by Huneker on Maeterlinck, whose sexy *Monna Vanna* had just become a popular success in London,[39] where it had once been forbidden a public performance on the grounds of immorality. Despite Maeterlinck's artistic integrity, boldness, and grasp of modern psychology, Huneker observed, few critics had taken him seriously or tried to understand him. Yet he was not really difficult, for the "symbol floats like a flag in his dramas." Maeterlinck's most poetic play, Huneker declared, was *Pelléas et Mélisande.*[40]

Several European dramatists and poets Huneker discussed were practically unknown in America. After reading a German translation of eleven one-act plays by Strindberg,[41] for example, he wrote, in March 1903, what was probably the most extensive American study of Strindberg that had yet appeared. The Swede was never pornographic, he noted, nor did he reveal a naked soul merely to provide charming diversion; his plays, moreover, grew progressively less abnormal in subject matter and treatment.[42] A year and a half later, Huneker informed his editor at Scribner's, Edward Morse, that Strindberg was the "biggest man now that Ibsen's life work is done. . . . I never saw a more terribly tragic play than *Fräulein Julie* in Berlin. But—impossible for us. It is too profoundly true."[43]

Also new to most educated Americans other than devotees of *M'lle New York* and modern French poetry was the name of Jules Laforgue, who had died in 1887 at the age of twenty-seven. On January 11, 1903, Huneker mentioned an "unexplored *Hamlet*, a study and recasting of his temperament . . . so profound, so original, so miraculously novel, that each time we read it we are aghast at the poet's temerity in shedding his own skin to enter Hamlet's. This Hamlet is the one that will be dearest and nearest to this age; it is the Hamlet ironical."[44] The article, one of the earliest in English on Laforgue, must have introduced a number of readers to the Frenchman's *Moralités légendaires*, which, with his poetry, was to exert a pronounced influence on American literature through Ezra Pound, T. S. Eliot, and Hart Crane.

As Huneker could not help noticing, the American drama was comparatively thin and circumspect. Less than two months after the 1902–3 season had opened, he was complaining that our theater was perishing for the "want of rich red blood, new ideas and artistic workmanship."[45] By April 1903, he had seen so many bad plays that another one, Richard Harding Davis' *The Taming of Helen*, produced this outburst on the tameness of American drama and literature:

Love, unless it be treated as a joke or a social gumdrop, is sternly waved away from managerial precincts. We are in darkness regarding an entire dramatic literature that Germany has enjoyed for the past quarter of a century. When we do get a few modern masterpieces they are mutilated, lines excised, sentiments expunged, and meanings suppressed. . . . In America the sentiment of the etiolated, the brainless, the prudish, the hypocrite is the censor. . . . Why is there absent the tragic note in America? Why are there so few shadows and inequalities? They exist, no doubt about that, but the vanilla-cum-lemonade school will have none of them. . . . The avoidance of all that reveals the soul; the elimination of poverty, crime, sin, despair; the selection of namby-pamby frivolous men and women, mostly in their teens; the abstaining from large emotional expression and the slurring over with sick music of false rhetoric all the cruel facts of life—these are the stock in trade of the American novelist and dramatist.

Not only Davis but far more talented writers such as Hawthorne, Poe, Henry James, Edgar Saltus, and F. Marion Crawford had become victims of the public opinion and spirit of compromise that, Huneker claimed, had tamed American literature.[46]

He slyly inquired whether the "great American play" might not be something of a cross between a Davis and a Fitch work in which the "Gibson girl will woo the Fitch boy and all end well."[47] In February 1903, when *four* of Fitch's plays were running on Broadway, Huneker analyzed his work at length and threw in a few broad hints about his personality. Considering his physical equipment, Huneker wrote, Fitch accomplished marvels with his "delicacy, tact, and a feminine manner of apprehending meanings of life" and his shrewd observation of the minor details of daily social interchange. But the intuitive perception in Fitch's dialogue was "not quite masculine," and he was not at his best when dealing with passion because he presented "no virile combinations in which men and women face each other, their souls stripped of conventional draperies." Yet his method of painting character in "subtle stippling" was "supremely clever in its genre," and though his subject matter was artificial, Fitch was among the few playwrights of his generation who had depicted real American men and women of the class he had chosen to portray. Huneker could not admire Fitch's selection, but he could appreciate his wit, irony, and knowledge of the world. A long rest, Huneker advised, would help him turn out a "masterpiece in miniature."[48]

The day after this article appeared, Fitch wrote John Corbin, the drama critic, that he was puzzled by Huneker's criticism. "He judges me outside, instead of in. He believes I'm insincere (like other people who don't know me, who seem to get it from the manner in which my hair is or isn't brushed, and the cut of my coat), and so can't understand or appreciate, or realize my sincere work."[49] Two months later, Fitch announced that he had deliberately fooled the critics by giving purposely inane lines in one of his plays to a group of women who all spoke at the same time—a bit of dialogue that the critics had called "brilliant." Huneker's rejoinder was neat:

Why not, Brother Fitch, why not? Making a dozen women talk all at once was a brilliant stroke to begin with; making them say absolutely silly things was tremendously truthful and brilliant. Playwrights are so under the iron dominion of feminine influence in this country that they put all the good speeches in the mouths of their women characters. Not to do this is to be as daring as an Ibsen; it is to tell the horrid truth. . . . [In criticizing] the next play of yours we shall be timid about the dialogue—the plots, being healthy and usually middle-aged, can take care of themselves. Their ocean trip always does them good before a New York appearance.[50]

Five months later, however, he declared that Fitch's new play, *Her Own Way*, was his best.[51]

At the end of April 1903, Huneker went abroad to see the newest theaters and the latest plays, to interview playwrights, and to gather material for his next major project, a biography of Liszt, paying his way as usual by writing articles for the *Sun* and various magazines. In five months, the busiest he ever spent in Europe, he attended dozens of plays, operas, concerts, and art exhibitions. He heard the Richard Strauss Festival in London and had a talk with Strauss. (Huneker claimed, in fact, that he was the first American newspaperman to interview Strauss.)[52] He reported in the *Sun* that Strauss had just recently come into his own in England (where even Arthur Symons had failed to do him justice),[53] and that though he had only begun his career, Strauss was already the greatest of musical narrators.[54] During his stay in England, Huneker finally met Symons and Havelock Ellis.[55]

In Paris, his next stop, Huneker found that his *Sun* articles on Maeterlinck won him free entry to every theater in the city.[56] On May 20 he was present at the heralded première of Maeterlinck's new play *Joyzelle*, to which eighty impresarios from all over the world had come, each ready to bid for the foreign rights,[57] and his review of it, apparently printed in the *Weekly Critical Review* as well as the *Sun*, brought Huneker letters from Remy de Gourmont, Huysmans, and Maeterlinck, whom he interviewed about this time.[58] (Huneker was a "remarkable erudite," Maeterlinck wrote Upton Sinclair long afterward, "although a little too much slave to ephemeral fashions.")[59] Huneker had just become more widely known in France through the appearance of excerpts from his *Chopin,* translated by Arthur Bles, in the bilingual *Weekly Critical Review,*[60] which boasted such contributors as Huysmans, Rodin, Symons, and Yeats—a company Huneker was proud to join. Bles, the editor of the publication, dedicated his translation to Jules Claretie, director of the Théâtre Français, and received a decoration from the Académie Française for his pains. ("What a farce," Huneker wrote Ziegler from Berlin, "and I am eating sauerkraut on the banks of the river Spree and on the edge of a table—unknown, unheard, unsung and *toujours* thirsty.")[61]

In Paris, too, Huneker interviewed the difficult Huysmans and had the honor of being called an *imbécile* by the reconverted ex-blasphemer because of his wayward Catholicism.[62] "His religious convictions seem to be sincere," Huneker commented in the *Sun.* ". . . But you never can tell. So great is the art of this erudite and magnetic man that he can make religious fiction more entertaining than the dreary erotics of his Parisian brethren."[63] Huneker also met Claude Debussy, whose flat face, prominent eyes, long hair, unkempt beard, and uncouth clothing were no less startling to Huneker than his revolutionary music. *Pelléas et Mélisande* was only a year old when Huneker saw it during this visit and wrote what he later called the first criticism of the opera in English.[64] He was tempted to call Debussy the "greatest of living De-composers," he said, for in *Pelléas* the "musical phrase is dislocated; the rhythms are decomposed; the harmonic structure is pulled to pieces, melts before our eyes—or ears." Though he detected no normal sequence in Debussy's idiom, Huneker admitted that perhaps it was because he was not accustomed to the "novel progressions and apparent forced conjunctions of harmonies and thematic fragments." Even if Debussy were a "literary" composer, needing a play, poem, novel, or picture to stimulate his imagination—the music of *Pelléas* was so completely wedded to the play, he remarked, that it had no separate identity —one could hardly quarrel with the methods of a man who could set to music difficult poems by Mallarmé and Baudelaire. Debussy certainly had an individual style, Huneker concluded, and his future should be watched "with suspicion" from all the critical watchtowers.[65]

Huneker took time off in Paris to put down on paper impressions accumulated during the previous three weeks. Between one Thursday night and the following Monday morning, he turned out 33,000 words, sometimes writing fourteen hours at a stretch.[66] Within a month he had

sent another 33,000 words to the *Sun* "for newspaper consumption—
and for cash, so much per word," he told Ziegler. ". . . Serious criticism will come later in the magazines."[67]

During one week in Berlin, shortly afterward, he saw fifteen plays,
including Gorky's *Nachtasyl,* which seemed to him the last word in dramatic naturalism.[68] (Josephine was more thrilled by a bow and salute
from the Kaiser on Unter den Linden.) Liszt's old housekeeper showed
Huneker the rich collection of manuscripts, trophies, jewels, pictures,
letters, and testimonials at the composer's Weimar home,[69] and he also
explored Goethe's residence, the superb Goethe and Schiller archives,
and the ducal library. In Weimar an attack of gout forced him to give
up beer temporarily, and on the stein-decorated postcard he sent Ziegler
from Pilsen, he wrote: "And nothing but a glass of water. . . . *Et ego
in Arkady!*"[70] He toured the Wagner house in Leipzig and the art gallery in Dresden, while in Vienna he saw a performance of *Monna Vanna*
and met the great conductor Arthur Nikisch. After visiting the Liszt
Museum in Budapest, Huneker spent most of August fighting fat at
Marienbad, where he lost sixteen pounds in fifteen days. "My fat belly
has gone, vanished, disappeared," he exulted. "Why it's worth all the
hard work to become acquainted with your own person."[71] Returning
to Germany from Holland in September, the Hunekers had a narrow
escape when several cars, including theirs, on the Amsterdam–Berlin
train left the track and rolled into a sand ditch, seriously injuring passengers in the cars just ahead of them.[72] It was a nerve-shattering climax to an exhausting summer.

By mid-October, not long after the New York drama season started,
Huneker was more disgusted than ever with the American stage. "After
scouring all dramatic Europe," he complained, "I am confronted . . .
with a collection of plays that might have been written A.D. 1200 for
all the connection they have with modern life."[73] Farce, melodrama,
and sentimental comedy succeeded each other monotonously: *The Virginian, The College Widow, A Fool and His Money,* and so on. Many
of these were enough to put Huneker to sleep. (When he read, at the
end of the season that someone in the audience at the Comédie Française had set off an alarm clock at the climax of a dull play, he dryly
commented that the timepiece might have been useful more than once
in New York's theaters.)[74] One performance of *Monna Vanna* in Yid-

dish—which, he reported, anyone with the slightest knowledge of German could easily follow[75]—was more exciting to him than most of these other plays combined. He declared that Mrs. Fiske's success with *Hedda Gabler* (which William Winter called a "long-winded, colloquial exposition of disease")[76] was not a sign of a pro-Ibsen reaction but rather a revolt by an intelligent minority against the "sentimental mush, the pious pap, and cheap vulgarities" on Broadway.[77] A course of Ibsen plays would be a welcome corrective to "our overweening national conceited optimism," Huneker declared, urging Heinrich Conried to undertake the project at the Irving Place Theater.[78]

In November 1903, when William Butler Yeats came to America on his first lecture tour here, Huneker described the leader of the Irish theater as "a playwright of poetic power . . . inevitably subtle in his suggestions of the strange and remote shapes, the fantastic dwellers of the human soul's threshold," and suggested that Yeats's plays be produced in America under his supervision.[79] John Quinn, the organizer of Yeats's tour and the chief American patron of Irish literature and art, wanted to introduce Huneker to Yeats, but for some reason Huneker asked that the meeting be postponed.[80] Shortly afterward, the *Sun* printed a long article by Huneker on Yeats and the Celtic revival,[81] which Yeats praised as being "precisely what journalism is not—detailed and philosophical and accurate."[82] Huneker sent clippings of these pieces to Yeats's sometime collaborator and friend George Moore, who replied that he read them with "great interest."[83]

Constantly quoting from American, English, and European magazines and newspapers, Huneker of course produced reams of words in the *Sun* on current theatrical topics and celebrities. He spoke out against a national endowed theater in Washington, for example, fearing that political influences would stifle it, and argued that a New York theater endowed by a millionaire, or better yet, a school for young actors and actresses, would be more desirable.[84] The musician's "naïve ignorance" of stage decoration and management annoyed him, and he would undoubtedly have cheered the Metropolitan's later use of Broadway directors. Equally irritating to Huneker, however, was the "ignorant naïveté" of theatrical managers on the subject of music. "Seldom it is that incidental music is successful," he remarked. "Then it is accidental." Usually the theater orchestra was a "public nuisance, driving men to drink and killing conversation outright."[85]

Among Huneker's favorite actresses were Ada Rehan[86] and, eventually, Julia Marlowe, with whom he corresponded. ("You looked superb across the footlights," he wrote Marlowe in 1909, after seeing her in *Antony and Cleopatra*. "We all envied the asp!")[87] Ethel Barrymore had a breezy, wholesome charm, a sense of humor, and a comely face and figure, he observed early in 1904, and though she was still angular and her art far from finished, he liked her in *Cousin Kate*.[88] ("*Is* there a drama critic in America?" A. B. Walkley, the distinguished English drama critic, asked Miss Barrymore in the following summer, and she immediately thought of Huneker.)[89] Perhaps the most important new personality that Huneker singled out in 1904 was John Barrymore, who had made his stage debut in the preceding year, and who, in Huneker's estimation, had easily topped the cast of Richard Harding Davis' *The Dictator*. "There is something droll about this young man, droll and individual," wrote Huneker. "He is handsome, devil-may-care and as time passes begins to recall his father, ill-fated, dashing Maurice Barrymore. . . . Like his brother Lionel, [he] may go far as a character actor, if he so wills it."[90]

Huneker's work in the *Sun* had soon attracted attention in America as well as Europe. To Edith Wharton, for example, he was "a breath of fresh air blowing through the stale atmosphere of the theatre,"[91] while one of his most competent colleagues, the *Press*'s Hillary Bell, lauded his absolute impartiality and his prose style. The *Sun*'s critic had the "wit of an Irishman, the grace of a Frenchman, the power of a German, and the versatility of an American," Bell stated in February 1903, predicting that Huneker would be "one of the great names in our literature."[92] In January 1904, theatergoers and showpeople would have seen some truth in the *World*'s flippant description of Huneker as a "mystic, an Ibsenite, a Maartin [*sic*] Maartenser, a Maeterlincker, and all that sort of thing that goes with Henry Meltzer and hair";[93] few, however, would have agreed with witty Maurice Barrymore, who, when Huneker once hesitated to enter the Lambs' with him because drama critics were not allowed in the club, had quipped: "Oh, that's all right, you're no drama critic."[94] Even the *World*'s philistine conceded that Huneker wrote "briskly, crisply, lightly and to the point." His fame had reached the hinterlands, too. "A dramatic critic has arisen in New York," reported the Johnstown *Republican*. "The clever work of James Huneker in the *Sun* marks the greatest step in advance that dramatic criticism has ever taken in America."[95]

But he was growing increasingly tired of poor plays and the pressures of daily journalism in general. He wanted more leisure to work on the Liszt biography, and he thought that he could now earn a living by free-lancing, choosing his own subjects and avoiding the growls of bad actors and cross editors, who wanted him to go easy on advertisers. "I've made no new ties during the past 2 years," he wrote Krehbiel on April 26, 1904, "for my heart is in the highlands—of music and not in this beastly miasma of the theater. . . . I find more and more every day that a position in a daily is a dangerous thing; your scalp is ever sought by the pushing throng."[96] Perhaps "passionate and punctilious press agents" had continued to send him anonymous letters, which had annoyed him in 1902.[97] Drama criticism was not a bed of roses, he told his readers on June 26, 1904, for "every man Jack thinks he knows as much as and more than the critic. . . . But we have upheld sound dramatic art and we have . . . decried the sloppy, second hand, sentimental, insincere stuff which masquerades as drama."[98] Whether any particular incident precipitated his action is uncertain, but at the end of the season Huneker left the *Sun*.[99]

ꝛ Twelve

FREE LANCE AND THE
ARTISTIC WINDMILL

In March 1904, Scribner's had published Huneker's *Overtones,* which was dedicated to Richard Strauss, the subject of its leading essay. This and a study—"Parsiphallic," Huneker aptly described it[1]—of Wagner's last opera were no doubt reprinted to take advantage of the wide publicity given to two events: Strauss's first visit to America, which began about the time the book came out, and the first production outside Bayreuth of *Parsifal,* which, despite legal action brought by the Wagner family and shouts of blasphemy raised by clergymen, had been repeated eleven times at the Metropolitan in the two months before the publication of *Overtones.*[2] ("If those purblind, reverend gentlemen . . . had only known how 'sacred' its roots really were," Huneker later remarked, referring to the relationship between Wagner and King Ludwig, "the conflict would have been tenfold greater than it was.")[3] Huneker was proud of his championship of Strauss, but even more pleased, perhaps, with the book's essays on Nietzsche, Balzac, Flaubert, George Moore, and Henry James—his first literary criticism in hard covers.[4] Though *Overtones* was hardly a best-seller, it increased his prestige in the eyes of the magazine editors on whom he now depended for a living.

During the spring and early summer of 1904, research on Liszt and writing for the magazines kept him busy. In January of this year he had begun to contribute regularly to the *Metropolitan Magazine,* a profusely illustrated middlebrow monthly containing fiction, verse, and criticism by such writers as Kipling, O. Henry, and Max Beerbohm, and by the spring of 1905, if not before, Huneker was the magazine's drama critic. Another main outlet for him was *Harper's Bazar* (as it was then spelled), edited by Elizabeth Jordan, whom he nicknamed "Brünnhilde" and sent charming notes and articles on women in fiction, music, and drama.[5] (He was apparently conforming to the *Bazar*'s taboos and not joking when he offered her an essay on "The Ibsen Girls" with the comment: "If you think the word 'girls' is too undignified or colloquial, how will 'The Maidens of Ibsen's Plays' do as a title?")[6] Huneker's work also appeared in *Scribner's Magazine, Lamp, Success Magazine, Theatre,* and *Smart Set.*

Free-lancing left him little time for relaxation, and he was forced to turn down all invitations to midweek dinners and parties. "I've been writing 5000 words a day, even more . . . for the past two months," he told Krehbiel in July 1904. "I'm fagged out and ready to cry at my own shadow. If this is to be the pace, I'll be damned glad to get back at the old leisurely newspaper grind—which after all is normal and more rhythmic."[7] But in one six-week period he earned $2,000, whereas on the *Sun* he had never made more than $125 a week, which he claimed was more than any other New York drama critic then received.[8] He hoped that he could now concentrate on the Liszt study without worrying over living expenses. "I must get out a standard book," he wrote Harry Rowe Shelley, "or let the job to someone else."[9]

In August the Hunekers again went abroad. Every day for four weeks he climbed hills in Marienbad, managing to lose weight, which he put on again just as soon as he could reach a supply of Pilsner. At Weimar he interviewed more people who had known Liszt and called on Nietzsche's cultivated sister. "Can't you see me moving around like a nervous nightmare among the books, letters, pictures, busts, and all the treasures of this artistic house?" Huneker wrote Rosebault, adding that he had been pleasantly surprised to find three of his own books on the library table.[10] One afternoon he and Josephine took a five-hour hike to Jena because he wanted to see if the plum trees were still as plentiful as when Heine had walked from there to visit Goethe in Weimar. They were, he reported, but so were the stones, and he and Josephine were both laid up with sore legs.[11]

He attended operas, concerts, and a cycle of Ibsen and Hauptmann plays in Berlin and then went to Stockholm to interview Strindberg. According to Huneker's earlier account of the episode, after seeing Strindberg's third wife perform in a play written by her husband, he was taken to the dramatist's home by an actress and a manager whom he had met at a café. It was past midnight when they arrived, but the actress threw gravel at the bedroom window until Strindberg awoke. When he learned of Huneker's mission, he heartily cursed him and disappeared, though afterward he sent Huneker a signed photograph of himself.[12] Why an experienced interviewer would choose such an hour and method is a mystery—unless Huneker had drunk too much at the café while working up the courage to tackle Strindberg. He later concocted the story that Strindberg, who hated Ibsen, had been in a bad humor because that very night his wife had played Nora in *A Doll's House*.[13] (As Benjamin De Casseres remarked, Huneker, like Remy de Gourmont, "was not guilty of the vice of mediocre writers of always being sincere. . . . When he felt like lying beautifully he did so.")[14] Stopping in Paris before going home, Huneker had a more conventional—and successful—interview with Paul Hervieu, whose *Le Dédale* he considered the "most significant French play thus far of the new century."[15]

Upon his return to America in November 1904, he found in his mail a volume of poems in German written by a twenty-year-old student at the College of the City of New York, who had introduced himself to Huneker at the Irving Place Theater. The grandson of Edwina Viereck, the famous German actress rumored to have been the mistress of Kaiser Wilhelm I, and the son of Louis Viereck, a Socialist friend of Engels and Marx, George Sylvester Viereck had been born in Munich in 1884 and had come to America in 1897.[16] Saturating himself with the poetry of Swinburne and Wilde, he had imitated them in the book he had sent Huneker, who liked the erotic, musical verse and informed Viereck that he would try to mention it in print.[17] A year later, Huneker read several rather daring poetic plays by the young poet and advised him that if he wanted to be a successful dramatist he would have to "sacrifice—especially in America—all notes of defiance, of rebellion against conventions and write for the many-headed monster of a public. Before you were born, *cher poète*, the world had its head filled, indeed packed with the concepts of duty, of love, of religion, of patriotism. You can't expect to drive out these *grundideen* in a few years. It will take centuries."[18] Nevertheless, Huneker showed the plays to several publishers, and Brentano's finally accepted them. "I think [the book] is rotten," the head of the firm told Viereck, "but Huneker says it is good, so I suppose we must publish it."[19] *A Game of Love and Other Plays* appeared in 1906, launching Viereck's checkered career as the *enfant terrible* of American letters, the Truman Capote of his day.

Another young writer Huneker encouraged was Benjamin De Casseres, a precocious Philadelphia journalist—at seventeen he was writing editorials and drama criticism for the Philadelphia *Inquirer*[20]—who had come to New York in 1899 and was pouring out somber essays and poems cluttered with adjectives, adverbs, capital letters, and epigrams. In 1902 his complimentary letter to Huneker had started a correspondence between them which grew warmer when the critic learned that De Casseres was Jewish and had been a friend of his playmate and favorite cousin, Joe Gibbons.[21] Huneker advised the worshipful De Casseres, sixteen years his junior, to simplify his style and lighten his tone. "But you are young, in the Orphic mood," he wrote in March 1904. "It will wear away. Pessimism will prove as empty as optimism—nothing is really worth while but the brain—the emotions are rank swindles. If a man possesses his skull, he is master of the stars. (I am in the De Casseres vein myself, just now!)"[22] A few weeks later, Huneker won the struggling writer's lasting gratitude by quoting him in the *Sun* and pointing out his "aptitude for saying clever aphoristic things in a manner which recalls Emerson, Nietzsche and Benjamin Franklin."[23]

On a typical day in 1905, Huneker would play Joseffy technics, Bach, and Liszt on the piano for two hours in the morning—"In my senility I may be able to teach piano," he had remarked a couple of years earlier, "or—play something brisk and 'lively' when the ladies get hold of a 'gentleman friend' from Brooklyn who opens wine!"[24]—read (mostly Liszt literature) and walk in the afternoon, and go to the theater or write articles and fiction at night. Occasionally he would feel the need for a "bath" of music at Carnegie Hall, but he seldom wrote about music now. "I'm invading the magazines and earning about treble over my income on the daily newspaper, and I have leisure," he told Finck in February. ". . . Envy me. I fear I'll die young (!) because of the jealousy of the gods."[25]

Iconoclasts: A Book of Dramatists, consisting of Huneker's most substantial drama critiques for the *Sun*, appeared in March 1905. No American dramatist was included; which one, indeed, could join the company of Ibsen, Shaw, Strindberg, Maeterlinck, Hauptmann, and Sudermann? (Shortly after it came off the press, Walter Prichard Eaton, assistant drama critic of the New York *Tribune*, asked Huneker what his new book was about. "The drama," he replied. "American?" inquired Eaton. "I said the drama," Huneker retorted with a smile.)[26] Though thin paper and full-set pages made it look small, *Iconoclasts* actually ran to more than 110,000 words, and Huneker had to omit studies of Pinero, Yeats, Echegaray, and others, as well as a thirty-page bibliography.[27] He was especially proud of the long essay on Ibsen, which, he claimed, was the first complete criticism of that dramatist in English.[28]

The critics considered *Iconoclasts* his finest book so far, and for many years it remained his best-seller, with *Chopin* a close second.[29] Scribner's informed him that no other collection of essays published in America at the same time sold as many copies in a year—over 3,300.[30] As one literary historian noted, it was the "first book by a major American critic to consider the drama as a subject for criticism" and (with the exception of a book on French playwrights published in 1888 by Brander Matthews, whom Huneker respected and frequently quoted)[31] the "first piece of criticism in this country to give serious attention to the Continental dramatists."[32] The *Outlook*'s reviewer declared that "no other book in English [had] surveyed the whole field so comprehensively."[33] "We may not have great drama ourselves," exclaimed Pollard in *Town Topics*, "but let us be thankful that we have one who can discuss great drama in a great way."[34]

Zoë Akins, a nineteen-year-old Missouri girl with ambitions toward playwrighting, praised *Iconoclasts* in *Reedy's Mirror*. "Not William Archer himself understands Ibsen as does Mr. Huneker," she stated, and the pinch of salt with which he took Shaw was "exactly the right size."[35] Replying to a letter written by Reedy on Miss Akins' behalf, Huneker advised her to avoid the stage—"a hell, morally and physically (mentally is an absent quantity)"—and added that he was not in a position to help her. "For a man who has been in theatricals here for 20 years, my acquaintance with actors and managers is lamentably small. I go not in their purlieus; and I am thus enabled to steer clear of alliances that might prove hampering."[36] (The young woman did not follow his advice, and went on to win the Pulitzer Prize in drama thirty years later.)

No review of *Iconoclasts* was to have greater personal significance to Huneker than the one signed "H.L.M." in the Baltimore *Evening Herald* of May 6, 1905. Its author was an energetic young Baltimore newspaperman named Henry Louis Mencken, then completing the first book in English on George Bernard Shaw. Huneker did not take Shaw seriously enough, Mencken wrote, but his judgment of Shaw's plays was usually sound. He was, moreover, the first English-speaking commentator to make an honest effort to discover the truth about Ibsen. Though Huneker's style, like A. B. Walkley's, was too allusive, much of the book's suggestiveness came from that very quality. A more glaring fault, in Mencken's opinion, was Huneker's tendency to exaggerate (which was to become, incidentally, the trademark of Mencken's own style). Nevertheless, Mencken concluded, *Iconoclasts* placed its author in the front rank of contemporary critics. "In England none but Mr. Archer and Mr. Walkley are his equal; and saving only Mr. [John] Corbin . . . there is no man in America deserving of being considered with him."[37] Mencken sent this review to Huneker, who replied: "When it comes to good fellowship you can't better a newspaperman's amiability to his fellow sufferer."[38] Thus began a friendship of two exceptionally congenial persons which was to grow much closer a decade later.

En route to Italy in August 1905, Huneker met the popular novelist F. Marion Crawford, from whom he had once expected great things, but who, Huneker had remarked in the *Sun* in 1904, had "contributed largely to the world's dust heap of inartistic novels [though] he is a man of brains."[39] Yet Crawford invited the critic to his villa in Cocuemella, overlooking the Mediterranean, and during his stay in nearby Sorrento, Huneker frequently swam out to Crawford's anchored yacht.[40] From the esplanade of the Hotel Vittoria on the Bay of Naples, Huneker watched the gorgeous fireworks of Mount Vesuvius in eruption, but on September 8 he slept peacefully, much to his chagrin, while a severe earthquake shook Sorrento and destroyed eighteen villages in Calabria, killing four hundred persons. Hoping for a "scoop," he hired a battered automobile and a young chauffeur, who stopped at every drinking place on the winding hills of Calabria, picking up friends to ride in the front seat with him, and almost wrecked the car. The trip took two days longer than it should have, but Huneker was still in time to see the King and Queen of Italy as they inspected the devastated area.[41]

Settling in Rome for a month, he visited places where Liszt had lived and examined the city's art treasures. "The Vatican library is maddening," he wrote Krehbiel. "You pass from one masterpiece to a million more—black letter works on music, first editions of Dante, manuscripts before Christ. Indeed Christ and Apollo are mixed up here."[42] On October 5 he joined a large group of German pilgrims at an audience with Pope Pius X. After the entire group was photographed with His Holiness, Huneker was introduced to him as an American music critic. Having recently abolished eunuch singers and ordered Catholic choirs throughout the world to sing Gregorian chants, the Pope asked Huneker how he liked music in Rome. Huneker replied that at Saint Peter's, of all places, he had been surprised to hear a mass by Milozzi in which one singer sounded suspiciously high-voiced. (That any male should be castrated seemed, of course, blasphemous to Huneker.) When asked if the Gregorian chant was popular in America, he answered, more truthfully than tactfully, that he was afraid it was not, whereupon an ecclesiastical aide poked him in the ribs. "Feeling that I was lost," Huneker recalled, "I fell on my knees and kissed the magic ring and the interview was at an end."[43] "I'm no better Catholic than I was," he confessed to Krehbiel. "How can one believe in the pagan city! Even the mass takes on a pagan tone. Why even Conried's *Parsifal* circus developed a more pious atmosphere."[44] But the audience furnished good copy for the New York *Herald*.[45]

When Huneker returned from Europe in November, *Visionaries,* his second collection of short stories, had just been published. Though most of these stories were written—or first printed, at least—in 1901–5,[46] in many ways they resembled those in *Melomaniacs.* Some of the same motifs are present: music as an evil force ("A Master of Cobwebs"); the conflict between the artist and his wife ("The Eternal Duel"); the triangle ("The Tragic Wall"); anarchism in art ("The Spiral Road"); the possibilities of new arts ("The Eighth Deadly Sin"); the American in Europe ("A Mock Sun," whose hero, Huneker later admitted, was modeled on Maeterlinck).[47] Again, traces of Huneker's experiences and bits of self-portraiture are scattered throughout the book: the critic in "A Master of Cobwebs" writes "brilliantly of music in the terms of painting, of plastic arts in the technical phraseology of music";[48] the East Side slummer in "A Sentimental Rebellion" encounters the anarchist leader "Yetta Silverman" (Huneker sent Emma Goldman a copy of *Visionaries*);[49] the fat man at Marienbad, in "The Enchanted Yodler," who dreamed he was "a very skeleton for thinness";[50] the burglar-pianist in "The Cursory Light," who studied under Theodore Ritter in Paris, is deft at sleight-of-hand tricks. The most "personal" story is "The Eighth Deadly Sin"—founded, Huneker later told Joseph Conrad, on an actual experience with Mrs. Leonora Piper, the "greatest medium (and swindler) in America"[51]—whose protagonist anticipates the autobiographical hero of *Painted Veils*.

In other ways, however, *Visionaries* differs from *Melomaniacs*. Its stories are, on the whole, more serious, more erudite, more ambitious. With the exception of the "insane" poet and painter in "Rebels of the Moon" (one of his own favorites),[52] a defense of the "mad" artist in a commercial society and a comment on Nordau's theory of the relationship between genius and insanity, Huneker's characters are not so pathological nor the situations so bizarre as those in *Melomaniacs*. Only a few of his "visionaries"—dwellers in the realm of art and ideas—are musicians, and in the most interesting and substantial tales the emphasis is on theology rather than psychology, Huneker not only uncovering his knowledge of the Bible and the sacred writings of other religions but also engaging in speculations that would have sent his mother scurrying to church to pray for his soul. It is doubtful if the Pope would have chosen to chat with the writer of a story ("The Third Kingdom") in which a Roman Catholic priest wonders whether the entire account of Christ's life was not a work of art, a great drama created by Philo Judaeus and based only on a "slight foundation" of fact. Nor would His Holiness have welcomed, perhaps, an author who had imagined that Judas took Christ's place on the cross,[53] or been amused by Huneker's levity in depicting Antichrist as a Greek Catholic's infant son baptized by a Roman Catholic Monsignor and "disconsolately roaming the earth, unwilling to return to his fiery home for fear of a scolding."[54] The smile of any Christian Scientist entertained by this playfulness would have suddenly vanished when he read "Nada," Huneker's irreverent projection of the battle for power precipitated by the death— which actually occurred five years afterward—of the "female pope,"[55] Mary Baker Eddy.

Visionaries reveals Huneker's penchant for "panoramic" prose— highly colored, richly textured catalogues of sound-evoking odors in "The Eighth Deadly Sin," illusional fireworks in "The Spiral Road," and fantastic cosmological music in "The Tune of Time." He must have had these passages in mind when he explained to Brander Matthews that he had attempted the "hopeless task of interpreting the content of music in prose—in a word, the evocation of emotion and ecstasy instead of the orderly narration of events in time and space."[56] Moreover, the book is studded with Huneker's epigrams, similes, and witticisms:

"Music is the memory of love." Parisian prostitutes are "over-decorated and under-dressed creatures." "The violinist presses his strings as one kisses the beloved." "She adored slender men, believing that when fat came in at the door love fled out of the window." The sealed bottles contained "ruined, otherwise miscalled preserved, fruit." The Wagner-hater named his two Maltese cats "Tristan" and "Isolde" because "they make noises in the night." And a woman anarchist advises the puri-tanical philanthropist who scorns her offer to become his mistress to "turn literary and edit an American edition of *Who's Who in Hell*."[57]

Dubious about the salability of Huneker's unconventional fiction, Scribner's printed 1,500 fewer copies of *Visionaries* than of *Melo-maniacs*.[58] The firm's fears were justified, unfortunately, as reviewers generally found the work weird, bookish, decadent, and morbid. In what Huneker called the "*first* sensitive, sympathetic and fair review,"[59] Edward G. Marsh pointed out in the *Bookman* that many of the charac-ters, most of the subjects, and, above all, Huneker's use of fiction as a vehicle for conveying ideas were French, as the book's dedication to Remy de Gourmont and its Baudelairean motto suggested. Huneker was a skillful evocator of moods, Marsh observed, and if his stories were static and undramatic, they displayed the exuberant Gallic fancy of a man who "creates dazzling shapes and colours of human life and tosses them off carelessly as soap-bubbles."[60] The volume's sale, in any event, did not encourage Huneker to leave criticism for fiction. It would be his last venture with "fantastic, exotic, erotic, esoteric, idiotic themes," he wrote Scribner's in November 1905. "I'm done. Three months with Italian paintings and Greek marbles have worked the cure —a permanent one. . . . To hell with dank tarns of Auber—or Chopin —and for me, glorious conventionalities. All of which may not interest you but may make for greater sales!"[61]

Since he knew that one Broadway success could end his money worries and allow him to concentrate on the Liszt biography, Huneker toyed with the idea of writing a play. Later in November, he optimisti-cally told Scribner's, the publishers of Edith Wharton's *The House of Mirth*, that he could make an "acting play" of the novel in three months,[62] though it is unlikely that he knew enough about stagecraft to do this effectively.[63] ("Criticism is the worst possible school for dramatic writing," he had once remarked. "Criticism freezes the emo-tions, kills the creative instinct—when it exists.")[64] Clyde Fitch eventually collaborated with Mrs. Wharton on the dramatization, and Huneker remained on the audience side of the footlights.

The most memorable of the articles on literature and music Huneker wrote for the New York *Herald* in the spring of 1906 was a poignant account of a visit to his old friend Edward MacDowell. After resigning as chairman of the music department at Columbia University in 1904 because he felt that the arts were not being properly taught there —an act that Huneker had privately commended[65]—MacDowell had suffered a mental breakdown, which ended his career. Huneker attributed the illness to overwork, lamenting that an artist of such caliber should have undertaken the drudgery of teaching, and predicted that MacDowell's piano sonatas would keep his name alive. On the afternoon of Huneker's call, a lightning storm had reminded MacDowell of the thunderbolt in his piano poem, *The Eagle,* and he had gone on to tell Huneker about finding water with a hazel wand on his New Hampshire farm. It was appropriate, Huneker remarked, that the last words he had heard from America's most poetic composer were of "bright fire and running water and dream-music."[66] A year and a half later, Mac-Dowell was dead at the age of forty-six. (Afterwards, according to Huneker, Mrs. MacDowell gave him a medal of Franz Liszt—dated Weimar, 1880—which Liszt had given her husband, and Huneker proudly wore it on his watch chain.)[67]

Summarizing the theatrical season of 1905–6 in the *Metropolitan Magazine,* Huneker still deplored the plethora of mediocre plays in New York. The American première of Shaw's *Man and Superman* and *Mrs. Warren's Profession,* the delightful performance by Maude Adams in Barrie's *Peter Pan,* and the superlative acting of Alla Nazimova in a Russian production of Ibsen's *The Master Builder* (when Huneker first saw her, he recalled, he "sat up and said, like a true believer in the Koran of art, 'Alla be praised!' ")[68]—even these did not compensate for the dozens of tiresome dramas he had suffered through.[69] One of the few native dramatists he found promising was Belasco's young protégé Channing Pollock,[70] also a drama critic, who sometimes dined with Huneker at the Maison Favre, an inexpensive restaurant located behind the Metropolitan Opera House on Seventh Avenue. (Almost forty years later, Pollock, author of many Broadway successes, spoke reverently of Huneker as "the greatest figure in criticism in this country.")[71]

Instead of going abroad in the summer of 1906, Huneker visited famous Eastern resorts which he described in a series of articles in the *Herald,* whose dignified Sunday supplement featured a meticulous coverage of society. In Atlantic City he saw his first professional baseball game and wondered why in the world full-grown men scampered madly about in the hot sun after a small ball. In the White Mountains he observed that the only justification he could see for lawn tennis was that it might make a pianist's wrist more elastic. From swanky Newport, where he felt out of place, he confessed that wealthy men often bored him because all they knew was wool, iron, copper, steel, oil, or railroads, missing what was most significant and beautiful in life, art, and literature. In plebeian Coney Island his encounter with a starving Russian family elicited from Huneker a rare outburst against the existence of poverty. The evangelical, temperance spirit of Asbury Park reminded him that the Puritan temperament was a "morbid growth."[72] "In America," he remarked shortly afterward, "the eradication of the Puritan microbe will be no easy task, taught as we are in our arid schools and universities that the entire man ends at his collar bone."[73] Yet on seeing Italian road workers dawdling in the Berkshires, he reflected that if the Latin race had settled New England they would not have accomplished "such wonders of landscape gardening, such persistency in the founding of homes and the development of industries" as the "cruel and holy Pilgrim Fathers."[74]

He arrived in Saratoga in time for the opening of the plush gambling club operated by the fabulous Richard Canfield, whom Huneker had apparently met some years earlier. To supplement his grammar-school education, Canfield had studied art and literature while serving a term in prison, and afterward had used the proceeds of his lucrative casinos to acquire one of the finest private art collections and libraries in the country. His collection of paintings by his friend Whistler—whose portrait of the clerical-looking Canfield was ironically entitled "His Reverence"—was one of the two major Whistler holdings. Canfield preferred to spend his leisure time with distinguished bibliophiles and connoisseurs of art, but he never tried to conceal his profession.[75] Huneker not only admired his taste but also found his freedom from pose refreshing when "pious proud persons" were looting financial institutions and heading charity lists. Men like him were a public boon, Huneker asserted, for they relieved congested wealth of its symptoms of apoplexy.[76]

Back in New York in the fall, he continued to write drama criticism for the *Metropolitan Magazine* until the end of the year. Perhaps the play that interested him most during this period was William Vaughn Moody's *The Great Divide,* undoubtedly the best American drama of the season. Declaring that no play ever produced in America had so concerned itself with sex, Huneker was particularly pleased by its ending—the heroine returns to her husband not because she considers it her duty but because she loves him—which he considered honest and true to life.[77] Another highlight of the season was the first English *Peer Gynt,* starring Richard Mansfield, whom Huneker had urged to attempt modern drama, preferably Ibsen—the first American edition of whose plays Huneker expected to edit.[78] While rehearsing the play, Mansfield invited the critic to discuss it with him, but wishing to remain completely independent, Huneker regretfully declined. The production was picturesque, Huneker thought, but lacked the spirit of Ibsen.[79]

He planned to leave for Europe in early October 1906, to hear Strauss's new opera *Salome* in Dresden and Leipzig,[80] but the trip fell through, probably because he could not afford it. He needed money to meet Clio's demand for $1,000 for twelve-year-old Erik's education and support[81] and also to allow him to complete the Liszt book without worrying about living expenses. ("The thing most to be desired is the leisure of the rich," he had wistfully remarked while visiting opulent Southampton. "What books one could write!")[82] He had apparently received offers from newspapers earlier in the year,[83] but he felt that if he went back to daily journalism he could not do as good a job on Liszt as he wanted. After Scribner's decided not to publish in 1907 a collection of his miscellaneous essays on which he had hoped to get an advance, Huneker asked for $500 against future royalties on the biography, pointing out that he had been receiving about $250 a year from the sale of his six books.[84]

He probably did not get the advance, for when William Laffan suddenly offered him the position of art critic on the *Sun,* a position that promised a steady income and time for outside work, he accepted it. Before the end of 1906 Huneker, within six years the music, drama, and art critic of a distinguished American newspaper, had performed a feat of versatility almost unparalleled in American journalism, while in England only one man could match it—Huneker's famous "friend," George Bernard Shaw.

🦋 Thirteen

IRISH TEMPERS AND ENGLISH REVIEWERS

Huneker's criticism of Bernard Shaw led to one of the liveliest—and most annoying—episodes of his life. During the late 1880's and the 1890's, Huneker had read the critical writings of Shaw, who emerged as a playwright shortly before Huneker became a drama critic, though no evidence has turned up to support his claim that he wrote about Shaw as early as 1888[1] (and the earliest reference to Shaw—or, at any rate, the earliest significant mention of him, particularly as a music critic—in the *Musical Courier* was probably the one printed in 1893).[2] Huneker remembered persuading Marc Blumenberg to buy an article of Shaw's which was published, he said, in the *Courier* in 1890 or 1891, "the first musical 'story' by Bernard Shaw to appear in an American publication";[3] as usual, however, his dates are wrong, the article actually appearing in the first European number of the *Courier*, dated "September, 1894,"[4] which was reproduced and distributed in America with the regular issue of September 26 of that year—the same issue that reprinted a portion of Huneker's review for the *Recorder* of the world première of Shaw's *Arms and the Man*, presented in New York nine days earlier.

This long review, which must have introduced Shaw to many American readers,[5] was, in all likelihood, Huneker's first substantial criticism of G.B.S. In it he described the play as a "charming, clever study, allusive, subtle, full of glancing, mocking sidelights and unpleasant, gibing remarks." Shaw was a doubter with a firm belief in humanity, he declared, but hated conventions and pseudo-idealists and rebelled against "hampering notions bequeathed us by the dead." Though he had much to learn about stage technique, Shaw had the dramatic sense and would "turn out a strong play by and by." The dramatist had written him a short letter in which he sounded like a "testy fellow," Huneker reported, as he "ought to be, with all his brains."[6] Seven months later, after seeing *Arms and the Man* for the fourth time, Huneker maintained that despite its cynicism and its bold attack on the "most sacred institutions," it had "more heart, more human nature, more underlying humor than a shipload of Wilde's plays."[7]

In the summer of 1896 he met Shaw at Bayreuth and congratulated him for having demolished Nordau in his reply to *Degeneration*. "He is one of the most delightful men imaginable," wrote the "Raconteur." "Like most literary egoists, he is in private life exceedingly modest. . . . The slight snap of Irish brogue in his speech is simply charming. If you fancy him a cynic, a harsh critic of men and things, you are mistaken. He is kindness itself, and the Celtic humor that peeps out gives piquancy to his slightest utterance." He noted, too, that Shaw seemed pleased by Huneker's enthusiasm over *Arms and the Man*.[8]

Early in 1899, however, Huneker observed that Shaw had rewarded his "hysteria" over the play by stating somewhere that the few American critics who had liked it had failed to comprehend it as much as those who had uncompromisingly damned it. Having read Shaw's *Plays, Pleasant and Unpleasant* (1898), Huneker concluded that *Arms and the Man* was no more than a "bit of harmless dramatic Gilbertian satire, loose in construction and shadowy in characterization," while *The Devil's Disciple* was merely "sardonic melodrama," though Shaw had undeniably demonstrated his "marked dramatic genius" in *Mrs. Warren's Profession* and *Candida*—"plays written for the twentieth century . . . [with] brilliancy, force, immeasurable scorn, humor, beauty, plenty of dramatic situations and admirable technic." At the same time, Huneker heartily praised Shaw's prose style and wit in his "extremely entertaining" book *The Perfect Wagnerite*, even if his economic interpretation of the *Ring* was not very convincing.[9]

Shaw's piquant personality seemed an ideal target for Huneker's own wit. When the erstwhile antimarriage propagandist and socialist married a wealthy woman in 1898, Huneker wondered, tongue in cheek, whether Shaw would bother with literature now that he now longer had to work for a living. (A week later, however, Huneker went out of his way to mention Shaw's generosity to charity.)[10] Not long afterward, Huneker described the author of *The Perfect Wagnerite* as "a sort of Twentieth Century Siegfried in Jaeger flannels," and, when Shaw had become involved in municipal government, was amused by the picture of the Irishman as a town councilor "sitting solemnly at some conclave wherein fat Philistines discuss poor rates." If Shaw should also take to boiled shirts, religion, roast beef, and beer, it would be as startling as if Mark Twain were to become a high executive in the Christian Science Church. Yet "we must always take G.B.S. seriously," Huneker realized, "simply because he says we mustn't."[11]

Upon the publication of *Three Plays for Puritans* in 1901, Huneker took a long look at Shaw, whose impressionistic criticism, he pointed out, stemmed from France and was nothing new. "Being a professional egomaniac myself . . . I knew the trick," he remarked, "for I, too, had read Heine, Baudelaire, and all the *raconteurs* of the Parisian boulevards. . . . It is all a pose, this egotistical blaring of tin horns and elaborate panoramas of one's intimate feelings." Shaw was simply a "man of brains, of fine sensibilities, an inverted sentimentalist, a fierce romantic and an idealist" who, knowing that the shortest road to publicity in England was the sensational, followed it and became "mountebank in ordinary to the British public and Jester to the Fine Arts." Contradicting his earlier remarks, Huneker denied that any of Shaw's plays were dramatic masterpieces:

It is the old Shaw masquerading again, this time behind the footlights. He is still the preacher, the debater of the Fabian Society, the socialist, vegetarian, lycanthrope and Irishman of the early days. . . . He can't be radical enough for me, for his admirers, for the tribes of persons he has educated to think for themselves. What I object to is using an art form—for the drama is, or rather *was*, an art form—as a vehicle for instruction, for the dissemination of Shaw doctrines. . . . [He] has translated into Shawese the ideas of Ibsen, Fourier, Nietzsche, Wagner and other heroes of Continental thought. He is not himself either a profound or an original thinker. . . . His plays are sermons—clever, rollicking, crazy, sincere, witty, brilliant and perverse—withal sermons. . . . He is a better bishop than a playwright.[12]

Yet in March 1903, Huneker recommended Shaw's plays to theatrical managers who bewailed the dearth of good comedy—*Caesar and Cleopatra,* he said, would "make the fortune of a clever pair of comedians"—and two months later he wrote a long article for the *Sun* on "The Quintessence of Shaw."[13] That summer Shaw warned Huneker in London never again to call him "benevolent," for since Huneker had mentioned Shaw's softheartedness, the latter complained, half the beggars of London were pestering him. Huneker reported that Shaw still looked as if a "half-raw beefsteak and a mug of Bass would do him a world of good." Privately he told Ziegler that Shaw was "very much pleased" with the *Sun* article.[14] At the end of October 1903, Huneker remarked in the *Sun* that although Shaw's newly published *Man and Superman* was delightful reading, it seemed unactable. His criticism that the play petered out into "talk, talk, talk" was sound enough, for he had no way of knowing that the last act would be omitted in the stage version. But his other comments were saucy and less than clairvoyant:

It is the work of a man whose mission in life (i.e., anarchism) has withered in his hands. Matrimony, one of the pursuing sex, may have thus deleted the life force of our Irish Ibsen. . . . Some day in the far future, let us hope, when the spirit of Bernard Shaw shall have been gathered to the gods, his popular vogue may be an established fact. Audiences may flock to sip wit, philosophy and humor before the footlights of the Shaw theatre; but unless the assemblage be largely composed of Shaw replicas, of overmen and underwomen . . . it is difficult to picture any other variety listening to *Man and Superman.*[15]

Less pleased by this review than by the earlier *Sun* piece, Shaw wrote Huneker on January 4, 1904:

I was sorry not to see more of you on your visit here, as you struck me as being a likeable old ruffian. My wife, since your review of *Man and Superman,* will not allow that you have a spark of intelligence, but you must come and mollify her in person when you are over next. It always amuses me to see Candida stirring up oceans of sentiment. I think I see you wallowing in it. . . . Who is Arnold Daly? Is he anything to the late Augustin?[16]

Shaw may have read Huneker's favorable notice of *Candida,* which actor Arnold Daly had presented in a trial matinee a month earlier. "Ten years ago such a grasping of the dramatist's intention would not have been possible," Huneker had asserted, "for Shaw was regarded as a cynic, a burlesquer in the robes of W. S. Gilbert. To-day we know him as something far more serious. He has educated his public as well as his actors." A few days later, Huneker had explained that the profound and far-reaching theme of *Candida* was: "Shall a married man expect his wife's love without working for it, without deserving it?"[17] After a regular run was announced for the play, Huneker predicted that when the public fully savored Shaw's witty, ironic comedies, it would cry for him[18]—and, indeed, *Candida* ran for 133 performances on Broadway and created a Shaw vogue in America.

Replying on April 6, 1904, to Huneker's request for the playwright's own interpretation of Candida, Shaw referred to his heroine as "that immoral female," who

seduces Eugene just exactly as far as it is worth her while to seduce him. She is a woman without "character" in the conventional sense. Without brains and strength of mind she would be a wretched slattern and voluptuary. She is straight for natural reasons, not for conventional ethical ones. Nothing could be more cold-bloodedly reasonable than her farewell to Eugene: "All very well, my lad; but I don't quite see myself at 50 with a husband of 35." It's just this freedom from emotional slop, this unerring wisdom on the domestic plane, that makes her so completely mistress of the situation.

And Shaw added: "As I should certainly be lynched by the infuriated Candidamaniacs if this view of the case were known, I confide it to your discretion."[19]

Huneker suggested another meeting with Shaw in London and asked for permission to print these remarks on Candida. Shaw answered on August 12, 1904, that he would be glad to see him in October, but that it would be useless to print the truth about Candida, for it would be considered an obvious invention of Huneker's.[20] In the August *Metropolitan Magazine*, however, before receiving this answer, Huneker had already quoted Shaw's interpretation of Candida.[21] If Shaw saw the article, he may have chastised Huneker in a postcard which the latter, taking the cure in Marienbad, described to the editor of *Success Magazine* on September 13 as "highly abusive but entertaining. He told me to stick to sawdust and water and I would not have to go to Marienbad for a reduction. But he only weighs 90 lbs. and looks like a stick of yellow taffy."[22]

In April 1905, shortly after the appearance, in *Iconoclasts*, of an enlarged version of "The Quintessence of Shaw," *Success* published another Huneker article on Shaw, in which he labeled *Candida* "diabolically clever" but "not an astounding play"; *The Philanderer* "futile"; *Mrs. Warren's Profession* "very strong, but the subject . . . a hopeless one for exploitation on the English speaking stage." (Six months later, Arnold Daly and his leading lady were arrested and charged with disorderly conduct after presenting one performance of *Mrs. Warren's Profession,* and though they were acquitted, the play was not seen again in America until 1907.)[23] *The Devil's Disciple,* Huneker continued, was "Voltaire smothered in melodrama"; *Captain Brassbound's Conversion* "a dime novel with an Ibsen ending"; and *Man and Superman* an "awful mess . . . overflowing with [wit and wisdom] but . . . not a play." Shaw's wittiest work, he maintained, was *Caesar and Cleopatra.* Shaw had the dramatic gift, but "casts it aside as worthless and hampering, so eager is he to make mouthpieces of his characters (his subsidiary characters, free to move without the counterweight of his theories, are most engaging and vivid)." Yet, concluded Huneker, one could not help "admiring and liking this wonderful bundle of contradictions, this perverse, intellectual, big-hearted, gifted ironical buccaneer . . . a wild Irishman sailing the seas of life in quest of moral plunder."[24]

The article's subheading—supplied by the editor, Huneker later insisted[25]—included the phrase "Rise from an Irish Peasant Lad." On May 9, 1905, Shaw jokingly informed Huneker that these words had compromised his sister's social position in Germany. "The Shaws peasants!" he exclaimed. "Good God! You know not what you say."[26] In the same month, Shaw wrote a preface—reproduced in the *Metropolitan* in January 1906[27]—for his reprinted novel *The Irrational Knot*; in it appeared this passage:

I protest that I will not suffer James Huneker or any other romanticist to pass me off as a peasant boy qualifying for a chapter in Smiles' *Self Help,* or a good son supporting a helpless mother, instead of a stupendously selfish artist leaning with the full weight of his hungry body on an energetic and capable woman. No, James; such lies are not only unnecessary, but fearfully immoral, besides being hardly fair to the supposed peasant lad's parents. My mother worked for my living instead of preaching that it was my duty to work for hers; therefore take off your hat to her, and blush.

At this point he added, in a footnote:

James, having read the above in proof, now protests he never called me a peasant lad; that being a decoration by the sub-editor. The expression he used was a "poor lad." This is what James calls tact. After all, there is something pastoral, elemental, well aerated about a peasant lad. But a mere poor lad; really, James, really!!![28]

Reviewing *Iconoclasts* in the London *Daily News* in April 1905, G. K. Chesterton found it witty and entertaining, if a bit too anarchistic for his conservative, Catholic taste. But he objected to the interpretation of Candida which Shaw had sent Huneker and which had been incorporated into "The Quintessence of Shaw" with the observation that its publication had been left up to his judgment. *"Candida*

always appeared to me not only as the noblest work of Mr. Shaw,"
wrote Chesterton, "but as one of the noblest, if not the noblest, of modern plays; a most square and manly piece of moral truth. . . . I assure
[Shaw] . . . that if he imagines he understands the character of Candida he is quite mistaken."[29] Three months later, A. B. Walkley, who
had written Huneker that he had enjoyed *Iconoclasts*,[30] described it in
the London *Times* as "a capital book, lively, informative, suggestive,"
though he disagreed with some of the opinions in it, particularly on
Shaw. Walkley pointed out, in passing, that Huneker had "blithely"
printed letters (*sic*) Shaw had confided to his discretion.[31]

At this juncture, thirty-three-year-old Max Beerbohm entered the
scene. Huneker never met or corresponded with him, but in 1895, when
Beerbohm was visiting America with his then more famous half-brother,
Beerbohm Tree, Huneker had described him as a "clever young man of
the Wilde-Beardsley type," a writer of "fantastically-garbed prose" popular with readers of the *Yellow Book*. (Beerbohm recalled, almost sixty
years later, that he had never read these words and that even if he had,
they would not have angered him or prejudiced him against Huneker.)[32]
At the same time, Huneker had told the famous story then making the
rounds in London: Beerbohm had announced that he was writing a
book to be called "The Brothers of Great Men," and was naturally
asked, "Aren't you the brother of Mr. Beerbohm Tree?" "Yes," he
replied, "he will be in it."[33] When the "Incomparable Max" replaced
Shaw as drama critic of the *Saturday Review* in 1898, Huneker had
identified him as "an insolent, clever person, who is brother to Beerbohm Tree, the actor," adding: "Mr. Beerbohm is given to acting,
too."[34]

Soon thereafter, however, Huneker had acquired more respect for
Max. In 1899, for example, he applauded Beerbohm's comparison of
London's two chief drama critics, agreeing with him that the outspoken,
allusive Walkley was more readable than the kindly, judicial William
Archer, and by 1902, indeed, Huneker was referring to Beerbohm as
a "brilliant drama critic and prose master."[35] As a matter of fact, the
two men had much in common. Though Beerbohm's tastes were more
romantic and sentimental than Huneker's (he preferred Jones to Pinero
and was not wholeheartedly in sympathy with Ibsen), he, like Huneker,
was a stylist, an individualist, an antisocialist, and a hedonistic skeptic
with a generally amiable disposition.[36]

But in July 1905, Max chose not to be amiable. Motivated solely (he claimed) by "deep dislike" of what seemed to him Huneker's "violently sensational" way of writing,[37] he blasted *Iconoclasts* (which Huneker had sent him) in a *Saturday Review* article ominously headed "A 'Yellow' Critic." He pretended that he had never heard of the American, who was apparently a young man—Huneker was actually fifteen years older than Beerbohm—for whom there might, therefore, still be hope:

Vitality he has, and ability. He may do very well in the future. I speak not of the immediate future. In the immediate future he will have to shape himself—learning to think, learning to write. Nor is this the first process for him to undergo: He must begin by *un*shaping himself. And this, I fear, will be no easy matter. For he is (considering his tender years) an extraordinarily hardened and perfect specimen of the sensational journalist. His writing is like a series of separate headlines which have, through a printer's error, been printed consecutively in small type. . . . The writing is so bad that you have generally to read between the lines to discover what Mr. Huneker means; and then, as often happens, he means nothing, and you naturally resent the waste of your time. . . . There is a difference (and I want to impress on Mr. Huneker the difference) between newspaper articles and a book. . . . [He] is not merely careless in form; his carelessness in matter is even worse. Self-repetition and self-contradiction don't much matter in "yellow" journalism. . . . If the doing of good work gives him no pleasure for its own sake, he ought to try to imagine that his readers won't stand bad work. . . . If he is not a young man, and so is beyond reclaim, he will yet be useful as an example to those of his young compatriots who are going in for literature. A drunken helot, even though he drink for drink's sake rather than for duty's, ought nowhere to be discouraged by mankind.[38]

Utterly disregarding Huneker's real service to Shaw in America, Beerbohm cited the essay on the playwright as a sample of Huneker at his worst, despite—or perhaps because of—the fact that he himself had once expressed opinions on Shaw similar to Huneker's. In 1899, for example, Beerbohm declared that the characters of *Mrs. Warren's Profession* lacked humanity.[39] In 1901 he remarked that Shaw did not have "enough of the specific art sense of writing" and that his work possessed the quality of a public speaker rather than a writer.[40] Two years later, while criticizing the published version of *Man and Superman* (which, he predicted, would be ineffective on the stage), Beerbohm complained that Shaw was "always trying to prove this or that thesis, and the result is that his characters (as soon as he differentiates them, ever so little, from himself) are the merest diagrams. Having no sense for life, he has, necessarily, no sense for art."[41] In 1904, however, when he praised *John Bull's Other Island*,[42] Beerbohm began to change, though he never fully made up, his mind about Shaw.[43] And in 1905, after seeing a production of *Man and Superman*, he made a celebrated recantation[44]—modified afterward, to be sure, by certain qualifications. In heaping insults now upon Huneker, Beerbohm, indeed, had all the enthusiasm of a recent, if somewhat temporary, convert.

No one can deny, surely, that Huneker's style is sometimes inconsecutive and contradictory, a quality emphasized in "The Quintessence of Shaw" because of his equivocal attitude toward the playwright. But even if Beerbohm's strictures were partly deserved, the incisive cleverness of his attack did not conceal its ugly tone. At least two American magazines bristled at what Mencken later termed an "idiotic assault."[45] Percival Pollard asserted in *Town Topics* that it sprang from Beerbohm's pique at the "unfailing success Mr. Huneker achieves in being readable on no matter what subject,"[46] while Harry Thurston Peck pointed out in the *Bookman* that though Beerbohm had bared Huneker's literary vices, he had not spoken a word about the many good things in *Iconoclasts*. Beerbohm was "as much addicted to under-thinking as Mr. Huneker is to over-stating," Peck wrote, "and he presented a broad, fair mark for a rejoinder if Mr. Huneker can only be induced to make one."[47] In the *Outlook* of November 25, 1905, an unsigned article on Shaw is headed "Yellow Dramatist," and elsewhere in the same issue Royal Cortissoz (later Huneker's friend) refers to Shaw as a "yellow" journalist[48]—both allusions, one suspects, to Beerbohm's review. Huneker objected to being called a yellow critic who wrote like a "drunken helot" because, as he eventually remarked, "every one knew that my color was purple" and "helots, drunk or sober, did not write at all,"[49] but he refused to answer Beerbohm publicly until long afterward.

Meanwhile, Shaw was describing the biographical remarks in "The Quintessence of Shaw" to Archibald Henderson, his future American biographer, as "pure romance."[50] (Huneker *was* "very careless" in his statements, Henderson himself recalled, but Shaw was "prone to attribute gross inaccuracies to anyone who made just *one* slip!")[51] Shaw disclaimed responsibility for having inspired Beerbohm's scarification, but he apparently approved of it, for on August 13, 1905, he wrote Huneker a long letter almost as vilifying as the review:

You really must come over here and have your mind properly trained: you will never be anything but a clever slummocker in America.
My object in the Irrational Preface was simply to relieve its fundamental

gravity by getting as much fun out of you as possible. That is the only use I can put you to at present.

The fact is, you are a horribly inaccurate ruffian, because your head is full of romantic idolatries, and you never observe anything. I have to defend myself against being set up in your temple with six arms, a gilt navel, and fat folded legs. You inform the world that I am a fierce ascetic, a misogynist, a good man, a heroic fighter against terrible odds. You lie. You say that nearly all my earnings went to the needy, and that this was "practical socialism." You lie. You say I lived on carrots, cabbage & brown bread. You lie. You say that the costume & the carrots were adopted because they were cheap and the money was needed by poorer folk. You lie. Mind: I do not contradict you because these statements are wounding or flattering to me, edifying or demoralizing to the world. I contradict them simply because, as a matter of fact, they are lies—gratuitous, thoughtless, shameless venal lies.

Worse, they are stupidities. This is not what men are like. You are quite right in saying that I have led the life of a saint: that is my trade. But a saint is not what you allege me to be. There is a convention that saints are disinterested and ascetic just as there is a convention that sailors are frank and generous and unsuspicious. You can get your living by picking up these conventions & retailing them at so much per thousand words. But you can also get your living by understanding saints and sailors and telling the truth about them. That is the only way in which you can interest me. When you try to make out that whilst I pose as Diogenes (I dont) I am at heart just the same sloppy, maudlin, coward-making-a-virtue-of-it as the feeblest of my readers, I fly at you promptly for debasing the moral currency. I am really a coward speaking with authority of the dangers of cowardice, a sort of converted prig who has found out the weaknesses of the current morality by practicing it, a voluptuary who founds himself not on the infinite illusions of a monastic imagination, but on a sufficiency of actual adventures, and a dozen other things that I have not time to enumerate. I confide this, not to your idiotic journalistic indiscretion, but to your discretion, if you have any. Walkley, in the *Times*, was quite right in his view of my phrase. To publish a letter confided to your discretion is an infamy that only an American journalist could perpetrate. I meant that you should know the view of Candida that I put before you; that you should criticize with that knowledge; that you should be guided by it (one way or the other); but I did not mean you to sling it into print thoughtlessly with its own words making it quite clear that it was not written for publication. In Walkley's own published collection of *Playhouse Impressions* there is a masterly critical passage founded on just such a letter; so that he spotted the state of the case at once. Of course it doesnt matter to me, because, knowing you to be an incontinent naive sort of a big baby, I knew the risk I ran, and even foresaw as an agreeable possibility that you would blurt the thing out & give me a chance to lecture you about it. But it does matter a bit to you. Use letters with discretion & you can publish more than ever was in them. Use them indiscreetly & you will shock the *Times* & become an outcast.—Someday I shall talk to you about music. . . . Last winter I heard Liszt's Faust Symphony played for the first time in London—old fashioned before it was born—an obsession with the new chords of the fifties. I have also a lot to say about your blathering but readable heretics. . . . Call on your way to or from home.[52]

Infuriated by this additional abuse, Huneker, who had just been editing a collection of Shaw's dramatic criticisms for Brentano's,[53] the American publisher he had recommended to the playwright in 1904,[54] answered Shaw heatedly in a letter which, unfortunately, has not survived.[55] Shaw's response on September 16 was hardly less patronizing than his previous letter:

Your chest now being relieved, we can resume cordial relations.

Need I say that I have not seen nor communicated with Max or Walkley since your book appeared? It was an excellent advertisement for me; and I got all the reviews, which were much more favorable than you deserved. Walkley went solely on your own quotation. . . . Max, who is not a Jew but a Dutchman, was very sweet indeed; and I should have been proud had I really inspired his article, which was richly merited.

The reason I call you a slummocker and heap insults on you is that you are very useful to me in America and quite friendly; consequently you must be educated, or you will compromise me. Your work is very good as far as it is a record of your first hand impressions from works of art. All the rest of it is execrable. All your assumptions as to the part of life that is not projected upon your sensorium by an artist's magic lantern are picked up out of the gutter, and not even pieced together with common care. Your impressions of compositions are those of an artist; but your composers are melodramatic figments. Now as you must, to make a really complete critical essay, continually provide a background of faithfully painted world to embroider your impressions on, you cannot use a shoddy background without spoiling the effect of your embroidery. And this is what you always do, and always will do until you come to London and are ground down by contact with men who dislike and despise cleverness, but who know in a prosaic way, a good deal, and will not value you until they are persuaded you know all that they do and more. Americans think cleverness fun, and play the game with you. Englishmen think it idiotic, and stare contemptuously until you are perfect in the prosaic part of your business. And that is what you want. The Englishmen not being available, you must put up with me. I know a lot more than you do, especially about music. What I said about Liszt's *Faust* is exactly accurate. Go and study the operas of Cornelius (delightful music) if you want to understand that particular moment.

Like all romantic men, when you discover the real man behind the work of art you think him a low ruffian. Thus, A.B.W. is a l.r.; Max is a l.r.; I am a l.r. &c. I assure you we are not. Your ideal men are illusions; your real men are disillusions: both equally false and hackneyed. Stick to me; and I will improve you. . . . If you return to London do not be afraid: I shall not eat you.[56]

One doubts that Huneker was this much of a romanticist—on the contrary, indeed, he often examined artists with a singularly unromantic, even clinical, eye—or that Shaw knew more about music than Huneker, who later took pains to point out that Liszt's *Faust Symphony* was not old-fashioned, as Shaw had stated, but was a pioneering work to which *The Barber of Bagdad*, by Liszt's pupil Peter Cornelius, was indebted.[57] Who but two such versatile and erudite Irishmen would argue over how much they knew? Believing he deserved more than humiliating lectures from a man for whom he had done so much in America, Huneker was not amused by the comedy of this exchange. In the April 1906 issue of the *Metropolitan*, Huneker answered the "merry little jest" on his romanticism which Shaw had made in the preface to *The Irrational Knot*. Shaw himself was the most perfect specimen of a Romantic, Huneker wrote, for "all reformers are Romantics. . . . Like all Romantic writers, Shaw is incapable of character creation. . . . He worships himself romantically, and when he does not write of himself, he no longer interests. . . . If he were a close observer of life as well as a superb satirist, he would be an objective dramatist."[58]

In his calm, friendly, if not warmly enthusiastic, preface to Shaw's *Dramatic Opinions and Essays*, published in 1906, Huneker did not mention their quarrel directly, but he took a mild slap at Shaw by implying that his criticism, "his best work, the very pith of the man," was more durable than his plays. One can read between the lines, moreover, in his description of the playwright as "a man of wrath and humors, a fellow of infinite wit, learned without pedantry, and of a charm —if one finds caviar and paprika charming." Yet Huneker acknowledged that Shaw's assaults on Shakespeare were really a plea for a saner critical attitude toward the bard, and that Shaw had been a Nietzschean before discovering the philosopher. At the end of his introduction, Huneker remarked briefly that Shaw's successor on the *Saturday Review* was that "gentle mid-Victorian, Max Beerbohm," an ironic nod, of course, to Beerbohm's slashing review of *Iconoclasts*.[59]

Pursuing Huneker relentlessly, Max pounced upon the English edition of this collection. In the *Saturday Review* of April 27, 1907, he found fault with the printing and format:

Scarcely less disfiguring to the book [he continued] is Mr. Huneker's intro-
duction. The writings of Mr. Huneker are, I am told, admired in America.
One sample of them—a pretentious and loudly muzzy book whose title I
don't remember—I gibbeted in these columns a year or two ago. If really
Americans are so illiterate as to think well of Mr. Huneker, then doubtless
Mr. Shaw stands in need of an introduction to them. But in England Mr.
Shaw needs no introduction; he has introduced himself so often and so ad-
mirably. And it is absurd that he should be introduced by a gentleman who
is almost wholly unknown here and so far as he is known merely excites de-
rision. When I devoted an article to him, I was under the impression that
he was a very young man, who might be educated to better courses. But I
learned later that he was well on in middle age; and thus it is not surprising
that his introduction of Mr. Shaw shows no advance in thought or in style.
His jocularity is as dismal as ever, and the platitudes howled by him are as
incoherent. Only in one passage does he express tolerably a not obvious
thing, and that is where he refers to myself as "a gentle mid-Victorian."
There you have a rather witty half-truth—one solid speck of brightness in
a dull deliquium. But it does not justify the deliquium. If Mr. Shaw wanted
a foil to his own journalism—an illustrious example of "how not to do it"—
he could not have chosen a better one than Mr. Huneker.[60]

Beerbohm was evidently not impressed by Shaw's statement—printed
in the book—that Huneker had done a better job of selecting and editing the dramatic essays than Shaw himself would have done.[61]

Angered by this notice, Huneker, nevertheless, made no direct public
reply. When an English edition of his next book, *Egoists,* was being
prepared in 1909, however, he asked Scribner's to request the English
publishers not to send a copy to the *Saturday Review*; if Max wanted
to attack *this* book, let him buy it.[62] (The unsigned and unfavorable
notice of *Egoists* which appeared in the *Saturday Review* on July 3,
1909, under the heading of "A Flamboyant New-Yorker" is in the Beerbohm vein, though he did not remember writing it.)[63] Moreover, Huneker was obviously still miffed at Max in 1910, when he remarked, in an
article that ridiculed the ignorance of H. G. Wells and Chesterton on
matters of art: "They don't know even as much as Max Beerbohm."[64]

Huneker never quite forgave either Shaw or Beerbohm for injuring
his vanity, and Shaw especially became his *bête noire*. The revival of
Mrs. Warren's Profession in the spring of 1907 reminded Huneker of
the lack of sexuality in Shaw's plays, though *Caesar and Cleopatra* delighted him so much that he almost forgot to remark that Shaw's chief
fault was his lack of architectonic. "How many personalities has St.

Bernard?" he wondered.[65] In September 1908, Shaw was the butt of
Huneker's satirical fantasy—twice reprinted—in which Hugo, Baudelaire, Flaubert, Sainte-Beuve, Richard Strauss, Wagner, Maeterlinck,
Manet, Ibsen, and Tolstoy appear at a banquet tendered to Shaw.
"Without me, and my books and plays," the guest of honor says to the
assemblage, "you would, all of you, be dead in earnest—dead literature as well as dead bones." Then Nordau enters, accompanied by Max
"Birnbaum,"[66] and everyone immediately scampers for cover under the
table.[67]

In 1910 Huneker denounced the insincerity of the book on Shaw by
G. K. Chesterton, a "much more gifted man" than Shaw[68]—who had
seemingly been horrified by Chesterton's inaccuracies, too, though he
considered it the best work of literary art he had yet provoked[69]—and
in 1912 he gleefully roasted Archibald Henderson's biography of the
playwright, observing that Henderson had to be a hot fanatic to write
so earnestly about his hero without seeing through the "very large
crevice in the millstone." "Perhaps when the author becomes an anti-
Shavian, as do most of the tribe," Huneker added, "he may refute
Shaw in fewer pages; that is, unless Shaw gets ahead of him and de-
nounces him as a devil's disciple."[70] (Shaw had already engaged in a
public dispute with Henderson over the book.)[71] When asked, a few
months before his death, about Huneker's apparently incredible claim
that Shaw had originally been grooming *him* as his biographer,[72] Shaw
answered obliquely that Huneker was "so recklessly inaccurate, and his
books about me so full of misprints, that they were worse than useless
to me. They were never ungenerous." And then Shaw quoted a line
from "The Quintessence of Shaw": "Bravery is Bernard's trump card."[73]

During the second decade of the century, Huneker usually managed
to spank Shaw and praise him at the same time. "The real Shaw," he
wrote in 1914, was a "kindly, humorous fellow—a reactionary chock-full
of old fashioned notions and exuding sentiment and prejudice of the
approved British variety"—who *might* have written "real plays, not
country lyceum discussions punctuated by clownish humor."[74] Four
months later, forty-seven years before *My Fair Lady* became the musical with the longest run in Broadway's history, Huneker described
Shaw's *Pygmalion* as a comic-opera libretto "fairly begging for a musical setting," weak though it was in characterization and "piffling" in

subject.[75] *Androcles and the Lion,* he remarked in 1915, was lowbrow—but vastly amusing.[76]

When Huneker wrote *Steeplejack* in 1918, the old insults still rankled. Realizing that the Shaw letters would enliven his autobiography, he quoted (without permission, it appears)[77] excerpts from them in the serialized version published in the Philadelphia *Press*—omitting, however, some of the most derogatory statements about himself.[78] In his full account of his relations with Shaw and Beerbohm, he answered their charges with traces of anger and almost petulant boastfulness, thus revealing how deeply he had been hurt. He explained, for example, that Shaw need not have offered to help him meet the "advanced spirits" in Vienna because he had already met them on his own hook.[79] As for Beerbohm's opinion of *Iconoclasts,* it was enough to say that other critics, including Remy de Gourmont, had disagreed with it.[80] Huneker, indeed, was more than generous to Max, whose "too few books," he wrote, "have been a source of joy to me as they are to lovers of prose as palatable as dry sherry. . . . [He] is a born classic, as readers of the delightful *Works* and *Zuleika Dobson* need not be told."[81] But Huneker could not resist one further attempt to even the score. Recalling that Beerbohm had been outraged by the statement in "The Quintessence of Shaw" that "if Mr. Shaw is brilliant on bran, what would he not be on beef and beer?" he quipped: "Perhaps I might have asked that Mid-Victorian if his imitation of the essay style of Charles Lamb did [not] sometimes turn out cold mutton."[82] Huneker was less gentle on Shaw, whom he blasted as a "sham and supersham slummocker" (the word Shaw had once applied to him) and a "Celtic Thersites . . . [whose] lack of virility permeates his dramatic characters."[83] The "sterile" Shavian drama, intended for half-baked amateurs, propagandists, and quacks, was moribund, Huneker concluded, and "like caviar, fly-blown, it will go down to the mother of Dead Dogs as do all such problem plays."[84]

Shaw proved so amiable, however, in allowing Huneker to print excerpts from the letters in the book form of the autobiography that Huneker decided to delete these angry phrases,[85] though his comments on Shaw remained strong enough. And one curious misprint was perpetuated in *Steeplejack*: in his letter of August 13, 1905, Shaw had clearly referred to himself as a "converted" prig, but in both the *Press* and the book the adjective reads "conceited."[86] Huneker may simply have made a mistake in transcribing the letter (at least two other words were misread), or the compositor may have erred in deciphering Huneker's difficult handwriting. One would prefer to think that he was not so bent on revenge that he was willing to indulge in the inaccuracy that Shaw had condemned. It may not have flattered him, but, at any rate, Huneker had the last word, during his lifetime, in the exchange of insults with his most distinguished "adversary."

℀ *Fourteen*

THE ART CRITIC

In August 1904, Huneker had written Charles Rosebault, now business manager of the *Sun*: "If I knew as much of painting as William Laffan Esq., I would get a job as critic on the *Sun*. But I don't; so I didn't ask for it."[1] The *Sun*'s "owner," a peppery Irishman with heavy spectacles (one eye was glass) and a brooding manner,[2] was a connoisseur of European art, particularly of the period from the Middle Ages to the end of the Renaissance, and an authority on Oriental porcelains. Familiar with all the famous public and private collections on two continents, he served as a trustee of the Metropolitan Museum and an influential member of its committee on acquisitions as well as the confidential adviser of J. P. Morgan, Henry Walters, and other prominent collectors. His tastes were conservative, but he was no diehard opponent of modernism,[3] and as an amateur sculptor, painter, and etcher, he knew at first hand something of the artistic impulse. As the *Sun*'s witty and colorful art critic, beginning in the late 1870's, he had convinced the skeptical senior Dana that a man who understood art could also write well about it,[4] and when Laffan himself assumed control he saw to it that the *Sun*—especially the *Evening Sun*, whose Dublin-born art critics, Charles FitzGerald and, a little later, Frederick James Gregg, were among the earliest and best-informed supporters of modern American painting—gave fuller coverage to the arts than any other newspaper in the country.[5]

Laffan probably knew that Huneker had studied pictures in America and Europe and had discussed them occasionally in the *Musical Courier*, that he collected engravings in a small way (Huneker had bought several good prints at the sale of his father's collection in 1894),[6] and that he was friendly with artists, and Laffan certainly knew that Huneker could write entertainingly. And so at the end of 1906, apparently on the recommendation of the circumspect FitzGerald—who was later appalled to discover Huneker quoting verbatim, and without acknowledgment, from art reference books[7]—Laffan hired Huneker as the *Sun*'s art critic and editorial writer, the arrangement being that Huneker would write his copy at home, submitting it directly to Edward Mitchell, the editor in chief, and would be paid at the rate of $20 per column.[8]

He made his debut as a regular art critic in mid-December 1906,[9] and soon three or four of his unsigned articles were appearing every week, many of them headed "Around the Galleries" and dealing with exhibitions in New York and other Eastern cities, while others were studies of individual painters, etchers, engravers, and sculptors. "Please don't say anything about the *Sun* job to your painter friends," he wrote Ziegler on December 26. "I want to get a good grip with my toenails in the sandy soil of American art before I sign or splurge. Mr. L. . . . wishes anonymity for the present."[10] Though all his art criticism during the next six years—at least 425 articles—remained unsigned, the secret was out by February 9, 1907, when the editor of the *American Art News* identified Huneker as the author of the *Sun*'s "charmingly written" essays and notes.[11] "It strikes me that 'Truthful James' or the Devil wielding his pen has come back to you," Frank Jewett Mather, Jr., the well-known art critic of the New York *Evening Post* and the *Nation*, wrote Laffan from Italy a month later. "You are lucky in getting a man who is at once so scholarly . . . so convinced of the value of the new movements and so thoroughly *au courant*."[12] Huneker was pleased by this letter, which Mitchell showed him, and flattered by the offers he soon received from several magazines to write about art, even if he could not accept them because the *Sun* had the sole rights to his work in this field.[13]

Won over to Impressionism by the famous exhibition brought to New York in the spring of 1886 by Durand-Ruel,[14] Huneker favored modern painters from the very beginning. "A man is to be pitied who is out of joint with his own artistic times," he remarked in October 1907. "He has no present or future—only a vague past."[15] New painters should not be measured by the extent of their conformity to tradition. "Let us study each man according to his temperament," he declared, "and not ask ourselves whether he chimes in with some older man's music. . . . To miss modern art is to miss all the thrill and excitement that our present life holds." If more masterpieces by contemporary painters were shown in this country, he maintained, pictures that seemed old-fashioned to Parisians would not strike New Yorkers as ultramodern; in matters of art New York was provincial.[16]

He was far more receptive to modern art than were the chief art critics of the New York press in 1907, Mather and Royal Cortissoz of the *Tribune*.[17] The scholarly, open-minded Mather, later professor of art and archaeology at Princeton, preferred old masters like El Greco and Goya, though eventually he could admire Cézanne and Matisse. Despite their difference in taste, Huneker respected Mather's more specialized and deeper knowledge, corresponded with him deferentially, and referred to him publicly as "one of the rare critics of art in his generation,"[18] while Mather rather ungratefully remembered Huneker as a delightful writer with "a big swallow for oddities and novelties," and at bottom a "charmingly irresponsible romantic."[19] Even less responsive than Mather to modern painting was Cortissoz, who had become the *Tribune*'s art critic in 1891 (and its literary editor in 1897).[20] An admirer of Whistler, Sargent, Thayer, La Farge, and Saint-Gaudens, he could see no beauty in the work of Cézanne, Picasso, Matisse, and others who, he felt, were exploiting technique for its own sake and flouting fundamental aesthetic laws. Other art critics such as Charles H. Caffin and Sadakichi Hartmann were much more modern-minded than Mather or Cortissoz but probably less influential.

One of Huneker's earliest subjects was Cézanne, who had died in October 1906—with hardly a mention in this country, Huneker told Mitchell.[21] Though his claim—not made until 1916[22]—that he met Cézanne at Aix in 1901 remains uncorroborated, in 1904 Huneker *did* attend the Autumn Salon in Paris, where Cézanne was the rage, and wrote about him (and, less extensively, about Toulouse-Lautrec, who had been dead for three years) in what was not only, in all likelihood, his first piece of art criticism for the *Sun*[23] but also one of the first discussions of Cézanne published in America, if not the first. A new king, Huneker reported then, had usurped the throne of the Impressionists— a painter "without taste, without the faculty of selection, without vision, culture . . . who . . . has dropped out of his scheme harmony, melody, beauty . . . and doggedly represented the ugliness of things. But there is a brute strength, a tang of the soil that is bitter and also strangely invigorating, after the false, perfumed boudoir art of so many of his contemporaries. . . . When Paul Cézanne paints an onion you smell it."[24] Huneker's "obituary" of Cézanne, which appeared in the

Sun in December 1906, was the first study printed in an American newspaper[25] of the man generally regarded as the most influential painter of the last fifty years. Never an unqualified admirer of the painter, Huneker felt that he lacked imagination and invention—"the Cézanne picture does not modulate," he wrote in 1906, "does not flow; it is often hard"—but admitted that he possessed "great vitality and a peculiar reserved passion." In his still life, Huneker asserted, Cézanne was the "great master of his century, greater even than Manet."[26] This opinion shocked academic American critics, who were still debating the merits of Manet.[27] A year later, Huneker told Rosebault, who had seen the Cézanne-dominated Autumn Salon in Paris, that the Frenchman was a "great painter—purely as a painter, one who seizes and expresses *actuality*. The same actuality is always terrifyingly ugly (fancy waking up one night and discovering one of his females on the pillow next to you!). . . . He could paint a bad breath." But ugliness existed in life, he added, and for artistic purposes it was often more significant and characteristic than prettiness.[28]

Another indication of Huneker's modernism was his criticism, in mid-January 1907, of young Pamela Colman-Smith, whose paintings were the first to be exhibited in a tiny gallery established in a brownstone house at 291 Fifth Avenue by two "advanced" photographers, Alfred Stieglitz and Edward Steichen. Huneker's description of her work as "memoranda of a spiritual exultation, of the soul under the influence of music, or haunted by some sinister imagining," helped to attract 2,200 persons to the show in less than three weeks and to publicize the "Little Galleries" as *the* showplace of new photography and painting.[29] During the next few years, indeed, he was "291's" most enthusiastic supporter among the critics. In January 1908, for example, he admired the exhibition there of Rodin's drawings, remarking that it was impossible to show them all in a city where the "exquisite plastic attitudes of a Salomé or a Thaïs" produced "drastic platitudes."[30] While most American critics scoffed at the Matisse pictures shown by Stieglitz in the following April, Huneker detected the painter's "brilliant, cruel temperament"—two years later he called him a man of "enormous talent, possibly genius"—and drew many visitors to an event that has been called the introduction of modern art to America.[31] Though he disliked the New Photography—a "smeary compound of mush and mezzotint," he called it—Huneker believed that Stieglitz had done so much to open the eyes of the philistines that in February 1910 he nominated him for the Hall of Fame.[32] No wonder Huneker was frequently quoted in *Camera Work*, the avant-garde art magazine edited by Stieglitz.[33]

Reflecting, perhaps, his father's interest in American painting, Huneker championed native painters more zealously than native composers, dramatists, or writers. "These fellows who have been buffetted and crowded out and subjected to the petty miseries of spiteful mediocrity —these are the chaps I'm after," he wrote Mitchell in February 1907.[34] One reason he praised "The Ten," a month later, was that this group, formed as an exhibiting unit in 1898 by Childe Hassam and nine other established American painters to secure more facilities for showing their work, encouraged other artists to be less dependent upon the Academy and, accordingly, more daring and original.[35] Several young painters received their first words of public praise from Huneker. "Donnerwetter!" he exclaimed on seeing Rockwell Kent's initial exhibition in April 1907. "He knocks you off your pins before you can sit down with these broad, realistic, powerful representations of weltering seas, men laboring in boats, rude, rocky headlands and snowbound landscapes. . . . He is very vivid, in style miniature, yet a style both personal and powerful."[36] A notice like this by New York's most famous critic was about the most exciting thing that could happen to a recent art-school graduate.[37] In the same year, Huneker also gave John Sloan his first favorable review,[38] and he was one of the first to salute the Manhattan street scenes of Jerome Myers.[39]

Huneker's greatest contribution to the cause of American painting was his outspoken support of the group known as "The Eight." Their dynamic leader, Robert Henri, had studied with Anschutz at the Pennsylvania Academy and had taught, during the 1890's, at the Women's School of Design in Philadelphia, where he met Sloan, William Glackens, George Luks, and Everett Shinn, all working as illustrators for the Philadelphia *Press*. Henri urged these men to become serious painters and to capture on canvas the down-to-earth scenes—streets, saloons, slums, riverfronts—they recorded as newspapermen. All five, living in New York by 1904, had haunted the more picturesque districts of the city, particularly the East Side, painting realistic pictures which had caught the eye of a few enlightened critics, notably the *Evening Sun*'s Charles FitzGerald (later Glackens' brother-in-law) and his friend

Gregg, both of whom may have stimulated Huneker's interest in the group.[40] The five were disturbed in 1906 by the amalgamation of the Society of American Artists with the National Academy, which made it even more difficult for nonconformist painters to sell their pictures, since there were only a few small galleries where they could show them. When the Academy, which had accepted the work of some of these men, turned down a picture by Luks in 1907, Henri angrily declared that its members were blind and the jury system indefensible. Joined by Maurice Prendergast, Ernest Lawson, and Arthur Davies (the group's only nonrealist), and aided by William Macbeth, a sympathetic dealer, Henri and his friends decided to give their own show.[41]

Opening on February 3, 1908, it soon caused a sensation, though neither the painters nor their subjects were unknown to the informed. Hundreds of people filled Macbeth's Gallery day after day, and within three weeks $4,000 worth of pictures by five of the eight exhibitors had been sold (Prendergast, Sloan, and Glackens being the unlucky ones).[42] The crowds continued to come when the exhibition was sent on to Philadelphia, Chicago, Detroit, Toledo, Indianapolis, and Pittsburgh. Cézanne had taught these artists that beauty could exist in ugliness (the same lesson that Crane, Norris, and Dreiser, their literary counterparts, had absorbed from Zola), but the public was startled by these honest revelations of urban existence. Accustomed to the pretty and the sentimental, most critics complained that the ugly and unclean were bad enough in life without being perpetuated in such "ash-can"[43] art—the same argument Huneker had opposed in his defense of realism in literature and drama. Admiring the sincerity, power, earthiness, and courage of "The Eight," some of whom—Henri, Lawson, Luks, and Sloan—he had already praised individually,[44] Huneker calmly pointed out that the Impressionists, now considered sound workmen even by Academicians, had also been derided. If some persons were now appalled, he wrote, what would happen to their nerves when Cézanne, Gauguin, and Van Gogh appeared? If "The Eight" were sometimes raw, crude, and harsh, it was because they were experimenting, as all true artists must. But the important thing was that they had new ideas to communicate.[45] Huneker had far fewer words to eat than other leading critics when all of "The Eight" went on to become acceptable even to the most conservative.

Two articles by Huneker on Luks, printed in 1907 and 1908,[46] were singled out by John Sloan as excellent examples of Huneker's "ability to *interest*" as a writer on art. "He's different from the average critic," Sloan noted, "in that they usually think they are sent by God to shield mankind from what they don't care for themselves."[47] Among other Americans who received favorable notices from Huneker in 1908 were Davies, whom Huneker described as the "most poetic and original painter in America";[48] George Grey Barnard, the sculptor, who in 1914 was to found "The Cloisters" museum and introduce medieval architecture and sculpture to America;[49] Childe Hassam, the American Impressionist;[50] and Henry O. Tanner, the Negro religious painter, a resident of Paris. ("Here in the land of the free and unequal," Huneker remarked, ". . . would we have accorded Mr. Tanner the recognition due him?")[51] In March 1909, he labeled the memorable Alfred Maurer–John Marin exhibition at the Little Galleries a "duet in fire and shadow" —Maurer supplying the fire and Marin the mist. He liked Marin's poetic symbolism and was impressed by Maurer,[52] who had developed a style which most critics found so incomprehensible that they practically ignored him until the 1920's, when he suddenly grew popular for a season.[53] Huneker's applause, in January 1910, for the rather traditional portraitist William M. Chase testified, moreover, that a painter did not have to be "advanced" to win his approval.[54]

Later in 1910, Huneker was more responsive than the other critics to an exhibition given by a group of young painters influenced by Matisse, among them Marin, Maurer, and Steichen. True, he was baffled by the work of Max Weber: Weber's "Summer" was a clever study of basic forms, he admitted, but in the meantime the picture had vanished, reminding him of the old hospital saying that the "operation was successful but the patient died."[55] Yet he spoke well of the other painters, who, says one art historian, "needed a Huneker on every paper . . . [to] sing them and urge them and announce them, if necessary, until the thinking of Americans had been changed. Then perhaps these young men might eat from the product of their labor."[56] Already eating—and still drinking—was George Luks, his first one-man show praised by Huneker in the spring of 1910, though the critic hoped that Luks was not deserting the East Side in favor of conventional, profitable portraits.[57]

Sometimes, to be sure, Huneker rebelled against art that had nothing to recommend it but blatant novelty. In April 1910, for example, he was impatient with the huge exhibition of Independent Artists, which he called "vaudeville in color." He saw only "wretched paint, draught-manship and composition" in so many of the pictures in what Sloan called "the best exhibition ever held on this continent"[58] that he wondered whether the pendulum had not swung from the insipidity and conventionality of the Academy to the other extreme.[59]

In June 1910 he wrote a lively appreciation of "Arne Saknussem," whom he identified as a New York "painter of genius . . . known to few."[60] "Arne Saknussem" (the name of the philosopher-alchemist in Jules Verne's *A Journey to the Center of the Earth*) was actually the far-from-unknown Albert P. Ryder, the bushy-bearded, beer-drinking, tenement-dwelling mystic, who had never exhibited at the Academy or given a one-man show but whose pictures sold for over a thousand dollars each.[61] Huneker thought that Ryder—whom he probably knew—deserved more recognition, however, and his hoax drew many letters of inquiry about "Saknussem."[62] In this year, too, Huneker commended John Quinn's faith in modern American art;[63] paid tribute to Winslow Homer[64] and to John La Farge, with whom he corresponded;[65] urged the nomination of Benjamin West, Rembrandt Peale, Homer Martin, A. H. Wyant, and George Inness at the next Hall of Fame election in 1915;[66] and visited important exhibitions by contemporary American artists in Washington and Philadelphia.[67]

Yet he did not, by any means, confine himself to native painters. He believed, indeed, that self-conscious Americanism was provincial. When Gutzon Borglum, the sculptor who later created the famous presidential portraits on Mt. Rushmore, was loudly denounced in 1908 as unpatriotic because he had deprecated the quality of American sculpture and architecture, Huneker quickly came to his defense. "The truth is that there is too much clotted nonsense written about an 'American' art," he asserted. "We must fight ugliness and mediocrity, and let originality take care of itself . . . [though] it is not a quality to be despised. . . . We are in our art infancy and we derive from the Old World in art."[68]

He strongly objected, of course, to the puritanical view that the painting of nudes was immoral. In 1909 he could not see why George Sauter's innocent picture "The Bridal Morning" had caused so much commotion in Pittsburgh. "There is nothing so terrible to some people as the human form divine," he remarked. "Banished from our 'literature' it is barely holding its own in painting and sculpture."[69] Four years later, he was in Europe when Anthony Comstock, complaining, reportedly, that the picture revealed "too little morn and too much maid," tried to prevent a New York art dealer from displaying a reproduction of Paul Chabas' "September Morn" on the grounds that this picture of a nude girl shivering in her lakeside bath was "demoralizing in the extreme and especially calculated to excite immodesty in the young."[70] Huneker would surely have chortled over an indignant art student's nude plaster caricature of the reformer in the same pose, which made the rounds of New York's studios.[71]

Huneker maintained that since a critic's primary responsibility was to the public, he need not be a painter himself to write of painting (painters, indeed, often made poor critics), but that he did need an artistic temperament and a *credo*. Huneker revealed something of his own *credo* when he declared that painting

exists in space, in two dimensions. It is quite rigid, though paradoxically it may suggest rhythm. It is representative rather than presentative (new schools believe otherwise). It is not as emotional as music, nor as definitive in form as sculpture. Yet by some temperamental magic, it can suggest emotion, invoke forms. . . . Painting . . . is no more to be understood *prima vista* than a Bach fugue or a Tanagra statuette. It requires a coordination of faculties not existent among people without culture. It necessitates long, arduous special training. It represents the victory of mind over matter.[72]

The great problem facing an art critic was how to use the medium of one art—literature—to interpret fully the materials of another. Since criticism was at "two removes" from its theme, it was, therefore, a makeshift, and, consequently, critics should be modest and make their work an "amiable art."[73]

In his own criticism, to attain greater expressiveness (and also because of his technical grounding in music, where he really felt most at home) Huneker habitually used musical terms, a device especially illuminating to those equally conversant with art and music, though not very helpful, perhaps, to unmusical artists. Together with his customary wit, gusto, sensitivity, tolerance, picturesque imagery, and curiosity about the artist as a human being, this mannerism produced a style that distinguished him at once from his colleagues. "There was no one like him," recalls Henry McBride, dean of American art critics and Huneker's successor on the *Sun*. "His strength lay in his knowledge of life and his ability to write."[74] "When the man *felt*," an art historian, Jerome Mellquist, has said of Huneker, ". . . he could impart a grace and a quality of spiritual audacity unsurpassed by any critic in his generation."[75]

In the spring of 1910, *Promenades of an Impressionist,* a collection of Huneker's essays on painting, was published under the supervision of the well-known literary critic William Crary Brownell, his new editor at Scribner's. Before turning to literature, Brownell had won a reputation as an art critic (a position he held on the Philadelphia *Press* in 1885–86,[76] when Huneker probably read his articles), having written an influential early study of Whistler in 1879[77] and the pioneering *French Art* (1892), in which he practically introduced Rodin to America. Urbane, aristocratic, and nonpolitical, he agreed with Huneker that the principles of art and literature were largely identical, and considered it legitimate to use the terms of one art to throw light upon another, while as a literary critic he, too, stressed the importance of a writer's personality. Otherwise, however, the two men were poles apart. Austere, reticent, and dignified, Brownell had little of Huneker's humor and charm. His style was crabbed and tortuous—he had no ear for music—and he lacked Huneker's flair for the picturesque phrase or the striking image. Like his favorite critic, Matthew Arnold, Brownell was judicial rather than impressionistic. His range of interests, moreover, was narrower than Huneker's; he seldom criticized drama or poetry, and the prose writers he analyzed were generally English or American "masters"—and almost always dead. "I am not so receptive to those vital eccentricities to which your more catholic mind is so hospitable," he tactfully wrote Huneker in 1914.[78] Allergic to "morally reprehensible" elements in literature and in personality, he believed that great art should proceed from, and lead to, good morals, was dismayed by crudeness, rawness, and sheer power,[79] and winced when he saw words like sodomy and flagellomania. Nevertheless, there developed between Huneker and Brownell a congenial author-editor relationship which lasted some ten years and which, considering their dissimilarities in temperament, method, and style and their importance in American culture, was one of the most remarkable associations in the annals of American publishing.

Since Huneker admired Brownell's capacity for sustained reasoning

—his forte as a critic—and was distrustful of his own impressionism, he was pleased when his editor assured him that *Promenades of an Impressionist* possessed "a great deal of close thinking and sound criticism" and was "a serious work in the best sense."[80] Some reviewers of the book still quarreled with Huneker's style,[81] but most of them realized that the essay on Cézanne contained the best account by an American critic of the aims and achievements of the Post-Impressionists.[82] The *New York Times* singled out as Huneker's pre-eminent virtue his "common sense in connecting the art with the artist," while the *Independent* noted that the book was the first in English to give biographical details about certain painters.[83] Mather's notice in the *Nation* and the *Evening Post* was "unusually bully," Huneker told him,[84] and Cortissoz's was also kind. (Huneker's note of thanks to the latter read, in its entirety: "My Dear Royal. Both by name and nature so.")[85]

Bernard Berenson, the Harvard-educated resident of Italy, whose important *The North Italian Painters of the Renaissance* Huneker had favorably reviewed at the end of 1907,[86] thanked him for a "most refreshing, sparkling, stimulating book." "What is more," Berenson added, "I came away with the feeling that the author must be just the kind of a man I should like."[87] Over forty years later, the world's foremost authority on Italian Renaissance painters regretted that he had never met Huneker (who had been forced, in 1903, to decline an invitation to meet Berenson, from whose criticism, he said then, he had almost gained a new sense of vision);[88] Berenson recalled that Huneker had written appreciatively about him when few others dared to, and was admirable as "a taster who wanted to tell others how to taste."[89] George Moore, whose name was frequently mentioned in *Promenades of an Impressionist,* wrote Huneker that he had found in it "all the qualities . . . that I admire in your writings—ease, grace, understanding, and all the subtle points in art which only the artist can understand."[90] And Ignacio Zuloaga—whom Huneker may have overrated—told Huneker that he had read the flattering essay on himself with special pleasure because he had thought that his work was disliked in America.[91]

Augustus John, not one of the subjects of *Promenades* (though Huneker liked his work), informed his patron, John Quinn, that he was "filled with admiration for the large, genial, and comprehensive outlook" of Huneker, whose "fresh and unfailing enthusiasm for a crowd of merits which lesser minds think mutually destructive" was splendid and unheard of. "This book," John concluded, "gives me the courage and humility of my boyhood." Three days afterward, he remarked to Quinn that he was astonished by Huneker's "huge, 'let 'em all come' attitude . . . his appetite—gargantuan and insatiable; and how he makes the best of a bad job and does justice to a good one."[92] Four decades later, John, then England's most distinguished painter, declared that he knew of no critic who filled Huneker's place, none with such vision and generosity.[93]

The liveliness of his style and his instinct for the new and neglected, qualities that attracted both the general public and art specialists, made Huneker the most popular art critic in America, especially after the publication of *Promenades*. Of course he did not please everybody; the conservatives were dismayed by his tolerance, while the ultramodernists felt that he was not sympathetic enough toward them. The latter were disappointed, for example, by his ridicule of Henri Rousseau's American debut in November 1910,[94] and by his emphasis on the "appalling ugliness" of Pablo Picasso's first exhibition here in the following spring, even though Huneker granted that the anarchic Picasso was not cultivating ugliness for its own sake but "searching after the expressive in the heart of ugliness."[95] (Most of the other critics found Picasso utterly incomprehensible.)[96] Yet less than two weeks after he made this observation, Huneker enthusiastically welcomed Jo Davidson's first important show, calling him a born sculptor and "a strongly individual artist in the field of contemporary sculpture."[97]

In the fall of 1912, when he left the *Sun* to become roving foreign correspondent for the *New York Times* (and, unofficially, a scout and amateur agent for John Quinn), Huneker again visited art galleries in Europe. He detected talent in the noisy Italian Futurists, but considered them " 'literary,' musical painters, not painters for the sake of pictorial loveliness."[98] Comparing the Autumn Salon in Paris with the one he had attended in 1904, he noted that Matisse, Picasso, Van Dongen, and others, who had "contemptuously pitched overboard everything that we oldsters consider as essential in pictorial or plastic art," now claimed the throne occupied a decade earlier by Cézanne and those "old masters," the Post-Impressionists. Though Huneker wondered whether a "still profounder level of ugliness and repulsiveness" could be reached, he prophesied that the work of a few of these new artists would stand the test of time, and among them he singled out Matisse, whom he had just interviewed in Paris.[99]

Huneker was living in Berlin (German painters, he thought, were deficient in color sense and a marked personal style)[100] when the famous International Exhibition of Modern Art opened in the Armory of the 69th Regiment in New York on February 17, 1913. Sponsored by the Association of American Painters and Sculptors, the huge Armory Show represented, in part, a culmination of the first phase of the battle Huneker had begun to wage six years earlier, for the show's main aim was to continue the revolt of "The Eight" against the intolerance within their profession; over 1,100 pictures—not so well publicized as those by foreign artists—by more than 300 American artists were included in the exhibition.[101] "You must make a brave showing," Huneker wrote John Quinn, incorporator and one of the two honorary members of the Association (the other one being Huneker's friend and ex-colleague Frederick James Gregg, art critic for the *Evening Sun*, chairman of the Show's press committee and author of the introduction to its catalogue).[102] "And I wonder if anyone remembers nowadays," Huneker added, "that I was the first man to write in America about Cézanne and Gauguin . . . ? It doesn't pay to play the part of a *premature* prophet in any country."[103]

Conservative critics of the Armory Show, which proceeded to popularize the Impressionists and Post-Impressionists and to introduce Fauvism, Cubism, Futurism, and Expressionism to the bewildered American public,[104] had reservations even about the Post-Impressionists, and they derided Marcel Duchamp, whose "Nude Descending a Staircase" was the show's big sensation.[105] Frowning at "some of the most stupidly ugly pictures in the world and not a few pieces of sculpture to match them," Cortissoz, for example, declared that Cézanne and Van Gogh "intermittently fumble their way into interesting achievement, but more often wrestle with their pigment and are sadly thrown"; called Gauguin "a bold craftsman and colorist gone wrong midway in the course of his artistic education"; derided Matisse's "pompous crudities" as "very absurd"; and dismissed Picasso and the Cubists as the wilder elements in the "farce."[106] Some critics, of course, hotly defended the ultramodernists, but even members of the sponsoring group—including Sloan and Luks—resigned in protest against the extremist painters, and the disagreement within the Association actually caused it to break up in 1914.[107] When the show came to Chicago, the Illinois legislature's "White Slave" Commission investigated charges of immorality brought against it, thereby increasing attendance, if not sales, but the fact that both Theodore Roosevelt and the mayor of the city inspected it without being corrupted ensured its respectability. A quarter of a million persons in New York, Chicago, and Boston eventually paid hard cash for the sensation of being shocked or edified, and over three hundred paintings were sold.[108]

Removed from the scene of the controversy, Huneker continued to take a rather ambiguous position on modern art. Aware of the fluctuation of fashion, the cycles of revolt and counterrevolt which kept the arts healthy, he observed from Europe that in emphasizing form at the expense of color the reaction against Impressionism was now producing art which many found ugly or abnormal. But beauty and ugliness, sickness and health were, after all, only relative terms. "The truth is the normal never happens in art or life," he remarked, "so whenever you hear a painter or professor of aesthetics preaching the 'gospel of health in art' [as he had once done himself] you will know that both are preaching pro domo. . . . In even the greatest art there may be found the morbid, the feverish, the sick or the mad." A lover of Velásquez, Vermeer, and Rembrandt—the "father, son and holy ghost of my paint religion"—need not close his eyes to originality, personal charm, or character in the newer men.[109]

Upon his return from Europe a few months after the Armory Show closed, Huneker repeated, almost verbatim, comments he had made six years earlier when criticizing "The Eight"; the tools of young American artists did not matter as long as they had individuality, for art was not a fixed quantity but an endless experimenting. Why must they "continue to peer through the studio spectacles of their grandfathers?" The only important question was whether they had something to say and a personal manner of saying it, and his answer was a "decided affirmative." He reported, also, that he had been told that Cézanne, Gauguin, Van Gogh—of the trio, he declared, Van Gogh was the greatest genius— and Matisse had been inadequately represented at the Armory Show.[110] Since the death of the three great Post-Impressionists, he asserted eight months later, Matisse was "the master of the field."[111]

After he joined the staff of *Puck* in the spring of 1914, proudly identified by the magazine as the greatest art critic in America, Huneker occasionally criticized pictures. Praising the work of Prendergast and others,[112] he deplored the slavish imitation by younger Americans of the Cubists, Zonists, and Post-Impressionists, but agreed, nevertheless,

that anything was better than a return to "benumbing academic methods," and that the freedom of the new forms might help these artists
"avoid the pitfalls of the obvious."[113] When George Bellows won an
important prize at the Spring Academy exhibition, Huneker happily
announced that his prediction that Bellows would "arrive" had come
true.[114] In 1914, also, two of John Marin's paintings of Manhattan
which had caught Huneker's eye, "Fifth Avenue" and "Woolworth
Building," were reproduced in *Puck*.[115] Later in the same year, he
briefly characterized some *sixty* lesser-known modern French painters
in an article of fewer than three pages![116]

Although he was less sympathetic than Stieglitz to the avant-garde,
Huneker continued to applaud the courage and determination of "291's"
dynamic leader. "I found [him] still the enthusiast and rebel against
the provinciality of American ideas in the region of art," he wrote in
late May 1914 after talking with Stieglitz for the first time in several
years. "He has fought a good fight, and for the sheer love of art; for
the profit of his soul and not of his pocket."[117] Upon *Camera Work*'s
commemoration, a year later, of Stieglitz's efforts on behalf of modern
art, Huneker went to congratulate him in person,[118] pleasing Stieglitz,
who had recently described Huneker as one of the very few writers in
this country who knew what he was writing about.[119]

Huneker confessed that on this last visit to "291" he had failed to
detect a portrait of Stieglitz in a design by Cubist Marius de Zayas.[120]
The Cubists, indeed, left Huneker cold. "They are as dead as a door-
nail," he wrote the venturesome Quinn in May 1915. "It's very fine
geometry, but it's not pictorial art." "All these petty revolutions," he
later added, ". . . will never even deflect for a moment the broad current of eternal art. . . . There is a norm, and these young chaps may
fume and sputter, but back to it they must revert else rot and drop from
the parent trunk."[121] He recommended Willard Huntington Wright's
Modern Painting, shortly afterward, as an excellent exposition of the
latest theories, but considered the author too sympathetic toward "some
of the crazy stuff. . . . 'Abstract Art,' as they call it nowadays, is not
art at all; it is an abstraction, and art is concrete or it is nothing. . . .
Music alone can express the inexpressible, but the arts of painting and
sculpture must represent."[122] Huneker's vision in art was thus more
limited, his viewpoint more equivocal, than in music, literature, or
drama.

He took issue, moreover, with Clive Bell's claim that there had been no great art in Europe between the Byzantine Primitives and Cézanne, astonished that anyone could ignore the great painters of the Renaissance. Cézanne was undeniably important, a "sign-post" for the generation that succeeded him, but to put him, Gauguin, and Van Gogh in a "pantheon superimposed on the historical pantheon" was, he said, "but another evidence that there is such a thing as disputing tastes."[123] It was this conservative strain, perhaps, as well as his reputation as an art critic that brought Huneker an invitation from Yale University's School of the Fine Arts, in the summer of 1915, to deliver two lectures there (on "Early Romanticism and Realism" and "Impressionistic and Decorative Tendencies in Landscape and Figure"). Huneker must have been delighted by this token of recognition, but the mere thought of speaking before an audience panicked him, and he gratefully declined.[124] He felt much more secure in his comfortable study, surrounded by his reference library and the books he was constantly reading.

Fifteen

BOHEMIAN IN BEDROOM SLIPPERS

During the years he was the *Sun*'s art critic, Huneker continued to free-lance in other fields, visiting galleries in the daytime and at night writing short stories, literary studies, and book reviews as well as art criticism.[1] From January 1906 until May 1907, for example, he contributed to the *New York Times* more or less monthly reviews of books on or by Ibsen, Balzac, Flaubert, and others. In January 1907 he finally broke into a major literary magazine (other than *Scribner's*); the *North American Review* printed his essay on Anatole France, which Bliss Perry, editor of the *Atlantic Monthly*, considered so "uncommonly brilliant" that he asked Huneker to send him something for the *Atlantic*.[2] (Huneker complied, his study of Maurice Barrès appearing there in the following August.) Before the year was over, his work was also published in the *Century* and the *Forum*. And, in addition, he was still working on the Liszt book.

When Josephine underwent a major operation in the late spring of 1907, Huneker was too worried to do much writing. Instead, to calm his nerves and to keep occupied, he phrased, fingered, and accented Chopin's more difficult, larger compositions for an edition published by Ditson's in 1908 as *The Greater Chopin* to supplement his edition of Chopin's more popular pieces issued by the same firm in 1902. He could never look at this second collection—which, he claimed, was based on information given him by "my venerable master," Georges Mathias— without thinking of Josephine lying in the hospital.[3] Medical bills then forced him to concentrate on lucrative magazine articles rather than on the Liszt biography, which, he decided, should come out in 1911, Liszt's centenary.[4]

His tight schedule left so little time for the old festivities that Ziegler accused him of becoming a hermit.[5] Occasionally, however, he managed to squeeze in a luncheon or dinner with friends at Mouquin's, Lüchow's, the Savoy, or the Hotel Seville, for no matter how pinched he was for time or money he refused to go to any café that did not offer well-prepared food and quiet, comfortable surroundings.[6] At the end of 1907 he wrote Rosebault, then homesick in Paris: ". . . Bath tubs, not Bohemia now-a-days for me. I loathe Paris to live in—unless one has steam heat and running water. . . . Once, when you are very young —then is Paris a fairy dream in its setting. But don't peep behind the scenes."[7]

Yet the embers of bohemianism were not completely dead. Benjamin De Casseres never forgot his first meeting with Huneker, which took place at two o'clock one Sunday morning in 1908 at Jack's restaurant. Wearing a flaming red tie and looking like a "fat Anarch Cherub straight from a conference with Lucifer or Bacchus," Huneker was sitting with Ernest Lawson, "Billy" Glackens, and Frederick James Gregg behind a row of empty beer mugs. De Casseres writes:

I literally seideled up to him (there's not much courage in beer).

"James Huneker, I'm De Casseres." He rose; his two little gray eyes squirted two shots at me that went through to my spine. He shoved a finger under my nose. His staccato voice came like a pistol-shot.

"Nietzsche or Schopenhauer?"

He was almost menacing. . . . "Nietzsche!" I whispered huskily.

Huneker's voice relaxed. His finger lowered. He exuded a titanic grin.

"Sit down and have a drink," he said. "Hell, Ben, Lafcadio Hearn is too artificial." He had caught sight of *Gleaning from Buddha Fields* [sic] under my arm.

What a night. I had met the most extraordinary talker America has ever produced. Seidel after seidel. The dawn peeped in through the window. Huneker had abolished time. He raced on: Chopin, Spencer, Roosevelt, Brillat-Savarin, Howells, Goya, Ireland, Cellini, Rembrandt, Lincoln, Culmbacher, Paracelsus, George Ehret, Poe, Harry Thaw, Renoir, William Penn— I know not.[8]

Afterward, the worshipful De Casseres made a point of waylaying Huneker wherever possible:

I . . . caught him [he recalled elsewhere] in the center of a Fifth Avenue traffic jam where he was in a flaming discussion with his friend, the cop, on the newest traffic regulations; planted before a bar . . . pouring the fascinations of the Great Beer Routes of Europe in the ears of Mix-'Em Mike, whose ears were wide agape; in the smoking room of the Metropolitan Opera House deep in the lower registers of a perfecto with "Billy" Guard; walking around the country lanes of Flatbush studying ornithology and rug beating.[9]

A pajama-clad Huneker once entertained De Casseres at the "dream barn" by playing Chopin for hours, cases of Pilsner and Chianti conveniently placed under the piano. One Easter morning, too, De Casseres had to call it quits at ten o'clock after trying to out-seidel Huneker, still going strong after a night of guzzling.[10] The older man encouraged De Casseres to be less pessimistic in his writings. "Wear the Epicurean badge of smiling, tolerant contempt for the foolish," he advised him in 1908. ". . . Believe me, it is the bravest, gayest philosophy. . . . It is moderate; it smiles at the inutile and fatuous and is only contemptuous of one thing—the man without a *sense of humor*; i.e., relativity, proportion. In the relativity of things lies the secret of personal salvation."[11]

In December 1907 the *Sun* raised Huneker's pay to $25 per column with the understanding that he was to turn in a total of four columns a week, including one special editorial in addition to his regular art criticism, and that he was not to write for any other daily newspaper on any subject or for magazines on the fine arts.[12] This arrangement did not ward off the financial crises which continued to beset him—Mitchell found Huneker "childlike in his conception of pecuniary relations," while Huneker himself admitted that he was "never a young Napoleon of Finance. *Hinc illae Lachrymae!*"[13]—though some of the crises were not his fault. Early in 1908, for example, he was jolted by the failure of both his bank and the bank where Josephine kept money of her own, and had to ask Mitchell for an advance.[14] To make matters worse, the magazines were not buying articles because of the business slump. The *Sun,* moreover, did not have room every week for four Huneker columns during 1908, William Dean Howells' letters from Rome and the presidential election crowding him off the editorial page, and he needed money so badly that fall that he almost asked the *Sun*'s music department for odd jobs. He suggested a new arrangement, accordingly, that would relieve his anxiety about the future: a fixed, year-round salary of $75 a week for three columns, and the privilege of being paid at his regular space rate for additional columns.[15] Whether Laffan accepted these terms is uncertain, but the *Sun* began to use more of Huneker's work and he was apparently satisfied.

The special, unsigned weekly editorials Huneker submitted were mainly book reviews and literary criticisms. His observations on vari-

ous French writers were actually by-products of close study reflected in
more substantial essays published in *Scribner's Magazine,* the *Atlantic
Monthly,* and the *North American Review.* In December 1907, when
some program designed to teach America the values of "pure" French
literature was suggested, Huneker protested that it was unnecessary and
insulting, for Hugo and many other "good" French authors were better
known here, he declared, than Zola or the purveyors of pornography.
Gallic literature was, of course, franker than English, but if Victoria
Cross and Elinor Glyn portrayed English life, why would it not be just
as appropriate, he wondered, to organize a league for the propagation
of pure English literature in Paris?[16] Decrying the crusade waged in
America against the alleged immorality of French literature, Remy de
Gourmont commended the *Sun,* in the *Mercure de France,* for telling
the truth about that literature and making it better known in this country, and called Huneker "one of the best informed of foreign critics,
one of those who judge us with the most sympathy and also with the
most freedom." Gourmont singled out Huneker's essay on Stendhal,
which the *Mercure de France* had translated from *Scribner's,* as one of
the best studies of the novelist that had been written in a long time.[17]

In the spring of 1909 this Stendhal piece—enlarged until it had
become, according to Huneker, the most extensive criticism of that
writer available in English[18]—was reprinted, together with essays on
Baudelaire,[19] Flaubert, Nietzsche, Ibsen, and others, in *Egoists: A
Book of Supermen.* Though these men were strikingly different in most
ways, Huneker believed that they had one important trait in common—
a devotion to individualism, the one philosophical principle upon which
his critical creed rested. Suspicious of oversimplified generalizations,
however, he did not worry too much about a unifying approach for his
book, preferring to suggest his central ideas on literature and life by
treating his subjects as unique individuals rather than fitting them into
some rigid, preconceived scheme. Constructing a sustained, closely-
knit argument to prove a theory was never his method, of course; he
chose instead to describe with intuitive understanding and immense
gusto those writers whom he found most sympathetic.

Egoists was dedicated to Georg Brandes, the cosmopolitan critic
par excellence, who had interpreted foreign literatures for Danes as
Huneker was attempting to do for Americans. "A group of the younger
men in America . . . look up to you as a leader, a light-bearer," he

wrote Brandes on March 29, 1909. "You taught us to understand Ibsen, Nietzsche, even Strindberg. . . . And in dedicating *Egoists* to you I am sounding the keynote of the book." Huneker's old friend Maurice Egan, professor of English at Catholic University until Theodore Roosevelt had appointed him Minister to Denmark in 1907, presented *Egoists* to Brandes, who had recently told George Sylvester Viereck in Copenhagen that Huneker was "strangely brilliant for an American."[20] Brandes was "very much flattered," Egan recalled. ". . . [He] was not especially fond of the writings of Americans . . . but I judge that Huneker was an exception—and then he knew the byways of French literature so well."[21] Brandes' gracious note of thanks brought a reply from Huneker, and the two men continued to correspond.[22]

Broad-minded, cosmopolitan critics admired *Egoists,* Huneker's own favorite among his books.[23] The *Sun*'s Mayo W. Hazeltine, who had published essays on French literature in *Chats About Books* (1883), stated that Huneker's volume contained "more knowledge and more thought" than a dozen ordinary treatises on philosophical and ethical questions, and that the essay on Ibsen was the best he had ever read.[24] "Many interesting pages with correct judgments and original points of view," commented the *Mercure de France*.[25] The *New York Times*'s reviewer applauded the book's charm, energy, sympathy, sound information, and freshness of observation.[26] But other reviewers quibbled with Huneker's choice of subjects and his lack of "general ideas." His old enemy, the Springfield *Republican*, complained, not unexpectedly, that enough had been written already about Nietzsche, that Ibsen no longer needed exposition to the American public, and that Flaubert was a "hackneyed subject if there ever was one."[27] Though Paul Elmer More informed Huneker that he was particularly pleased by the book's unity of effect, its clear point of view, he obviously believed that Huneker's "eccentrics and maniacs" were unworthy of serious study. (How, More wondered later, did Huneker summon up the will power to read authors who would kill More with ennui in a week?)[28] The usually liberal William Reedy called Huneker's egoists "abnormalities, sensitives, pathological morbidities," while the *Outlook* labeled Stendhal, Baudelaire, Huysmans, Nietzsche, and Stirner a "singularly unpleasant group, all touched with insanity," and wondered whether their contribution to literature was as important as Huneker thought.[29]

Even William James, whose lucid style and open-mindedness Huneker greatly admired (but whose pragmatism he had derided in 1908 as a wishy-washy philosophy, floating "serenely in the tepid waters of opportunism"),[30] balked at Huneker's tolerance. "You seem to have French literature at your fingers' ends," James wrote Huneker in April 1909, thanking him for *Egoists,* "but why not call Stendhal the awful cad he was, and why give so many serious pages to that cad in putrefaction, Huysmans? Surely almost the *nastiest* contemporary phenomenon!"[31]—a remark that annoyed Huneker. "The New England philistine—pragmatic pedant!" he reportedly sputtered as he showed the letter to De Casseres, whom he happened to meet right after he had received it.[32] He proceeded to "explain" Huysmans to James, who then graciously apologized for the statement, admitting that he really knew very little about Huysmans. More astonishing to James than this spirited defense of Huysmans was Huneker's disclosure, in the same letter, that he had been "brought up" on the writings of James's father. "Most strange," exclaimed the philosopher, struck by this incongruity.[33] He, in turn, sent Huneker a copy of his new book, *A Pluralistic Universe,* which Huneker reviewed favorably in the *Sun* six weeks later in an article James termed "extraordinarily racy and ingenious."[34]

Huneker informed his brother John that some critics of *Egoists* failed to understand that it was not an exploitation of bizarre characters but a study of individualism:

The damn ignoramuses speak of me as digging up queer birds &c. When as a matter of fact Stendhal created the entire modern school of psychological fiction, Meredith, Bourget, Hewlett & the rest, while the influence of Baudelaire on poetry has been profound; without Baudelaire there would not have been the exotic note in Swinburne. . . . And Ibsen! Who changed the theatrical map of Europe! The damned asses write as if they had never followed the great intellectual currents of the 19th century. . . . In what back alleys of the brain live our provincial critics.[35]

A review of the book in the *Harvard Advocate* suggested that Huneker was leading the younger generation, at least, on exciting intellectual safaris. Observing that the author, "far too alert" to be an American, was French in temperament, "T.S.E." added:

Mr. Huneker's style may impress us as unpardonably hasty, crammed, staccato. . . . But (among American writers, still further distinction) a style it decidedly is, and shares with that of Mr. Henry James . . . a conversational quality; not conversational in admitting the slipshod and maladroit, or a meagre vocabulary, but by a certain informality, abandoning all the ordinary rhetorical hoaxes for securing attention. In the matter of English style, by the way, his criticism of the later Henry James is illuminating. . . . Mr. Huneker's book titles are a little noisy, and in this case vague and unsatisfactory. But the Egoists are all men—French and German—of highly individual, some of perverse and lunary, genius. Particularly good is the critique of Huysmans, the genius of faith, also the note on Francis Poictevin, a forgotten literary specialist.[36]

This was the impression Huneker made upon the young T. S. Eliot, who, unreceptive in his maturity to Huneker's point of view and method, recalled, over four decades later, that as an undergraduate he had found Huneker's essays

highly stimulating because of the number of foreign authors, artists, and composers whom he was able to mention, and whom I had then never heard of. Later it came to seem to me that the actual value of his criticism was slight, and the parade of names . . . rather tiresome. But I think his work may have performed a useful service for others as well as myself, in bringing to their attention the names of distinguished contemporaries and men of the previous generation, in the various arts.[37]

Among Yale literati Huneker was very popular, according to George Soule, a Yale alumnus and later editor of the *New Republic*, one reason being that the editorial board of the *Literary Magazine* on campus was eager to print student essays on little-known European writers, painters, and musicians, and Huneker, who "could mention more potential celebrities in a given number of words than any other author in the library," was a favorite source of subjects.[38] Seeming to be the only essayist to have read a contemporary book or heard modern music, Huneker, as Van Wyck Brooks remarked, "shoveled into the minds of the young precisely what they did not learn in college."[39] "In the years that I read him, 1914 to 1921," says Ben Hecht, "I regarded [Huneker] as my alma mater,"[40] and the studies in *Egoists* were eye-openers as well to the youthful Floyd Dell, Kenneth Burke, Malcolm Cowley, S. N. Behrman, and Edmund Wilson.[41]

On August 31, 1909, Huneker left for Europe—his first visit since 1905—to tour art galleries in Holland, Belgium, and Spain, the most noteworthy result of the trip being a series of articles on Spanish art for the *Sun*. When he came back in late October or early November, he was shocked to discover—from a newspaper clipping, the wire sent to him having gone astray in Spain—that his fifty-year-old brother Paul had died during his absence.[42] He was jolted again, in November, by the sudden death of William Laffan, which not only saddened him personally but made him uneasy about his future on the *Sun*, since he could hardly expect the newspaper's new owner to be as interested in art as Laffan was. Mitchell continued as editor, however, and Huneker's columns still appeared frequently—which was fortunate because Josephine, almost dying of peritonitis before the year ended, required the expensive services of two doctors and a nurse.[43] In February 1910 Huneker began a Sunday department, "Seen in the World of Art," which became a regular outlet for articles that could not be fitted into the daily editorial page. When the art season was over, he spent the summer of 1910 grinding out editorials, writing a preface to Joseffy's edition of *Selected Piano Compositions* by Brahms (published in 1910),[44] and trying to finish the Liszt biography.

There were signs now that the celebrity worshiper was becoming something of a celebrity himself. In the spring of 1910 Huneker must have smiled in the direction of Shaw and Beerbohm when he was elected to the Authors' Club of London, his name being proposed by no less a personage than Thomas Hardy and seconded by Joseph Conrad. "Few American authors are members," Huneker wrote his brother on May 13, 1910. ". . . It's an honor, if only an empty one. I get so little help on this side of the Atlantic—for the old chaps regard me with suspicion, and I'm old fashioned! with the younger crew (Phillips, Chambers, etc., good friends all of them)—that it is a pleasure to have my work appreciated in England."[45] In December a reporter from the New York *Telegraph* interviewed Huneker in the "dream barn," impressed by the critic's personality and the good taste of the furnishings in his study— the pictures, books, piano, rare clock, samovar, fine rugs, blending tapestries, and autographed photographs of Symons, Maeterlinck, Olive Fremstad, and other famous persons.[46] About the time the interview was printed, Theodore Presser's flourishing journal published a biographical sketch and portrait of Huneker in the "*Etude* Gallery of Musical Celebrities."[47]

Frank Weitenkampf, the distinguished curator of the Lenox Library's Print Room, which Huneker visited from time to time, provides an unusual glimpse of the critic around 1910. One Saturday afternoon

at the library, Weitenkampf remembered, the boyish Huneker exuber-
antly pulled from his pocket a bunch of bills, his pay from the *Sun*
(wanting to see what it looked like, probably, before spending it). He
suggested to the librarian that the cool cellar next to the engine room
in the library be turned into a rathskeller, promising to be its first and
best customer. And Weitenkampf never forgot Huneker's habit of walking the streets with his cane held straight up before him a foot or so
from his chest, the handle at collar level, which caused some wag to remark that he carried it as if he were handling a stein of beer.[48]

At the request of Theodore Dreiser, now a successful editor of pulp
magazines and women's fashion journals, Huneker read, in the late
spring of 1911, the manuscript of *Jennie Gerhardt,* Dreiser's first novel
since *Sister Carrie,* and sent Dreiser a detailed criticism of it. The critique deserves to be quoted at length not only because it contains some
of the best advice Dreiser ever received but also because it furnishes
the most graphic evidence of Huneker's seldom-exhibited ability as a
"practical," even a "textual," critic:

It is a big book this new one of yours. I'm not yet certain whether I like it
better than *Sister Carrie.* . . . What made me happy while reading it was
the fact that it attempted to prove nothing; didn't advocate Socialism, or
Christian Science, or any of the new thought Breakfast Foods. A moving
and vivid picture of life, nothing else. And that spells a lot in these days
of wild-eyed, inartistic propagandists who have strayed into fiction.[49] . . .
Your story is very human, simply conceived, probable, sympathetic—though
not invariably well told. Your prose style is still opaque, moves too slowly,
lacks rhythmic variety; and is too "literary." You may smile at this, but
it's the main fault I find. When you begin to get solemn, to preach, you
write chunks of bookishness; even several of your characters talk bookish.
Despite this handicap the story shines through; the characterization is masterly—hard to beat—the sequence of events logical. Your fashionable women
are not well realized. I like Lester's brother—the real, cold American business man, hard as nails—old Gerhardt, Lester, Jennie, her mother, and that
delightful child. Indeed, I thought at one stage the book ought to be called
"Lester Kane," but it has the precise title. To make an essentially weak girl
sympathetic, without pulling out all the lachrymose stops of pity and indig-
nation, is a difficult undertaking. Of course, there will be a yowl of woe from
the dyspeptic moral critics. With few exceptions you have kept your hands
off the girl and not disfigured the book by moralic [*sic*] reflections. But
these exceptions spring to the eye and they made me groan. Chapter X is
full of them. Why? It interrupts the swing of the narrative. And that inter-
polated chapter dealing with old Gerhardt's habit of miserliness—why do

you place it where you have done—just before the return of Jennie and Lester from Europe? Shouldn't it be fitted in somewhere else—though I find it quite superfluous—about the time when Father Gerhardt comes from Cleveland to Hyde Park? Another bad thing, perhaps the most offensive (to me, understand) in the book is your *epilogue.* Again, in the name of Flaubert and Maupassant, why? Your ending, on what musicians would call a suspended harmony, is superb. I take off my hat to you Theodore Dreiser—that funeral scene and the last paragraphs about Jennie's future (in the last chapter but one) are those of a master. Don't spoil that ending for the sake of moralizing no matter how symmetrical or ethical that moralizing may be. Your story ends there. Let it end there. Above all, the appeal is to the imagination in those last cadences. We see the gray, dusty end of the girl's life. This is only the opinion of one man. But I know the best fiction—the Russian—and there is page after page in *Jennie* that recalls the best of the Russians. I admire your courage in tackling such a purely American theme, and giving it such a dreary setting. I've lived in the Columbus (O.) hotel you describe—in 1887. And I know Cleveland and Chicago. Local color is perfect. Again I say a big book, eloquent in its humanity, *too long*; too many repetitions (you ride certain words to death, such as *big*) and the best fiction I have read since that of Frank Norris.[50]

Grateful for this "excellent criticism," Dreiser soon replied to Huneker that he had removed nearly all the objectionable repetitions and moralizings, invited him to dinner,[51] and later that year sent him an inscribed copy of the book. "I'm sorry . . . you kept in that . . . postscript," Huneker replied.[52] (When the novel was reprinted in 1924, however, the epilogue was dropped.)[53] Dreiser came to rank Huneker with Mencken and Charles B. DeCamp (a former editorial assistant of Dreiser's) as superior critics, "as grim critically as any [critics] I know."

Huneker apparently did not review *Jennie Gerhardt* or *The Financier,* the first volume of the Cowperwood trilogy, which came out in the fall of 1912 when he was abroad (though he wrote Dreiser that he had been "bowled over" by its color and documentation).[54] But he did criticize two of Dreiser's later novels. In *The Titan,* Huneker observed in 1914, Dreiser's penchant for moralizing and his stylistic weaknesses were still apparent, but he was, nevertheless, a "master of numbers, crowds, confusion, and swarming cities." And there was a "bigness about the work which overshadows its petty faults. The height, depth, breadth, and mass of this ugly but very significant and modern fictional architecture may repel at first, but in the end impresses by sheer sincerity."[55] Huneker did not care for Dreiser's next novel, *The "Genius."* It was far too long, he remarked early in 1916, and its painter-hero a "shallow bore" and a "wooden Indian as to character after he leaves the Middle West to settle in New York." To call "such a nonentity . . . a 'genius' because he manufactured East Side pictures with the pity motive as a tag" was ridiculous.[56] Huneker knew, moreover, that in the first decade of the twentieth century, such paintings—suggested in part by those of John Sloan and Everett Shinn—could hardly have been as lucrative as Dreiser indicated, since, after all, only seven canvases in "The Eight's" exhibition had been bought, and Sloan himself had not sold a single painting until 1913.[57]

Huneker's low opinion of *The "Genius"* and his failure to take an active part in defending the book against charges of obscenity may have led to a coolness between him and Dreiser, for a passage about the latter in the serialized version of Huneker's autobiography (omitted in the book, where Dreiser is virtually ignored) is rather sharp. "Dreiser we must accept with his faults, full-blown," he asserted here. "He is dull yet powerful at times." *Jennie Gerhardt* was more individual than *Sister Carrie* and had not been surpassed by the incomplete Cowperwood trilogy or *The "Genius,"* but his most readable book was *A Hoosier Holiday.* "Nevertheless the Zola influence . . . has mortised his work with materialism," Huneker concluded. "Theodore Dreiser has a ponderous style and he lacks vision."[58] Despite this comment, Dreiser seems to have maintained a fairly high opinion of Huneker as a critic, though he felt that the extent of Huneker's pioneering had been somewhat exaggerated. After Mencken had complained to him in 1920 about Huneker's "senility"—he objected to certain passages in *Steeplejack,* as we shall see—Dreiser replied: "Many of Huneker's earlier critical estimates and interpretations are excellent—quite generous and fascinating. . . . He was & is a fine writer, interpretative and illuminating. He was certainly very much needed over here."[59]

Having read proofs of his Liszt book—finished at last—and obtained an advance from Scribner's as well as an increase in royalties from 10 to 15 per cent,[60] Huneker sailed for Europe in late August 1911. After two weeks in Antwerp and Bruges, he started on a tour of German art galleries, but on September 20, while getting off the train in the poorly lit station at Cologne, he tripped over some baggage and bruised his side so severely that he was laid up under a doctor's care. "I told Jozia . . . that it was the first time I broke my heart since I met her," he scribbled painfully to Rosebault a week later, his ribs still aching.[61] Physically unable to write at length, he managed to see pictures in Cassel, Frankfort, Darmstadt, and Berlin, and to hear twice in Dresden, where it had received its world première earlier in the year, Strauss's opera *Der Rosenkavalier*. (In 1910 Huneker's edition of songs by Strauss had been published by Ditson's.) He decided, however, that since he was not earning expenses, he could not afford to go to Budapest for the important Liszt Festival. To top off his bad luck, he had trouble getting steamer accommodations home—and then the crossing was uncommonly long and stormy. When he reached New York in early November, he was weary, disappointed, and $1,200 poorer.

Moreover, *Franz Liszt*, published in October, had failed to materialize into the biography Huneker originally projected. As he confessed in a note at the end of the volume, he had not had the time and patience to do a first-rate life of the multifaceted Liszt. He told Finck, to whom the book was dedicated, that it was "botched," that it should have appeared in 1902 when his enthusiasm had not cooled[62] (and, one might interpolate, before he had been sidetracked into drama and art). The most readable part of the book is the opening chapter, a lively survey of Liszt's entire career, while the most useful, for reference purposes, is probably the section on his compositions, a series of program notes in which Huneker too often quotes Finck, Philip Hale, and other experts instead of relying on his own judgment. The chapter "In the Footsteps of Liszt," where Huneker discusses his visits to European cities associated with his subject, throws light on his own life but is not always relevant to the task at hand; his account of his audience with the Pope, for example, may supply "Roman atmosphere" but it does not tell us much about Liszt. To musical specialists the most interesting feature of the book was undoubtedly Huneker's insistence on Liszt's unappreciated originality as the inventor of a new form, the symphonic poem, and as the creator of ideas which other composers—especially Wagner— shamelessly borrowed without acknowledgment. Although the almost pedantic array of evaluated authorities and carefully selected quotations makes *Franz Liszt* his most "scholarly" achievement, rather than a unified biography Huneker produced a source book helpful to critics and subsequent biographers of Liszt[63] but too choppy, repetitious, and poorly organized for the discriminating layman. Yet as late as 1925 it was described in a reputable history of American music as "decidedly" the best life of Liszt in existence.[64]

In early September 1911, while Huneker was in Holland, his one-time friend and colleague Percival Pollard had suddenly lashed out against him in a biting poem printed in *Reedy's Mirror*. Though Huneker's name was not mentioned, "To Our Canniest Critic: on Gautier's Birthday" (his centenary) was obviously addressed to him, the reference to Gautier being Pollard's crafty way of suggesting Huneker's indebtedness to the Frenchman. The poem read as follows:

> He never wore a scarlet coat
> Nor joined a losing fight;
> If safety lay toward the wrong,
> He did not choose the right.

> He never wore his heart in sight,
> Nor spilt his youth in song;
> Made foes of none, but friends of all
> Who to the Powers belong.

> The fine Italian hand he wrote
> His canny cunning showed,
> For though he wrote of Anarch Art,
> And for the Moderns glowed,

> His Moderns and his Anarchs all
> Were never close at home.
> But—lived and worked far overseas
> In Paris, Zurich, Rome.

> High though his shrewdness carried him
> In his own native land,
> To not one fellow-countryman
> He lent a helping hand.

> His was the genius of the Jew
> With Jesuit craft combined;
> A dextrous skill in juggling words,
> A grasping, copious, mind.

> He will go down to fame as one
> On foreign fodder grown,
> Who never wrote a stupid word
> Nor—any of his own.

He never fought in rebel cause;
No windmill drew his lance;
His pen dripped jewels only for
Cash Down, and In Advance.

He never wore a scarlet coat,
Nor advertised Romance,
His pact, in literature, was with
The Devil, not Dame Chance.[65]

What was the story behind this attack? The facts seem to be that for several years Pollard, unable to get his books accepted by major New York publishers, had become increasingly embittered by his lack of recognition as a novelist, playwright, and critic.[66] He had begun, consequently, to vent his anger and frustration upon "friends" who had become more famous than he, though he felt they were no more talented, and perhaps even less so. In his outspoken *Their Day in Court* (1909), a book consisting mainly of *Town Topics* reviews, he added ugly overtones to his generally amiable notice of *Egoists*[67] and repeated the claim that Huneker had practically ignored the arts in America. "Certainly he abstained most cannily," he wrote, "from any such iconoclasm, or such appreciation of home-grown iconoclasts, as might have brought about and upon him the destructive, crushing power of all those mighty forces leagued together in America to make plain speaking perilous." (Huneker suspected that this was a reference to his refusal to share Pollard's high regard for Ambrose Bierce, whose enemies, Pollard believed with an almost paranoid intensity, were determined not to give Bierce his due.)[68] "Aside from the canniness in the adoption of this scheme of criticism," Pollard went on, "apart from the equation of personal success involved, he was quite right in his survey of the home field; there were not enough creative giants here to make brilliant criticism worth while." Huneker had supported American painters, Pollard conceded, but the art criticism had not yet been given permanent book form, and thus it could not be admitted as evidence of Huneker's "Americanism."[69] *Promenades of an Impressionist* gave Pollard more ammunition, a year later, since, as he quickly pointed out, it did not contain a single study of an American painter.[70]

Most of the creative artists Huneker found significant and exciting were, of course, European. But the accusation—to which he had made himself vulnerable by failing to collect his scattered essays on American subjects—that he was indifferent to native literature, drama, music, and painting was absurd, as every careful reader of his work in New York newspapers and magazines could surely attest.[71] Had any other critic, had Pollard himself, so persistently pleaded for a freer, less provincial artistic atmosphere in America? Huneker therefore resented Pollard's unjust remarks and nasty tone, especially since he had frequently praised Pollard's earlier books,[72] and publicly ignored *Their Day in Court*. "Some of the dearest friends, like Jim Huneker, kept most cannily silent," Pollard complained to his friend Mencken in February 1910,[73] and he had nursed his grievance for more than a year before gaining revenge with his lampoon[74]—published a few weeks after Huneker's tribute to Gautier upon his approaching centenary appeared in the *Sun*.[75]

It is worth pausing to note that Pollard's recognition of Huneker's affinities with Gautier shows that even a bad-tempered, vindictive critic could be perceptive. Few, if any, American reviewers had remarked that consciously or unconsciously Huneker may have modeled himself upon *"le bon Théo."* (George Moore, himself influenced by Gautier, saw the resemblance. "Like Gautier," he wrote Huneker in 1906, "you came into the world to produce a great deal of 'copy.'")[76] Though aesthetic ideas popularized by Gautier—individualism, "art for art's sake," the inutility and amorality of art—were the common property of Flaubert, Hugo, Baudelaire, and other French writers, and had circulated in America via the more accessible writings of Wilde, Moore, Symons, and Ellis, Huneker had undoubtedly read Gautier long and well, for he often quoted or alluded to him.[77] Surely he had pondered over Gautier's dictum—originally published less than two months before Huneker's birth—that criticism should be a "demonstration of the beauties, not a search for the faults" of a work of art, and that the critic's mission was not to "mark and grade an artistic production in the manner of a school-teacher correcting examination papers," but to study and understand it and to help others appreciate it.[78] In the Frenchman, Huneker had encountered a kindred spirit whose personality and career bore remarkable similarities to his own. Gautier, who disliked sports as a lad because of bad health, hated school discipline, and took refuge in books from the taunts of "rough" boys,[79] became a nonmaterialistic, apolitical lover of good living, pleasure, and beauty, who preferred creative work to criticism but spent forty years of "slavery" in journalism criticizing all the arts; yet he managed to "create" by making criticism a personal vehicle for fine prose based on taste, sympathy, color, rhythm, an enormous vocabulary, and the device of discussing one art in terms of another in an attempt to break down artistic barriers and reveal the interrelationship of the senses. The genial Gautier, too, had composed humorous sketches satirizing or parodying his more eccentric contemporaries,[80] as well as serious short stories with spiritual overtones.[81]

Naturally there were important differences in the careers of the two men. Gautier's fiction is far better than Huneker's, and the latter's few attempts at light verse cannot be compared, obviously, with the polished poems of the author of *Amaux et Camées*, a landmark in French poetry. Gautier's chief technical knowledge was in painting, of course, instead of music, and he was not as sympathetic as Huneker to modernism in art and literature, preferring Delacroix to Manet, for example, and historical to realistic drama. Knowing no English, moreover, he lacked the firsthand familiarity with English literature that Huneker had with French. But Huneker more than any other American writer resembled Gautier in his range, interspersing fiction, improvisations, and travel sketches among countless critiques of the most distinguished literary creators and actors of many countries; and his sensitivity, gusto, style, and method were also reminiscent of Gautier. If Huneker deliberately emulated such a model, in an America only slowly awakening to the attractions of art, it was no mean aim. Pollard recognized the style as Gautier's, though others might have thought it Huneker's own.

If Reedy's purpose in publishing Pollard's poem was to stir up a controversy, he succeeded, for within two weeks it had elicited so many letters to the editor that he decided to make his own position clear. The verses were clever, he said, but Pollard had overstated his case; Huneker *had* "worn a scarlet coat" (a reference, of course, to Gautier's wearing a rose-colored waistcoat at the famous première of Hugo's *Hernani*, symbolizing his courage in standing up for his convictions and his desire to shock the bourgeois) in his *M'lle New York* days and *had* aided his countrymen, as Reedy knew from personal experience, for Huneker had once contributed articles to the *Mirror* for "small and mighty slow pay." Moreover, he had "helped many a writer, many a painter, many a girl with a passion for the stage, along the rough, unfeeling ways of Gotham," and had shown "thousands of . . . younger men and women

worlds new, beautiful and strange for their conquest and enjoyment."[82]
One of the writers Huneker had assisted, Reedy observed, was the ver-
milion-coated George Sylvester Viereck, the most daring purveyor of
sex and paganism in American letters. After Reedy printed a letter by
"A Visiting Englishman" who saw no virtue in Huneker's discovery of
Viereck,[83] the latter also protested against the poem. "I owe my own
literary impetus in this country very largely to the same 'canny critic,' "
he declared,[84] recalling, no doubt, that Pollard had condemned his
Nineveh and Other Poems in 1907 whereas Huneker had generously
hailed him in the same year as a "youthful prodigy."[85]

Reedy probably hoped that Huneker would fan the flame by replying
to Pollard in the *Mirror,* but Huneker (who may not have actually seen
the verses until after Pollard's death in December 1911, for he wrote
Scribner's on the following January 1, asking for a copy of the lampoon)[86] wisely remained silent. On the same day, he hinted to Viereck
that Pollard's fatal disease might have affected his mind—which is, indeed, quite possible. "Was I right in not worrying over what the poor
sick chap wrote? All his friends knew and said nothing; all got the same
sort of letters."[87] The episode came to an ironic end in Baltimore when
Ambrose Bierce told Mencken grotesque jokes as they drove to Pollard's
cremation.[88]

Pollard's attack made Huneker sensitive about his "Americanism."
When Mencken was gathering material for an article about him in 1916,
he asked Mencken not to endorse Pollard's "legend." "All my life," he
said, "I've toiled in the cause of American poets, painters, musicians,
prosateurs, critics," and someday, he added, he would print a volume
on American arts and date it, and Mencken might be surprised.[89] He
never got around to doing this, but he was careful to include at least
one "American" essay in each of his collections published after 1911.
Yet it was as an importer of "poisonous honey" from Europe rather
than as a press agent for the home product that Huneker made his mark
on American culture, and though he had already done his most important work by 1912, when his era was approaching its cataclysmic end,
there were a few importations still to come.

Sixteen

FOREIGN CORRESPONDENT

By January 1912 William C. Reick had bought a controlling interest in the *Sun* and had instituted a factual reportorial style which robbed it of its chief distinction.[1] The effect of this new policy, together with a tightened budget, was to reduce the number of Huneker's contributions printed on the editorial page throughout the following months, and in midsummer he apparently resigned as the *Sun's* art critic. Having agreed to write feature articles from abroad for the *New York Times's* Sunday pages, edited by Alden March, Huneker gave up the "dream barn," stored the furniture, and sailed with Josephine for Europe in late August.

After two weeks in Holland and Belgium and two in Paris—where he interviewed Henri Bergson as well as Matisse—Huneker went to London mainly to meet his favorite contemporary novelist, Joseph Conrad.[2] Huneker had praised Conrad at least as early as 1905, when he commented on the insufficient recognition given to that "man of genius . . . surely an apparition in dusty English literary life with his formal perfections, his glow, his color, his vitality!" In the spring of 1909 he had started a correspondence with Conrad by sending him a copy of *Egoists*. "I will not conceal from you that I take it in the sense most flattering to myself," Conrad replied. ". . . What's more delightful than to find one's own half-formed thoughts expressed with force, conviction and charm in an unexpected and authoritative book coming to me from over the seas?" He was surprised, shortly afterward, to learn that Huneker was one of his "reviewers" in America. "I have seen very few criticisms from your side; and the few I've seen were not calculated to stimulate my curiosity as to the others." It was comforting to know that he had a band of faithful readers in America, he admitted, for "to live (artistically) one needs the feeling that one is believed in."

On the afternoon of October 12 Huneker talked for three hours with

Conrad at Conrad's farmhouse in Kent. He found the writer "a man of the world, neither sailor nor novelist, just a simple-mannered gentleman, whose welcome was sincere, whose glance was veiled, at times faraway, whose ways were French, Polish, anything but 'literary,' 'bluff,' or English." With his love of Chopin and other Poles, his cosmopolitanism, his high regard for French literature, and his friendship with Conrad's great American friend Stephen Crane, Huneker made an excellent impression on Conrad. Replying to his guest's note of thanks for extending such warm hospitality to a "stranger," Conrad graciously assured him that he was no stranger:

> Ever since I first heard from you [he wrote] you have been one of the men who count in our existence, often thought of, frequently spoken about. I have had from the first the greatest respect for your attitude to life and art and a very sincere admiration of your penetrating intelligence and illuminating judgment of men and things. That is why I have prized highly your generous appreciation of my work. To these sentiments is added now a profound sympathy for your person. It was difficult to tell you how much I thought of you while you were here. The time was so short; and when I feel deeply I am not quick in expression. I only hope that I shall have the delight of seeing you and grasping your friendly hand once more before your return to the States.

On November 17 the *New York Times* printed Huneker's account of the meeting, which, he claimed, was the first interview of Conrad published in America. He described Conrad here as the only man in England who belonged to the "immortal company" of Meredith, Hardy, and Henry James, a judgment he revised two years later, when, as Conrad's most enthusiastic American supporter, he ranked him not with England's but with the world's greatest novelists—Flaubert, Turgenev, Dostoevski, and Tolstoy.[3]

At the Richard Strauss festival in Stuttgart, Huneker heard the world première of *Ariadne auf Naxos* (his verdict: "a melange of styles and a weak book") as well as performances of *Feuersnot, Elektra, Salome,* and *Rosenkavalier,* the "most beautiful of all 'comic' operas," according to Huneker. Fremstad sang "wonderfully" in *Salome*[4]—as she had at the Metropolitan in 1907, when the "immoral" opera had been suppressed, much to Huneker's disgust, after one performance.[5] Salome herself should be a "slight, cynical young person—half Flaubert, half Laforgue," Huneker remarked in 1912, not "a mature pussycat at mid-

summer," as Mary Garden had played her.[6] (If Huneker and Garden
were good friends by 1909,[7] when her sexy French Salome was inevitably compared with Fremstad's more subdued, better-sung interpretation of the role, and if he admired her then as much as he did later, he
would hardly have printed this remark—even if he felt, as George Jean
Nathan once hinted,[8] that he could not praise Garden while her "rival"
was performing at the Metropolitan without jeopardizing his friendship
with Fremstad.[9] At any rate, when he composed his famous rhapsody
on Garden seven years later, he must have hoped that nobody remembered his earlier comment on her.) Strauss would live, he predicted,
because of his *Till Eulenspiegel, Don Quixote*, and *Elektra*.[10]

At Stuttgart Huneker also saw Frank Wedekind, the dramatist, on
whom he was to write an article published a few months afterward.[11]
In Munich he interviewed Max Liebermann, the leading modern painter
of Germany, and signed a contract with publisher George Müller for the
publication of his *Chopin* in a German translation by Lola Lorme, a
young Austrian writer and translator.[12] "If the sale is good," Huneker
wrote Mitchell from Vienna, "the *Chopin* is to be followed by all of my
books—coals to Newcastle in my opinion, for I owe much to German
culture."[13] After visits to Prague and Dresden, he wearily settled in
Berlin at the end of November to write new articles and put old ones
together for his next book.

With three fine symphony orchestras and thousands of concerts,
operas, and recitals every season, Berlin was the music center of the
world.[14] Its theaters, moreover, were staging exciting new works by
modern German dramatists, while Ibsen plays could be seen every night
in a dozen playhouses.[15] It was no less important to the far-from-affluent
Huneker that steam-heated apartments were available at low rentals, and
that food was reasonable, if not always appetizing.[16] To get a change
from heavy German cooking, the Hunekers went one night to a place
called "Tonello's" and briskly ordered spaghetti. "Pardon me, sir," the
waiter replied, "this is a kosher restaurant." They settled for roast goose
and knockerl—which turned out to be one of the most delicious meals
they had ever eaten. "The secret was not the Hebraic chef," Huneker
explained, "but the tiny flavoring of garlic in the sauce—garlic, which
is the C major of all flavoring."[17]

His pride, too, was fed on December 18 when he had what he called
his "little quarter of an hour" at a music and reading program in the

Kleiner Beethoven-Saal in Vienna, where Lola Lorme gave a paper on Huneker's work and a German actress read Mme Lorme's translation of his short story "The Lord's Prayer in B."[18] The honor flustered him so much, it seems, that in one letter he said that he had attended the affair, while in another he said that he had not (which was more likely, considering his fear of speaking in public).[19] It pleased him, in any event, and was good publicity for the German *Chopin*, proofs of which he was reading by the following March. Later, an article on Vienna, printed in the *New York Times* on April 13, 1913, won Huneker a free-dom-of-the-city award from the Austro-Hungarian capital.[20]

His comments on Berlin's music, drama, and art appeared in the *Times* at irregular intervals during the first half of 1913. Especially significant was a report on Arnold Schönberg, Strauss's successor as the most controversial composer in Europe. In December 1912, Schön-berg's *Lieder des Pierrot Lunaire* reminded Huneker at first of "the sound of delicate China shivering into a thousand luminous fragments. In the welter of tonalities that bruised each other as they passed and repassed, in the preliminary grip of enharmonies that almost made the ears bleed, the eyes water, the scalp to freeze, I could not keep a central grip on myself. It was new music, or new exquisitely horrible sounds, with a vengeance. The very ecstasy of the hideous!" "If such music making is ever to become accepted," he concluded, "then I long for Death the Releaser. More shocking still would be the suspicion that in time I might be persuaded to like [it]."[21] Huneker also gave special attention to plays by Schnitzler, Sudermann, Hauptmann,[22] and espe-cially Wedekind, whose eroticism and hatred of shams strongly appealed to him. Wedekind's "most original, if not most finished drama," he reported, was a treatment of puberty, *The Awakening of Spring*, a mile-stone in the modern theater's fight against sexual taboos. "The caprice, the bizarre, the morbid in Wedekind are more than redeemed by his rich humanity," Huneker wrote. But "on the English stage he would be emasculated. And I wonder who would have the courage to pro-duce his works."[23]

Though no expert, certainly, on politics and economics, Huneker was not blind to what was going on in Germany. While America hailed the Kaiser as a peacemaker on his Silver Jubilee in 1913, Huneker muttered against the high taxation levied on foreigners who lived in the country more than three months. "Germany has the best-equipped army in the world," he remarked, "but she is paying a killing price to maintain it. . . . I feel at times as if I was sitting over a big boiler that is carrying too much steam. If an explosion ever comes it will be felt the world over."[24]

Dedicated to John Howard McFadden, the Philadelphia cotton magnate, art collector, and philanthropist, whose relationship with Huneker is rather obscure, *The Pathos of Distance* appeared in the spring of 1913. A charming potpourri of personal reminiscences and brief essays —most of them reprinted from the *Sun*—on music, drama, painting, literature, and philosophy, Huneker's tenth book covered a wider range than any of the earlier ones, and may well be his most readable and representative volume. "It's very personal," he explained to Quinn. ". . . I've been told by so many reviewers that I should put more of 'myself' into my work (as if that were possible) that I let her rip."[25] The last chapter, "A Belated Preface to *Egoists*," was a reply to those who had decried his lack of general ideas, or, more reprehensively, had questioned the importance of his "Supermen." (It resembles the preface to *La Culture des idées*, in which Remy de Gourmont engagingly admits that his book was merely a collection of articles and was not held together by any "common idea.")[26]

The reviewers liked this "new" personal note. "The best thing in [it] is Huneker himself," remarked Reedy, mentioning him for the first time since the Pollard fracas.[27] The critic was "neither an eccentric nor a disciple of eccentrics, but a very human person," Duncan Phillips keenly observed in the *Yale Review*. ". . . When we lay [the book] down we *know* Huneker."[28] Especially impressed by the essay on New York architecture, Holbrook Jackson commented in the London *Bookman* that Huneker's intelligence, which "soars above that of the modernist art-tasters of the coteries," reflected the omnivorous, eclectic mind of his cosmopolitan race and its age.[29] If he considered such a cosmopolitanism typically American, Jackson surely overestimated Huneker's countrymen, but he recognized, nevertheless, Huneker's inherent Americanism. ("I had rather be a fried oyster in Philadelphia than the Lord Mayor of London," the homesick traveler had declared a few months earlier.)[30] The sweetest words about *The Pathos of Distance*, however, came from Joseph Conrad. "Apart from the temperamental sympathy I feel for your work," Conrad wrote him in 1913, "the lightness of your surface touch playing over the deeper meaning of your criticism is very fascinating. One feels grateful to you for your pages of acute and sincere judgment familiarly expressed—as a friend talks."

Old Fogy, a collection of the light musical sketches contributed to *Etude* over a period of twenty-seven years (two had appeared in 1912), came out shortly after *The Pathos of Distance*. As one might expect, it is rather disjointed and mixed in tone: the crotchety "Old Fogy" is not even present in two of the papers, and burlesque and parody are combined with serious criticism and autobiography, "A Visit to the Paris Conservatoire" being an embellished account of Huneker's fateful audition in 1878.[31] Sometimes "Old Fogy" completely contradicts himself, as, for example, in the two essays on Liszt. ("I'm having fun with my old opinions," Huneker told Theodore Presser, the book's publisher, "just letting off gas for the sake of being contradictory.")[32] While "Old Fogy" echoes Huneker's own admiration for Chopin, Bach, Brahms, Pachmann, and Joseffy (to whom the volume is dedicated), his cantankerous objections to Wagner, Liszt, Tchaikovsky, and Strauss are designed to ridicule diehard musical conservatives. "After Mozart give me Strauss," says the old man, "—Johann, however, not Richard!"[33] But when he counsels his readers, elsewhere, to "enjoy the music of your epoch, for there is no such thing as music of the future,"[34] it is clearly Huneker himself speaking.

Yet *Old Fogy* contains some prize passages of Hunekerian humor. "A College for Critics," for example, gently but effectively satirizes the prejudices and pretensions of music critics, including several of his thinly disguised friends ("Blink," "Slehbell," and "Sanderson" are obviously Finck, Krehbiel, and Henderson).[35] In "Musical Biography Made to Order," Huneker parodies the sentimental biographical anecdote with delightful results. "Old Fogy Writes a Symphonic Poem" is an amusing burlesque on program music, and "A Wonder Child," written as early as 1888, is one of his funniest pieces. Racy and witty remarks are not lacking in the other essays. "A man in love with his wife and that man a musician!" "Old Fogy" exclaims, apropos of Robert and Clara Schumann. "Why, the entire episode must seem abnormal to the flighty, capricious younger set, the Bayreuth set, for example."[36] "The story could not come clear," he says of a performance of *Die Walküre*, "although I saw I was in trouble when I read that the hero and heroine were brother and sister. Experience has taught me that family rows are the worst, and I wondered why Wagner chose such a dull, old-fashioned theme."[37] It was these antics and quips that led Mencken to declare that if he had to choose one Huneker book and give up all the rest, he would instantly choose *Old Fogy*, because in it Huneker was "utterly himself."[38]

To maintain the slight pretense that "Old Fogy" was anything other than a fictitious creation, Huneker was identified only as the book's "editor," but *Etude* practically gave away the "secret" in prepublication notices, and few readers were fooled.[39] Issued by a music publisher, *Old Fogy* was not widely advertised or reviewed, and, consequently, its sale was unusually small; during Huneker's lifetime, indeed, royalties covered less than half of the $250 advanced to him.[40] "It is due to the pious friendship of the publisher," he remarked in the charming introduction, "that these opinions are bound between covers."[41] Yet he undoubtedly felt that this was the least that Presser, now a millionaire, could do for him in return for his help in establishing *Etude*.

At the end of April 1913, Huneker left Berlin. After two weeks in Belgium, he proceeded to London to confer with Chapman and Hall, the English publishers of his *Franz Liszt*, over legal action brought against them for having reprinted without permission or payment a copyrighted translation of Heine's reminiscences of Liszt (the matter was apparently settled out of court).[42] Huneker also saw some of his English friends and met other writers and newspapermen through the Authors' Club. "Wells is a decent chap, so is Chesterton," he wrote Edward Marsh. "Any quantity of invitations. . . ." He had not "run across" Shaw, who was rich and "waxes pompous," he added, nor did he have an opportunity, it seems, to visit Conrad, "the most lovable of the lot." The *Saturday Review* offered Huneker a job, he stated, which he might have taken, perhaps, were Beerbohm—who had left the magazine in 1910—still on the staff, if only to enjoy the sweet revenge of being Max's colleague; but he decided that the pay was too low[43] and the English weather too depressing. The only signed article by Huneker printed in the *Saturday Review*, a critique of Runciman's *Wagner* written in a carefully pruned style, appeared later that year.[44]

In June Huneker made his first trip to "dear old dirty but adorable Dublin," primarily to see the Municipal Gallery's fine collection of modern art gathered by Sir Hugh Lane, though he found the people on the streets as interesting as the pictures during his five-day visit. Too many able-bodied men and women were taking orders and filling convents, he observed, instead of marrying and having families, and there was too much dirt and poverty.[45] This comment and a humorous reference to the Fenian invasion of Canada angered at least one Irish-American, who sent a sharp letter to the editor of the *Gaelic-American,* complaining that it was unbecoming for anyone with Irish blood to make slighting remarks about the homeland.[46]

A cable from his brother requesting his presence in Philadelphia for the transaction of urgent family business[47] brought the Hunekers back to America on July 1, but six weeks later they sailed again from New York, this time for Holland. On August 28 Huneker covered the opening of the magnificent Peace Palace at The Hague. "It was a great day for Mr. Andrew Carnegie and the hopeful persons who believe war is to be abolished by sentiment . . . ," he reported. "When its utter futility is finally demonstrated I think it will make one of the handsomest restaurants and cafés in all Europe. As such it will be useful and provocative of peace."[48] (More indecorously, he had confided to his young Nietzschean friend Willard Huntington Wright, editor of *Smart Set,* that the structure would do more good as a *piece* palace.)[49] After short stays in Amsterdam, Zandvoort, and Haarlem, and a quick trip to strike-bound Dublin in early September,[50] Huneker settled in Utrecht for a few weeks to catch up on his writing.

Here he had several talks with the director of Amsterdam's famous Central Institute of Brain Research, Dr. C. U. Ariens Kappers, whom he had met in 1909. Huneker had always found science absorbing. For years at Philadelphia's Academy of Natural Sciences he had heard lectures by distinguished scientists such as Joseph Leidy and Edward Cope,[51] and he had collected material on tornadoes.[52] He was familiar enough with investigations in modern physics and mathematics to mention, in his short story "The Disenchanted Symphony" (published in *Melomaniacs*), the fourth-dimension theories of Zöllner and the speculations of Cayley, Abbot, Clifford, and Newcomb.[53] Intrigued by biological theories of man's development and personality, he had written for the *Sun* at least one editorial on anthropology and also a review of H. Archdall Reid's *The Laws of Heredity.*[54] Therefore, when Dr. Kappers, a brilliant neurologist who had attempted earlier to interest Huneker in his experiments,[55] invited him to visit the Institute and offered to introduce him to Hugo De Vries, the world-renowned Dutch botanist, he quickly accepted. In his laboratory at the Amsterdam Botanic Garden, De Vries showed Huneker evidence supporting his famous theory of the mutations of species and supplied data which, with Kappers' help, Huneker fashioned into an essay on the evolution of man. Although this —and an article about the Peace Palace and the towns and arts of Holland—did not appear until 1914,[56] his earlier writings on Dutch art, the most recent of which was a study of Vermeer published in the *Times* in January 1913,[57] won Huneker a royal decoration bestowed upon him before he left Utrecht.[58] (With professional wistfulness, perhaps, Kappers later lauded the "excellent and sparkling brain" of his American friend.)[59]

Huneker retained an informed layman's interest in science, which he called the "most honourable profession in the world."[60] In 1916 and 1917, for example, he reviewed *Creative Involution* by Cora L. Williams, a mathematician, and Claude Bragdon's *Four Dimensional Vistas*.[61] An essay "On Re-reading Mallock," published in October 1916, reveals Huneker's awareness of the wonders of contemporary science:

A new world has come into being. And what discoveries: spectral analysis, the modes of force, matter displaced by energy, the relations of atoms in molecules—a renewed geology, astronomy, palaeontology, biology, embryology, wireless telegraphy, the conquest of the air, and, last but not least, the discovery of radium. The slightly worn evolution theory is now confronted by the Transformism of Hugo De Vries. . . . And the brain, that telephonic centre, according to Bergson, is become another organ. Ramón y Cajal, the Spanish biologist, with his neurons—little erectile bodies in the cells of the cortex, stirred to motor impulses when a message is sent them from the sensory nerves—has done more for positive knowledge than a wilderness of metaphysicians.[62]

Nor did the new psychology escape his attention. Though one might expect, considering the bent of his mind, that Huneker would have been fascinated by Freud's theories, or willing, at least, to listen, he seems to have shut his mind to Freudianism. Surely Huneker himself often sought an artist's "naked soul" (a pet phrase of his) by examing his sexual nature, as his essays on Whitman, Tchaikovsky, and Wagner amply testify.[63] If he did not practice literary psychoanalysis —"In literature nowadays," he remarked in 1907, ridiculing the pathologic theory of genius set forth by Nordau and Lombroso, " 'psychiatrists' rush in where critics fear to tread"[64]—he often appeared to be more curious about the artist than his work. "So far as I can recall," Mencken declared, "he never wrote a piece of criticism without adding to it a piece of biography."[65] Indeed, as Huneker once told Mencken, with as much truth as humor, *Melomaniacs* and *Visionaries* had been called "valuable documents for alienists."[66] On the other hand, he was too conscious of an individual's uniqueness and of the complexity of human nature to be convinced by any pat "explanation" of behavior. Perhaps he feared that Freud's theory of the artist as a successful neurotic tended to disparage the creative act without really accounting for it, or that Freudianism, like Nietzscheism, would be misinterpreted by the Greenwich Village intellectuals and their counterparts as a misty justification for the free love and riotous living which no longer seemed to promise happiness to the aging Huneker.[67]

It would be surprising if anyone as *au courant* and as curious about abnormal psychology as Huneker had not read some psychoanalytical literature by this time. If he had not cared to tackle Freud in German, by 1910 he could have obtained an English translation of the important *Three Contributions to a Theory of Sex* or seen a popularized article or two on psychoanalysis in American journals.[68] At any rate, Huneker referred to Freud at least as early as November 1914, pointing out that a dream sequence in Leo Ditrichstein's adaptation of Molnar's play *The Phantom Rival* was "a bit . . . which would be approved by Professor Freud."[69] In 1916, when the popular magazines were discovering psychoanalysis, Huneker's sharply etched "character" of "The Mock Psychiatrist"—who can diagnose "anything from rum-thirst to sudden death" and who tries to assume the "outward appearance of a veritable man of science"[70]—was probably aimed more at Lombroso and Nordau than at the psychoanalysts. Three years later, however, in discussing Baudelaire's letters to his mother, Huneker remarked that Albert Mordell, Freudian author of *The Erotic Motive in Literature* (1919), could have found Baudelaire "a better subject than Stendhal for his Oedipus-complex."[71] The incidental use of Freudian terminology also found in *Painted Veils* (in which, Huneker once admitted, his "suppressed 'complexes,' as the Freudians say, come to the surface")[72] indicates that he was certainly familiar by the middle of 1919 with the jargon of psychoanalysis.[73]

Later in 1919 Huneker made it clear that he thought *all* psychia-

trists were partly fakers—and none more so than those who attempted
to account for genius as a disease or a sign of decadence. He traced the
degeneration theory from Morel's *Traité des dégénérescences* through
Charcot, Nordau, and others to

the so-called new school of Freudian psychoanalysis, which exploits to the
reductio ad absurdum the von Hartmann theory of the subliminal consciousness, with a little spice of soothsaying and dream-book twaddle thrown in to
lend an air of novelty. We learn from Dr. Freud that dreams are the result
of unfulfilled desires—which may mean anything—that authors unconsciously reveal themselves in their writings. What an astounding discovery!
. . . Cut out the erotic element in this "new" theory and the world would
pass it by.[74]

But Freud had his revenge in the psychoanalytic 1920's, when a young
professor detected a mother complex in Huneker—a diagnosis that
Josephine hotly denied.[75]

Leaving Utrecht in mid-October 1913, Huneker proceeded to Brus-
sels for a few days and then to London for nearly two months of plays
—he could not help being amused by Shaw's *Androcles and the Lion*
and *Great Catherine*—sculptures, and pictures. He was impressed by
Jacob Epstein's strangely daring, powerful "dreams in stone," though
rather puzzled by his latest style. Huneker's highest compliment was
paid to Augustus John, "a great personality (with greater potentiali-
ties)." Vyvyan Holland, Oscar Wilde's son, took his friend John Mc-
Fadden and Huneker to Sir Hugh Lane's house in London to see a
Gainsborough that was for sale, but though he knew Holland's identity,
Huneker tactfully said nothing to him about his father.[76] It appears
that Huneker even sat through the banquet given for Georg Brandes in
London on November 27, which was attended by H. G. Wells, Israel
Zangwill, and other literary celebrities, and also the dinner given for
Anatole France on December 10, when the company included Kipling,
Galsworthy, and Shaw.[77] And he visited the Cancer Research Labora-
tory, founded by McFadden, and the Lister Institute of Preventive Medicine, partially subsidized by the Philadelphia philanthropist, to gather
material for an article on the latest developments in the study of cancer
and syphilis—another indication of his interest in science.[78]

Tired, homesick, and irritated by the fog and gloom, the Hunekers
gladly left London for New York, arriving in late December. Unable

to find a suitable apartment they could afford in Manhattan, they took one in the Flatbush section of Brooklyn near the home of Josephine's youngest sister. At the end of the following February, they moved into the five-story Westminster Court, at 1618 Beverly Road, where they had a flat on the top floor so that Huneker, increasingly sensitive to noise, would not be disturbed by commotion overhead and could have more freedom in playing the piano. The houses and green lawns reminded him of a well-kept English country village, while Manhattan now seemed a "filthy factory town haunted by the worst class of European muckers imaginable." Yet he felt lonely in the suburb, at first, though he could reach the city in twenty minutes by subway, and the nearby cemeteries were depressing. But even more discouraging was the thought that now he had to "begin all over again." "Two years away from Broadway and you are a stranger here," he wrote Frida Ashforth, dipping his pen into the inkstand she had given him many years before.[79] His nerves almost as shaky as his bank account, Huneker, in his fifty-eighth year and suffering from a kidney disorder, was soon on the lookout, once again, for a regular job and a steady income.

✌ Seventeen

THE 'PUCK' PERIOD

In the spring of 1914 Huneker joined the staff of *Puck* (his salary was $50 a week, later increased to $75 and finally to $100),[1] for which he wrote, during the next three years, a column of miscellaneous criticism called "The Seven Arts." The oldest humorous weekly in America, *Puck* had recently been bought by Nathan Straus, Jr., the twenty-five-year-old, Heidelberg-educated scion of the prominent New York department store family. To make the once-brilliant *Puck* a "clever periodical for cultured people,"[2] an American counterpart of the famous German *Simplicissimus,* Straus and his editor, Hy Mayer, the noted illustrator and cartoonist, improved its format, solicited contributions from talented writers and artists—and acquired the services of Huneker. *Puck*'s long-established barbershop clientele liked its slightly bawdy cartoons and jokes, and, even more, the girlie pictures—many of them reprinted from the erotic magazine *La Vie Parisienne*—that drew protests from the YMCA. Higher-brows could also enjoy the impertinent comments on the news; the sophisticated scoffing at Christian Science, quack medicines, Billy Sunday's evangelism, and Prohibition; deft and witty light verse by George S. Kaufman, Arthur Guiterman, A. A. Milne (who made his first American appearance in *Puck*), and others; serious poetry by Richard Le Gallienne and James Joyce; satiric prose sketches by Stephen Leacock; and drama criticism by George Jean Nathan.

In "The Seven Arts," which made its debut on April 11, 1914, Huneker discussed books, pictures, music, plays, and even motion pictures. Sometimes, too, as in the "Raconteur," he filled his department with short stories or humorous sketches and, when desperate for copy, reprinted his earlier articles. Cropping up frequently in his pages were the names of Flaubert, Nietzsche, Anatole France, and the Russian novelists. Russian writers were popular, partly because of improved English translations—most notably, Constance Garnett's version of Dostoevski

—and partly because of the interest in Russia aroused in the West by
its participation in the war. Huneker found "extraordinary" imaginative power, for example, in Mikhail Artsybashev's sex-filled novel *Sanine*
(1907), which had been proscribed as pornographic in Russia and elsewhere but had finally been translated into English in 1914.[3]

On June 6, 1914, at the Hotel Astor in New York, Huneker met and
talked with Georg Brandes, who had been lecturing on Shakespeare
during his only visit to America, and was about to sail for home. In
his account of the interview, printed in *Puck*, Huneker called Brandes a
"pathfinder and iconoclast of the first order," ranking him with Sainte-
Beuve and Taine, and marveled at the alertness and continual pro-
ductivity of the seventy-two-year-old critic. "I've long known [him]
through correspondence," Huneker concluded, "but I found the man
even more refreshing than his letters."[4] Brandes thanked him privately
a month later for "speaking so warmly about me, you who are yourself
a master."[5]

Showing, once again, that he was no slave to European literature,
in 1915 Huneker urged American writers to read the fiction of elderly
(and, to the younger generation, anachronistic) William Dean Howells
to learn a "sense of proportion, continence of expression, the art of exquisitely simple prose, and vital characterization"; historians, he maintained, would go to these novels for a "truthful study of men and women
and manners during the last quarter of the Nineteenth Century in New
England and elsewhere (and not to the vermilion prose of the present
crowd of melodramatists between covers)."[6] In the following year,
Huneker again complimented Howells in an article on "The Great
American Novel," which pleased Howells so much that he wrote Huneker a letter about it.[7]

In 1916, also, Huneker reported that Van Wyck Brooks, the "cool-
headed and admirable" author of *America's Coming-of-Age* (1915),
had dethroned "our Yankee demi-gods of plaster and plush" from their
"musty, dusty pedestals." He found "many truths" in the sweeping
judgments of Brooks's courageous, if socialistic, attack on American
materialism. "We are such a self-satisfied nation," Huneker remarked,
"that it takes courage to state the facts concerning our provincial, colo-
nial, even parochial art and literature."[8] Almost forty years later, after
Brooks had published a long, picturesque history of American literature
in which he dropped his earlier iconoclasm in favor of an affirmative

quest for a "usable past," he felt that in this early book he had not attacked the New England writers quite so indiscriminately as Huneker had suggested; though he had generously acknowledged, in his history, Huneker's contributions to American culture, the older Brooks detected in this review an indication of Huneker's "blindness" to almost everything in the past.[9]

A younger American writer Huneker seems to have known only by her rather bizarre reputation was Gertrude Stein. If he had read the little-known books she had published, *Three Lives* (1910) and *Tender Buttons* (1914), or seen her word-portraits of Matisse and Picasso published in Stieglitz's *Camera Work* in August 1912 (about the time he left for Europe), he made no mention of them. Apparently his only public reference to her came in *Puck* in April 1915, where he had the hero of one of his fantasies recite words from Lewis Carroll's "The Jabberwocky," Huneker himself commenting: "That beats Gertrude Stein."[10] It is a pity that with his knowledge of abnormal psychology and modern painting, his sympathy for literary experimentation, his sensitivity to prose rhythm, and his eye for the picturesque personality, Huneker did not come to grips with Stein, who would have been an ideal subject for him. But he must have failed to understand her literary cubism (and how many critics did, or, for that matter, do yet?), just as he was unable to see much in Picasso and the cubist painters.

Huneker thought that the most encouraging sign of cosmopolitanism in the American theater of 1914 was the increasing freedom allowed playwrights in the treatment of sex. Why, in one recent play, he exclaimed, the heroine had actually spent the night before her marriage in the room of her bridegroom-elect! It would not have been difficult to guess the fate of a play with such a scene during "Willie" Winter's heyday.[11] Another step in the right direction was the establishment of the pioneering Washington Square Players, a group of Village amateurs formed early in 1915 to produce new or seldom-seen plays (preferably American) at low admission prices, a group that was to launch the distinguished careers of Katharine Cornell and Robert Edmond Jones and to lead, three years later, to the formation of the finest play-producing unit in America, the Theatre Guild. Though their productions were not as yet top-rate, Huneker wrote in the midst of the Players' second season, their ambition, industry, and high purpose were "bound to bring success."[12]

Huneker preferred even a mediocre play, however, to the best movie, an art form now competing with the legitimate stage. In 1914 he described a sample of this "canned" drama as

a monstrous olla-podrida of incidents, a jumble of movements, all without sense or relevance, nevertheless so filled with action that the eye is raped by the sheer velocity of the film. No story can ever be definitely related, for the essence of photography is the arrest of motion, and despite the ingenious mimicry of movement there is no narrative, only poses. The very faults of photography are exaggerated; the figures in the foreground are giant-like, in the middle distance or distant perspective they are those of pigmies. . . . The truth is that the moving pictures are a remarkable mechanical device, but never for a moment can be considered in the category of art. . . . They demand a minimum of thought from their spectators . . . and give to the eye the maximum of sensation. . . . You watch untouched by emotion the most "thrilling" spectacles and hair-breadth escapes. . . . This shadow-land is never dramatic, never poetically suggestive, never human. The absence of the human voice . . . is depressing. . . . The substitute, usually vulgar, noisy music, is an impertinence. A diversion for children, an aid to science, anything you will, but not an art for intelligent people.[13]

The best thing he could say about silent motion pictures was that, like gum-chewing, they spared the ear the "rasping, raucous, nasal enunciation and pronunciation—and mispronunciation—of the average acting male and female of our theaters."[14] One wonders what he would have thought of the modern film.

He predicted jokingly that some day another art would supplant the movies, and even wrote an amusing (and, in the television age, not too far-fetched) fantasy in which entire dramas were condensed in free "Luminovelocious Shows"—"vivid flashes of luminosity in a key higher than the violet rays of science." In this bright new world of speed, "there were no longer books and newspapers; the news was announced free of cost by monster phonographs." The venerable, pious Bernard Shaw, he added, would be writing for the "Lumies."[15]

"The Seven Arts" was widely read and admired. Fanny Butcher of the Chicago *Tribune* remarked that Huneker was the only man in America who knew enough about art, music, literature, and the drama to criticize all of them without sounding ridiculous.[16] Arthur Brisbane, no mean columnist himself, told Straus more than once that Huneker's column was generally considered to be the most authoritative department of criticism in the country.[17] In June 1915, Don Marquis, the popular

conductor of "The Sun Dial" in the *Evening Sun*, went out of his way
to compliment Huneker, who was always one of his "great admirations,"
though they never met:[18] reporting that a law had been proposed to require music teachers as well as doctors and lawyers to pass state examinations, Marquis ironically suggested that the idea be extended to painters, poets, novelists, and dramatists, and that a national committee for
each of these last four arts—he omitted music—be established, with
Huneker, a member of all four (no other person was to serve on more
than one), having the deciding vote on each board.[19]

Huneker's relations with Straus were extremely cordial.[20] At the editorial conferences also attended occasionally by the little-known George
S. Kaufman and (eventually) George Jean Nathan, Straus, awed by
Huneker's knowledge of the arts, beer, and women, listened almost spell-
bound as Huneker did most of the talking. Afraid that a loose expression or an unconventional idea in "The Seven Arts" might get *Puck* in
trouble, Straus once sent a note to Huneker (who usually worked at
home), asking him not to be "needlessly obscene." Huneker replied
gaily that he did not mind being told that he was obscene, but what did
Straus mean by "needlessly"?[21]

Before the war began to cut down the demand for his work, this was
a pleasant period for Huneker. His closest friends now were John Quinn
(also his attorney) and Frederick James Gregg, the trio constituting the
"Three Musketeers" of Huneker's last years. Advised by Huneker,
among others, Quinn, the Ohio-born corporation lawyer and power in
the Democratic Party, had acquired such an outstanding collection of
books, manuscripts, paintings, and sculptures that by the time he died,
in 1924, he was probably the "twentieth century's most important patron
of living literature and art." His collection was eventually to sell for
almost a million dollars, and would have been worth far more if it had
been kept a few years longer.[22] The well-read, incredibly energetic
Quinn, a virile bachelor, had a Celtic temperament and a Rabelaisian
wit similar to Huneker's. He was a close friend and patron of Joseph
Conrad, T. S. Eliot, James Joyce, Matisse, and Picasso, among others.
After the Armory Show, he became even more enthusiastic about modern art. He increased his purchases and, in February 1914, bought an
interest in a commercial gallery, the Carroll, where exhibitions of advanced European and American painters were given. He discussed

many of his acquisitions with Huneker and Gregg, and proudly displayed them to his two knowledgeable friends in his large apartment on Central Park West, crammed with some of the most striking specimens of ultramodern art and with shelves of first editions, rare books, and manuscripts. Huneker had pleased Quinn by publicly praising Irish writers whom Quinn patronized, and, indeed, one of the most memorable parties Huneker attended at Quinn's apartment was a dinner given in the spring of 1914 for Yeats, then lecturing in America.[23]

Born in Dublin, where he had gone to school with Yeats, the scholarly, witty Gregg had been regarded as a promising poet in Irish universities. Turning to journalism, he had been the *Evening Sun*'s art critic and editorial writer for years, his preference for modern art ("The Eight"—and especially Luks—were his special American favorites),[24] his personal charm, and his Irish sympathies ingratiating him with both Huneker and Quinn. In 1910 Huneker had dedicated *Promenades of an Impressionist* to Gregg, and five years later he was to dedicate *Ivory Apes and Peacocks* to Quinn.

Huneker's kidney condition put him on the water wagon intermittently, but during the intermissions one of his pet saloons was Knirim's Pilsner Sanatorium, a dark, roomy establishment in Hanover Square frequented by businessmen, office workers, and ship reporters based at nearby Battery Park. After he had happily reported, on discovering the place in 1911, that "Doctor" Knirim practiced the art of curing with Pilsner instead of pills,[25] Huneker was an especially welcome guest there. On the question of how (or how much) Pilsner should be drunk, Huneker agreed with the Teutonic, anarchistic Knirim (another saloon he had run had been a center for German revolutionaries), who claimed that most of the world's troubles could be ascribed to the drinking of cold beer, and would silently move among his customers with a thermometer, testing the temperature of each stein's contents.[26]

Often accompanied by Joseffy, Ziegler, Victor Herbert, or Leo Ditrichstein, Huneker went two or three times a week to Lüchow's, where young writers and artists sometimes came to catch a glimpse of him. ("My first visit to Lüchow's Restaurant was inspired by the fact that I had read somewhere that Huneker went there," recalled S. N. Behrman, the playwright, who had read every Huneker book in the public library of his hometown before graduating from Harvard in 1916 and coming to New York not long afterward. "I asked the head waiter if my hero was around, allowing him to believe that I was an important figure in Huneker's world, and when I was told that he was not, I went out on Fourteenth Street to Walton's [a "one-arm" restaurant] for lunch. I have often wondered what would have happened if Huneker *had* been there.")[27] Veteran employees of Lüchow's still remember Huneker. If Josephine was not with him, the erect, slow-walking, cross-looking critic would always sit in the front room at the "Stammtisch," the round table reserved for regular male diners. His favorite dishes were boiled beef with horseradish sauce, pig's knuckles and sauerkraut, and steak tartare, and he usually drank—with no apparent effect—ten to fifteen glasses of Pilsner from nine in the evening until two-thirty in the morning.[28] All the waiters liked him because he ordered slowly and quietly, often in German, and sometimes even discussed philosophy and poetry with them.[29]

One night at the end of 1914 or the beginning of 1915, Huneker spent over thirteen consecutive hours in the company of Maurice Sterne, the artist, whom he had met through Jo Davidson and whose work he had given a favorable notice several years earlier. They lunched at the Brevoort from one to four, stayed at the bar there until eight, and then adjourned to Lüchow's, where they remained until two-thirty. Throughout this spree, Sterne recalled, Huneker's "flow of beer and brilliant talk was never interrupted."[30] Ben De Casseres, an expert on New York's drinking places, had similar experiences with Huneker. "Jim, do you know you emit an aura?" Ben once asked. "It's the essence of ten thousand Holy Grails of Pilsner!" Huneker replied, lifting his glass.[31]

In June 1914 he attended the "seventieth" birthday party given at Lüchow's for sixty-two-year-old Max Heinrich, who liked to pretend that he was older than he really was so that he would be considered remarkably spry for an old man. Realizing, perhaps, that if the friend of his early days were taken to be seventy, Huneker's pretense that he himself was only fifty-four might appear transparent (since he looked even older than he really was), Huneker challenged Heinrich's claim, all the more readily because the lively, pugnacious Heinrich persisted in treating him like a not-too-bright pupil.[32] Two years later, Huneker and his one-time mentor were still arguing over the point. Yet Heinrich's death, shortly afterward, touched him deeply—and reminded him of his own mortality.[33]

Now that he was occasionally criticizing music again, he saw more of the old cronies from whom he had somewhat drifted away in recent years. In the summer of 1914 he almost quarreled with the crotchety Finck, who commented in the *Evening Post* that Huneker "was guided by a correct instinct when he printed his remarks on *Parsifal* in a comic periodical." The obvious rejoinder, Huneker replied in *Puck*, was: "But not half so comical as the musical criticism of Mr. Finck in the column of a serious newspaper." "How's that as a Roland for an Oliver, Heinrich!" he exclaimed.[34] The quarrel did not materialize.

The great explosion of World War I foreseen by Huneker struck him as "an abomination of desolation."[35] The political and economic issues at stake did not concern him nearly so much as the cultural and psychological repercussions he anticipated. "National neurasthenia," he wrote in October 1914, "—with its attendant train of ghost worshippers, fortune-tellers, charlatans, who will take advantage of the diminished vitality—degeneration, moral and physical, is a sure outcome. . . . As for art and literature, it always suffers." To offer prayers for peace, as churchmen did, seemed hypocritical and futile to Huneker. "Let us not tap God so familiarly on the shoulder, telling Him it is high time for peace and prayer mills," he remarked, "for it will be admitted by the most hardened mythomaniac that He knows what He is about . . . and that He is usually on the side of the heaviest artillery. Furthermore, the vilest wars, in which the carnage was the most tremendous, have been religious wars." "Personally, I would run a mile if I saw a cannon cracker alight," he added. "I hate noise, and I dearly hate cant and superstition and hysteria."[36]

He was disgusted, too, by the shrill "open-letter" writers, patently ignorant of Europe and too busy voicing their racial antipathies and their "painful provinciality" to view the war objectively. When both sides tried to win sympathy by boasting of their great men, he himself pointed out that genius had no country by listing over sixty names of famous persons neglected or persecuted during their lifetime by their own countrymen.[37] Torn between his Teutonic background (which, however, he never admitted) and his tie to German music, on the one hand, and his deep love of French literature on the other, he found it impossible to take sides, though almost fifteen years before the war started he had recognized and commented on the superiority of the German army to the French, and had predicted that with her "magnificent" civilization the future belonged to Germany, even if, as he remarked in 1911, in her general culture there was "more light than sweetness."[38] In October 1915, after Quinn, a Francophile whose hatred of Germans was second only to his dislike for Jews,[39] had charged Huneker with being pro-German, Huneker replied: "Please don't call me pro-anything. I'm neutral, I'm also cosmopolitan and I have good friends in all the battlefields. I only said that a certain nation would pull out ahead. Thus far it has,—and there my interest ceases. Pilsner is my only solicitude. Otherwise let the brutes kill each other."[40]

Not until New York's supply of Pilsner had run short, indeed, did the war really begin to affect him. "If all the world drank beer," he had once written, "war would cease, destroyers and Dreadnoughts would be converted into scrap iron, not for ploughshares but for brewery utensils."[41] One night in April 1915, Frederick L. Hackenburg, a prominent lawyer (later a judge), who used to join Huneker's group at Knirim's, found the saloon deserted except for a dozing waiter. Hearing a noise in the cellar, he went downstairs, and there, beneath the flickering light of a single candle fastened in the neck of a bottle, stood Huneker and Knirim, dejectedly tapping the last keg of Pilsner.[42] The war had hit home.

In Huneker's eyes the growing clamor for prohibition was a form of hysteria more dangerous to America than the conflict overseas. He was afraid that Vance Thompson's incredible potboiling[43] temperance tract, *Drink and Be Sober* (1915), would be used as propaganda by the Prohibition Party—the "most detestable set of politicians that have thus far appeared on the national horizon." Drunkenness could not be prevented by legislation; psychotherapy, not prohibition, was the only cure. Since "true temperance consists in moderation," why should the personal liberty of the moderate drinker be infringed upon? "Drinking is one of the seven arts," he concluded. "Cultivate it, but don't abuse it. Don't be afraid of life."[44]

Equally obnoxious to him was Billy Sunday, whose packed revival meetings (and collection plates) were front-page news. Religious fanaticism alone was bad enough, he thought, but combined with prohibitionist zeal it was insufferable. Excessive churchgoing led to marked deterioration of character, Huneker slyly observed, young men who went twice during the week and twice on Sunday and visited the YMCA in the interim being "hopelessly decent chaps, who never drink, smoke, or swear; they also seem to have an aversion to matrimony."[45] He countered Billy Sunday's lurid religiosity with a public prayer of his own, printed in the *Sun*:

Let us pray that we are not struck by religious zeal. Religious people are not always good people; good people are not envious, jealous, penurious, censorious, or busybodies, or too much bound up in the prospect of the mote in their brother's eye and unmindful of the beam in their own. . . . Let us pray for the misguided folk who, forgetful of Mother Church, her wisdom, her consolations, flock to the tents of lewd itinerant mumbo-jumbo howlers, that blaspheme the sacred name as they epileptically leap shouting glory kingdom come, and please settle at the captain's office! . . . Conversion is silent and comes from within, and not to the din of brass bands and screaming hallelujahs. . . . Paganism in its most exotic forms is preferable to this prize-ring Christianity. . . . Let us pray for those imbeciles and for the charlatans who are blinding them.[46]

(If Sunday saw this, he might have made the same remark about Huneker that he reportedly made about Mencken: "Mencken? Mencken? I never heard of him, but he's just some cheap jack trying to get a reputation by attacking me.")[47]

Nor was Huneker sympathetic to the woman suffrage movement then approaching its climax, for he had little faith in the political sagacity of the average American of *either* sex, and did not believe that giving women the vote would improve the unruly democratic process. Moreover, he felt that women were happiest in the kitchen or bedroom (from which they already ruled America), and that the "New Woman" was unbecomingly masculine. Woman should be the certain "inspirer of the Seven Arts" rather than the dubious elector of presidents.[48] Perhaps he was prejudiced against the suffragettes because Clio, whose mother had been one of the first to join the cause in America, had herself become the secretary of the Greenwich Equal Franchise League in Connecticut, and together with her parents, brother, sister, son, and second husband had joined the gigantic suffrage parade in New York on May 4, 1912.[49] What the agitators really wanted, Huneker thought, was activity, excitement, and notoriety. "What will become of the suffragettes when women get the vote?" he inquired in 1914. ". . . How will the girls fill in the time and their purses then?" An anti-gum-chewing league, he suggested, would keep them busy for years and accomplish something of social value.[50]

On the night of November 19, 1914, after Caruso and Farrar had taken their first-act curtain calls in the Metropolitan's revival of *Carmen*, Huneker walked out to the lobby. As he stood there, he felt a tug at his coattail and turned to face a tall, slim, well-dressed woman in her late twenties, who introduced herself in a low-pitched voice and told him how much she admired his work.

"I'd . . . I'd like to know you better," she finished, intimidated a little by the ferocious expression his hardened features gave him.

"Madame," he replied gruffly, focusing his steel-gray eyes on her, "I'm impotent."

"That's the best news I've heard in a long time," she quickly replied.

"Then what do you want from me?"

"Everything you can give me," she said.

Amused and curious, he invited her to join him at Browne's chop-house across the street. Thus began the most unusual friendship of Huneker's last seven years.

Granddaughter of a duchess, Lydia Barrington—not her real name, since she wishes to remain unidentified—had been born in London and educated by a governess, then at a convent, and finally at the University of London, where she obtained a Master of Arts degree in English literature. She had studied piano and art from an early age, and in her grandmother's drawing room and in London and Continental society circles had met many of the artistic celebrities Huneker knew or criticized. Though raised a Catholic, she followed the rules of the Church no more closely than Huneker did. At the time she met him she was married to a titled Englishman and living in New York.

Not long after their first encounter, Huneker was dropping in every week or two around noon at Lydia's apartment on Fifty-fifth Street off Sixth Avenue, near Carnegie Hall, usually staying for lunch. She was careful not to press him, but if he was in the mood they would talk about Chopin, Nietzsche, Aquinas, Cardinal Newman, Italian painting, and dozens of other subjects. Often he would play the piano for Lydia, who played so well herself and knew so much about music that he sometimes let her substitute for him at a minor recital and used her criticism in his notice. From the start it was a master-pupil relationship, purely platonic, for, as other evidence suggests, Huneker had probably not been joking about his impotence,[51] and she certainly had no romantic interest in him. She found him the most stimulating person she had ever known, while he was charmed by her voice, poise, vivaciousness, and—what he seldom discovered in a woman—intelligence. A facet of her personality that fascinated him even more, one suspects, was her abhorrence, which she did not conceal from him, of sexual intercourse or, as Huneker called it, "horizontal refreshment." Her extreme frankness, indeed, once led him to assert that she had the "manners of a duchess and the morals of an alley-cat," and to wish that he had met her earlier, when he might have been able to convert her or, in any event, would have enjoyed the attempt. Josephine apparently did not know about Lydia, but the latter introduced Huneker to her husband (who was often out of town) and the two men got on well enough, though the Englishman did not fully understand his wife's intellectual need for Huneker.

She managed to persuade him to attend several of her parties, which his wit enlivened. "I understand you were at another affair before you came here," a conceited tenor said to him at one of these parties. "Were there many musicians there?" "Yes," replied Huneker, "and a few singers." On another occasion he squelched a lady making a nuisance of herself by loudly proclaiming how wonderful it was to have a child. "The trick," snorted Huneker, "is *not* to have them."[52]

Two collections of Huneker's essays appeared in 1915—*New Cosmopolis* in the spring and *Ivory Apes and Peacocks* (the comma after the first word was somehow omitted) in the fall. The former, fittingly dedicated to Vance Thompson "En Souvenir of *M'lle New York*," consisted mainly of chatty sketches, printed in the *Times* in the late summer and early fall of 1914,[53] on the restaurants, museums, subways, parks, waterways, theaters, roof gardens, and picturesque sections of New York City, together with prose portraits of European cities and of two American summer resorts—Atlantic City and Newport—he had visited in 1906. Though not one of his more substantial books, it contains material valuable to social historians, particularly the chapters on the East Side and on Gotham's celebrated cafés. The *Times*'s reviewer, Joyce Kilmer, admired Huneker's humor, his "tremendous" power of appreciation, and the poetic use of language which could produce, for example, this striking description of the Manhattan landscape: "In twilit tunnels beautiful churches are lost like stone needles in metallic haystacks."[54] (Huneker was so pleased by the notice that he looked up the young poet and thanked him in person.)[55] Most reviewers, indeed, found *New Cosmopolis* charming—even in England, where the London *Daily Chronicle* described Huneker as a "critic's critic" and "a rich and merry personality," and the sober *Athenaeum* found "many graces and virtues" in his style.[56]

In *Ivory Apes and Peacocks*, with its important essays on Laforgue, Whitman, and Conrad, Huneker was back in his more serious role of aesthetic scout. One of the most perceptive reviews of the book was written by Francis Hackett, who indicated what Huneker had meant to all the younger critics by calling him a "fine audacious exception" to the general aesthetic cowardice of academic criticism. If Huneker were in the main tradition of American criticism, Hackett added, instead of writing about apes and peacocks he would be "implanted in that dim academic grove where the constants of the mind are the owl and the hen, where nothing is esteemed so impressive as the serenity of the dove or the dignity of the dodo."[57] When the study of Laforgue—which Philip Hale, an expert judge, considered fully worthy of Huneker at his best[58]—first appeared in the *North American Review* in July 1915, T. S. Eliot had been reading and emulating him for six or seven years, and Ezra Pound had recently discovered him; but, as Huneker had remarked in 1914, the French poet who had so strongly influenced modern poetry was "direfully neglected by criticism and the public."[59] Indeed few, if any, critiques of Laforgue's work had been written by Americans since Huneker's *Sun* article of 1903.[60]

The reminiscence and criticism of Whitman disturbed those who felt that Huneker underestimated Whitman's poetry (which he did) and that it was bad taste, if not outrageous libel, to suggest openly that Whitman was a homosexual.[61] Too skeptical to swallow a spiritual interpretation of Whitman's gospel of love among men, Huneker implied more about the poet's sexual activities than could be proved, but he helped to focus attention on a matter that subsequent American critics, following the lead of Continental Whitman students, have not been able to ignore. One conservative literary historian, Fred Lewis Pattee, later called Huneker's study the most penetrating brief estimate of Whitman in existence.[62]

Joseph Conrad must have been pleased with the essay on himself in *Ivory Apes and Peacocks*. "The . . . book is good and immensely characteristic of our extremely 'alive' friend," he wrote Quinn. "What mental agility! What a flexible liveliness of style! And, of course, he is very far from being shallow—very far; but the light of his intelligence has such wonderful surface play that one is dazzled at first. It's only after a while that one sees how deep he can go—when he likes."[63]

In September 1915 Huneker went to Atlantic City for a brief vacation, his first in more than a year. On the New Jersey seacoast he took his initial ride in an airplane. "It beats music," he wrote after the flight, "it beats love, and is far superior to automobiling."[64] It seemed less dangerous than automobiling, too, for in the previous December a taxi accident had left him with a splintered rib, sprained thumbs, two missing teeth, and a broken nose—which ruined his profile, he said, and made him look like George Luks's "caricature" of him[65] reproduced in *Vanity Fair* a month before the accident.[66] (Four years later, however, Huneker's former pilot and a passenger were both killed during a flight at the resort.)[67] Though he was almost sixty and had not been on skates since his youth, Huneker also got up the nerve, a few months after his vacation, to go ice skating in Central Park, and survived to write an entertaining account of the experience for *Puck*.[68]

Theodore Roosevelt—who, like Huneker, had been contributing articles to the Sunday *Times* during the fall of 1914—invited him and John Quinn to Oyster Bay for lunch on November 2, 1915. Roosevelt did not know, of course, that in 1901 Huneker had privately called him a "loud-mouthed, bumptious epileptic,"[69] but in 1907 he might have read, in the *Metropolitan Magazine,* Huneker's slightly two-edged comment that Roosevelt "would have made a remarkable actor if he had chosen the boards instead of that other stage in the Washington political hippodrome. He is endowed with a multiple personality . . . [and] can play a half dozen parts in one evening. . . . Each year he handles life and his contemporaries with more mastery."[70] In Huneker's estimation, Roosevelt's interest in the arts, unusually extensive for a politician, was perhaps his greatest virtue.[71] The library and pictures at Oyster Bay appealed to Huneker more than Roosevelt's belligerent anti-German views. "I don't think there would have been a *Lusitania* incident if I had been President," said Roosevelt,[72] who, when the ship had been sunk in the previous May, had written a famous editorial urging war against Germany. "The Roosevelt family seems ideal," Huneker wrote Quinn a few days after the visit, thanking him for having secured the invitation, "—the good, old solid American ideal. The Colonel is a human dynamo. His force and versatility are as extraordinary at close hand as in public. Altogether, I had a 'bully' time."[73]

In 1915 George Jean Nathan[74] became *Puck*'s drama critic,[75] a position he held until March 1916. Born in Indiana in 1882 and educated in Europe and at Cornell University, he had been hired by the New York *Herald* in 1905 as reporter, special Sunday writer, and assistant drama critic, and had first met Huneker a year later when the latter called on Charles Frederic Nirdlinger, Nathan's uncle and Huneker's former colleague on *Town Topics* and the *Criterion*, with whom Nathan was living. Attracted by Huneker's cosmopolitanism, erudition, and hedonism, Nathan joined the bright young men who regularly gathered around Huneker at Scheffel Hall or Lüchow's to hear the spiced, sparkling pronouncements on art and life that were already legendary, and to marvel at his ability to identify every known brand of beer by the slightest taste.[76]

In 1908 the new owner of *Smart Set*, a magazine of sophisticated fiction and verse which had been founded as a literary journal for society by *Town Topics'* Colonel Mann, hired Nathan as drama critic and H. L. Mencken, two years Nathan's senior, as literary critic. Bold, high-spirited stylists, these two bachelors proceeded to direct their lively criticism toward the man or woman who had "lived in large cities, and read good books, and seen good plays, and heard good music, and [was] tired of politicians, reformers, and the newspapers"[77]—thus making *Smart Set*, in effect, the successor of *M'lle New York* and the precursor of *The New Yorker*. Ever since he had first read Huneker in Baltimore at the turn of the century, Mencken had considered him the critic in America from whom he could learn the most.[78] ("Where would the rest of us be if we didn't steal his ideas every day?" read Mencken's generous inscription—dated 1912—on Huneker's copy of Mencken's *The Artist*.)[79] Supporting such writers as Ibsen, Nietzsche, Conrad, Twain, and Frank Norris, and lambasting Hamlin Garland, Upton Sinclair, Jack London, and Comstock, among others, Mencken soon demonstrated in his *Smart Set* reviews how much he had in common with his teacher. "If a merciful Providence had not sent James Gibbons Huneker into the world," he observed in 1909, "we Americans would still be shipping union suits to the heathen, reading Emerson, sweating at Chautauquas and applauding the plays of Bronson Howard. In matters exotic and scandalous he is our chief of scouts, our spiritual adviser. . . . Let us not neglect to reward him with loud praises to his face while he is yet with us."[80] Huneker's allusiveness put heavy burdens on most readers, to be sure, Mencken declared in 1913, but Huneker conducted the postgraduate courses, not the ABC's, of criticism. For fifteen years he had been the "teacher of our teachers, the critic of our critics."[81]

In 1913 *Smart Set* had reprinted two of Huneker's more daring short stories (one involving prostitution and the other satanism),[82] and in the following year, when Nathan and Mencken became joint editors of the magazine, they invited him to submit others, eventually printing four more[83] (though Mencken considered three of these second-rate and bought them only out of friendship).[84] Mencken met Huneker through Willard Huntington Wright—the exact date is unknown, but evidence suggests that it was no later than July 1913[85]—and the two critics began to correspond regularly at the end of 1914,[86] after Huneker had given a favorable notice in *Puck* to *Europe After 8:15*, a travel book written by Nathan, Mencken, and Wright.[87]

During Mencken's monthly visits to New York, he and Nathan always made the rounds of their favorite bars and restaurants, usually winding up at Lüchow's,[88] and here one day occurred a session with Huneker that Mencken never forgot:

We sat down to luncheon [he wrote] at one o'clock; . . . at six, when I had to go, the waiter was hauling in [Huneker's] tenth (or was it twentieth?) *Seidel* of Pilsner, and he was bringing to a close *prestissimo* the most amazing monologue that these ears (up to that time) had ever funnelled into this consciousness. What a stew, indeed! Berlioz and the question of the clangtint of the viola, the psychological causes of the suicide of Tchaikovsky, why Nietzsche had to leave Sils Maria between days in 1887, the echoes of Flaubert in Joseph Conrad (then but newly dawned), the precise topography of the warts of Liszt, George Bernard Shaw's heroic but vain struggles to throw off Presbyterianism, how Frau Cosima Wagner saved Wagner from the libidinous Swedish baroness, what to drink when playing Chopin, what Cézanne thought of his disciples, the defects in the structure of *Sister Carrie*, Anton Seidl and the musical union, the complex love affairs of Gounod, the early days of David Belasco, the varying talents and idiosyncrasies of Lillian Russell's earlier husbands, whether a girl educated at Vassar could ever really learn to love, the exact composition of chicken paprika, the correct tempo of the Vienna Waltz, the style of William Dean Howells, what George Moore said about German bathrooms, the true inwardness of the affair between

D'Annunzio and Duse, the origin of the theory that all oboe players are crazy, why Löwenbräu survived exportation better than Hofbräu, Ibsen's loathing of Norwegians, the best remedy for Rhine wine *Katzenjammer*, how to play Brahms, the degeneration of the Bal Bullier, the sheer physical impossibility of getting Dvorak drunk, the genuine last words of Whitman. . . .

I left in a sort of fever, and it was a couple of days before I began to sort out my impressions, and formulate a coherent image. Was the man allusive in his books—so allusive that popular report credited him with the actual manufacture of authorities? Then he was ten times as allusive in his discourse—a veritable geyser of unfamiliar names, shocking epigrams in strange tongues, unearthly philosophies out of the backwaters of Scandinavia, Transylvania, Bulgaria, the Basque country, the Ukraine. And did he, in his criticism, pass facilely from the author to the man, and from the man to his wife, and to the wives of his friends? Then at the *Biertisch* he began long beyond the point where the last honest wife gives up the ghost, and so, full tilt, ran into such complexities of adultery that a plain sinner could scarcely follow him. I try to give you, ineptly and grotesquely, some notion of the talk of the man, but I must fail inevitably. It was, in brief, chaos, and chaos cannot be described. But it was chaos made to gleam and coruscate with every device of the seven arts—chaos drenched in all the colors imaginable, chaos scored for an orchestra which made the great band of Berlioz seem like a fife and drum corps.[89]

At each subsequent meeting Mencken, no wallflower himself at barroom repartee and reminiscence, remained entranced by Huneker, whose most casual talk was so full of wit, Mencken stated, that it made his lively books appear "almost funereal," bathing "everything that he discussed in new and brilliant lights. I have never encountered a man who was further removed from dullness; it seemed a literal impossibility for him to open his mouth without discharging some word or phrase that arrested the attention and stuck in the memory."[90]

Though he was more than twenty years older than they—four decades later Mencken still referred to Huneker affectionately as "the old man"—Nathan and Mencken found him *en rapport* with their ideas. He had done much, of course, to interest the former in the modern European drama which became Nathan's specialty, and sympathized with the young critic's acrimonious attacks on sentimentalism, moralism, and commercialism in the American theater. "Paris is where . . . [Nathan] ought to be," Huneker wrote Mencken in 1915, after reading Nathan's first volume of drama criticism, *Another Book on the Theater*. "There he would be appreciated. Here he only bruises his brain against the eternal box-office."[91] In "The Seven Arts," shortly afterward, Huneker described his colleague as "witty, wise and cruel . . . the Bad Boy of New York drama criticism."[92]

Unlike Huneker and Nathan, basically aesthetes detached from the "practical" stream of American life, Mencken did not ignore politics and economics but, on the contrary, gloried in them. He felt the call to keep pounding away, with weapons of laughter and scorn, at the platitudes of democracy or the prejudices of philistinism which stood in the way of civilized, pleasurable living. He liked to contrast Huneker with the arid, frigid, ultraconservative "professors"[93] (one of whom, Fred Lewis Pattee, he chided in 1916 for not even mentioning Huneker in his pioneering history of modern American literature),[94] eventually realizing, however, that Huneker was not the militant anti-academician that Mencken himself professed to be. "For all his enterprise and daring," Mencken later wrote, ". . . there was not much of the fighter in him, and though he was the greatest of all the enemies that the guardians of tradition had to face, it was seldom that he tackled them directly. . . . He was always loath to set himself directly against a concrete champion of orthodoxy; he could never get quite rid of the feeling that he was no more than an amateur among such gaudy doctors, and that it would be unseemly for him to flout them too openly."[95]

The middle-aged Huneker, it is true, never loved a fight for its own sake, as Mencken sometimes seemed to, and had neither the energy nor the financial security to battle vigorously for a principle. When, for example, the New York Society for the Suppression of Vice virtually suppressed Dreiser's *The "Genius"* in 1916, Mencken marshaled the opposition even though he disliked the book, while the only action taken by Huneker—whose objections to censorship were equally strong—in response to Mencken's plea for help[96] was to describe the book publicly as "moral to the sermonizing point."[97] Huneker, moreover, was more "feminine" than Mencken—which is what Huneker must have meant when he said that Mencken was too fond of roast beef to like Chopin;[98] Mencken, that is, was inclined to interpret literature more as a reflection of society than as an expression of an individual artist. Yet he was well read in modern literature, sharing many of Huneker's tastes, and, despite his dislike of Chopin, his love of music (he was himself a superior music critic[99] and a competent amateur pianist) almost matched Huneker's and formed one of the strongest bonds between them.

A hearty companion, good listener, and faithful correspondent, Mencken repeatedly demonstrated his unabashed admiration for Huneker. "Really I'm becoming alarmed at the sight of my name with your signature," Huneker wrote him in April 1916. "—I'll never live up to all the things you say of me! And I needn't add, that you know how grateful I am for your lonely, but golden voice in the wilderness."[100] Friendship with such a disciple—who was soon to become more famous than his mentor—brightened a little the days growing increasingly dark in Brooklyn.

ℜ Eighteen

FULL CIRCLE

By the summer of 1916 the poor quality of *Puck's* paper and the virtual disappearance of its colored illustrations (the European artists who had supplied them were now at the front)[1] indicated that it was in trouble, and later in the year Straus sold out. Faced with dropping circulation, the new owner immediately attempted to cut expenses, and one of his early moves, apparently, was to reduce Huneker's salary—with the result that he resigned on December 1.[2] In August, fortunately, he had joined the editorial staff of the *Sun,* which Frank Munsey had recently purchased and merged with the *Press,*[3] Mitchell remaining as editor and giving Huneker his usual freedom. He now received only $15 per column,[4] but was glad to get the job, for he was having a hard time selling work to the magazines (though one of his best short stories, "Husband of Madame," appeared in *Scribner's Magazine* in November 1916).[5]

"Only the dogs of war make money with their pens or typewriters," he complained late in 1915. "If I could only write a 'Somewhere in Pants' and drag in a lot of lies about *les Boches* raping infants and cutting off old ladies' ears! Ah! Assassins of English and of the truth!"[6] This might be a good time, he thought, to try to fulfill his old dream of writing a successful play, and so at the end of 1915 he and his friend Leo Ditrichstein, the popular actor-playwright then enjoying a smash success in *The Great Lover* (which ran until the following June), signed a contract with the firm of Cohan and Harris to furnish, by October 1, 1916, a drama about Chopin.[7] They worked on it during much of 1916,[8] but the play was apparently never completed or staged, the idea being eventually scotched, perhaps, by the production, in November 1917, of Philip Moeller's *Madame Sand,* starring Mrs. Fiske.

By November 1916, however, following his return from a visit to Havana in September,[9] Huneker had finished two other theatrical pieces:

a narrative outline for a three-act play entitled "All's Fair in Love and Air" and a one-act play called "The New Jealousy." The former, as bad as its title, was never published or produced; the only thing worth noting about it is the appearance of an airplane in its plot, an idea stemming possibly from Huneker's first flight a year earlier. The latter, which was dedicated to—and undoubtedly written for—Leo Ditrichstein, and which deals with a philandering actor whose long-suffering wife turns the tables on him by making him jealous, reveals much more dramatic skill, though Huneker's use of the aside is old-fashioned and his dialogue stiff. It, too, was neither published nor produced,[10] and Huneker wisely went back to writing criticism.

His first column for the *Sun* in August 1916 was an enthusiastic review of *Casuals of the Sea,*[11] a novel by William McFee, whom Huneker, still on the lookout for literary talent, was almost the first to discover. (McFee never forgot this "very good" notice, sent to him in Egypt where he was serving in the British navy.)[12] Six months later, in February 1917, he scored a far more memorable scoop when he reviewed *Portrait of the Artist as a Young Man* (published in New York in the preceding December) by James Joyce, another Irish writer Quinn had taken under his wing[13] and told Huneker about. "I read *The Dubliners* at a sitting and with decided pleasure," Huneker wrote publisher B. W. Huebsch on January 31 asking for *Portrait,* shortly before reviewing it, and for information about the author.[14] Though Joyce was not completely unknown in America—two stories from *Dubliners,* his first pieces of fiction to be published here, had appeared in *Smart Set* in May 1915—he was obscure enough so that Huneker could begin his review by asking "Who is James Joyce?" "Indubitably a fresh talent," he went on, Joyce was "potentially a poet, and a realist of the De Maupassant breed. . . . He is as truthful as Chekhov, and as gray . . . as implacably naturalistic as the Russian in his vision of the somber, mean, petty, dusty, commonplaces of middle-class life, and he sometimes suggests the Frenchman in his clear, concise, technical methods."[15] Ernest Boyd sent this review to Joyce, who thanked Huneker briefly but warmly from Zurich for a "very favourable" notice.[16] Thus Huneker seems to have been the first prominent critic to discuss Joyce in an American publication; at any rate, Huneker's *Unicorns,* in which the review soon reappeared, was the first book by an American to contain more than a passing reference to Joyce.[17]

Huneker apparently overlooked two other important modern writers, André Gide and D. H. Lawrence. Not many of Gide's books were translated into English during Huneker's lifetime, it is true, but this should have been no great obstacle to Huneker. One might have expected that Gide's preoccupation with homosexuality, as well as his concern with technique in the writing of fiction, would have captured Huneker's attention. He surely would have been gratified by Gide's devotion to the piano—if he had to earn his living, the novelist once said, he would become a piano teacher—and Gide's veneration of Chopin, his favorite composer,[18] would have endeared him to Huneker. Huneker's unawareness of Lawrence, whose lyric prose and frank eroticism might well have appealed to him, is even more surprising. A dozen books by the Englishman, including novels, plays, poems, and short stories, were published during the last decade of Huneker's life without any notice on his part. His comments on Lawrence's view of sex would doubtless have been lively and illuminating, and reviews by Huneker of *Sons and Lovers*, *The Rainbow*, and *Women in Love* (the last privately printed in 1920 for subscribers only, to be sure, and thus not generally reviewed) might have popularized Lawrence in America years before he was "discovered" in the 1920's.

For some eight months Huneker averaged about an editorial a week in the *Sun*—usually a book review. Two days after America declared war on Germany in early April 1917, for the first time in his old newspaper an article by him was signed "James *Gibbons* Huneker" to counteract his German-sounding surname. But the "Gibbons" was not potent enough to keep the ailing *Sun* from letting him go on April 10,[19] thus ending an association that had lasted some eleven years, off and on. Krehbiel certainly should not complain at having been put out "to pension" by the *Tribune*, Huneker confided, shortly afterward, to Grenville Vernon, a young *Tribune* reporter, adding: "Now I'm usually dropped after the juice has been squeezed from the orange."[20] His departure from the *Sun* was not only a milestone in his own career, he sensed, but also a symptom of the passing of an epoch. "Newspapers have lost their personal flavour," he wrote in 1918. "Huge syndicates have taken the colour and character and quality from daily journalism. I am quite sure that if ever a comprehensive history of the *Sun* is written my name will be absent simply because I would be considered a myth, a figment of a fantastic imagination."[21] And sure enough, neither in Frank M. O'Brien's *The History of the Sun* (1928) nor in the history published in the newspaper's 100th anniversary number of September 2, 1933, is Huneker even mentioned.

At the age of sixty, he was without a regular job, and now that the country was at war he could sell even less to the magazines, which wanted propaganda or action stories rather than essays on aesthetics. Although the 1,000 marks sent by the publisher of the German translation of his *Chopin,* published in 1917,[22] was a godsend—royalties for the second edition, issued in 1920, were paid in practically worthless marks[23]— Huneker's financial condition was soon more precarious than ever. "I'll have nothing to do this summer—besides starving—except to read proof of a fall book," he wrote Mencken, who had himself been dropped by the Baltimore *Sun* because of his embarrassing war views and had taken a job on the New York *Evening Mail* (the publisher of which was arrested and jailed, a year later, for having received financial aid from Germany, a charge that surprised Mencken as much as anyone).[24] "Let us pray, Henri, *mon cher ami! Maintenant seulement la langue fran-çais*[e]!"[25] "Now [one must use] only the French language" was, of course, a grimly humorous allusion to the anti-German sentiment which had engulfed Mencken and which Huneker had feared enough not only to have added the "Gibbons" to his signature but also to have told Mencken (in 1916) the lie that he did not have a drop of German blood in him.[26]

Though he may have allowed Mencken to believe that he sympathized with Mencken's views on the war, Huneker was patriotic—or hungry?—enough to permit his study of Villiers de l'Isle-Adam to be reprinted in 1917, shortly after America entered the war, in an unabashedly propagandistic volume of poetry, prose, and drawings entitled *For France,* the contributors to which included some two dozen of the country's best-known writers and artists, among them William Dean Howells, Booth Tarkington, Vachel Lindsay, Edgar Lee Masters, Ellen Glasgow, Charles Dana Gibson, John Sargent, and Robert Henri; Huneker's contribution was probably the least sentimental of the lot, but Mencken was undoubtedly shocked at the company Huneker was keeping. (Theodore Roosevelt, who wrote the Introduction, declared that every man who had been a pacifist or pro-German, or had failed to support preparedness from the outset of the war in 1914, had been "false to America, and false to humanity.")[27]

The sunniest day for Huneker in the otherwise gloomy summer of 1917—to make matters worse, his kidneys were acting up again, and he suffered attacks of vertigo, aggravated, possibly, by anxiety during his enforced idleness—came on July 21, when the *Evening Mail* printed a long, highly complimentary article on him by Mencken, based partly on biographical material furnished by Huneker himself. Deploring the low order of critical writing in America (the "normal" American book reviewer, he said, was "virginal and afraid of bugaboos, . . . her customary attitude one of fascinated horror") and calling Brownell and Paul Elmer More "Victorians, sonorous pundits, critics of the *Nation* school," Mencken described Huneker as the only American critic "whose vision sweeps the whole field of beauty, and whose reports of what he sees there show any gusto. . . . No better volume of criticism than *Iconoclasts: A Book of Dramatists* has ever appeared in America, save it be *Egoists: A Book of Supermen.*" If the United States had any contact, however remote, with aesthetic developments in the "more civilized" countries, Mencken concluded, no man could claim a larger share of the credit than Huneker.[28] When Mencken included a revised version of this article in his first volume of critical essays, *A Book of Prefaces,* published in the following October, Huneker was immensely pleased to be placed in the company of Joseph Conrad and Theodore Dreiser, subjects of two of the three other essays. "A newspaper man in a hell of a hurry writing journalese is not to be dumped into the seat of the mighty so easily," he gratefully told Mencken.[29] (He must have been almost as disappointed as Mencken when, largely because of Mencken's unpopularity during wartime, the book received only three favorable notices.)[30]

Huneker could use the publicity for *his* new book, which came out shortly after Mencken's. "The meaning has gone out of the past; and what is rolling up is incomprehensible," Vance Thompson had written Huneker in the spring of 1917. "Anyway it needs interpretation—the interpretation you gave, explicitly and once for all, to the last generation of thinking, searching men. I wish you would publish (in 1917) a Hunekerism of what is coming down the road of the new twenties."[31] While the essays in *Unicorns* on Henry James and Joyce certainly pointed to the future, Huneker did not attempt anything so ambitious in this book, though with its studies of Chopin, Wagner, Brahms, Cézanne, Huysmans, Wilde, George Sand, and others (most of them written for the *Times, Puck,* and the *Sun* during 1915–17) it is one of his most varied, cosmopolitan collections.

Too few readers, unfortunately, were in the mood for aesthetics or agreed with Israel Zangwill that "Hunicorns," as he was tempted to rename the book, was "a great relief from the war," a reminder that there was a time when men bothered about Art.[32] Not many reviewers were as condescending, however, as Paul Elmer More, who may have been miffed at Mencken's scoffing at the *Nation* and his upgrading of Huneker at the expense of critics like More. "Volume after volume devoted to the mud gods of Russia and France become a little tiresome in the end," complained More. "Would it be unkind to intimate that [Huneker] is writing, or at least publishing, in 1917 and not in 1897, and that the world has grown, for terrible reasons, rather weary of trifling with morality?" More admitted that Huneker was frequently sound as well as clever, but lamented that his "unicorn" commonly turned out to be a "rhinoceros snouting in the mud."[33] Mencken replied in *Smart Set* that Huneker was worth "not only a whole herd of Harvard poets and essayists, but the whole of Harvard"[34] (where More had studied and taught).

"I'm glad our names are so often linked nowadays," Huneker wrote Mencken in early December 1917.[35] They had just been rather unpleasantly linked in the *Nation* by Stuart P. Sherman, the Harvard-educated protégé of More and Irving Babbitt, and a professor of English at the University of Illinois. Angered by Mencken's attacks on academic critics and on "Puritanism," Sherman had caustically reviewed *A Book of Prefaces*, assailing Mencken's pro-German sympathies. "Probably the root of our difficulty," he wrote, "is that, with the exception of Mr. Huneker, Otto Heller, Ludwig Lewisohn, Mr. Untermeyer, G. S. Viereck . . . and a few other choice souls, we have no critics who, understanding what beauty is, serenely and purely love it. Devoid of esthetic sense, our native Anglo-Saxon historians cannot even guess what ails our native literature." Mencken exhibited "a certain Teutonic gusto," Sherman added, "in tracing the 'Pilsner motive' through the work of Mr. Huneker."[36] But neither Mencken's praise nor the slurs of More and Sherman made *Unicorns* a money-winner, and, meanwhile, Huneker had gone back to music.

In the fall of 1917 Alden March, who had recently left the *New York Times* to become editor in chief of the Philadelphia *Press,* hired Hune-

ker to cover the Quaker City's chief musical events. Although he had
not written music criticism regularly since he had given up that department on the *Sun* and resigned from the *Musical Courier* in 1902, Huneker had not lost touch with his first love. In *Puck,* for example, he had
discussed Moussorgsky, Debussy (of whom he never grew very fond),
Charles Martin Loeffler (whom he considered the leading American composer), and young Leo Ornstein,[37] whose dissonant compositions, he
declared, made Schönberg sound tame. Noting in 1914 that the "immorality" of *Der Rosenkavalier* had lifted eyebrows at the opera's New
York première a few months earlier, Huneker asserted with his old-time
vigor that there was no such thing as moral or immoral music, "only
well-written or badly-written music. As for the plot of a light opera—
do we go to the theatre for sermons?"[38] Later in the same year, he had
greeted as a "red-letter day" the return to the concert hall of Olive Fremstad, who had just ended a distinguished career with the Metropolitan,
and he described Toscanini as the first operatic conductor in America
who could be placed in the same category as Anton Seidl.[39]

Piano music, especially Chopin's, was never far from Huneker's mind
and fingers. In the spring of 1915 he wrote the biographical sketch
and prefatory notes for Joseffy's edition of Chopin's *Complete Works
for the Pianoforte* (1915–16), which was left incomplete by Joseffy's
death in June 1915. (Huneker's heartfelt tribute to his teacher and
friend appeared soon thereafter in the *Times*.)[40] In the fall of this year
he wrote the program notes, published as a pamphlet called *The Development of Piano Music,* for a series of six recitals played in 1915–16
by the "many-sided, richly endowed, and charming" Ossip Gabrilowitsch (the admiration was mutual), who had given the same cycle of
programs a few years earlier in Munich and Berlin with great success.[41]
During this period Huneker also began editing a collection of piano
pieces in various moods and styles, published in 1919 by Schirmer as
Romantic Preludes and Studies. "I am told 20 times a month to stick
to my last—music criticism," he informed Quinn in April 1916, "and
begad I think people are right."[42]

At the end of 1916, moreover, he had agreed to write a booklet com-
memorating the seventy-fifth anniversary of the New York Philharmonic
Society, a task for which Krehbiel and Aldrich, the editors of the fiftieth
anniversary publication, were better suited than Huneker, for in addition to lacking the talents of a historian,[43] he had once been sharply
critical of the organization. "The Philharmonic Society was sixty years

old last week," he had remarked in 1902. "It has been dead for ten years, but it is considered bad taste to mention the fact; so people keep up the illusion of life by attending sixteen dreadful concerts every season"; he had observed, too, that the Society was "largely devoted to the suppression of the new in music."[44] Now, however, needing the $500 he received for the work,[45] he did his best with essentially dry material. "I'd rather go to the trenches than tackle such a job again," he told Felix Leifels, manager of the Society.[46] When the pamphlet was distributed in 1918, Leonard Leibling declared in the *Musical Courier* that Huneker could make even statistical data fascinating with his "luminous style," but the author himself rightfully considered it only a potboiler.[47] He felt the same way toward *The Steinway Collection of Paintings* (1919), in which pictures by American artists on musical subjects, commissioned by the piano company for use in an advertising campaign, were handsomely reproduced together with Huneker's prose portraits of great composers.[48]

In October 1917, the *Press* proudly announced that it had obtained the services of "America's most eminent critic,"[49] and it was rumored in Philadelphia that for three articles a week Huneker was being paid more than some of the newspaper's top editors.[50] He was earning more in twenty-four hours than he had earned on Park Row in two weeks, Huneker told Krehbiel.[51] "It's hard luck to get into harness at my age, just after 15 years' escape," he explained to Quinn, "but what am I to do? Here, if I take a job as music critic it means slavery for 7 days a week and not more than 50 plunks."[52]

He came to Philadelphia on Fridays and Saturdays (Tuesdays instead of Saturdays when the Metropolitan was in town) and, except for the tiring two-hour train trips, liked his new position, finding the work easy and the surroundings congenial. Though he had once chastised its members for arguing over the admission of musicians,[53] he joined the Art Club, to which his brother John and old friends belonged. Cultured natives considered him a real catch and basked in reflected glory. Annoyed by Mencken's comment in *A Book of Prefaces* that Huneker had miraculously emerged from Philadelphia, "that depressing intellectual slum," one resident, indeed, had protested in another local newspaper that the city must have been an "intellectual pleasure garden" to have produced him.[54] (Huneker himself had remarked in 1916 that Philadelphia's fried oysters were better than her aesthetic culture.)[55]

Theodore Presser even proposed a public dinner to his former editor —"dotage, anecdotage, and table d'hôtage," Huneker once called such affairs[56]—an honor that he quickly declined in favor of a quiet luncheon. "I never make speeches," he wrote Presser, "because I can't (though I can, when pressed, converse fluently with a barman)."[57] This reply was more restrained than the one he had made in 1914 to an invitation to speak before women's groups, when, to illustrate his stage fright, he cited the story of an old Russian peasant, who, pursued by a large, hungry bear, at last reached his hut in safety; the bear was only a few feet behind—and had to swim all the way.[58]

His "return" to his native city naturally brought back many memories to Huneker, who felt the urge to revisit his old neighborhoods. On one street he noticed a furniture store which bore the same name it had forty years earlier. Standing in the doorway was a young man who looked so much like the proprietor Huneker had known long ago that he spoke to him and learned that he was, indeed, the son of the original owner. "My father's inside at his desk," he said. "Go in. He'll be glad to see an old friend; you won't find him much changed." Huneker glanced in, and, as he recalled a year later, the man "did look many years younger than he should have, considering that he was my contemporary." Afraid that he himself had changed so much that he would not be recognized, Huneker decided not to go in. "Your father is busy," he said as he left. "Never mind my name. I'll surprise him again."[59]

In Philadelphia he often lunched with March, J. W. Magers, the *Press*'s business manager, and Richard Beamish, the newspaper's managing editor and an intimate friend of Huneker's brother John. The *Press* executives had formerly frequented the huge dining room at Green's Hotel, but when Huneker remarked that the music there was as bad as the food (music distracted him at mealtime because he tended to chew on the beat),[60] they switched to Dooner's. For two hours, usually, they would sit at a large round table in the main dining room of this "men's" restaurant,[61] telling stories and sometimes arguing while they ate Dooner's famous food, and ending the session with a word game ("Ghost") at which Huneker's huge vocabulary stood him in good stead. Linguistic disputes could easily be settled at the Mercantile Library (where Huneker had spent so much time in his youth), conveniently located across the street. Afterward, if Huneker did not have to attend a concert, the men sometimes adjourned to March's office for a "conference," which, on one occasion at least, as Mrs. Beamish discovered, turned out to be a crap game.[62]

Popular among the *Press*'s employees, Huneker never failed to exchange pleasantries with Theodocia Walton, March's former secretary who had turned to reporting but was occasionally called upon to decipher the handwriting in Huneker's copy. She was struggling with "sadist" one day when he stopped by her desk and spelled it out with obvious embarrassment, assuring her that nice young ladies could hardly be expected to know such words.[63] He was friendly, also, with Benjamin F. Glazer, music critic, book editor, editorial writer, and general handy man on the *Press* (he later became one of Hollywood's best film writers, winner of two Academy Awards), with whom he used to go to concerts. "It was not always comfortable for a young fellow to have to write about books and music in the shadow of a real critic like Huneker," Glazer remembered. "But if I felt that way it was not from anything Jim did or said."[64]

At the Academy of Music, where long ago he had so often stood in line to get a ticket for the cheap top gallery, no seat in the house was too good for the world-renowned critic of the *Press*, almost as much of an attraction as the artists on the stage. This must have been a great satisfaction to him after all the unhappiness he had experienced in his native city—the years of floundering through the study of law, giving monotonous piano lessons to untalented pupils (when he could find them), suffering the breakup of his marriage and the death of his infant daughters—as the black-sheep son of a bourgeois family trying to find his niche in a world that might well have considered him, as he probably considered himself, a failure at the age of thirty. Now he listened comfortably to concerts by the Philadelphia Orchestra, generally admiring the virile, poetic interpretations of thirty-five-year-old Leopold Stokowski, then in his sixth year as conductor of the Orchestra, who was, Huneker declared in March 1918, without doubt "*facile princeps* as an interpreter of modern music."[65]

Huneker still had an eye, too, for a pretty face and a trim shape. ("A woman is as old as her figure," he once wrote, "a man as old as his eyes; the advent of fat in the one and the absence of fire in the other, tell tales of the approaching end.")[66] After hearing Frances Starr's stirring reading in Elgar's *Carillon* at the end of February 1918, Huneker stood outside the Academy's stage door to get a close look at her as she left, and later sent her a charming note. "It was quite fascinating for a young woman to interest this fabulous and famous older man," the actress recalled. ". . . Too bad I wasn't older and more aware of the beautiful compliment [he] was paying me."[67]

Yet there were signs of age. Most modern singers squealed and shouted, he complained to Frida Ashforth at the height of the operatic season of 1917–18, and they could scarcely compare with the singers of the past.[68] The great exception, of course, was Caruso; one note from Caruso's golden throat, Huneker had remarked in 1905, was "worth, in a purely tenoric way, all of Jean's [De Reszke's] voice."[69] In December 1917, after a round trip to Philadelphia on the Metropolitan's special train—Huneker frequently returned to New York with the company following the Tuesday night performances, doing much to make the dreary train rides bearable for baritone Thomas Chalmers[70] and others—he reported that prosperity had not spoiled the big-hearted, fun-loving Caruso (who admired the critic and called him by his first name).[71] In 1919, when the tenor reached his silver jubilee as a singer and completed his fifteenth year with the Metropolitan, Huneker described him as not only a great artist but "something rarer, a genuine man," whose presence had been an "artistic boon at a period when the art of singing has fallen from its once noble estate."[72]

The feature articles Huneker wrote for the Sunday *Press* in addition to his biweekly criticism appeared regularly until the end of May 1918, a number of them being verbatim reprints of earlier essays on music, literature, and art (though not many of the newspaper's readers would know this, for the writings were still engaging and not greatly outdated). As the music season drew to an end, Alden March, realizing that Huneker had virtually no income apart from his *Press* job,[73] suggested that he write his memoirs for serial publication in the newspaper. Having long toyed with the idea of recording his vivid recollections, Huneker eagerly accepted March's offer of $100 a week for the serial rights during the five months the memoirs would run in the *Press*. "Alden, the Lord bless you, but it was the Devil himself that put this flea into your editorial ear," he wrote March on May 20. "My summer is lost. No music. No outings. Ten thousand words weekly—i.e., 2500 for four days weekly. And hell, and writer's cramp, and I can't typewrite, I can't dictate. But oh! what a beautiful flow of language is gushing up from my sub-conscious, what a dazzling rainbow mist of vocables!"[74]

He did not project a strictly factual story of his life. As he explained to March, he preferred to give the series a "strong autobiographical coloring at the beginning; thereafter men and events will rule, connected by a slender thread of autobiography."[75] Shortly after the serialization began, Krehbiel, the "date-hound," pointed out some errors. "I am not writing a history of music in N.Y. or elsewhere," Huneker replied. "It is to be a book of personal ties, in art, music, literature, and it will be a large varied gallery." As for the mistakes, he meant to correct them before the book was issued.[76]

Boomed by the *Press* as one of the "more notable and significant literary productions of the war period"[77]—Huneker put one of the eight-foot sheet-poster pictures of himself used to advertise the memoirs into his bed covered with blankets up to the neck, startling his wife into hysterical laughter[78]—"Avowals of a Steeplejack" made its debut on June 9, 1918, and, after the first week's installments were reprinted, continued to appear six days a week until November 9. Keeping up with the demand for copy was hard work. "I'm nervous as a mud-hen, but patient as a prostitute," he wrote Quinn on June 12; "10,000 words a week till October—and the great drama in the world's history going on! . . . He who lives by the pen shall perish . . . by the pen."[79] But he was pleased that his work was being well received. "The priests are beginning to write nice things," he informed March on July 3. "We have the Irish vote; now for the Jewish!"[80] When the task was finished by September 1, he was so worn out that he went to Atlantic City for a month's rest.

Happy on the *Press*, Huneker seriously considered moving back to Philadelphia as the newspaper's full-time music critic and editorial writer,[81] but the position failed to materialize, probably because of the *Press*'s shaky financial condition (it was sold in 1920), and instead he became temporary music critic of the *New York Times*, a job he had turned down earlier.[82] William B. Chase, who had joined the *Times* in 1916 after twenty years on the *Sun*, had taken over the post when Aldrich went to Washington on military duty, but discovering that he could not handle it alone and that Huneker was available after all, had generously suggested that his friend be appointed chief critic and he the assistant.[83] "After 15 years' absence the wheel has come full circle," Huneker wrote Cortissoz, "and I'm once more a convict, a galley-slave to tone."[84] Despite his recent vacation, he was plainly not looking forward to the exhausting grind ahead when he greeted the season in late October with a piece headed "The Droning Tune of Things."[85]

The war was coming to an end, at last, and that was something to be thankful for. Huneker had refused to succumb to the wartime hysteria against music by German composers,[86] which had resulted—much to his disgust—in the ban of Wagner at the Metropolitan from November 1917 (preventing the return of Olive Fremstad, who had been engaged to sing German roles during that season)[87] until 1921–22. At Carnegie Hall one night, when anti-German feeling was so strong that even the language was taboo, Huneker saw his musician friend Paolo Gallico walking up the aisle in the middle of a number. *"Wo gehst du hin?"* Huneker asked the embarrassed Gallico in a booming voice, his eyes twinkling—and then sat serenely through the concert, ignoring the glares of his neighbors.[88] In 1918 he was dining at the Voisin Restaurant with Leo Ditrichstein—whose loyalty to America had been questioned because the theater orchestra at one of his openings had failed to play the "Star-Spangled Banner"[89]—when he encountered the now notorious George Sylvester Viereck, editor of two rabidly pro-German magazines, who had just been expelled from the Poetry Society of America and from the Author's League because of his disloyalty. Huneker shook hands warmly with his former protégé. "George," he said, as Viereck was leaving the café, "you are the bravest man in America."[90]

Four days after the war ended, Huneker covered the Metropolitan debut of young Rosa Ponselle as Leonora in a revival of Verdi's *La Forza del Destino*. "She possesses a voice of natural beauty that may prove a gold mine," he wrote. "It is vocal gold, anyhow, with its luscious lower and middle tones, dark, rich, and ductile."[91] More than three decades later, after a twenty-year career as a Metropolitan star, Mme Ponselle recalled that Huneker's comment on the "vocal gold" of her voice was still quoted by music historians and critics. "What singer," she added, "would not remember with gratitude such a critic!"[92]

On November 20 he attended the first American piano recital of twenty-seven-year-old Sergei Prokofiev, who played some of his own compositions. Walking out of Aeolian Hall, afterward, into the comparative quiet of Forty-second Street, Huneker was silent for a long time. "New ears," he said, finally, to Ben Glazer, his companion. "New ears for new music"[93]—the phrase with which his review began. The "gifted young man's" music was "volitional and essentially cold," he wrote, its immense technical difficulties deafening one to the "intrinsic poverty of ideas" of a composer who was a "psychologist of the uglier emotions—hatred, contempt, rage—above all, rage—disgust, despair, mockery, and defiance." There could be no doubt of Prokofiev's "instant success," Huneker declared, but whether his music would last was another question.[94] After hearing Prokofiev's *Piano Concerto #1*, three weeks later, Huneker remarked that the piano was "shrieking, groaning, howling, fighting back, and in several instances it seemed to rear and bite the hand that chastised it." Yet Prokofiev might be the "Cossack Chopin for the next generation," he added, for the "human ear soon accommodates to such monstrous aberrations." Prokofiev would not give an encore at the concert, he reported—which demonstrated that the "Russian heart may be a dark place but its capacity for mercy is infinite." On the following day, however, when he heard Prokofiev for the third time, he found a group of his little piano pieces "piquant" and "full of the unexpected and epigrammatic." "The composer has evidently many strings to his bow," he concluded, "a mastery of old forms not being the most inconspicuous."[95]

Huneker was less impressed, apparently, by another, more popular and less "difficult" Russian composer-pianist, Sergei Rachmaninoff, who was making his second American tour late in 1918. His piano-playing seemed to interest Huneker more than his compositions, reminding the critic of Von Bülow—"the same cold white light of analysis, the incisive touch, the strongly marked rhythms, the intellectual grasp of the musical ideas, and the sense of the relative importance in phrase-groupings proclaimed that [he] is a cerebral, not an emotional artist." When Huneker heard him, Rachmaninoff happily did not play his famous *Prelude in C-sharp minor* (which Huneker had described in 1899 as "a feeble imitation of Henselt and Jadassohn . . . sonorous—and empty"),[96] disappointing the "amiable fanatics" who followed him around from place to place to hear it, Huneker wrote, "like the Englishman who attended every performance of the lady lion tamer hoping to see her swallowed by one of her pets."[97]

Two months later, Huneker covered the Carnegie Hall debut of a pianist who was to rival both Prokofiev and Rachmaninoff and to become perhaps the most popular virtuoso of his day. A youthful prodigy when he first toured America in 1906, Artur Rubinstein, better known at that time in Europe than in this country, had returned to New York in his early thirties to display his more mature artistry. Huneker, who had heard him play in London five or six years earlier, was disappointed by the recital he gave on February 20, 1919, conceding, however, that he may have been nervous because of the debut. Huneker reported (with more technical details than usual) that the pianist was a miniaturist with a limited scale of dynamics, "a trifle old-fashioned in style," following the "Viennese school, with its light action keyboard, the lack of depth in his chord playing, the too-rapid scales, also superficial in tone; above all, his pedalling after, instead of before, his attack. The triceps play a minor role. . . . His tone was occasionally hard and his phrasing not ductile, but slightly angular." Rubinstein was "out of his depth" in Beethoven and Bach, Huneker continued, and though his Chopin was better, it was "less Polish than we had expected," speed usurping the place of eloquence. With Debussy and Albeniz, Rubinstein was at his best; "his color scheme became richer, his rhythmic gifts proved delightful." He had undeniable qualities, Huneker concluded—"finger velocity, and a staccato, brilliant, incisive with a splendid left hand . . . coupled with a sweet singing touch and a musical temperament; traits sufficient to equip a half-dozen pianists."[98] Huneker thought the Pole's second performance, three weeks afterward, was vastly improved, heading his review "A Brilliant Piano Recital." Rubinstein still tended to play Beethoven too fast, but he had found his triceps and, consequently, a deeper, larger, and more varied tone. In Debussy, Ravel, and Albeniz, Rubinstein was "simply fascinating." The Spanish music was "positively electrifying," Huneker declared, and the "diabolic verve, color scheme, and dash would alone make the reputation of a less musical artist."[99]

To the *Times*, whose prestige and circulation were rapidly rising as a result of its excellent war coverage, Huneker was a real asset. His lightness and charm were so refreshing that the *Musical Courier* was soon dreading the "analytical, historical, statistical, supererogated, soporific music reviewing" that would be resumed on Aldrich's imminent return.[100] Aldrich himself feared that Huneker was not always sober when he wrote those casual, often playful, criticisms[101]—and he may have caught Huneker in the act of reprinting old work as Sunday feature articles, especially after the regular season ended.

With the staff of the *Times* Huneker was exceedingly popular. Lovable "Billy" Chase worshiped him, as did Sigmund Spaeth, Huneker's

part-time assistant in the spring of 1919. "He was the best music critic
I ever met—which includes Henderson, Krehbiel, Gilman, H. T. Parker,
and all the current crop," Dr. Spaeth declared thirty years later. "He
had the broadest outlook, the greatest tolerance, and the most human
reactions. He was constructive rather than destructive."[102] T. R. Ybarra,
then a *Times* reporter, recalls that Huneker made so many amusing remarks in the city room that whenever he was there his colleagues sat on
the edge of their seats, wondering what he would say next. He startled
a prim stenographer, one gloomy afternoon, by murmuring: "What a
terrible day! What is there to do on a day like this except wreck a
home?"[103] He threw the room into an uproar, on another occasion, by
passing around his review of a poor musical play which he had attended
to satisfy some *Times* dignitary. "This is art," it began, "with a capital
F."[104] (The sentence was censored.) The compositors liked him because he used to come into the composing room and help them decipher
his handwritten copy. At a café opposite the Times Building, Huneker
would sit at the head of a table, surrounded by editors and reporters,
whom he regaled with quips, racy stories, and anecdotes of his own adventures. The younger men were naturally awed by him, but he went
out of his way to put them at ease. He seemed like a second father,
indeed, to Neil MacNeil, a giant Nova Scotian working on the *Times*'s
war desk. "You're too young to write," Huneker once told him. "You
haven't suffered enough. Better wait before you turn out that important
first book."[105]

In early December 1918, the *Musical Courier* assigned a young
woman to interview its most distinguished alumnus. Huneker did not
answer her letter, and she was told that the only thing to do was to
corner him at a concert or opera. Someone pointed him out to her at
Carnegie Hall, but just as she was about to speak to him friends stopped
him, and then before she had a chance to introduce herself he went off
with another critic. Having heard him say that he would be at the Times
Building at six that evening, she decided to phone him there. A voice
she immediately recognized as Huneker's answered the phone and asked
her whom she wanted.

"Sorry," he replied. "Mr. Huneker is out. This is Chase, his assistant. Is there anything I can do for you?"

"Thank you, but I wanted Mr. Huneker. I'm anxious to interview
him. I saw him at the concert this afternoon, but I . . ."

"Awful looking mess, wasn't he?" interrupted Huneker.

"No, I thought he was handsome."

"Well, I'll tell him that, and he's sure to give you an interview."

"Thank you so much, Mr. Chase. You know, I've never met him."

"Small loss. This fellow Huneker is a red faced, rough sort of chap, who drinks hard, very hard indeed."

"Thank you, Mr. Chase, that's very interesting."

"I'll give Huneker your message."

The interview—which never proceeded beyond this conversation—soon appeared in the *Musical Courier*.[106]

In mid-December, Huneker was elected to the literary section of the National Institute of Arts and Letters, along with Edgar Lee Masters, the poet; Albert Bigelow Paine, Mark Twain's biographer; Walter Prichard Eaton, the drama critic and historian; William Bishop, a writer-diplomat; Jefferson Fletcher, Dante expert and professor of comparative literature at Harvard and Columbia; Charles Hazen, professor of history at Columbia; and Stuart P. Sherman.[107] Mencken and Nathan were astonished when Huneker accepted the invitation to join this august body. Mencken, whose *Prejudices: First Series,* published in September 1919, contained a blast against "Six Members of the Institute," felt that after Huneker had been passed over for so long in favor of "all sorts of cheapjack novelists and tenth-rate compilers of college textbooks," the invitation was insulting—"almost as if the Musical Union had offered to admit a Brahms";[108] moreover, joining any group to which the anti-Teutonic Sherman belonged, not to mention Mencken's other bête noire, Theodore Roosevelt, a charter member of the Institute, seemed traitorous to Mencken.

Though Huneker eventually told him that he had merely allowed himself to be elected "to please certain people remotely connected with the publishing business," and that he had never even possessed a rosette of the Institute (which was probably not true) or attended their affairs (which probably was),[109] he was obviously proud of the honor; he surely agreed with Gautier, another one-time scoffer at institutional approval, who had been delighted to accept an appointment as Officier de la Légion d'Honneur, that no matter how much fun you poked at such institutions, when they opened up their doors and "you acknowledged receipt of the brevet, you are in your heart of hearts completely enchanted, and you stroll about the town all the week, with your bit of red ribbon, brand-new, in your buttonhole."[110] (Long afterward, in 1950, Mencken himself, though never elected to the group, some of whose members he had called "humorless omphalopsychites" as late as 1947,[111] accepted the National Institute's Gold Medal for Essays and Criticism—much to the unrelenting Nathan's disgust.)[112]

Before Huneker could explain, however, his irrepressible friends chided him for his "apostasy" at a luncheon at Sherry's in April 1919. Dressed in a cutaway morning coat, an ascot, and a pearl-gray Homburg adorned with a green feather, Huneker was greeted by a solemn-faced Mencken and Nathan each wearing around his neck a specially designed pendant of the "Order of Chastity, Third Class." After lunch, the pair, aware of Huneker's increasing sexual debility and his bladder trouble, crowned him with a warming pan.[113] "All right, all right for you lads," he wrote Mencken. "I'll get uneven later."[114] Mencken recalled that it was the last time he saw Huneker,[115] but Nathan thought it was in 1920 when he and Mencken played another joke on Huneker, taking him to the apartment of a lady acquaintance of theirs, who gave the "old man" a new kind of thrill by retiring from the drinking festivities at a pre-arranged signal and casually reappearing covered with the snakes that she used as a professional entertainer.[116]

The most talked-about criticism that Huneker wrote as music critic for the *Times* was a barrage of purple prose about Mary Garden, a long-time favorite of his,[117] though it is not clear whether they had ever met before this season. According to the picturesque tale Mencken related to James M. Cain (the novelist) in the 1920's, Huneker had told Mencken that he had been having an affair in Paris with Sybil Sanderson, the famous American-born singer for whom Massenet wrote *Thaïs*, at the very time her protégé, Mary Garden, then an impecunious young student, was living at Sanderson's apartment, and that their first "morning in" was interrupted by the protégé's joining them for breakfast. When, as a celebrity, Garden was afterward "introduced" to Huneker, she conveniently forgot this earlier meeting—a bit stuffy on her part, Huneker thought.[118] (The story is dubious, however, for during the time Garden was staying with Sanderson—a few months beginning in November 1899[119]—Huneker was in America, and there is no other evidence linking him romantically with Sanderson, though he undoubtedly heard her sing the title role in the Metropolitan's first *Manon* in January 1895, and may even have written the interview with her published in the *Musical Courier* a week after the performance.)[120] In her seventies Garden recalled that she had met Huneker only twice in her life—both times in 1919—and Huneker's statement, published in that year, that he never saw her off-stage, seems to confirm her account.[121]

In 1919, at any rate, Garden, starring in two operas never before heard in New York, Février's *Gismonda* and Massenet's *Cléopâtre*, and singing her celebrated roles in *Pelléas et Mélisande, Le Jongleur,* and *Thaïs* (which Huneker liked to call "Thighs"),[122] was *the* attraction of the opera season. Judging her an excellent sitter for a flamboyant portrait, an "orchidaceous Circe . . . uncommon or Garden variety,"[123] he conducted what amounted to a one-man publicity campaign for the "nearest approach to Duse on the lyric stage,"[124] beginning in late January 1919, a week before the Chicago Opera's opening night, and continuing even beyond the company's month-long stay. Garden was so gratified by his criticism of her performance in *Pelléas*—"Mary Garden was Mélisande," he had remarked. "No further praise is needful"[125]— that she wrote him it was the "first time since I have been in America that I have read something about myself that *absolutely pleases* me."[126] By mid-February his enthusiasm was so effusive that an anonymous letter writer—probably one of the female singers who used to press a grease-painted nose so hard against the windows of Lüchow's to see if Huneker was lunching with a rival that the window-washer had to scrub the panes with sandpaper[127]—accused him of being madly in love with the soprano. He answered the charge in an article called "The Baby, the Critic, and the Guitar" by citing Saintsbury's anecdote to the effect that one need not like babies to admire pictures in which they appeared. "If I were a young chap I should pay no attention," Huneker added, "but being as old as I am I proudly confess my crimes, merely pausing to ask, who isn't in love with Mary Garden? . . ." "Why doesn't your wife put you behind bars?" wired a "sympathetic singer." "Which one?" asked Huneker.[128] He had been fetched out of more than one bar by Josephine, whom he once called a "sort of Lead Kindly Light in petticoats."[129]

His outburst of panegyric reached its gaudy climax on April 13 with a three-column spread headed, in large capitals ranging across the entire width of the story, "Mary Garden: Superwoman." While other critics were still debating whether she could sing, Huneker rhapsodized her as a

swan. . . . A condor, an eagle, a peacock, a nightingale, a panther, a society dame, a gallery of motion pictures, a siren, an indomitable fighter, a human woman with a heart as big as a house, a lover of sport, an electric personality, and a canny Scotch lass who can force from an operatic manager wails of anguish because of her close bargaining over a contract; in a word, a Superwoman. . . . She does not represent, she evokes. She sings and she acts, and the densely woven web is impossible to disentangle. Her Gallic temperament is of an intensity. She is white hot, a human dynamo with sudden little retorsions that betray a tender, sensitive soul, through the brilliant, hard shell of an emerald personality; she is also the opal, with its chameleonic hues. . . . She is eminently cerebral. And yet her chief appeal is to the imagination. Not a stroke of her camel's-hair brush, not the boldest massing of colors, are left to chance. . . . Not a tone of her naturally rich, dark voice but takes on the tinting of the situation. . . . Despite her Scotch birth, she has remained invincibly Yankee. . . . She is Our Mary.[130]

("Criticism in general is a chameleon that takes on something of the pattern upon which it imposes itself," George Jean Nathan once wrote. ". . . There is . . . some of Mary Garden's spectacular histrionism in [Huneker's] essay on her acting.")[131] A few days afterward, according to Miss Garden, Huneker's skeptical colleagues presented him with a baby's milk bottle[132]—a reference to his "Baby" article rather than a suggestion that he had embarked upon his second childhood.

About the time the "Superwoman" story appeared, Huneker called on its subject at the New York home of her sister, and several days later she was the guest of the Hunekers at a matinee of Edward Knoblock's hit play, *Tiger! Tiger!*[133] (to which Huneker had apparently taken Olive Fremstad earlier without bothering to tell Josephine).[134] Aware of the persistent rumor of her "affair" with him, Garden remarked, long past her own prime, that Huneker, the "greatest music critic this country ever had," must have been a handsome man when he was younger. "If I had known him then," she said, "I might have been attracted to him."[135] In 1919 it was much too late, alas, for any satisfying romantic attachment on Huneker's part—except in his still lively, potent imagination.

THE FLESH: 'PAINTED VEILS'

I've fallen head over heels desperately in love with your daughter," Huneker wrote Clio on March 18, 1919, the day after he saw her and eleven-year-old Mona Bracken at the opera, ". . . and, subject to your maternal approval, I am sending her the enclosed love letter with two little pictures. . . . You are wonderful dear, your eyes are eternally young—and—; but this is not a love letter to you but to Mona. . . . You are a great sculptor in flesh and blood, Clio. Your living statues are all beautiful." This was a far cry from the stiff notes he had sent his former wife from time to time regarding Erik. "I fear I'm suffering from suppressed paternity," he added in a postscript. "There is no cure for this disorder which attacks elderly persons only." He told Mona that the pictures of her mother and himself would show her how they looked when they were little and "rolled their hoops in dreamland where the birds and children play under the trees listening to what the leaves say to the wind." "You know that trees talk to each other," he explained, "their leaves are their tongues. They told us in green whispers of you and Barrie [her brother], and Erik on the other side of the moon where all the dream children await" until their mothers send for them.[1]

Though in his autobiography he had disgorged himself of many memories, Huneker continued to ruminate over the past—especially during the first three weeks of May 1919, after the music season ended, when he was laid up following an operation for the removal of a cyst on the bladder. Warned not to touch alcohol because of incipient diabetes, he could only dream of glorious prewar Pilsner and other, headier pleasures. After forty years of good times, he wrote Frida Ashforth on May 18, the only "vices" he could now enjoy were tea and tobacco.[2]

But he was also worried about the present. A few days before his operation, Josephine had undergone a more serious one, and the double dose of medical bills produced a heavy drain on the Huneker finances.

He had recently notified Brownell that other publishers were bidding for his autobiography, and that he would not even ask Scribner's to make an offer because he was discouraged by his small royalties[3]—which, from 1916 through 1918, had averaged a little less than $500 a year for twelve books, plus a total of some $600 for *Unicorns* in 1917 and 1918.[4] His *Times* salary of $100 a week ($75 during the off-season from June to October)[5] covered little more than living expenses, however, and when Scribner's, after all, offered him advances of $1,500 each for the autobiography and a collection of essays to be published in 1920, he quickly accepted. In June he was reading proofs for the former and arguing with Brownell over the inclusion of the Shaw letters, which he thought would help the book's sale. "Well, my dear W.C., this is 1920, isn't it?" he wrote Brownell, who objected to printing Shaw's references to flagellomania and sodomy. "We are in for a puritanical suppression of individuality at all costs, so I'm taking time by the forelock (not foreskin, as you may think)!"[6] They finally agreed to print the letters *without* the offensive words. To turn out a money-maker, for once in his life, was also one of the chief motives behind his major undertaking in 1919, the writing of *Painted Veils*.

An idea for a long piece of fiction had been in the back of Huneker's mind for so many years that by 1893, when his autobiographical story "The Corridor of Time" was first published, he must have already identified himself with his protagonist, who spends ten years laboring on a novel and completes only the title page and the first sentence.[7] In 1905, when he told two friends that he was working on a novel,[8] he had probably outlined the scenario for a book to be called *Jet*, whose heroine he described as a composite of Fremstad and Calvé.[9] This may well be the germ of *Painted Veils*. Seven years later, however, he had still not started the actual writing. "In January I hope to begin that infernal new book," he wrote Brownell at the end of 1912. ". . . Only about 90,000 words, straight narrative and not a trace of mucilage in a single chapter. For 10 years I dreamed of it and now it seems thin, insipid, stale—like the fumes of a far off carouse."[10] But again he could not afford to take time off to write the book. He was thinking about the same story, in all likelihood, in July 1915, when he asked Mencken if *Smart Set* would be interested in a "30,000 word novelette [about] . . . a warm Prima Donna Wagnérienne. I've got the scenario."[11] Though

Mencken liked the idea and urged Huneker to tackle it,[12] the novelette did not materialize.

Going back to his original plan and hoping that a full-length novel could be serialized in *Smart Set* before being published in book form, Huneker finally found time to concentrate on the project during the late spring and the summer of 1919. Working like a beaver, he had built the "dam" with "many damns," he informed T. R. Smith of Boni and Liveright, the publishing firm, on June 17; now all he had to do was write the book.[13] If the dates that he placed at the end of *Painted Veils* are correct, he began writing on July 9, and by the following August 25 he had finished (except for slight revisions) a novel of over 70,00 words.

As Huneker confessed to Alden March and others, *Painted Veils* was a sequel to *Steeplejack*, bringing his "suppressed complexes" to the surface.[14] *Steeplejack*, indeed, contained so little about Huneker's love life (he "didn't wish the publishers to go to jail," he explained)[15] that, as Mencken later observed, it gave the impression that his early days were spent "in the fashion of a Y.M.C.A. secretary."[16] Under the cover of thinly disguised fiction, however, he could expose something of his *vita sexualis*. Not that everything in *Painted Veils* is based on fact; to find a parallel in his experience for every situation, an original for every character, would now be impossible, of course, even if he had invented nothing. One would hesitate to seek out any real-life event or prototype if Huneker did not explicitly state that it existed. To Frida Ashforth, portrayed in the novel as "Frida Ash," he described its setting as New York, artistic and bohemian, of 1895–1905.[17] "The story itself is largely true," he told Quinn. "I know—and knew—Istar. She is a composite of—well, I'll tell you some day. Mona is in town today; and the little slut, Dora, still lives and ceased fornication. . . . She cries when we meet. . . . Ulick is we all."[18]

Huneker informed Burton Rascoe, who had suggested in his review that the book's most sensational features, the Holy Rollers incident and the banquet orgy, owed something to Huysmans' *Là-bas* and *A Rebours*, respectively,[19] that both episodes were, in fact, taken from life. While strolling between Franconia and Littleton, New Hampshire, in 1899, he explained, he had run into Brother Rainbow, Roarin' Nell (their actual names), and the other Holy Rollers, and had in fact experienced the event depicted in *Painted Veils*, though there was no such person as Istar. The bacchanalian scene was an "exact transcription" of the notorious Pie Girl Dinner given by millionaire Henry W. Poor to Augustus Saint-Gaudens, the sculptor, at the Sixteenth Street studio of James Laurence Breese, an amateur photographer. It was here, Huneker added, that he met Dora.[20]

These claims contain a puzzling mixture of truth and error. The Pie Girl Dinner *was* given—on May 20, 1895—by Poor, a prominent art and book collector,[21] not for Saint-Gaudens, however, but for John Elliott Cowdin, a noted polo player, on the occasion of Cowdin's tenth wedding anniversary (Mrs. Cowdin being conveniently in Europe). It *was* held at the Sixteenth Street studio of James Laurence Breese, a member of New York's most exclusive society and a leading photographer, whose secretary, according to Georgiana Carhart, was Josephine.[22] Among those invited were Saint-Gaudens; architects Stanford White, Charles F. McKim, and William Rutherford Mead; Charles Dana Gibson, the famous illustrator; painters J. Alden Weir, John H. Twachtman, Robert Reid, Edward Simmons, and Willard Metcalfe—five of "The Ten"; George Barnes, the writer; William Astor Chanler, explorer and Congressman; Nikola Tesla, the distinguished inventor; John Ames Mitchell, founder and editor of the old *Life*; and Robert Bacon, Secretary of State, briefly, under Theodore Roosevelt, and later Ambassador to France. Huneker's name was not on the printed menu which listed all the guests, but it seems that two or three of those originally invited did not come (including Saint-Gaudens)[23] and others were substituted in their place. Thirty-three men and two unidentified women—models—sat down to a sumptuous dinner, which was said to have cost Poor $3,500.

If the newspaper account of the affair is accurate, it appears that the dozen naked serving girls Huneker placed in the novel were products of his imagination, his reading, or his memory of another party, and that he also reduced the number of male guests to an even dozen. Thus his version of the banquet was not, in all likelihood, an "exact transcription." As in the novel, however, the *pièce de résistance* at Poor's feast was a huge pie—actually a sphere of galvanized iron with a crust of pastry—from which, when the top was cut, emerged a bevy of canaries and a stunning, sixteen-year-old model dressed in flimsy black gauze with a blackbird perched on her head. Did the entertainment end here, as it assuredly did not in *Painted Veils*, or was a punning feature writer hinting at after-dinner familiarities when he remarked that the girl "bore her honors meekly. . . . Such honors are sometimes rather depressing at first"?

On October 13, 1895, the *World* came out with a sensational page about the party, reporting that Susie Johnson, the Pie Girl, had recently disappeared from her New York home, and suggesting that these "midnight revels" may have started her on a life of sin.[24] Poor's guests were horrified not only at finding their names in such a scandalous article but also at being charged with responsibility for the girl's "downfall," and through their organ, *Town Topics,* replied that the story was merely another outrageous attack by Joseph Pulitzer on persons of high society because they would not associate with him.[25] (William Randolph Hearst was so impressed by the scoop that he induced the editor of the Sunday *World,* Morrill Goddard—whose last name Huneker may conceivably have borrowed for the character in his novel—to leave the *World* and join the *Journal* with his entire staff.)[26] If Henry Poor was courageous enough to give another such extravaganza before he went bankrupt in 1908, he managed to keep it unrecorded, and though accounts of it had cropped up once or twice in chronicles of conspicuous consumption,[27] even his most notorious social venture was practically forgotten until Huneker revived and decorated it in *Painted Veils.*

Huneker's claim that he had actually participated in the Holy Roller orgy is more difficult to assess. This much is true: he *was* in New Hampshire in the late summer of 1899, and by that time a Pentecostal sect that was officially known as the First Fruit Harvesters but commonly called Holy Rollers (founded in Rumney, New Hampshire, in 1897 by Joel A. Wright) *was* active in the White Mountains.[28] There is no evidence, however, that the group's services—usually held in schoolhouses, private homes, rented halls, abandoned stores, and tents—took place in the Franconia-Littleton area in 1899, and no permanent congregation of Harvesters was ever established there. But by 1906 a few converts were living in Jefferson, twenty miles northeast of Littleton, where, late in 1908, they remodeled an old farmhouse into a chapel, in which, it was soon rumored, they engaged in "immoral" rites, muttering ecstatic gibberish ("talking in tongues"), shouting wildly to the accompaniment of tambourines, cymbals, and drums, and even rolling on the floor. Such charges, together with Wright's outspoken condemnation of other churches and the grange, so aroused the community that on the night of December 8, 1908, a mob of over a hundred men destroyed the chapel with battering rams, axes, and dynamite,[29] thus ending the movement in Jefferson and driving the faithful to Rumney, where the sect continued to flourish for years.

Huneker, who had gone to Jefferson for relief from his hay fever in 1900 and again in the summer of 1906,[30] might have heard about—or even seen—the Holy Rollers there. But it is more likely that "Billy" Chase, whose family homestead was in the adjacent town of Whitefield, later told him about them and the incident of the razed "temple," adding the colorful touch that the cult's leader was a gigantic Negro whose "orgies" with his followers had produced mulatto children—the same story he told Grover C. Loud, his colleague on the *Times,* who repeated it later in his book *Evangelized America.*[31] The Negro leader is the only part of the story about which there seems to be any doubt, for although former residents of Jefferson, including a member of the raiding party of 1908, still remember the tall, dark-complexioned, flat-nosed "Brother Rainbow" (his real name?), who, as head of the sect, associated with an alcoholic woman convert known as "Roaring Nell," no one considered him a Negro or recollected *any* colored man in the Jefferson group. (Chase or his informers may have confused Brother Rainbow with a Negro minister from Manchester, Vermont, who sometimes conducted services in the area, or with an itinerant Negro evangelist who lived with his white wife and mulatto children on Sugar Hill, near Franconia, around the turn of the century.) Isolating and dramatizing the sexual fireworks in Chase's account, it appears, and probably not unmindful of the Black Mass orgy described in *Là-bas,* Huneker, at any rate, inserted the "Holy Yowlers" into the first chapter of *Painted Veils*; but having promised Chase, as did Loud, not to embarrass descendants by revealing the real name of the town,[32] he used the Franconia area as his setting rather than Jefferson. Certain features of the terrain between Bethlehem and Franconia match the description in the novel—notably the "dusty road" (the South Road shortcut) on which Huneker had actually walked to Franconia in 1906.[33]

Before attempting to pin down other autobiographical elements or to identify the prototypes of characters in Huneker's "key" novel, it might be helpful to summarize the plot. At an orgiastic meeting of the "Holy Yowlers" in a New Hampshire summer resort, Ulick Invern, a restless, Paris-born American writer, has intercourse in the darkened room with someone he thinks is Esther (called Easter) Brandès, an ambitious, opportunistic, amoral singer, though he does not even know her name. Afterward, she comes to New York to study voice, moving into the Maison Felicé, and is befriended by a fellow boarder, Alfred Stone, a cynical music and drama critic, who helps her enroll in the Conservatoire Cosmopolitaine as a student of Frida Ash. Then she meets Ulick, another Maison Felicé boarder, and they recognize each other. Greatly attracted to her, he takes her to the famous Lilli Lehmann, who immediately recognizes her great possibilities. Easter also becomes friendly with Paul Godard, a millionaire dilettante, and Allie Wentworth, a rich Lesbian pupil of Ash, and financed and accompanied by both of these friends, she goes abroad to study with Lehmann.

Mel ("Milt") Milton, a theological student and friend of Alfred Stone's, then introduces Ulick to his sister Mona, who takes Easter's place in his affections, though he also becomes a regular customer of Dora, a prostitute he meets at a studio stag party, and whom he eventually shares with Godard. The neglected, sex-hungry Mona finally throws herself at Ulick—who breaks with Dora—and becomes pregnant by him, losing the child, however, in an automobile accident.

Returning to America as a heralded Wagnerian singer, Easter, now known as Istar, makes a brilliant debut at the Metropolitan. Falling under her spell again, the highly susceptible Ulick pursues her, but is treated so shabbily and ungratefully that he goes back to Dora for physical relief, having decided not to make further advances toward Mona. The perverse Easter, now jealous of the prostitute, tracks them down and revolts Ulick by displaying sexual interest in the drunk, acquiescent Dora, as she had in Mona, whom she had met through Ulick. After seducing Mona's ascetic brother because his purity annoyed her, Easter horrifies Ulick by revealing that it was not she but Roaring Nell whom Ulick had enjoyed in New Hampshire, *her* partner having been Brother Rainbow.

Years afterward, Alfred Stone, a parasite on Easter, ends the story by telling what happened to the others: Ulick suffered a paralytic stroke (probably syphilitic) at Dora's apartment and finally returned to Paris, where he soon died. Mona married Paul Godard and raised a much-desired family. The repentant Milt entered the priesthood and served as a missionary in China. Dora becomes "a fashionable modiste—a Madame. All her customers are men." And Easter, having committed almost every possible sin, still lived and sang—"the great Singing Whore of Modern Babylon."

Painted Veils is thus the story of a deracinated, highly-sexed American writer and his relations with three women, and, secondarily, of a ruthless opera singer's rise to fame. The title—originally *Istar: Daughter of Sin* (Istar or Ishtar was the Assyrian goddess of love corresponding to the classical Venus, while the subtitle is a pun on the name of Sin, the Babylonian moon god)—and the use as a structural device of the "stripping" motive borrowed from the obscure Babylonian poem "Istar's Descent into Hades" indicate that Easter is to be the protagonist; as the action develops, however, it is clearly Ulick, Easter almost vanishing during the static middle section of the novel.

The situation of Ulick (the name, incidentally, of the musician-critic in George Moore's *Evelyn Innes*, which Huneker described in his memoirs as the best novel about operatic singers that he knew)[34] was clearly closer to the author than Easter's. The plight of the Parisianized American—"my own case," Huneker informed Senator Henry Cabot Lodge, though he disclaimed being the "sorry hero"[35]—a critic of the Seven Arts, "Jack of all, master of none,"[36] so much influenced by French masters that he risked the loss of his own personality, was essentially Huneker's. The theme of deracination, touched upon in his short story "The Supreme Sin" (published in 1916[37] but probably written much earlier), whose protagonist appears in the novel only slightly revised as Ulick's elder brother, is not, however, central in *Painted Veils*. Huneker focused, instead, on the love life of a man whose middle names, we are told, are *Shamus* Fitz*gibbon*,[38] and who is, in fact, so much like Huneker that whole pages of the book read like an intimate gloss of *Steeplejack*.

Huneker veiled his identification with Ulick by changing his character's family background, modeling it, in part, one suspects, on that of his friend Stuart Merrill,[39] the expatriate poet raised (but, unlike Ulick, not born) in Paris, where his father was legal counselor of the American legation. Ulick also differs from his creator in several respects which may indicate wish projection by Huneker: he is well-to-do, the graduate of a university (Jena, from which Vance Thompson received his Ph.D.), no longer a music critic, and still in his twenties when the story opens in about 1895, when Huneker himself was thirty-seven—another manifestation, perhaps, of his desire to be considered younger than he actually was. And Ulick is a teetotaler and nonsmoker, Huneker apparently minimizing his protagonist's other vices in order to emphasize his passion for women.

The cynical, sharp-tongued Alfred Stone, one of the most vivid characters in the novel, was undoubtedly based on Albert Steinberg, Huneker's longtime colleague, but the prototypes of the two other important male characters, Paul Godard and "Milt" Milton, are conjectural. Godard (or Goddard) had appeared previously in two of Huneker's short stories. In "The Last of the Valkyries," written and published immediately after his visit to Bayreuth in 1896,[40] Godard, portrayed as a native New Yorker, rich, college-educated, a dilettante piano student of Joseffy's, a friend of Edgar Saltus, and an admirer of Chopin, Wagner, and Nietzsche, resembles Ulick-Huneker. In another story with personal overtones, "The Rim of Finer Issues" (1896), which deals with the breakup of a marriage between two "prima donnas," Goddard is a rich young music-lover, who runs away with the married heroine.[41] Moreover, Huneker's statement to Burton Rascoe that Paul "really married" Mona—who is surely a portrait of Clio—makes one wonder whether the Godard of *Painted Veils* might not have been suggested in part by Clio's second husband, William Barrie Bracken, whom Huneker knew by reputation as a successful bachelor-about-town and member of the Opera Club before Bracken married Clio, though the two men had probably not met.[42] The character of "Milt" may contain something of Clio's brother Erwald (nicknamed "Waldy"), a charming, ineffectual Christian Scientist, who died two years before *Painted Veils* was written.[43]

Easter is largely a composite of the two singing actresses Huneker knew best—Fremstad and Garden—with touches of Sibyl Sanderson (who Mencken thought was Huneker's chief model).[44] Like Easter, to be sure, Sanderson was American-born (a Californian, while Easter is a Virginian) whereas Fremstad and Garden were both immigrants; Sanderson, moreover, prettier than either of the other two, a charming actress, and, in addition to her other distinctions, rumored to be Massenet's mistress and inspiration, was perhaps the most publicized American singer of 1895–1900, her love life receiving almost as much attention as her art. Unlike Easter, however, she was a lyric rather than a dramatic soprano, specialized in French, not German, opera, and was never a big success in America. Easter's physical appearance resembles Garden's more than either Sanderson's or Fremstad's; her nose, for example, "too

large for canonic beauty . . . boldly jutting, not altogether aquiline,"
is reminiscent of Garden's.[45] But otherwise the character contains much
more of Fremstad, who studied in New York and then in Berlin with
Lilli Lehmann, made her operatic debut in Germany, and became a celebrated Brünnhilde, Kundry, and Isolde. The Lesbian element seems to
have been Huneker's own spicy invention. To forestall any identification
with one of these three singers, Huneker took pains not only to mention
all three in the story by their own names but also to distinguish Garden
and Fremstad from their "rival," Garden being "younger than Easter,"
he observed, while Fremstad "had visited New York before" his heroine
(qualifications which, incidentally, happen to fit Sanderson, who was
born in 1865 and made her American debut in 1895, the year in which
the novel opens); Easter's Isolde, furthermore, lacks Fremstad's "exquisite tenderness" in the second act.[46] In these three respects, at least,
the description also fits Georgiana Carhart, who took voice lessons from
Frida Ashforth and sang Wagnerian roles in Germany—and by no means
limited her romantic attachments to Huneker. It would be surprising,
indeed, if "Georgie" did not figure in some way in this account of Huneker's amours.

Mona Milton and Dora represent two other kinds of women in Huneker's life. Mona (Clio's favorite name) closely resembles Clio, both in
appearance and family background, her parents, the Miltons, being portraits of the Hintons. Ulick and Mona meet in Central Park and talk
about "dream children" just as "Jamie" and Clio did during their court-
ship.[47] The main difference between Mona and Clio is that the former
lacks her prototype's artistic interests, Huneker probably realizing that
the role of woman-as-artist was filled by Easter, and that he needed a
maternal type to balance his plot. The name of Dora's original is unknown,[48] but she was undoubtedly one of those "charming morganatic
ladies, *les belles impures,* who make pleasanter this vale of tears for virile
men," to whom Huneker dedicated the novel "in all gratitude."

Traces of Lizzie and Josephine are difficult to find in *Painted Veils,*
but Huneker may have been thinking of them (and himself) when he
wrote—with typical exaggeration—of the newspaperman Bell:

Some wags said that he was more divorced than married, more sinning than
sinned against. He admitted that he had to pay common-law alimony, as he
called it, to his common-law wives. They were legion. . . . He had been
divorced four times in four different states by duped women.[49]

Other disguises, apart from the characters, are transparent. The Maison Felicé, with its poker-playing proprietors, is obviously the Maison Félix, while the Conservatoire Cosmopolitaine is the National Conservatory, whose director, Mrs. Thurber, is portrayed as Madame Meyerbeer. The *Chanticleer* and the *Clarion* represent two New York newspapers, the first of which is probably Steinberg's *Herald*. Huneker makes no attempt, of course, to veil many of the artistic celebrities that give the novel verisimilitude and piquancy, mentioning as part of the musical and literary background or introducing briefly as minor characters over a dozen such personages, including the De Rezskes, Melba, Farrar, Huysmans, and Remy de Gourmont. Except for brief scenes in New Hampshire and Atlantic City, the action takes place in the New York of the nineties, which Huneker attempted to evoke through suggestion rather than naturalistic detail. The characters frequent many of the cafés and resorts described in *New Cosmopolis*, especially those in the Union Square area.

The dedication to *"les belles impures"* set the temperature of *Painted Veils*, which was so hot that no publisher would touch it for more than a year. Accustomed to the frankness of French fiction, Huneker may have seen nothing objectionable in his story; but a novel that contained a mass sex orgy by a religious cult, an acquiescent "rape" of a white woman by a Negro, an attempted rape of an intoxicated woman, a stag party with nude waitresses and "entertainers," a liaison with a prostitute, a scene in which a "nice" girl begs a man to sleep with her, an extramarital affair resulting in a pregnancy, a seduction of a theological student, and a Lesbian relationship—such a novel was obviously too torrid for the America of 1919. It was with good reason, he told Henry B. Fuller—who had himself daringly written a delicate, ironic study of inversion, *Bertram Cope's Year* (1919), which Huneker admired—that the "imps of the perverse" had rechristened the volume "Painted Tails."[50]

Though Huneker's treatment was not, by present-day standards, minutely physiological or, with one or two exceptions, bawdy merely for the sake of bawdiness, his hero's comments on sex were so pervasive and so colorfully phrased that they quite overshadowed the serious theme of the book, which indeed was never fully developed. Chapter XI of the "Fourth Gate" section, which Mencken singled out as "Huneker to every last hitch of the shoulders and twinkle of the eye,"[51] is especially ful of sparkling epigrams either invented or recalled:

Whether or not the tenor is castrated, he sings like a eunuch.
He knew that when the flesh moved him the spirit took a holiday.
A virile man is as rare nowadays as a chaste one.
No one with a particle of taste seduces a young girl nowadays; they wait
till she is married—it saves time and trouble.
Love is not a sentiment, it's a sensation.
In the cuisine of love, there are flavours for all tastes.
Food, shelter, fornication, the fight for daily existence—these are the
prime levers; not sentiment.
There are no illegitimate children; babies are always born legitimately.[52]

Elsewhere, one of his characters remarks that "the twin pillars of all
religions have been, still are and ever shall be, superstition and fornication."[53] "Little Dora knows your fine society dames, your artistic ladies,"
Huneker's prostitute exclaims, "—whores, the whole lot of them."[54]
Paul Godard relates the remark of a singer whose husband was bisexual:
"We never quarrel unless we fall in love with the same man."[55] And
Alfred Stone tells the ribald story of a man of sixty who begged his doctor for enough sexual potency for one more experience with his mistress,
who "never deceived her lover, except with the aid of her legitimate husband"[56]—a story that reminds one of Huneker's own impotence, especially since the man who supposedly passed it on to Stone is given the
name of Huneker's real-life doctor (who actually told him the tale).[57]
    Although it is a valuable document for Huneker's biographers and
for literary historians, *Painted Veils* will never be mistaken for an important novel in the mainstream of American literature. It belongs, rather,
to a minor development of modern fiction, the cosmopolitan-bohemian-
stylistic tradition begun here by Edgar Saltus and continued by James
Branch Cabell and Carl Van Vechten.[58] The characters are drawn too
superficially to be convincing, and their motivation is not always clear.
Furthermore, Huneker's delightful discourse—he was far better at monologue than dialogue—on sex, art, and religion inevitably makes the book
"talky." George Moore, who in the 1880's had touched, rather more
subtly, upon the Lesbian theme in *A Drama in Muslin* ("Lock her up—
she's a woman lover!" Huneker had scribbled in his copy of this book,
prompting Carl Van Vechten, who later acquired it, to wonder what comments Huneker would have found suitable to inscribe on the margin of
Painted Veils),[59] declared in 1921 that although Huneker's novel starts
well, "he loses himself in details, and is always dropping the thread of
his narrative."[60] "I started to write a psychological study of character,"
Huneker wrote Mencken in November 1919. "I didn't succeed."[61] With

his usual perceptiveness, he realized that the novel's chief weakness was that it failed to touch the emotions—the result, he said, of doing in seven weeks what should have taken seventy months.[62]

On September 27, 1919, the day on which Cabell's *Jurgen* appeared, Huneker wrote De Casseres that *Painted Veils* was "slated for Oct., 1920, i.e., if the police, prompted by Mr. Sumner of the . . . Society for prevention of cruelty to imbeciles, don't intervene."[63] He was referring, of course, to the New York Society for the Suppression of Vice, which had prevented the sale of Dreiser's *The "Genius"* since 1916, and which was shortly to effect a ban on *Jurgen*. Huneker optimistically suggested to Mencken that *Painted Veils* might be serialized in *Smart Set* "without police interference,"[64] but Mencken, who described the manuscript to a friend as "the best thing he has ever done [though] absolutely unprintable . . . not merely ordinarily improper . . . a riot of obscene wit," and wondered whether Huneker was perpetrating a practical joke in submitting it to *Smart Set*,[65] replied that it could only be published privately —which Huneker did not want to do because he felt that there was no money in such a venture. The character of Istar, he replied, could easily be bowdlerized—"my wife says disinfected; it's not all obscene."[66]

After months of negotiations with Scribner's, Horace B. Liveright, and Alfred Knopf,[67] during which a suit was filed against the publishers of *Jurgen*, Liveright agreed, in the late summer of 1920, to publish *Painted Veils* in a subscription edition of some 1,300 copies, with Huneker receiving a total of $1,800. (Huneker gladly added his name to the protest against *Jurgen*'s suppression signed by Mencken, Nathan, Dreiser, Rascoe, Knopf, and Liveright, among others.)[68] Since the vague laws regarding obscenity might still have been invoked against his novel despite its private publication, Huneker was disturbed in early October by the arrest of the editors of the *Little Review*, which had been serializing James Joyce's monumental *Ulysses*. (Huneker selected some extracts from *Ulysses* to send to Quinn, the editors' defense attorney, with the comment that if these passages were passable—Joyce, he said, seemed to be suffering from aberrations of the smell and fetishism—there would be hope for *Painted Veils*.)[69]

Publicity, then, was the last thing he presumably wanted for *Painted Veils*, and he seemed to be surprised by the appearance of a review of it in the New York *Evening Post* on October 30.[70] The reviewer, twenty-three-year-old Kenneth Burke (later the well-known critic), who had read Huneker since his high school days, called the book a remarkable essay in assimilation, as I suppose a novel by a critic should be. With marked Baudelairean morals, it also has bits after the St. James version, a generous application of psychoanalytic nomenclature, passages in the manner of our newest fragmentary writers, a few sentences of the thriller type, and most of all, frequent borrowings from James Huneker, the critic. . . . It is hard to believe, when you read *Painted Veils,* that Mr. Huneker was once a contemporary of waxed flowers and anti-macassars, family albums, and the sheaf of wheat. . . . There is no break between the Huneker of ethicless criticisms and the Huneker of *Painted Veils.* His treatment is completely unhampered, and will prove decidedly too unhampered for those who prefer calling a spade a teaspoon.

Indeed, the novel's frankness, Burke observed, placed it in the category of *The "Genius"* and *Jurgen.*[71]

On December 8, 1920, shortly after the novel was ready for distribution to subscribers, more "unwanted" advertisement came in the form of a review in the Chicago *Daily News* by Burton Rascoe. Formerly the literary editor of the Chicago *Tribune* (which reprinted, at Rascoe's suggestion, the column Huneker wrote for the *Times* during the summer and early fall of 1919),[72] this young Midwestern member of the Huneker-Mencken school had begun a brief correspondence in 1919 with Huneker, whom he had described as "probably as near an approach to a perfect critic as we have had."[73] Late in that year, T. R. Smith had sent the manuscript of *Painted Veils* to Rascoe, who had recommended it for publication in a limited edition, and had also suggested some minor corrections to Huneker.[74] In his review, now, Rascoe called the book "a strange and unusual literary performance, rich in matter, gleaming with the iridescent words of an apt and inexhaustible vocabulary, the very personal creative effort of a varied and interesting experience." Huneker's gift for humanizing his characters was meager, to be sure, but Huneker himself, "a man of astounding sensitivity [with] a prodigious memory and an infinite capacity to enjoy," was a fascinating sight. And Rascoe tried to forestall moralistic attacks on the novel by maintaining that Huneker made sin "bizarre and a trifle ghastly," and was therefore a moralist in the Huysmans tradition.[75]

Rascoe suggested, long afterward, that Liveright or Smith may have sent *Painted Veils* to reviewers—if they so requested—hoping they would disregard the request not to review it and, instead, denounce it publicly as lewd and lascivious, thus creating a demand for the unnumbered copies that were often printed in a "limited edition" of a book which might attract lovers of pornography; since the novel was issued privately, the publisher felt reasonably safe, and Huneker did not have to be told about the maneuver.[76] If this is what happened, and if Mrs. N. P. Dawson, the New York *Globe*'s squeamish book critic, was one of the recipients (as Rascoe suspected), the scheme certainly succeeded: in a review printed on December 24, 1920, she pounced on Huneker as she had on Dreiser, Cabell, and Joyce:

Every admirer of Mr. Huneker into whose hands *Painted Veils* comes should put it in a bag (with a brick) and wander in the dark of the night in the direction of the North or the East River, or down to the bay, and chuck it in—and say no more about it. . . . If sex obsession is as clean and natural as eating or drinking, why does not Mr. Huneker, with others of his way of thinking, write books wholly given up to orgiastic descriptions of men and women stuffing cabbage or guzzling home brew? The fact is, of course, that there are some things that most civilized, and uncivilized, people prefer in private view, so to speak, rather than in public exhibition. . . . There are disgusting scenes in *Painted Veils* that "outstrip" anything that has ever been put in print before. Mr. Huneker does not even put his readers to the trouble, as does Mr. Cabell, of searching out the symbols for themselves.[77]

Untouched by the law, and having collected his money for *Painted Veils*, Huneker was amused by all this commotion. The novel had aroused the "barnyard school of fictionists and its critics—much to my joy," he told Mencken on January 22, 1921. "Anything to make imbeciles realize their imbecility."[78] He was pleased, too, by the compliments paid him by Rascoe, the spokesman, as it were, for the younger generation, whose taste Huneker had done so much to mold for the riotous decade that had just started. At the age of sixty-three, indeed, Huneker had sounded one of the first notes of the Jazz Age he had foreseen but whose wildest music he was not destined to hear.

THE 'WORLD': LAST SEASONS

Throughout the summer of 1919 while he was writing *Painted Veils*, Huneker was contributing weekly copy to the *Times*, mostly material published previously in the Philadelphia *Press*, the *Sun*, *Puck*, and even the *Musical Courier*, and also reading proof for *Steeplejack*, the publication of which was suddenly postponed until 1920 by a printers' strike. Since Aldrich was returning to his old post in the fall, Huneker was mulling over the *Times*'s offer to send him abroad as European correspondent[1] when he received and accepted, just before leaving for a rest in Atlantic City, an offer to become music critic of the New York *World*.[2]

Ralph Pulitzer was now the head of this popular newspaper, but for ten years after his father's death those who had upheld its reputation were Joseph Pulitzer's hand-picked men, especially Frank I. Cobb, editor from 1911 until his death in 1923, and Charles M. Lincoln, managing editor until the fall of 1920. Ralph Pulitzer's fair-haired boy was Herbert Bayard Swope, who had risen from reporter to "consulting editor" and was soon to replace Lincoln. The *World* had always distinguished itself far more by its campaigns for civic betterment, its news enterprises, and its terseness and accuracy than by its coverage of the arts. Though Joseph Pulitzer collected paintings and loved music— among his public benefactions were bequests of almost a million dollars each to the Metropolitan Museum of Art and the Philharmonic Society[3] —and though Cobb occasionally wrote editorials on music, art, literature, and drama,[4] the *World*'s handling of the arts had never matched that of other leading New York newspapers. But in 1919 the ambitious Swope had decided to change all this, the acquisition of Huneker being the first step in the development of the famous page opposite the editorial page ("op ed" to the staff), which was to contain, a few years later, the brilliant writings of Franklin P. Adams, Heywood Broun, Deems Taylor, Alexander Woollcott, and Harry Hansen[5]—probably the most gifted group of critics and columnists ever associated at the same time with an American newspaper.

Huneker's first article for the *World*, a "special" printed on October 5,[6] was called "Noise Our National Neurosis," a sign that he was in a cranky mood as another music season drew near. (When Swope eventually learned that Huneker had trouble concentrating in the noisy Pulitzer Building in Park Row, he graciously invited him to use the executive editor's quiet office.) Given free rein in subject matter,[7] Huneker wrote Sunday features on painting and literature as well as music, his main province. Readers familiar with his work found few changes in his opinions or style. They could not have helped smiling, for example, at his witty, if ungallant, comment on hefty Emmy Destinn's voice upon her return to the Metropolitan: her trying war experiences, he said, had shattered everything but her bulk.[8] Perhaps his most perceptive criticism of 1919–20 was devoted to the young American composer Charles T. Griffes, whose *The Pleasure Dome of Kubla Khan* he warmly praised and whose untimely death in the following spring he considered a great loss to American music.[9]

He also applauded (with reservations) the symphonic poem *Salome* by another American composer, Henry Hadley.[10] Mrs. Hadley met Huneker for the first time on January 29, 1920, at a Metropolitan rehearsal of her husband's new opera *Cleopatra's Night*. Geraldine Farrar, whom Hadley had wanted for the main role, which Frances Alda had won by persuading Gatti-Casazza that she was the only one who could sing English properly, joined Huneker and Mrs. Hadley in the orchestra as they watched the stage. Alda made her entrance in a ridiculous costume, which included French heels. "What kind of a costume do you call that?" Farrar said to Huneker. "Does she look like Cleopatra? Now, Jim, you know that my legs—bad as they are—look better than hers."[11] This was probably Farrar's retort to Huneker's celebrated quip that there had been "two very good reasons" why Alda had been chosen for the role of the Princess in *Marouf*—"her right and left leg."[12] A few days afterward, Huneker described the prelude of *Cleopatra's Night* as the "leg motive" and remarked that Alda's two costumes, "especially the one she didn't wear in the bath, were brilliant." He was too grateful to quibble over the *baritone* eunuch in the opera, and he observed that the legs of the tenor were unusually robust; but "faint legs," he added, "never won a fair lady!"[13]

He found little merit in the Metropolitan's most publicized production of the season, the world première of an opera based on Maeter-linck's renowned play *The Blue Bird,* which the dramatist himself attended on his first visit to America. The fact that Huneker was left off the committee named to officially welcome Maeterlinck moved "Billy" Guard, the Metropolitan's publicity chief, to write a letter to the editor of the *Evening Post*—it was printed on December 23, 1919, the day Maeterlinck arrived in New York, two days after a long article by Huneker on the writer's career appeared in the *World,*[14] and four days before the première—in which he expressed amazement at this slight to one who had done "more than anyone else in the country" to make Maeterlinck known in America.[15] The omission probably made it easier for Huneker to ridicule the opera (the bird, he reported, re-fused to fly),[16] the mediocrity of which was soon confirmed by its dis-appearance from the repertory.

He was also disappointed by another memorable musical event at the Metropolitan in 1919–20, the first American operatic production of Tchaikovsky's *Eugen Onegin,* which was presented on March 24, 1920. The score, he wrote, was "weak, pretty, inconsequential." Observing that the composer was said to have wept when he first heard it in public, Huneker remarked: "No wonder. The man who wrote such master-pieces as the fifth and sixth symphonies, the symphonic poems, or even such a single song as 'Nur wer die Sehnsucht Kennt' . . . should have wept over such ineptness as may be found in this opera."[17] It, too, dis-appeared from the repertory after the following season.

There seemed to be no end to the operas and concerts Huneker had to cover. "I have the N.Y. Symphony at Carnegie Hall at 3 P.M.," he wrote Smith, "another concert in the evening same place, and between the two, I earn my living—as the little girl said of her legs; i.e., I write my criticism at office, bolt my dinner and rush into the Philharmonic fray at 8:30. A hell of a life for a lazy man, as I am."[18] As he was leav-ing the Metropolitan on a cold, wet night in February 1920, Huneker met S. Jay Kaufman, the *Globe* columnist. After talking for a while, they walked toward Fortieth Street, passing the fancy automobiles parked around the opera house. In his "Round the Town" department Kaufman observed that instead of getting into one of these luxurious cars the "ablest man of letters in America" took a subway, while a man who made bristles for shaving brushes went home in his eight-cylinder affair.[19] On the following day, multimillionaire Otto Kahn called Kaufman and said that if Huneker would let him know what nights he would be at the opera, Kahn would put one of his automobiles at his disposal.[20] Huneker was amused by Kaufman's "socialistic" comment, but he continued to use the subway.

Bedouins, the first of three Huneker books published in 1920, came out at the end of February. He had wanted to call this volume of mixed essays and short stories "Mary Garden,"[21] but Brownell rightfully objected because less than a sixth of its contents was about her, and they compromised by featuring her name in the subtitle. Though Huneker had hoped that the book would appear a month earlier, at the height of the Chicago Opera's visit to New York,[22] it did receive some free publicity on February 27, when Garden starred in the role of a scantily clad courtesan in the heralded New York première of Camille Erlanger's *Aphrodite.* Huneker reported that those who had come to see the singer "attired in moonlight" were disappointed, for nothing happened, "not even the fall of a safety-pin."[23] Thinking of the trouble he was having getting *Painted Veils* published, Huneker added, in a bitter aside, that the unexpurgated version of the "beautiful book" on which the inferior opera was based, Pierre Louÿs' *Aphrodite,* was available only in a privately published edition, "thanks to meddlesome censorship that seeks to elevate literature in this 'free' land to the dignity of a laundry."

Many readers naturally assumed that the purposely ambiguous dedication of *Bedouins*—"*A la très-belle, à la très-bonne, à la très-chère,*" a line from Baudelaire's *Les Fleurs du mal*—was addressed to Mary Garden. But Huneker told De Casseres, who wrote at least *four* reviews of *Bedouins,*[24] that it was dedicated to "my own beloved Jozia, my lawful wedded wife! If this gets into the news I lose forever my reputation as a bohemian—and I'm an old bourgeois! She is worth the whole shooting match of singers, actresses, and other 2 legged nuisances."[25] A number of reviewers, including even De Casseres,[26] felt that Huneker's portrait of Garden was extravagant. Mencken doubted whether any opera singer was worth so much "polyglot rhapsody" and suggested that Huneker go back to Bach and Brahms, for mummer-worship was "William Winterism."[27] Henry Finck observed, with unconscious irony, that it was no wonder Garden had excepted Huneker when she had recently called the New York critics "dried-up old men."[28] In the Philadelphia *Press,* Ben Glazer headed his notice "The 'Great Lover' of American Criticism."²⁹ "A wonderful book," Vance Thompson wrote his old friend from Nice. "I forgive your Mary Garden—you've hung such tapestry on her. . . . Your future biographers are going to have a lot of fun when they come to the 'Bedouin period.' "³⁰

Though the *Tribune*'s reviewer, Heywood Broun, was no fan of Garden's, he admired Huneker's "nimble mind," his eloquence, and his determination that "his views of the world of music and letters should not be one whit less exciting than the story of the second half of the Harvard-Princeton football game or the latest turn of events in Russia."³¹ Burton Rascoe found in *Bedouins* a "fascinating phantasmagoria of verbal sound and color."³² The same feature inspired Don Marquis to write a poetic tribute to Huneker for the fantastic erudition and command of language displayed in "A Masque of Music," a richly imaginative prose-poem reprinted in *Bedouins* (it had first appeared, in a slightly different version, in the *Musical Courier* twenty years previously and had reappeared, more recently, in the *Times*),³³ in which Huneker traces musical history and reels off a long list of obscure, oddly-named instruments. Entitled "A Mask of Music," Marquis' delightful parody was printed in the *Evening Sun* on March 10:

> Harken to Huneker playing on
>   The Sam-i-sen and the Cem-bal-o!
> The Pentachord and the Pantalon!
>   The Rebab! Gekkin! Shunga! Yo!
>   —How many instruments does he know?
> But the one of them all that I prefer
>   Is neither the Salpinx nor the Sho:
> I like the sound of the Huneker!
>
> This polyphonic phenomenon
>   Sets the quaint words singing all in a row
> As he smites the Shawns of Solomon
>   Or the Ophicleide or the Theorbo—
>   How many instruments does he know?
> When he sweeps his fist o'er the clavier
>   The vocables gallop to and fro—
> I like the sound of the Huneker!
>
> Better than Zither or gay Genkwan
>   Or Re-bec or Flute or Ya-*mat*-o-ko-*to*,
> Or Ceylonese Ra-*van*-a-stron,
>   Or Shofar that blew over Jericho,—

(How many instruments *does* he know?) —
Clavichord, Virginals, Dulcimer,
   Or Sackbut or Domra or Piccolo,
I like the sound of the Huneker!

James! You're a wizard, and I'll say so!
   How many instruments *does* he know?
Oh, hear that language whizz and whirr!
I like the sound of the Huneker![34]

The literary criticism Huneker himself wrote during this period consisted largely of brief comments on books—mostly by Americans—for the Sunday *World*. In January 1920, for example, he recommended *In the Garret* by his colleague Carl Van Vechten,[35] the Iowa-born music and drama critic, whose penchant for the exotic, the *outré*, the ultra-modern, and the outspokenly sexual in art had been strengthened, if not, indeed, inspired, by Huneker's example.[36] The subjects and even the style of Van Vechten's graceful essays resembled Huneker's, while one of the racy, sophisticated novels he was to write during the 1920's, *Peter Whiffle* (which contains a tribute to *Old Fogy*),[37] evokes the tone and aesthetic ideas of *Painted Veils*. The two men did not mix in the same social circles, but they met occasionally at musical events and complimented each other both privately and publicly.[38] Another young journalist Huneker praised (though never met) was Christopher Morley, conductor of the "Parnassus on Wheels" department for Philadelphia's *Evening Public Ledger* when Huneker was working for the *Press* in 1917–18, and "The Bowling Green" columnist in the New York *Evening Post* in 1920.[39]

Yet Huneker did not neglect his old favorites. In May 1920 he discussed Henry James's recently published letters, describing the portrait that emerged from them as that of "a kindly gentleman . . . and a scholar . . . a character abounding in the finest human traits, more lovable, more intimate, than his literature."[40] In a more elaborate review of the letters for the May *Bookman,* Huneker denied that James was a Puritan and, moreover, labeled him "invincibly American" despite his change of citizenship.[41] And as late as 1919 Huneker lauded William Dean Howells' "pellucid sentences so free from the overblown" and his "admirable character etching."[42] (When Howells died, a year later, De Casseres claimed that now Huneker was—or ought to be— the "Dean" of American letters.)[43]

Throughout the spring of 1920 Huneker suffered from advanced diabetes and intercostal neuritis. "My father always warned me not to bet my kidneys against the brewery," he wrote Mencken, "but I did. I've lost."[44] When Mencken, an ardent student of medical symptoms, pointed out that diabetes originated in the pancreas, not the kidneys, the suffering Huneker, still able to laugh, remarked to his doctor that wherever it began, it "ends in the *pissoir*." "I wound up last night with a brief, but brilliant, indigestion," he added. ". . . At present I think I have gall-stones, dyspepsia, a large and intelligent tumor on the heart, a peristaltic rib, a floating erection. . . . I'd better see a preacher."[45]

At times, however, his ill-health, together with financial worries and annoyance over the delay in finding a publisher for *Painted Veils*, exacerbated his irritability to the point of crankiness. Prohibition was almost the last straw, for even though he himself had been forced to stop drinking, he considered the Eighteenth Amendment a constraint on individual liberty and protested vociferously against it. "Like other tyrannical devices to enslave the will of mankind," he had declared in May 1919, seven months before the new law went into effect, "it will be tested, found wanting, and dropped. And the best way to hasten the decease is to enforce rigidly the law."[46] In "The Art of Being Sixty," printed in the *World* on February 1, 1920, the day after his sixty-*third* birthday—the few persons who knew his real age must have chuckled at his remark that it was "simply a question of the Will-to-Enjoy that keeps men and women younger than their official years"—he pictured himself as an oldster bored by English fiction, disgusted with the drama because of the rasping voices and poor diction of actors and actresses, uninterested in New York's deteriorating cuisine, unable and unwilling to play cards, and disinclined to sit around at a club with other old grouches, especially since there was now nothing to drink. His only refuge against boredom was his beloved piano.[47]

Though ill and busy, he took the trouble to answer a letter from a Harvard senior, Leonard S. Saxe, the nephew of one of Huneker's friends, the pianist Leopold Godowsky. (Interest in his work was "ever strong among the undergraduates," the Harvard Library informed Huneker a few months later, and he was so flattered that he sent it a copy of *Steeplejack*.)[48] Having studied literature under Kittredge, Copeland, Babbitt, and Bliss Perry—who advised him not to follow Huneker's habit of quoting too much—as well as music history, Saxe wanted to become a music critic and thought that perhaps Huneker, his idol, could use an assistant.[49] Huneker advised the young man to finish college and get a job as a newspaper reporter in order to come in contact with the "raw material of life, . . . get the vaporish idealism knocked out of you, the spiders swept clean from your cerebral ceiling.[50] *Then* start in at music reporting. In 40 or 50 years you may know music but you will be no richer, indeed, poorer, as I am at the end of a long, toiling career."[51] (After a short fling at reporting, Saxe eventually became a successful lawyer and law professor, confining his writing to articles in legal periodicals.)

By the end of June, however, when he sailed with Josephine for England to cover the London season for the *World*, Huneker felt somewhat better. During the voyage he met Monsignor Francis C. Kelley, founder and longtime president of the Catholic Church Extension Society of the United States, editor in chief of *Extension Magazine*, author of several books, and later Bishop of Oklahoma City and Tulsa. Huneker, who usually got along well with priests,[52] made this one forget all his thoughts of seasickness. "We . . . listened to him for three hours today," the Monsignor wrote. ". . . They went like fifteen minutes."[53] Huneker, in turn, had so much faith in his new friend's open-mindedness that he later sent him a copy of *Painted Veils*. "I read the book," Monsignor Kelley replied, "but of course you know how a clergyman would feel about it. He could not say that it would suit the parish library. Still I was deeply interested—especially in the theological student; but I was never very confident of him."[54] The cleric gave Huneker one of his own books, *Letters to Jack* (1917), a collection of ethical essays addressed to a young Catholic—not exactly the kind of literature Huneker would read willingly, even out of friendship. (It bears, at least, none of the bawdy or sarcastic annotations provoked by writers who tickled his sense of the ridiculous or aroused his ire.)[55]

In "The Escape from U.S. Sahara," printed in the *World* the day after Huneker sailed for England, he took another slap at Prohibition and censorship. "The small town has conquered," he asserted. "Its crammed soul and bone head have entered politics and with the aid of pernicious petticoats we may as well bid goodbye to America, once the land of the free, now the home of humbuggery."[56] The English, he soon observed, did not have to get their liquor on the sly or drink it as criminals in dank cellars,[57] nor did they blanch at the open sale of such books as Dr. Marie Stopes' "sensible and informing study," *Married Love*, banned in America. "Yet we Americans," he remarked, perhaps recalling his own outspoken attacks on the English, "apply to [them] the very name we best deserve—hypocrites."[58]

It rained in London almost continuously as Huneker shuttled between theaters and concert halls in search of new material. The weather was so depressing and his schedule so exhausting—in five weeks he turned out ten long articles for the Sunday *World*—that he could muster up little enthusiasm for London's attractions except for Sir Thomas Beecham's memorable revival of *The Beggar's Opera*.[59] He had hoped to bathe in the hot springs at Bath, but the weather there was just as bad. "You can't take a cure in a bath tub," he told Dr. Williams. "So I drank Pilsner."[60] Perhaps he had a premonition that this would be his last visit to Europe, for he felt an "insane desire" to see Paris[61]—the "beautiful Paris" of his youth—before going home, and in late July or early August managed somehow to slip away alone to the French capital and to spend a day examining the cathedral at Chartres with Lydia Barrington; shortly afterward, he also met her in Rome to look at paintings for a couple of days.[62] Then on August 12 he sailed from England on his twentieth-odd—and final—crossing of the Atlantic.

He was too tired and irritated, upon his return to New York, to take much interest in the advertising campaign prepared for *Steeplejack*, the publication of which had been delayed so long that it seemed stale to him. "I only hope [it] will pay expenses," he told Maxwell Perkins, his new editor at Scribner's. "Anything more I dare not expect for fear of shell-shock and heart failure!"[63] When he received copies of his handsome two-volume autobiography, however, pride temporarily overshadowed his disgust over the slender royalties his books had always brought. "It's not often that a man lives to enjoy such a gift . . ." he wrote Arthur Scribner, "not even if he has worked 21 years as I have under the fostering wing of your house. A beautifully made book, a frame for a mediocre picture!"[64]

Reviewers rightly preferred Huneker's story of his early life in the first volume of *Steeplejack* to the more disordered, less personal jumble of celebrities, letters, and even fiction in the second. Probably the first to discuss the book, De Casseres was, as usual, the most enthusiastic, describing it as "an arsenal of epigrams, an Odyssey of psychic and

physical adventures, a symphony of gossip, a violent purge for sentimentalists. It is easily the non-fiction book of the year. It is the chal-
lenge of a cultural superman to his generation."[65] At the other extreme
were the English critics who still found fault with Huneker's "flamboy-
ancy" and his "excess of emphasis and ornamentation," though credit-
ing him with being a "shrewd and trustworthy judge of men and
movements."[66] Yet Havelock Ellis considered *Steeplejack*, with its "remarkable pages of concentrated and . . . felicitous criticism," Huneker's finest achievement since *Chopin*.[67] The remark Huneker might
have relished above all others came from Georg Brandes. "What a pity
that we saw each other only a half-hour in New York," Brandes wrote him
on March 20, 1921, after reading both *Steeplejack* and *Painted Veils*.
"We were made to understand each other and to teach each other many
things."[68] But Huneker never saw this letter.

The person most disappointed by *Steeplejack* was the one who, having done more than anyone else to place Huneker on a pedestal among
American critics, expected the most from his hero—H. L. Mencken.
What especially disturbed Mencken, who had been reviled and threatened
bodily for his courageous but unpopular views during the war, was that
Huneker's brief account of his visit in 1915 with Theodore Roosevelt
(whom Mencken had recently derided in *Smart Set*)[69] seemed to be an
endorsement of the ex-President's belligerently anti-German prejudices,
which Mencken knew Huneker had privately opposed.[70] The forth-
right Mencken felt that this smacked of hypocrisy and deserved, as he
wrote Dreiser, a reprimand with "good German artillery."[71] Moreover,
Mencken had not forgotten Huneker's apparent defection to the
"enemy" in his acceptance of election to the National Institute of Arts
and Letters. And finally, he saw that though Huneker's autobiography
had its moments, it fell short of revealing the inner man and eventually
degenerated into a "feeble stream of inconsequential reminiscences, relieved here and there by a chapter that is obviously half fiction, conceived and written years ago," and which, he suspected, was interpo-
lated after the *Press* serialization had run its course. In late September
1920, accordingly, Mencken announced in the *Evening Post* that Huneker, "for a whole epoch the gadfly and the bugaboo of all right-thinking
men—a Bolshevik of the bozart, a preacher of sickening anarchies in
color and tone . . . a sly apologist for lamentable carnalities," had now
become a "respectable Philadelphian with the gilt-edged purple of the

National Institute of Arts and Letters in his buttonhole, . . . one fetched by the braggadocio of the late Roosevelt, a 100 per cent American."[72]

First publishing his memoirs at the height of America's war effort, Huneker, to be sure, had reluctantly decided not to risk antagonizing the touchy public by including his prewar experiences in Germany, and he had stipulated, also, that the *Press* version be signed by his full name so that the "Hun" would be removed from his patronymic;[73] he did not add any material on Germany to *Steeplejack,* which was the only one of his books with the "Gibbons" in his signature. But apart from one statement which *was* rather uncharacteristic and uncourageous of Huneker— "My cosmopolitanism peeled off like dry paint from a cracked wall when President Wilson [for whom Mencken had no use, either] proclaimed our nation at war. . . . Our country first"[74]—there was nothing in *Steeplejack* that could be called "100 per cent Americanism," and the single war issue mentioned in the page-and-a-half section on Huneker's visit to Oyster Bay was Roosevelt's remark concerning the *Lusitania.*

Mencken's review surprised and upset Huneker, who tried to pass it off lightly, however, when he wrote Mencken in early October. "I'm sorry you don't see [*Steeplejack*]," he remarked, "but what's a book review between pals?" Mencken had been so kind to him for so long that he "blushed" to explain that he recalled no 100-per-cent-American talk and that he was a "good American, even though I criticize my country; rather, criticize the mutts who are running it." Answering Mencken's comment about later interpolations, he maintained that "every line" in the two volumes had appeared in the *Press* (which was not true, a passage on his Jewish friends and a prose poem having been added to *Steeplejack*)[75] and that, on the contrary, three chapters on Philadelphia art collections printed in the *Press* were deleted from the book. He was going to have some fun in the *World* over Mencken's review, he concluded, "simply to stop the mouths of the condoling friends who seem to think we are at loggerheads."[76]

Huneker's public reply to Mencken appeared four days later. "Occasionally the worshipper of a wooden god (with clay feet) up and smites his deity," Huneker began, using the same expression that Shaw had once thrown at *him.* Mencken, he went on—with something less than complete accuracy or logic—had "invented" a Huneker that did not exist. "I never was a *chef d'école,* a propagandist, a radical, a pioneer, as he so politely said I was in his *Book of Prefaces*. . . . I never preached aught but the beauty of art; I didn't even spell beauty with a big B. Not that I don't love art, but because I love life the more." If he had chosen to do a gossipy, anecdotal autobiography rather than the kind Mencken would have preferred, that was his privilege; he had written enough serious criticism elsewhere (and, indeed, there was plenty of it in *Steeplejack*). Surveying the American scene from his study window in Baltimore, Huneker continued, and observing that "an old chap, umbrella in hand, though the sky is sunny, is toddling along, dreaming and humming old tunes," Mencken had immediately wired George Jean Nathan that " 'old Jim is getting sentimental. It must be stopped. . . . I'm sorry, but I'll have to write his obituary. If Stuart Sherman hears of this he will triumph.' " (The last sentence is Huneker's single, oblique reference to the "desertion" that had riled Mencken.) Mencken's chief asset was a strong personality, and his essential quality the power of detecting shams and smashing them; imaginative sympathy, which produced the "highest type" of criticism, was, however, generally absent from the work of a critic whose favorite weapon was the battle-axe. Having so brilliantly reviewed *Steeplejack*, he said, Mencken should now read it. " 'Consider your verdict,' said the King to the jury," Huneker ended, quoting from *Alice in Wonderland*. " 'Not yet, not yet,' the Rabbit hastily interrupted. 'There's a great deal to come before that!' In this particular instance I am the Rabbit—an Irish not a Welsh Rabbit. Garcon! Make the order two rabbits and two mugs of musty for two thirsty cronies."[77]

Both men cared enough for each other's friendship not to carry the "quarrel" any further. Huneker, indeed, even sent Mencken a clipping of his reply (which he rather immodestly recommended to De Casseres as a "specimen of not only turning the other cheek but also of polishing off a question without raising one's voice").[78] "Did you see this?" he wrote Mencken in November. "No bones broken."[79] About this time, also, he gave Mencken a card inscribed "for *Steeplejack* with best wishes from a flayed victim."[80] Much kinder and gentler in his personal relations than his booming, often lethal writings would lead a stranger to expect, Mencken could not be angry with Huneker and, in fact, generously softened his second review of *Steeplejack*, published in the December *Smart Set*[81]—the last service he could render his friend and teacher during Huneker's lifetime.

This public exchange was a good advertisement for *Steeplejack*, which sold fairly well. To further stimulate sales, Maxwell Perkins wanted Huneker to attend the "Authors' Night" at the annual book exhibition at the National Arts Club on November 17, assuring him that he would only have to autograph copies of his book and perhaps make a little speech. The other Scribner writer there, Perkins hoped, would be twenty-four-year-old F. Scott Fitzgerald (a friend and protégé of George Jean Nathan), whose *This Side of Paradise* was the firm's best-selling novel. "I want him to meet you," wrote the tactful editor, "and I think you will find him an interesting personality."[82] But the possibility of having to make a speech was enough to scare Huneker off, and the meeting between these key representatives of the old and the new generations, the symbolic figures of the 1890's and the 1920's, never materialized.

Huneker's worry about his health and finances[83] and his disgust with the repressive, materialistic atmosphere in America are reflected in the articles he wrote for the *World* upon his return from London. In one of these he lamented the disappearance of the New Yorker who had leisure for conversation and the arts; the national melting pot, he remarked, had thus far melted nothing but the native American, of whom there was little trace left.[84] He admired Edith Wharton's new novel, *The Age of Innocence,* an artistic "evocation of the town when it was still civilized, before the advent of the barbarians."[85] But though he had no desire to mix with the "pigmy races with dolichocephalic heads" that jammed the thoroughfares of Manhattan, he condemned the racial or religious persecution practiced by the Ku Klux Klan and other bigoted groups.[86]

He reiterated, too, his familiar diatribes against the movies[87] and the phonograph, and composed new ones against the automobile and the telephone, the "most sinister agents in the decivilization of mankind. One slays out of doors, the other invades your privacy indoors."[88] He objected strenuously to a proposed Sunday observance law, predicting a strong reaction to all the prohibitive measures that were making Americans the "laughing stock of more civilized nations."[89] "Literature in America wears blinders," he complained. "The human shape, which should be divine, is a crime unless a corset advertisement. It won't be long before music will be indicted as subversive to public morals."[90]

The season of 1919–20 had scarcely ended before a tired Huneker

was dreading the thought of the next one. "I long for [its] completion
. . ." he had written, "because I then shall be one year nearer the cremation urn"[91]—a prophecy not quite fulfilled. On the eve of a Carnegie
Hall concert opening the season of 1920–21—which turned out to be
the most active in New York's history—Huneker moaned over the prospect of "six months wasted time, temper, nerves, over piddling poddlers
and slithering pianists."[92] Yet he had no alternative, for the $125 a
week the *World* paid him[93] was almost his only income. Though he began to suffer frequent attacks of vertigo and exhaustion after a few days
of rushing from concert hall to opera house to the *World*'s office, climb-
ing countless subway stairs—"My legs have aged more quickly than my
skull—anyway I hope so," he wrote Mencken in late December[94]—he
remained on the job.

During the early weeks of the season, Huneker passed final judgment on two composers whose works he had heard for three decades.
"Puccini doesn't wear well," he declared on November 23, reviewing a
performance of *Tosca*, the American première of which he had covered
almost twenty years earlier. "With the progress of time his meretricious
music becomes balder and balder."[95] (Shortly afterward, Huneker admitted privately that he disliked Puccini because of his "innumerable
'appropriations'" from other composers—Smetana, for example, from
whose *Bartered Bride*, Huneker believed, Puccini had stolen the introduction to *Madame Butterfly*.)[96] But he predicted that Richard Strauss,
who had "in all probability given his best work," would eventually be
ranked with Wagner, Berlioz, and Liszt.[97] Huneker demonstrated, also,
that he could still recognize new talent when he praised the "fresh,
sweet, vigorous, well-trained" voice of Beniamino Gigli, whose Metropolitan debut he attended on November 26.[98]

His criticism of Verdi's *Don Carlos*, produced at the Metropolitan
for the first time a month later, was lukewarm. Its plot "inchoate," the
opera was a "huge, lumbering machine with an unequal score," he
wrote, though interesting to the student of Verdi's artistic development.
Several duos, one trio, and some solos were "dramatically intense," to
be sure, but the style lacked homogeneity throughout, as Verdi "wabbles
from the sublime to the trivial." The dramatic accent was never
absent, however, and as a "traditional type" in the composer's artistic
evolution, Huneker concluded, *Don Carlos* was worth seeing and hearing.[99]

A note of appreciation Huneker received about this time from a feminine reader evoked a charming reply. "There is only one thing an elderly person can do," he wrote, "after receiving such a touching letter as yours: arise, solemnly bow, wipe his glasses to remove the suspicious moisture and then sit down—and wish he were 25 instead of 60." While she was wishing him luck, he hoped she would wish him "across the Atlantic and away from noisy New York and detestable musical criticism. Both are killing." He was delighted that she had enjoyed his books and had told him of the pleasure they had brought her. "Luckily for all of us," he added, "joy is a more easily communicable quality than sorrow; else—crape would hang on every heart."[100] He felt (but never admitted) his age again on hearing of the death, in early January 1921, of his old Philadelphia mentor, Dr. Nolan.[101]

On January 15 Huneker, as symptom-conscious now as Mencken and Nathan, informed the latter that he was having spells of vertigo and nausea, which he ascribed to the effect of eye strain upon the stomach. "*Vita sexualis* very low indeed," he complained. "Guts are going. . . . What is there to live for?"[102] But he had little time for brooding over his health. A concert by the La Scala Orchestra conducted by Toscanini—who could make even a melodeon or a phonograph eloquent, Huneker reported, but was more convincing as an interpreter of opera than of symphonic music[103]—was followed, on January 24, by the opening of the Chicago Opera's six-week season in New York. Music lovers were anxious to read what Huneker had to say about Mary Garden, now that the heroine of *Bedouins* was the director as well as the star of the company, and he had to attend the first production of each opera in the repertory. On Tuesday, February 1, Erik saw his father at the Manhattan Opera House and noticed that he did not look well. "I feel awful," he said, "and these singers don't help any."[104] A day or two later, he wrote an article for the Sunday *World* on Reyer's opera *Salammbô*, suggesting it as a vehicle for Garden;[105] it was fitting that Huneker's last extensive piece of writing should feature Flaubert, his lifelong hero, whose centenary he had looked forward to celebrating that year.[106]

Suffering from a cold he may have caught in a drafty subway station,[107] Huneker went to Carnegie Hall on Saturday afternoon, February 5, to hear the Boston Symphony and managed to complete a short, impatient review for the next day's paper.[108] It was his final bit of criticism. On returning from an opera matinee, Josephine found him ill and put him to bed. He said he would be all right in the morning, but he apparently sensed the seriousness of his illness, for on the same day he wrote a one-sentence unwitnessed will (not valid in New York) leaving royalties and all he possessed to Josephine.[109] He was worse on Sunday, and Dr. Williams, hurriedly called, discovered that Huneker had pneumonia.

During the following three days, he remained outwardly cheerful. Erik phoned on Sunday and was told by Josephine that his father was very sick but would be alarmed if Erik visited him.[110] On Monday, Huneker was seemingly better, though Erik was asked not to disturb him by phoning again. When Josephine's sister Ruth came to see him on Wednesday, the 9th, he frowned at her dark dress and asked her to wear something brighter next time.[111] (Could the punster, witty to the end, have been thinking of Goethe's famous last words, "Light—more light"?) Later that afternoon, he grew restless, protesting that he had to get up and go to the Pulitzer Building to do his Sunday article so that all the work would not fall on the shoulders of his assistant. Shortly afterward, however, he slipped into a coma from which he never awakened. When Dr. Williams arrived at 6:30 that evening, he found Huneker dead.[112]

So many people wanted to pay their last respects to Huneker that Josephine reluctantly agreed, at the insistence of his brother (who paid for the funeral),[113] to public memorial services, which were held at noon, Sunday, February 13, in the new Town Hall. Over 1,200 persons, among them many singers, musicians, conductors, actors, and producers (though few painters or sculptors and apparently only one well-known writer, Richard Le Gallienne), were present at the greatest tribute paid in New York to anyone in the world of music since the funeral of Anton Seidl. Far from well herself, Olive Fremstad nevertheless came to the services,[114] as did Mary Garden, who asked to see the remains privately before the ceremony started and, visibly shaken, bade Huneker an emotion-packed farewell.[115] One of the Metropolitan Opera House ushers loaned for the occasion unwittingly added a touch of irony when he happened to seat Georgiana Carhart in the balcony box next to Josephine's; Georgie, who had not seen her one-time rival for twenty years, prayed that Josephine had not recognized her.[116] (Erik sat with the widow, but Clio was home ill—and probably would not have come anyway.)[117] The simple, nonreligious services began with the playing of Mozart's "Ave, Verum Corpus" by a string quartet composed of Huneker's friends. Eulogies were then delivered by John Quinn, George W. Wickersham, Henry Krehbiel, and Francis Wilson, after which the unopened coffin was borne from the hall to the strains of Schumann's "Träumerei."[118] The body was taken to Fresh Pond Crematory on Long Island—where, exactly two decades earlier, Huneker had attended the pathetic last rites of Albert Steinberg which he had feared might be his own fate. The ashes were preserved to be mixed with Josephine's.[119]

The public farewell that perhaps most movingly expressed an entire generation's affection and esteem for Huneker came from the usually unsentimental George Jean Nathan:

The greatest of American critics. . . . A man of no country and no people save that of beautiful things and of those who loved them, [Huneker] made possible civilized criticism in this great, prosperous prairie. He taught us many things, but first of all he taught us cosmopolitanism, and love of life, and the crimson courage of youth. . . . Huneker's books are our foremost university. The man himself was our foremost cultural figure. . . . He did more to free America from its slavery than any Lincoln. . . . His hair was gray and his mind was a . . . storm-lashed cathedral of experience, but his heart was the heart of Huck Finn. Good-bye, dear Jim . . . God rest your splendid soul.[120]

✒ Twenty-one

EPILOGUE

Nathan's tribute was only one of many that followed Huneker's death. The *Musical Courier*, for example, proud of his long (and sometimes forgotten) connection with it, for six weeks reprinted excerpts from his "Raconteur" columns.[1] The death on February 8, 1921, of Harvard's professor emeritus of English, Barrett Wendell, author of *A Literary History of America* (1900), which someone once called "an intellectual history of Harvard (with incidental glimpses of minor writers . . .),"[2] suggested a revealing comparison to—of all publications—the *Nation*: whereas Wendell represented the New England tradition with its love of "culture," its gentility, academic prose, class consciousness, and Anglophilism, the equally learned Huneker, only two years younger than Wendell, had what the latter "never had, a sense of the many-stranded complexity of modern American life."[3] It is not surprising that three decades later, Van Wyck Brooks began *The Confident Years*—a study of the breakdown of Anglo-Saxon domination of American literature—with Huneker's arrival in New York in 1886.

In June 1921, the *Century* printed a warm, colorful portrait of Huneker by Mencken, who tenderly recorded his vivid recollections of the rakishness and defiance of Huneker's hat and cravat, the exoticism of his tastes, the charm of his torrential conversation, and the gusto and richness of his criticism. Even his "slips," said Mencken, meaning Huneker's deference to less talented co-critics and his unbelligerency, were "grounded upon qualities that are certainly not to be deprecated— modesty, good-will to his fellow-men, a fine sense of team-work, a distaste for acrimonious and useless strife."[4] About the same time, some 770 books and pamphlets from Huneker's library were presented as a memorial gift to the New York Public Library by a group of his friends, led by Edward Ziegler.[5] Twenty-six years later, Mrs. Huneker gave a number of Huneker's manuscripts and letters to Richard H. Mandel, a businessman and collector, who included them in the sizable Huneker collection he presented to his alma mater, Dartmouth College;[6] except for Huneker's music and music books, which went to the New York Public Library, Josephine bequeathed the rest of his papers and books to Dartmouth.[7]

In November 1921, Scribner's issued *Variations*, an aptly named collection of Huneker's last writings, which revealed once again the astonishing range of his aesthetic interests, even if many of the essays—almost all of them printed in the *Times* and *World* in 1918–20, though a few first appeared much earlier—were rather thin. (The one with the most curious history, surely, was an obituary of Caruso, composed when the tenor was seriously ill during the early winter of 1920–21 but not published in the *World* until his death in August 1921—by which time both Huneker and the printer who had set the article were also dead.)[8] To anyone aware of the repetitions, the claim in the jacket blurb that Huneker died at the "very height of his career" was a bit absurd. Of the book's relatively few but generally kind reviewers, the best known, Richard Le Gallienne, was the most discerning, praising Huneker's "vitality, magnetism, verve, knowledge, sensitiveness, humor, sparkle, and, above all, generosity of appreciation," though gently deploring the hurry and restlessness of his style.[9] Benjamin De Casseres was, as usual, Huneker's most rhapsodic champion.[10]

Following Mencken's suggestion,[11] and aided by T. R. Smith and Frederick James Gregg, Huneker's widow collected much of his huge correspondence and edited a selection of it for publication. In March 1922, Scribner's gave it advance advertisement by running an essay on Huneker by Norman T. Byrne, a graduate student in philosophy at the University of Oregon who had written the essay for a graduate course in literature, basing it entirely on his reading of Huneker's books.[12] Lavishly commending the taste and prose style of America's "most vital" critic, Byrne nevertheless annoyed some of Huneker's friends—especially Alden March, who complained to Maxwell Perkins[13]—by overemphasizing Huneker's "hatred of theory" and "scorn for the intellectual" and pointing out the "disconcerting number of misquotations, unacknowledged quotations, unauthentic data and utter falsification" in his work. Even more irritating, perhaps, was Byrne's more debatable (but not untenable) Freudian suggestion that the "mother *imago*" dominated Huneker's unconscious (which might, indeed, help to account for his interest in abnormal psychology), though Byrne's conclusion that this "aberration"—he suspected that Huneker was unmarried—held Huneker within the bonds of the Roman Catholic Church and kept him from being completely fair to anti-Catholic writers is hardly supported by the mature Huneker's irreligiousness. All these charges, together with Byrne's amply justified reference to Huneker's partiality for the "pale beverage of Bohemia,"[14] also upset Josephine, who was not entirely mollified by Perkins' explanation that an academic estimate of Huneker was overdue and that this one would be considered high praise in university circles[15] (not to mention the fact that the article, selected by the *New York Times* as one of the ten best magazine articles of the month, would help to sell the forthcoming volume of letters). After this experience, Josephine distrusted academicians even more, as several would-be biographers of her husband discovered.[16]

Published in the following October, *Letters of James Gibbons Huneker* was well received,[17] the most significant review being the one written for *Vanity Fair* by young Edmund Wilson, who was to become for his generation what Huneker had been for the preceding one—the great "popularizer."[18] Wilson remarked that the book gave

an extraordinarily attractive picture of Huneker as an honest, candid, courageous and spontaneous man. He had a gift for brilliant and pithy writing which is here sometimes seen at its best. Even his letters were shot with those bright shifting colors which we already knew in his books—colors of a singular clarity, clouded, crystalline or flushed. His books were like the floral bombs and the close-packed rockets of fireworks. When they exploded we all held our breaths and were caught up for a moment to the sudden cluster which opened green and red corollas in a shower of golden gouts. If the sparks faded out in the sky and left no fixed stars in the firmament it was not that the fiery beauty had not left its colors in our hearts.[19]

In November 1924, Boni and Liveright issued, in a limited edition, a second volume of correspondence, *Intimate Letters of James Gibbons Huneker,* which included letters Scribner's had considered too indelicate to print[20]—Mencken had wondered, privately, how they had managed to "delouse" the first collection[21]—though they are actually no more "intimate" or revealing than the others. For subscribers only, the book was not generally noticed, apparently the only major review (possibly the *only* review) appearing in the *New York Times,* where, fittingly enough, Huneker's old friend Henry B. Fuller lauded his zest, catholicity, perspicacity, and knowledge.[22] The book did not sell well, but thanks to the efforts of T. R. Smith, it was reissued in 1936 by Liveright, and still remains in print.[23]

In the spring of 1925, Benjamin De Casseres brought out a little volume somewhat misleadingly entitled *James Gibbons Huneker*, which consisted almost entirely of De Casseres' reviews of *Bedouins*, *Steeplejack*, *Variations*, and *Letters*,[24] plus an admittedly incomplete bibliography of Huneker's writings compiled by the book's publisher, Joseph Lawren, a one-time Harvard student.[25] Huneker was "the greatest of twentieth century Americans," De Casseres insisted, "the most extraordinary man—with Poe, Whitman, Saltus and Bierce—that America has produced, and in his field their equal."[26] Five years later, loyal Ben was still loudly proclaiming that no one had taken Huneker's place in the country's aesthetic life,[27] and until his death in 1945 he was always eager to sing the praises of his hero.

As Huneker had predicted,[28] neither he nor Liveright fully benefited from *Painted Veils*. From September 17 to December 10, 1925, the German weekly *Die Bühne* ran a serialization of Lola Lorme's translation of the novel—which Mrs. Huneker claimed was unauthorized.[29] In America, moreover, the book sold for as much as eighty dollars, and the demand grew so great that a pirated edition containing forgeries of Huneker's signature was printed. Though most of these bogus copies were seized and destroyed,[30] the piracy caused Liveright to publish in 1928 and again in 1929 a limited, unexpurgated edition for the general public,[31] now more accustomed to frankness in American fiction. The book was issued by Random House in a popular-priced "Modern Library" edition from 1930 to 1942, and in 1932 it also joined Liveright's "Black and Gold" series.[32] On December 23, 1947, an adaptation of the novel was presented on the Columbia Broadcasting System's radio program "Studio One," starring James Mason and Mercedes McCambridge, with the then relatively little-known soprano Eileen Farrell singing Easter's arias.[33] And decorated by a cover no more lurid, for once, than the text, *Painted Veils* emerged six years later as a paperback, the first printing of which numbered almost a quarter of a million copies.[34]

By the spring of 1929, Huneker seemed to be a legend and a symbol[35] rather than an operative force in criticism, his books selling so poorly that it was becoming impracticable for Scribner's to keep them in print.[36] Deciding that a selection by Mencken—then at the zenith of his fame—

of Huneker's best work might revive interest in him, the firm published *Essays by James Huneker* in October 1929. If Huneker was no longer widely read, Mencken remarked in his sprightly introduction, it was not because his doctrine was unsound but because of the swing back to the "pious, pseudo-intellectual frummery" that Huneker abhorred—by which Mencken meant the Neo-Humanism of Babbitt and More; yet Huneker's influence, surviving him, was "a formidable obstacle to complete surrender. In the midst of the prayer-meeting one hears anon his ribald laugh and his reassuring 'Grüss Gott!' "[37] (Mencken's jaunty assertion that Huneker had emerged from the "spiritual slums of Philadelphia, soberly bred and badly fed"—a gibe first made, in a slightly different form, in *A Book of Prefaces,* and aimed at the Quaker City rather than the Huneker household Mencken had once labeled "extraordinary"[38]—was misinterpreted by Huneker's brother and sister, who probably encouraged two vigorous public replies, one of which irritated the increasingly testy Josephine by ignoring *her.*)[39]

Although C. J. Bulliet, the Chicago art critic, reiterated, in the revised edition of his *Apples and Madonnas,* that Huneker was "easily the best critic of the arts America has produced,"[40] the newer literary critics were unsympathetic to Huneker's impressionism, demanding, as F. O. Matthiessen pointed out (in, ironically, a dual review of *Essays* and the *Life and Letters* of Stuart P. Sherman, who had died in 1926), a "firmer intellectual grasp, a more solid sense of structure, a deeper perception of the relation of art to life in all its phases."[41] "We can recognize [Huneker's] capacity for the kind of thing he sought to do," wrote Granville Hicks in 1930, "his brilliance, his independence; but his work is seen to be—O damning phrase!—of merely historical importance."[42] To leftist, social-minded critics of the 1930's such as Matthiessen, Hicks, and Bernard Smith, who judged him even more harshly,[43] Huneker's antipathy to socialism and his apolitical attitude probably indicated a shallow intellect, while the emerging school of textual exegetes naturally felt that he seldom came close enough to a work of art.

If the *Essays* did not create a Huneker revival or prevent all of the Huneker books published by Scribner's from going out of print by 1954[44]—the last survivor, *Ivory Apes and Peacocks,* was reprinted in 1957 in a paperback edition of 10,000 copies by the Sagamore Press in its "American Century Series" as one of the cultural milestones in America between 1830 and 1930[45]—the book did undoubtedly help three literary historians make up their minds about Huneker. Fred Lewis Pattee, once chastised by Mencken for ignoring Huneker in his earlier history,[46] now devoted five pages to him in *The New American Literature, 1890–1930,* describing him as the "most remarkable" literary figure of the period and in "certain areas of contemporary European art and literature, the most erudite critic that America has yet produced." Though Huneker seemed undeservedly headed for oblivion, Pattee observed, a hundred years later he might be rediscovered as was Herman Melville and be rated as "first magnitude in the new American ephemeris."[47] In his *Literary Criticism in America,* George E. DeMille, later a leading Anglican clergyman and scholar, startled more than one reader of his forty-page essay on Huneker by associating him with the great French critics of the nineteenth century, Sainte-Beuve, Taine, and Lemaître, and placing him in the "very front rank" of American critics with Lowell, Poe, and Henry James.[48] Detecting the major weakness of Huneker's style—"sentences and paragraphs cohere not through inner logic but by virtue of a viscous quality"—Ludwig Lewisohn nonetheless acknowledged in *Expression in America* that the entire modern period of American culture was "scarcely thinkable" without Huneker's efforts.[49] Henceforth, no literary historian would ignore Huneker—as evidenced, for example, by Oscar Cargill's *Intellectual America,* Alfred Kazin's *On Native Grounds,* Harry Levin's essay in the *Literary History of the United States,* and Van Wyck Brooks's *The Confident Years.*

Huneker's Catholicism, wayward though it was, made him especially attractive to Catholic graduate students searching for thesis topics. Literary undergraduates of all faiths undoubtedly wrote papers on him—Kenneth Fearing, the poet and novelist, won a prize at the University of Wisconsin in 1924 with an essay on him[50]—but a musical Xaverian brother, Jason Black, wrote what seems to be the first master's thesis on Huneker in 1927.[51] ("I do not think that in his heart he ever entirely forsook the religion of his youth," wrote Brother Jason, who remained fascinated by Huneker even after learning that he had abandoned his faith,[52] "but . . . at any rate, if he was not a Catholic, he was nothing else.")[53] And surely Huneker would have savored the delicious bit of irony that the first person, apparently, to begin a doctoral dissertation on him, thus ensuring his academic respectability, was a nun of the Religious Sisters of Mercy, the very order whose Philadelphia convent he had happily frequented as a child, when he had promised the good sisters to become a priest. Irish-American and Pennsylvania-born, Sister Miriam Gallagher, a poet, essayist, editor, lecturer, and teacher of English literature, had been introduced to Huneker's work by a Midwestern priest and had found it stimulating, though "James G. Huneker: Failure" was the title she intended to give her study—suggested to her by the same professor at Catholic University (Arthur Deering) who had interested Brother Jason in the critic. "Huneker and I are strange mental bedfellows," the charming, fifty-year-old nun wrote Mencken, who was so pleased by the prospect that he graciously loaned her his Huneker books and letters and even recommended her to Mrs. Huneker. In 1938 the two women met and discussed the project, but Josephine decided that no nun (or anyone else, for that matter, while she herself was still living) could fully interpret her earthy husband, and declined to cooperate. Not long afterward, Sister Miriam, never too comfortable about the topic, gladly dropped it.[54]

To make amends, perhaps, for not having helped his famous (but proud) brother financially during those last hard years, John Huneker, who died in 1931, left a large trust fund to his nephew Erik, "cutting off" Josephine, of whom John had never quite approved because she was not Catholic,[55] with $2,500. He also attempted to honor his brother's memory with bequests to Philadelphia institutions: the Home of Incurables to establish and maintain the "James G. Huneker Free Bed"; the School of Industrial Art to set up the "James G. Huneker Fund"; and the Little Sisters of the Poor to provide a suitable memorial.[56] Because the half-million-dollar estate shrank during the depression, however, none of these bequests could be honored.[57]

Before the end of the 1930's most of Huneker's close friends and colleagues had died: Krehbiel in 1923, Quinn in 1924, Thompson in 1925, Finck in 1926, Hale in 1934, and Aldrich and Henderson in 1937. When Edward Ziegler passed away in 1947, it marked the end of an era, as the eighty-three-year-old Josephine sadly remarked at the funeral.[58] In 1950, three decades after her husband's death, her own ashes were finally mixed with his.[59] Only the childless Erik—whose mother had died in 1925[60]—was left to carry on the family name.

Though the present writer pointed out in 1951 that Huneker's centenary would take place in 1957 instead of 1960, as was commonly supposed,[61] it passed unnoticed in 1957, and even three years later only two writers, it seems, publicly observed it. Huneker's work was not as well known to contemporary readers as it might be, Irving Kolodin declared in the *Saturday Review*, but his influence was "still felt through the critics who read him as they grew up." In a time of such able American music critics as Finck, Krehbiel, Henderson, Gilman, and Aldrich, Huneker was their "universal choice as elder statesman," Kolodin stated, "not only for erudition and wit, but also for the racy fluency of his writings. . . . To paraphrase Hilaire Belloc it might be said that if his prose was sometimes scarlet, his books were read."[62] (Privately, Kolodin called Huneker "without question the most gifted writer on music this country has ever produced.")[63] In the only other anniversary essay —much longer than Kolodin's, and printed, ironically (in view of Huneker's antipathy to the early phonograph), in *High Fidelity Magazine*— Van Wyck Brooks, who had paid his respects to Huneker more than once, again drew a colorful portrait of him. "Agile and humorous at his best, and sometimes a beautiful writer," concluded Brooks, "he was learned, always alive, and certainly unique."[64]

Almost the final tribute paid to Huneker by one who knew him well came, appropriately, from William J. Henderson, the last survivor of the "Big Five," who always turned aside praise of his own excellent criticism with a nod to the incomparable "Jim the Penman";[65] it appeared, with equal appropriateness, in the newspaper for which Huneker had done his best work, the *Sun*:

Bubbling over with human kindness, but with a satirist's eye always on human folly, ever throbbing with life in the midst of the life around him, his mind meanwhile fashioning . . . glowing phrases . . . —that was Jim. . . . In his books he lives, flamboyant, multi-colored, orotund, Turneresque, in a prose that baffles description; Jim, the flaming comet of criticism, whirling in his own orbit through the unbound ether of the seven arts.[66]

Notes

NOTES

All newspapers cited (e.g., *Sun, Herald, Times, World*) are (or were) published in New York City, except where otherwise indicated. The parentheses at the end of an entry indicate where the item was found. In most instances no distinction has been made between original unpublished letters and copies; where both are available, the original is listed. If a published letter is also available in manuscript (holograph or copy), the more accessible printed version is invariably cited, unless it differs significantly from the manuscript; then the manuscript is cited and the difference indicated.

Abbreviations used in the Notes are as follows:

AFN: Autobiographical fragment, Notebook, Dartmouth College
ATS: Arnold T. Schwab
Dart: Huneker Collection, Baker Library, Dartmouth College
EHH: Erik H. Huneker
INT: *Intimate Letters of James Gibbons Huneker*
JGH: James Gibbons Huneker
LET: *Letters of James Gibbons Huneker*
Ltr: Letter
MA: *Morning Advertiser* (New York)
MC: *Musical Courier* (New York)
NYPL: New York Public Library
REC: *Recorder* (New York)
Scrib: Archives, Charles Scribner's Sons, New York
STJ: *Steeplejack*

Full titles and publication data are given only for works not listed in the Sources.

CHAPTER ONE

1. Baptismal Records, St. Augustine's Church, Philadelphia. See ATS, "Huneker's Hidden Birthdate."

2. A typewritten statement by JGH's second cousin, George E. Walton, contains genealogical data, some of which JGH used in *STJ*, I, 18–21 (EHH).

3. See unlabeled clipping containing two limericks by Vance Thompson (Dart); Mencken, *A Book of Prefaces,* p. 165; Sonnenschein, p. 3; and ltr, EHH to ATS, April 6, 1950.

4. Gerson, pp. 88–90.

5. Ltr, Cemeteries Office, Archdiocese of Philadelphia, to ATS, May 15, 1950.

6. A copy inscribed to "my dear grandson Master James Huneker with the affectionate regards of his grandfather" is at Dart.

7. She was not a high school principal, as JGH stated in *STJ,* I, 51 (ltrs, Add B. Anderson, Secretary and Business Manager, School District of Philadelphia, to ATS, May 3, 1956, and May 8, 1956).

8. Ltr, Mary Huneker Lagen to John F. Huneker, "Wed. A.M." [1929?] (given to ATS by Mrs. Richard J. Beamish, whose husband received it from his friend John F. Huneker). The career of Mrs. Lagen, who usually wrote and acted under the name of Diana Huneker, is partially recorded in her scrapbook, owned now by EHH, who allowed me to examine it.

9. *LET,* p. 311. See undated ltr, JGH to Henry James, son of William James and nephew of the novelist (Dart).

10. See Federal Census, 1870: Philadelphia, Ward 20, vol. 73, p. 297; Philadelphia *Press,* July 10, 1918, p. 8; and *STJ,* I, 62.

11. AFN, p. 31.

12. Campbell, p. 515.

13. Egan, *Recollections of a Happy Life,* p. 54.

14. *Catalogue, Register and Prospectus of the Broad Street Academy* (Philadelphia, 1864), *passim.*

15. Dart

16. The information on JGH's school record is contained in Broad Street Academy catalogues, the only extant collection of which seems to be that in St. Joseph's College in Philadelphia; catalogues for 1866–67, 1867–68, and 1868–69 are missing, however, and none was printed for 1870–71.

17. *Times,* Oct. 24, 1915, Sec. 4, p. 13.

18. JGH, "Looking Backward," *Theatre Magazine,* XI (May 1910), 143.

19. *Broad Street Academy Catalogue,* 1871–72, pp. 26–27.

20. *Ibid.,* p. 7. See *Catholic Standard,* July 6, 1872, p. 4.

21. *STJ,* I, 42.

22. Henry Ridgely Evans, *History of Conjuring and Magic* (Kenton, Ohio: International Brotherhood of Magicians, 1928), pp. 79–80.

23. See Egan, *Recollections,* p. 123. The collection is described briefly in the *Tribune,* Dec. 12, 1894, p. 4.

24. W. S. Baker's *The Origin and Antiquity of Engraving* (Philadelphia: George Gebbie, 1872). Dart has a copy of the review.

25. Ltr, JGH to Dr. Percy Fridenberg, March 21, 1919 (Clifton Waller Barrett). See E. C. Savidge and William Anderson, *A Gallery of Eminent Men of Philadelphia* (Philadelphia: Henry L. Everett, 1887); Philadelphia *Evening Bulletin,* Jan. 14, 1882, p. 1; and Elizabeth Robins Pennell, *Our Philadelphia* (Philadelphia: Lippincott, 1914), p. 376.

26. Brooks, *John Sloan*, p. 3; Goodrich, p. 73.

27. Egan, *Recollections*, p. 23.

28. AFN, p. 30.

29. See JGH, *Unicorns*, p. 329.

30. Edward J. Nolan, *A Short History of the Academy of Natural Sciences of Philadelphia* (Philadelphia: The Academy of Natural Sciences, 1909), pp. 11, 21–22; ltr, James A. G. Rehn (Nolan's successor at the Academy) to ATS, Nov. 9, 1950.

31. *LET*, p. 54.

32. *STJ*, I, 83.

33. AFN, p. 32.

34. AFN, p. 31; *STJ*, II, 23.

35. Ltr, JGH to John F. Huneker, June 25 ["1874" added in pencil] (Dart).

CHAPTER TWO

1. Egan, *Recollections*, p. 59.

2. *STJ*, I, 119.

3. Reproduced in *INT* in front of p. 96. The location of the original is unknown.

4. Ltr, EHH to ATS, March 19, 1960.

5. Ltr, Charles L. Lagen to EHH [April, 1960], excerpt sent to me by EHH (undated ltr [April, 1960]).

6. Rosebault, p. 14. See Clarke, p. 226.

7. Egan, *Recollections*, p. 59.

8. *REC*, May 7, 1893, p. 14; *MA*, March 18, 1896, p. 5. See *MC*, XXII (April 29, 1891), 416.

9. Gerson, pp. 158–60.

10. *MC*, XXX (March 13, 1895), 23.

11. JGH, *MC*, XIX (Dec. 12, 1894), 21.

12. Ltrs, Edith C. Heinrich (Heinrich's daughter) to ATS, April 17, 1957, and April 25, 1957; Brister, *passim*; Gerson, pp. 126–27; Bispham, pp. 31–33, 52.

13. JGH, *MC*, XIX (Dec. 12, 1894), 21.

14. AFN, p. 32; ltr, Sarah Baer, Director of Admissions and Records, Judson College, to ATS, April 25, 1957.

15. AFN, p. 32.

16. Aubertine Woodward Moore, "Rubinstein's Meteoric Tour of America," *Etude*, XXIX (Nov., 1911), 731–32.

17. Moore, "Some Hitherto Unpublished Letters of James Gibbons Huneker," p. 533. See also JGH, *MC*, XLI (Nov. 10, 1900), 24.

18. Dart.

19. *Puck*, LXXV (May 23, 1914), 16.

20. The church is identified in ltrs, Msgr. Cletus J. Benjamin and Rt. Rev. Msgr. John V. Tolino, pastor of the church, to ATS, July 23, 1954, and Aug. 7, 1954, respectively.

21. *Francis Wilson's Life of Himself* (Boston: Houghton Mifflin, 1924), p. 344.

22. Atlanta *Georgian,* Nov. 18, 1935, p. 3, and Atlanta *Journal,* Dec. 19, 1935, p. 12.

23. JGH's account in *STJ* (I, 188) is confirmed by Louise Barili (Alfredo's daughter) in ltr to ATS, Dec. 4, 1950.

24. For a discussion of JGH's knowledge of the classics, see Pritchard and Raines.

25. "The Comet"—written on July 4, 1876, and, according to Huneker, printed ten years later in a Philadelphia journal, *The Telephone. (STJ,* I, 122). No manuscript or printed copy of the story seems to have survived.

26. *STJ,* I, 195. The essay—not in the *Atlantic Monthly,* as JGH suggested here—may have been the one in the *Fortnightly Review,* VI (Oct. 15, 1866), 538–48. Whitman *is* mentioned favorably, by an unknown writer, in "The Contributors' Club," *Atlantic Monthly,* XL (Dec. 1877), 749–50.

27. Moore, "Walt Whitman and American Music," p. 5.

28. JGH, "A Visit to Walt Whitman," *Puck,* LXXVI (Nov. 21, 1914), 8, 20 (reprinted in *Ivory Apes and Peacocks,* pp. 22–31) and *STJ,* I, 195–98. JGH recalled the date of the visit as July 1877 and stated that he called upon Whitman only once in Camden (*Ivory,* pp. 23, 27), but the entry in Whitman's notebook—now owned by Charles E. Feinberg, who allowed me to examine it—containing Huneker's signature and address as well as Whitman's notation as to the month and day of the visit, was obviously made in 1878. I have not found Huneker's copy of the 1867 edition of *Leaves of Grass,* in which he claims to have pasted Whitman's autograph dated "Camden, New Jersey, July, 1877" (*Ivory,* p. 22).

29. Ltr, Wickersham to JGH, March 20, 1909 (Dart).

30. Campbell, p. 414.

31. Egan, *Confessions of a Book-Lover,* pp. 76–77.

32. Egan, *Recollections,* p. 38.

33. JGH, *MC,* XXX (March 13, 1895), 23.

34. The day was not Tuesday, as Huneker recalled (*STJ,* I, 199).

35. Rose, p. 35.

36. Goodrich, p. 36.

37. *STJ,* I, 221.

38. Huneker marveled that so much money—$5,000—was paid for such commonplace music (*STJ,* I, 122).

39. The criticism of the performance printed in the *Evening Bulletin,* March 14, 1876, may be JGH's.

40. *Unicorns,* p. 318.

41. James D. McCabe, *The Illustrated History of the Centennial Exhibition* (Philadelphia: National Publishing Co., 1876), pp. 77–80; Joseph Jackson, *Encyclopedia of Philadelphia,* 4 vols. (Harrisburg, Pa.: National Historical Association, 1931–1933), II, 500.

42. Marta Milinowski, *Teresa Carreño* (New Haven, Conn.: Yale University Press, 1940), p. 121; JGH, *Unicorns*, p. 177.

43. Death certificate, Dept. of Health, Bureau of Vital Statistics, file no. 48135-16, Pennsylvania.

44. Bureau of Marriage Licenses, Philadelphia, License No. 310.

45. EHH, interview, May 2, 1950; Georgiana Carhart, interview, Dec. 28, 1950. But Miss Spitzmueller does not confirm the tradition, and JGH's sister said nothing of it in her interview with H. L. Mencken on August 10, 1943 (copy of his account of the interview, sent to me by Mencken on Nov. 26, 1951).

46. Ltrs, Rupert Hughes to ATS, Oct. 29, 1950, and Nov. 4, 1950.

47. Information about Lizzie's family and appearance was furnished by Miss Emma T. Spitzmueller, whose sister, Mrs. Carl Dambman, lived across the street from Margaret and Franz Schubert and was a close friend of theirs (interview, Aug. 25, 1955). Mrs. Schubert, who survived her husband by thirty-four years, died on July 24, 1941, the last of her family (Philadelphia Register of Wills, No. 1817 [1941].

48. AFN, p. 32. The words are partially obliterated.

49. Divorce records, Elizabeth T. Huneker vs. JGH, Court of Common Pleas No. 3, June term, 1891, no. 6, County of Philadelphia.

50. AFN, p. 33.

51. Notebook (Dart).

52. *Old Fogy,* p. 122.

53. Lizzie testified that she accompanied Huneker to Paris (divorce records, 1891), confirming Georgiana Carhart's recollection that Huneker had told her that Lizzie had been there with him (interview, December 28, 1950).

54. AFN, p. 33.

CHAPTER THREE

1. See "Old Fogy Abroad," *Etude,* XXI (Dec. 1903), 472, and "The Seven Arts," *Puck,* LXXVIII (Aug. 21, 1915), 10, 21.

2. Georgiana Carhart remembered JGH telling her about this episode (interview, Dec. 28, 1950).

3. See ATS, "Huneker's Hidden Birthdate."

4. JGH, *MC,* XXI (Nov. 5, 1890), 452. See *MC,* XXXII (Feb. 19, 1896), 20–21, and *Old Fogy,* pp. 120–28.

5. Edward Lockspeiser, *Debussy,* 3d ed. (London: J. M. Dent, 1951), p. 9.

6. Isidore Philipp, who knew Ritter well, never heard of Doutreleau (ltr to ATS, April 2, 1952).

7. The pieces he studied are listed in a notebook (Dart).

8. *Evening Bulletin,* Dec. 7, 1878, p. 5.

9. *Ibid.,* Dec. 14, 1878, p. 1.

10. *Ibid.,* Dec. 23, 1878, p. 1.

11. *STJ*, I, 258–59.

12. *STJ*, I, 230.

13. JGH, "The Magic Lantern," *Century Magazine*, LXXIV (July, 1907), 417–21 (reprinted in *The Pathos of Distance*, pp. 3–15) ; *Sun*, July 17, 1910, p. 6.

14. Brander Matthews, *These Many Years* (New York: Scribner, 1917), pp. 186–89.

15. John Drew, *My Years on the Stage* (New York: Dutton, 1922), pp. 60–61.

16. *Evening Bulletin*, May 1, 1878, p. 4.

17. See JGH's ltr, *Evening Bulletin*, Jan. 7, 1879, p. 2.

18. See Rose, p. 230.

19. He placed work by Degas and Cassatt in the Salon instead of the Exposition (*STJ*, I, 266), and associated Renoir and Sisley with the Exposition (*STJ*, I, 241–42), whereas Renoir was actually represented at the Salon only (elsewhere JGH states that he saw a Renoir portrait there [*Promenades of an Impressionist*, p. 243]), and Sisley did not participate in either show.

20. Rewald, p. 333.

21. Glackens, p. 54.

22. *STJ*, I, 241.

23. Lawrence Gilman, *Edward MacDowell: A Study* (New York: John Lane, 1909), pp. 6–7.

24. Sam Franko, *Chords and Discords* (New York: Viking Press, 1938), pp. 29–30.

25. JGH, "A Musical Primitive: Modeste Moussorgsky," *Forum*, LIII (Feb. 1915), 275.

26. *Evening Bulletin*, April 26, 1879, p. 1. See Richard M. Gipson, *The Life of Emma Thursby* (New York: New York Historical Society, 1940), pp. 203, 396.

27. *Evening Bulletin*, Jan. 29, 1879, p. 2.

28. *MC*, XXIV (March 16, 1892), 7.

29. *Evening Bulletin*, March 24, 1879, p. 1.

30. *Ibid.*, Jan. 22, 1879, p. 2.

31. The date (but not the place) of the birth is given in AFN, p. 33.

32. *STJ*, I, 265–66.

33. "July 20," superinscribed "1881"—the last "1" written over a zero —is given in AFN, p. 33.

34. *Vaderland*'s passenger list (National Archives).

35. *Evening Bulletin*, p. 2.

36. *STJ*, II, 23.

37. AFN, p. 33. He advertised in the *Evening Bulletin* beginning Sept. 15, 1879, and continuing, at fairly regular intervals, until March 12, 1880.

38. AFN, p. 30.

39. Copy of marriage certificate, dated Feb. 28, 1869, on which is noted

the fact that the marriage is recorded in Vol. II, p. 22, of the marriage records in St. Michael's Church in Philadelphia.

40. AFN, p. 33. Barili was in Atlanta by Nov. 15, 1880 (*Evening Bulletin,* Nov. 15, 1880, p. 4).

41. Notebook (Dart).

42. Ltr, Martin M. Alsher, Executive Secretary, Congregation Rodeph Shalom, to ATS, March 20, 1956; *Musical America,* XVII (Feb. 22, 1913), 40; and Philadelphia *Evening Bulletin,* Feb. 13, 1913, p. 17.

43. JGH, *MC,* XXXIII (Oct. 21, 1896), 23; ltr, Mrs. Paul Popenoe, Stankowitch's daughter, to ATS, Jan. 29, 1956.

44. Brister, p. 45. The occupation listed on Schubert's marriage license in 1885 is "decorative artist" (Bureau of Marriage Licenses, Philadelphia, License No. 310). See *Etude,* IV (June 1886), 152.

45. Heinrich was teaching at Judson Female Institute during 1878–79 (ltr, Judson College to ATS, Sept. 4, 1954), but is listed in the Philadelphia City directory during 1880–83.

46. *Evening Bulletin,* Nov. 15, 1879, p. 1.

47. Mellquist, pp. 79–81.

48. Goodrich, pp. 84, 86–87.

49. *Ibid.,* p. 57.

50. *INT,* p. 112; Moore, "Walt Whitman and American Music," p. 22.

51. *Unicorns,* pp. 329–30.

52. *Dwight's Journal of Music,* XXXVIII (Oct. 26, 1878), 327.

53. *Unicorns,* p. 333.

54. Church records (ltr, Msgr. Cletus J. Benjamin, Chancellor of the Archdiocese of Philadelphia, to ATS, Jan. 25, 1951).

55. *MC,* XL (May 2, 1900), 22.

56. AFN, p. 33; divorce records (1891); ltr, Msgr. Benjamin to ATS, Jan. 25, 1951.

57. Baptismal records, Cathedral of SS. Peter and Paul.

58. Divorce records (1891).

59. JGH's reading notebook (Dart).

60. *Evening Bulletin,* Nov. 2, 1880, p. 7.

61. See, for example, Dec. 20, 1884, p. 11.

62. *LET,* p. 212. The newspaper has no record of his connection with it. The article in the *Evening Bulletin,* Dec. 12, 1924, p. 8, in which appears the statement that JGH began to write for Philadelphia papers on his return from Paris, is apparently based on an unsigned sketch written in 1901, according to which he was "writing for Philadelphia papers" [sic] after his return from Paris in 1882 [sic] (ltr, Melville F. Ferguson, editor of the *Evening Bulletin,* to ATS, Nov. 27, 1950).

63. *LET,* p. 22. The "1881" was not a typographical mistake for "1891," according to Walter Prichard Eaton, who examined the original ltr (ltr, Eaton to ATS, Nov. 21, 1950).

64. Dart.

65. AFN, p. 33.

66. Lloyd Lewis and Henry Justin Smith, *Oscar Wilde Discovers America* (New York: Harcourt, Brace & Co., 1936), pp. 71ff; Philadelphia *Evening Bulletin*, Jan. 18, 1882, p. 5.

67. Hesketh Pearson, *Oscar Wilde: His Life and Wit* (New York: Harper, 1946), p. 55.

68. *INT*, p. 115; *Unicorns*, p. 214.

69. See Egan, *Recollections*, p. 97.

70. *STJ*, I, 310–11.

71. *STJ*, II, 144, 149.

72. JGH, *World*, Nov. 27, 1920, p. 11.

73. See [JGH], *MC*, XXXVI (June 15, 1898), 20.

74. *STJ*, I, 121.

75. *Evening Bulletin*, Dec. 29, 1883, pp. 4–5.

76. Elizabeth Robins Pennell, *Charles Godfrey Leland*, 2 vols. (Boston: Houghton Mifflin, 1906), II, 112–13.

77. Church records (ltr, Msgr. Cletus J. Benjamin to ATS, Jan. 25, 1951).

78. Ltr, James Francis Cooke, editor emeritus of *Etude*, to ATS, March 23, 1956.

79. "1883 — Twenty-fifth Anniversary — 1908," *Etude*, XXVI (Jan. 1908, 62–63.

80. See *Publisher's Weekly*, CLXXI (May 20, 1957), 11.

81. Cooke, p. 73, and ltr to ATS, Dec. 12, 1949.

82. JGH states that he helped to found *Etude* in 1883 (ltr to Frederic T. Hoppin of Scribner's, Aug. 23, 1911 (Scrib). See *Etude*, LXIV (June 1946), 312.

83. See *MC*, XIX (Dec. 12, 1894), 21; *Old Fogy*, p. 8; and *STJ*, I, 143.

84. The original tintype, inscribed on the back "Easter Monday April 6, 1885, Die ganze familie," is at Dart. Edith C. Heinrich identifies the person standing in the photograph as her uncle, Franz Schubert (ltr to ATS, June 1, 1960).

85. *MC*, XXXIII (Nov. 11, 1896), 20.

86. See *Etude*, IV (July 1886), 162.

87. Dart.

88. The penciled date [of receipt?] on the ltr is August 20, 1885. All the Huneker-Bloomfield letters quoted herein, together with typed transcripts of two letters from the pianist to Huneker, are owned by Mrs. Amelia S. Zeisler, the second wife and widow of Sigmund Zeisler.

89. Ernest B. Zeisler, the pianist's son, states that his mother preserved "many letters" from Huneker (ltr to ATS, April 22, 1952), but Mrs. Amelia S. Zeisler informed me that she destroyed all but eight of them when she went through her husband's papers after his death in 1931 (interview, July 9, 1956).

90. Ltr, JGH to Fanny Bloomfield-Zeisler, Oct. 17, 1910.

91. Ltr, JGH to Fanny Bloomfield-Zeisler, May 16, 1906.

92. *STJ*, I, 309; undated, unlabeled clipping (Dart). See Philadelphia *Press*, Sept. 16, 1885, p. 3, and *Evening Bulletin*, Oct. 31, 1885, p. 5.

93. "Mechanical Aids to Piano Playing," *Etude*, III (May 1885), 103–4.

94. Ltr, Isidore Philipp (author of *Exercises in Extension of Fingers* [1906] to ATS, March 27, 1952.

95. *LET*, pp. 3–4.

96. Divorce records (1891).

97. *Etude*, IV, 55.

98. Divorce records (1891).

99. *STJ*, II, 5.

100. Divorce records (1891).

CHAPTER FOUR

1. *STJ*, II, 148.

2. Vincent Sheean, *Oscar Hammerstein I: The Life and Exploits of an Impresario* (New York: Simon & Schuster, 1956), pp. 44–45; Binns and Kooken, p. 31.

3. Rewald, pp. 390ff.

4. *Tribune*, Feb. 17, 1886, p. 5.

5. *Ibid.*, Feb. 23, 1886, p. 6.

6. *STJ*, II, 11–13; JGH, *MC*, XIX (July 3, 1889), 5.

7. *MC*, XIX (Nov. 13, 1889), 406.

8. *Unicorns*, p. 174; *STJ*, I, 154, and II, 71. See *MC*, XXXIII (July 1, 1896), 18, and Catherine Drinker Bowen, *'Free Artist': The Story of Anton and Nicholas Rubinstein* (New York: Random House, 1939), p. 295.

9. Egan, *Recollections*, p. 122. See ltr, JGH to Fanny Bloomfield-Zeisler, April 21, 1887 (Mrs. Amelia S. Zeisler).

10. Egan, *Recollections*, pp. 121–22.

11. Maurice Francis Egan, *Modern Novels and Novelists* (New York: William H. Sadlier, 1888), pp. 27, 55, 121, 176.

12. Egan, *Recollections*, p. 122. See *STJ*, II, 38.

13. Egan, *Recollections*, pp. 123, 144.

14. Churchill, pp. 16ff.

15. *Times*, Feb. 20, 1921, Sec. 3, p. 14.

16. Ltr, Walter Damrosch to JGH, June 1, 1909 (Dart).

17. JGH states that he was the Cardinal's cousin (ltr to John Quinn, Dec. 25, 1903 [NYPL]), but the exact relationship is unknown (ltr, John Tracy Ellis, Cardinal Gibbons' biographer, to ATS, June 30, 1950). See Clarke, p. 223.

18. *MC*, XIX (Nov. 20, 1889), 427.

19. JGH, *MC*, XXIX (Nov. 7, 1894), 10; ltr, Louise Barili to ATS, Dec. 4, 1950.

20. *Etude*, IV (Oct. 1886), 232.

21. *STJ*, II, 92ff; Mary K. Neff, ed., *Personal Memoirs of H. P. Blavatsky* (London: Rider, 1937), pp. 56, 127, 281.

22. *Home Journal,* Oct. 9, 1889, p. 1.

23. Egan, *Recollections,* p. 124.

24. *Ibid.,* pp. 122–23.

25. *Ibid.,* pp. 124–25. See Lionel Trilling, *Matthew Arnold* (New York: Norton, 1939), p. 395.

26. *LET,* p. 5.

27. See "Correspondence," II (March 1887), 5–6, and (April 1887), 24; *American Art Journal,* XLVII (June 4, 1887), 107.

28. *American Art Journal,* XLVII (July 16, 1887), 195, and (Oct. 1, 1887), 369–70. The manuscript of "Wagner and Swinburne," with JGH's notation, "first article ever written in New York," is at Dart.

29. Meltzer, "The Huneker of Early Days," unnumbered page.

30. *INT,* p. 205. See Cecil Y. Lang, "Introduction," *The Swinburne Letters,* 2 vols. (New Haven, Conn.: Yale University Press, 1959), p. xlix.

31. *Etude,* V, 83.

32. *Ibid.,* (July 1887), p. 94, and (Dec. 1887), p. 185. See JGH, *MC,* XVIII (April 10, 1889), 283.

33. *Etude,* V (Aug. 1887), 105–6; *American Art Journal,* XLVII (July 16, 1887), 195.

34. *STJ,* II, 18; AFN, p. 34.

35. Arthur Loesser, *Men, Women and Pianos* (New York: Simon & Schuster, 1954), pp. 562–64; *MC,* VI (Jan. 3, 1883), 2.

36. Waters, p. 194; *MC,* LXVI (April 2, 1913), 20–21.

37. Ltr, Arthur M. Abell to ATS, Nov. 29, 1950. See A. J. Goodrich, *MC,* LXVI (May 21, 1913), 24.

38. See Klein, p. 277; Finck, *My Adventures in the Golden Age of Music,* p. 404.

39. Waters, p. 195.

40. *STJ,* II, 21–23.

41. *Ibid.,* pp. 16ff.

42. *Times,* Nov. 10, 1918, Sec. 4, p. 4. See JGH, *MC,* XVIII (March 13, 1889), 203, and *World,* Dec. 28, 1919, Metro. Sec., p. 4; Baehr, p. 230; Richard Aldrich, *Musical Discourse from the New York Times* (New York: Oxford University Press, 1928), pp. 287–89; and *Musical America,* XXXIII (Feb. 19, 1921), 7.

43. JGH, *MC,* XVIII (March 13, 1889), 203.

44. *MC,* XLII (April 17, 1901), 36; *Evening Post,* April 16, 1901, p. 3; Neilson, *My Life in Two Worlds,* I, 94; JGH, *MC,* XVIII (March 13, 1889), 203; and *STJ,* II, 17.

45. Richard C. Aldrich, "Introduction," in Richard Aldrich, *Concert Life in New York: 1902–1923* (New York: Putnam, 1941), pp. ix–x; Mrs. Richard Aldrich, interview, April 30, 1950; and *Times,* June 3, 1937, p. 25.

46. See *Home Journal,* April 13, 1892, p. 4 (on Krehbiel and Henderson); *MC,* XXX (May 15, 1895), 19, and XXXIX (Dec. 6, 1899), 25 (on Finck).

47. *Egoists,* p. 95.

48. *MC,* XVI, 143–44 (reprinted in *Old Fogy,* pp. 183–95).

49. *Melomaniacs,* p. 221.

50. Unlabeled clipping (Dart).

51. Churchill, p. 157.

52. *MC,* XXXV (Dec. 8, 1897), 23.

53. Meltzer, "The Huneker of Early Days," unnumbered page.

54. *North's Philadelphia Music Journal,* III (Jan. 1888), 5.

55. The precise year in which this occurred is uncertain, but Arthur M. Abell dates it "probably about 1889" (ltr to ATS, March 12, 1952).

56. *Egoists,* p. 91.

57. *STJ,* II, 22.

58. *MC,* XVIII (Jan. 30, 1889), 96; XIX (Sept. 18, 1889), 257–58; XXI (Aug. 27, 1890), 220; XXII (Jan. 28, 1891), 88; and (June 3, 1891), 595–96; XXIII (July 11, 1891), 68, 70; (Aug. 26, 1891), 228; (Oct. 21, 1891), 465; (Oct. 28, 1891), 495–96. See *MC,* XL (May 28, 1900), 500, and *STJ,* II, 22.

59. Ltrs, Arthur M. Abell to ATS, April 16, 1952, and April 24, 1952. By Jan. 1, 1892, Driggs was listed as Secretary and Treasurer of the *MC* Co. (*MC,* XXIV [Jan. 6, 1892]), and he must have been with the magazine for some time before that.

60. *MC,* XXX (March 6, 1895), 22.

61. *MC,* XVII, 186.

62. *Ibid.* (Oct. 17, 1888), p. 278.

63. The exact year is uncertain, but it was sometime between April 21, 1887, the date of an extant ltr addressed to Fanny Bloomfield-Zeisler from the Seventh Avenue address (Mrs. Amelia S. Zeisler), and an unspecified month in 1889, when Helene von Schewitsch was living in Roselle, New Jersey (Princess Helene Von Racowitza, *An Autobiography,* trans. from German by Cecil Mar [London: Constable, 1910], pp. 381, 389). JGH states that he knew her in New York "about 1885" (*Sun,* June 26, 1910, p. 8).

64. Ford, *Forty-odd Years in the Literary Shop* (New York: Dutton, 1921) pp. 165–69; Brooks, *The Confident Years,* p. 15.

65. JGH, "A Half-Forgotten Romance," *Bookman,* XXVI (Oct. 1907), 148–54; *STJ,* II, 30.

66. *STJ,* II, 173.

67. JGH, *New Cosmopolis,* pp. 5–6, 27.

68. See Emma Goldman, *Living My Life* (New York: Knopf, 1931), p. 119; Morris, *Incredible New York,* p. 278.

69. *Visionaries,* pp. 227–48. See *LET,* p. 40.

70. Ltr, JGH to Edward P. Mitchell, Dec. 27, 1906, published in part in Mitchell, p. 383; JGH, *Overtones,* p. 219.

71. *MC*, XLII (April 3, 1901), 26.

72. *MC*, XXXII (Jan. 1, 1896), 20. See Lionel Trilling, *The Liberal Imagination: Essays on Literature and Society* (New York: Viking Press, 1950), pp. 69ff.

73. JGH's heavily annotated copy of the book is in the Huneker Collection, NYPL. See Sonnenschein, p. 4.

74. JGH, *Puck*, LXXVII (May 22, 1915), 11.

75. *Ibid.*

76. *Visionaries*, p. 243. See *New Cosmopolis*, p. 5.

77. Egan, *Recollections*, p. 124.

CHAPTER FIVE

1. Ltr, James Francis Cooke to ATS, Dec. 12, 1949.

2. Excerpt from Abell's unpublished notes of a conversation with Huneker in the summer of 1893, enclosed with his ltr to ATS, June 8, 1950. Abell believes that JGH had finished his studies with Joseffy by 1889 (ltr to ATS, March 12, 1952), and Gustave L. Becker states that JGH studied with Joseffy "about 1888 or 1889" (interview, Dec. 27, 1950).

3. Paderewski and Lawton, pp. 251–52; Klein, p. 274.

4. The apartment of Jeannette Portor, whose sister, Laura Spencer Portor (who lived with her), wrote "On Living Next to James Huneker."

5. "Mephisto's Musings"; ltr, Arthur Farwell to ATS, Feb. 3, 1951.

6. Gustave L. Becker, interview, Dec. 27, 1950.

7. Mrs. Reginald De Koven, *A Musician and his Wife* (New York: Harper, 1926), p. 162.

8. *MC*, XVIII (Feb. 27, 1889), 163. See JGH, *World*, July 4, 1920, Metro. Sec., p. 4.

9. *MC*, XIX (Nov. 20, 1889), 427.

10. *MC*, XXI (Dec. 10, 1890), 596.

11. *MC*, XXV (Nov. 9, 1892), 6–7.

12. *MC*, XXXII (May 27, 1896), 19.

13. Ltr, James Francis Cooke to ATS, Dec. 12, 1949.

14. Ltr, JGH to Theodore Presser, Feb. 26, 1920 (Dart). See *MC*, XXXIII (Nov. 11, 1896), 20, and XXXIV (April 28, 1897), 22.

15. Ltr, Isidore Philipp to ATS, March 9, 1952.

16. AFN, p. 34; *LET*, p. 212.

17. Finck, *My Adventures*, pp. 274–75.

18. Waters, pp. 53, 55.

19. *MC*, XIX (Oct. 23, 1889), 357, and XXXIII (July 1, 1891), 4.

20. Ltr, Mrs. Le Gallienne to ATS, May 19, 1950.

21. Gustave L. Becker, interview, Dec. 27, 1950.

22. *Times*, May 18, 1919, Sec. 4, p. 5.

23. Leonard Liebling, *MC*, LXXXII (Feb. 17, 1921), 21; Ltr, James Francis Cooke to ATS, Dec. 12, 1949.

24. James Francis Cooke, *Etude*, LII (Feb. 1934), 73.

25. With explanatory ltr, Mrs. Thurber to Scribner's, Oct. 6, 1921 (Scrib).

26. Ltr, Arthur M. Abell to ATS, June 8, 1950.

27. *MC*, XXXV (Oct. 6, 1897), 21–22.

28. *LET*, p. 276.

29. *Times*, May 18, 1919, Sec. 4, p. 5.

30. Boston *Musical Herald*, XIII (May 1892), iii, and (June 1892), iii; Finck, *My Adventures*, p. 282.

31. Walter Damrosch, *My Musical Life* (New York: Scribner, 1932), p. 62.

32. *MC*, XXV (Sept. 14, 1892), 6.

33. *MC*, XX (April 16, 1890), 348.

34. Neilson, *My Life in Two Worlds*, I, 143.

35. Paul Stefan, *Anton Dvořák*, trans. Y. W. Vance (New York: Greystone Press, 1941), p. 201. See interview of Dvorak, *Herald*, May 21, 1893, p. 8, and Anton Dvorak, "Music in America," *Harper's New Monthly Magazine*, XC (Feb. 1895), 429–34.

36. *STJ*, II, 67–68; *Times*, Oct. 27, 1918, Sec. 8, p. 4. JGH was not impressed by Arthur Farwell's Indian songs (ltr, Farwell to ATS, Feb. 3, 1951).

37. Neilson, *My Life in Two Worlds*, I, 143.

38. *MC*, XXVII (Dec. 20, 1893), 37–38.

39. *Sun*, Nov. 26, 1911, p. 8 (reprinted in *The Pathos of Distance*, p. 46).

40. *World*, Dec. 1, 1920, p. 15; *STJ*, II, 67.

41. *Philadelphia Musical Journal*, IV (May 1889), 7, and (Dec. 1889), 9; *MC*, XVIII (May 1, 1889), 343, and XIX (July 17, 1889), 66.

42. *MC*, XVIII (May 1, 1889), 343. See *MC*, XVIII (Feb. 20, 1889), 143.

43. See JGH's review of Bispham's autobiography, *World*, March 21, 1920, Metro. Sec., p. 5, and Bispham's ltr to JGH, March 27, 1920 (Dart).

44. Her self-description inserted in copy of *INT*, opposite p. 128 (Dart).

45. Josephine's notation on Scott's autograph, JGH's autograph book (Mrs. John J. Lonergan, Josephine's niece). Josephine apparently continued painting professionally until at least 1904 (see unpub. ltr, JGH to Florence Mosher, Jan. 5, 1904 (Clifton Waller Barrett).

46. Marriage record, New York City. Her birthday was July 14 (ltr, Mrs. Vera Kasow [her niece] to ATS, Aug. 8, 1950.

47. Mrs. Josephine Huneker to ATS, interview, March 20, 1950. Max Laski is listed in the New York City directory for 1887 only; the address given is 40 Seventh Avenue.

48. This is what JGH told Georgiana Carhart (Mrs. Carhart, interview, Dec. 26, 1950).

49. Not, most likely, in the 1870's, as JGH implied (*STJ*, I, 198). An unlabeled, undated clipping of the story at Dart contains an advertisement

of a Philadelphia druggist, thus suggesting that the story was published in the West Philadelphia *Telephone* (Rose, pp. 149, 151, 237).

50. *INT*, facing p. 128.

51. Georgiana Carhart, interview, Dec. 28, 1950; *STJ*, II, 26.

52. *Times,* Dec. 11, 1890, p. 8.

53. Ltr, Surrogate's Court of New York County to ATS, Dec. 1, 1960.

54. Gustave L. Becker, interview, Dec. 27, 1950.

55. Mrs. Josephine Huneker, interview, March 20, 1950.

56. Basil Rauch, "The First Hundred Years," *Town and Country*, C (Dec. 1946), 129.

57. For information about Hinton, see *Times*, April 2, 1920, p. 15, and Feb. 13, 1925, p. 17.

58. Ltr, EHH to ATS, July 24, 1961.

59. *MC*, XX (Feb. 12, 1890), 132.

60. *Times,* Dec. 21, 1921, p. 19 (the handwritten original and a typed copy of a more extensive obituary of Mrs. Hinton are in possession of EHH). See Richard Le Gallienne, *Vanishing Roads: And Other Essays* (New York: Putnam, 1915), pp. 229ff. The original of "Luccia" in Le Gallienne's essay is identified as Mrs. Hinton in Whittington-Egan and Smerdon, p. 435.

61. Unless otherwise indicated, the source of the information about Clio, her family, and her marriage to JGH is their son, Erik H. Huneker, via interviews with, and numerous ltrs to, ATS.

62. For a contemporary description of Clio, see *Home Journal*, Oct. 2, 1895, p. 1.

63. [Unsigned], "Personals," *MC*, XXII (May 20, 1891), 523.

64. Georgiana Carhart, interview, Dec. 28, 1950.

65. Philadelphia Registration of Deaths, Book No. 20456, 1891, p. 220. For obituaries, see *MC*, XXII (May 6, 1891), 450; *Catholic Standard*, May 9, 1891, p. 5, and May 23, 1891, p. 5.

66. Divorce records, 1891.

67. Ltr, Walter Prichard Eaton to ATS, Nov. 24, 1950.

68. Ltr, Mrs. Philip Hale to ATS, July 21, 1950. JGH's ltr. to Philip Hale, in which he mentioned the luncheon, has apparently not survived.

69. See Philadelphia *Public Ledger*, Feb. 21, 1907, p. 9.

70. Miss Emma T. Spitzmueller, interview, Aug. 25, 1955; Lizzie's death certificate, file no. 48135-16.

71. Philadelphia *Press*, April 18, 1916, p. 9, and April 19, 1916, p. 13; church records, Archdiocese of Philadelphia.

72. Original owned by Mrs. Richard J. Beamish of Harrisburg, Pa.

73. Marriage records, New York City, certificate No. 1226.

74. Clio's testimony, divorce records, New York City, file no. EJ954, 1899.

75. At 89 Clinton Street (1892) and 15 Spruce Street (1893) in New York City (city directory, 1892 and 1893, and divorce records, 1899).

76. *STJ*, II, 156–57.

CHAPTER SIX

1. *INT*, p. 141.

2. See N.Y. *Dramatic Mirror*, XXV (Feb. 21, 1891), 5; Seitz, pp. 186–87.

3. Notation by Josephine on clipping—labeled Philadelphia *Telephone*, June 20, 1891—which mentions JGH's connection with the *Recorder* (scrapbook, Dart). Edgar Smith Rose guesses that JGH's first contribution to the newspaper appeared on Feb. 19, 1891 (Rose, p. 170).

4. Rose, p. 170; "About Walt Whitman," *Recorder*, Nov. 1, 1891, p. 26.

5. JGH, *MC*, XXII (April 8, 1891), 330–31, and (April 22, 1891), 388–89; Friedheim, pp. 23, 213, 218.

6. Herbert Weinstock, *Tchaikovsky* (New York: Knopf, 1943), pp. 342–43.

7. *MC*, XXII (May 13, 1891), 482–83; XXV (Oct. 27, 1897), 23; and (Oct. 20, 1897), 22.

8. Quoted in Phillips, p. 164.

9. *MC*, XXIII (Nov. 18, 1891), 585. The article—unsigned but JGH's— is reprinted in Phillips, pp. 160–62. See Paderewski and Lawton, pp. 251–52, and Phillips, pp. 160ff.

10. Ltr, JGH to W. D. Moffat, Feb. 12, 1901 (F. L. Rodgers Collection).

11. *Home Journal*, April 13, 1892, p. 4.

12. *MC*, XLII (Feb. 27, 1901), 26.

13. *MC*, XXIII (Dec. 2, 1891), 643.

14. Philip Hale, "Music in Boston," *MC*, XXVI (Jan. 25, 1893), 19.

15. *MC* (March 29, 1893), 9.

16. Ltr, Arthur M. Abell to ATS, Feb. 28, 1954.

17. *Ibid.*

18. Ltr, Matilda E. Frelinghuysen (for Mme Eames) to ATS, May 25, 1950.

19. Henry T. Finck, New York *Evening Post*, Feb. 19, 1921, Sec. 1, p. 12 (reprinted in Finck's *Musical Laughs*, p. 262). I have not found the quip in JGH's writings.

20. *Sun*, Jan. 24, 1901, p. 7.

21. *Sun*, Jan. 2, 1902, p. 5.

22. *World*, Jan. 28, 1921, p. 13.

23. *Times*, Dec. 15, 1918, Sec. 4, p. 4 (reprinted in *Variations*, p. 235).

24. *MC*, XXII (April 29, 1891), 413.

25. Ltr, Mrs. Charles J. Rosebault to ATS, Aug. 9, 1954. I have not located the remark in print.

26. Rose, p. 192.

27. *REC*, June 25, 1893. See Rose, p. 176.

28. JGH, *MC*, XXIX (Dec. 5, 1894), 22.

29. *MC*, XX (Feb. 12, 1890), 132.

30. *STJ*, II, 167.

31. *MC*, XXII (March 18, 1891), 252.

32. *MC*, XXIII (Dec. 16, 1891), 709.

33. See *Times*, Dec. 27, 1931, Sec. 8, p. x9, an account denied by Josephine (copy of ltr, Josephine Huneker to editor of *Times*, Dec. 27, 1931 [Dart]).

34. Friedheim, pp. 225–26.

35. *STJ*, II, 42–43; *MC*, XXIII (Dec. 16, 1891), 723. JGH often told his son this story (ltr, EHH to ATS, April 9, 1961).

36. Ltrs, Mrs. Richard J. Beamish to ATS, June 11, 1950, and Sept. 7, 1952. Mrs. Beamish believes she heard this story from Huneker himself, but is not sure when he said the incident occurred.

37. *STJ*, II, 206–7.

38. Preface, vol. VII, New York Edition of Henry James (reprinted in Henry James, *The Art of the Novel: Critical Prefaces* [New York: Scribner, 1950], pp. 96–97).

39. *MC*, XXIII (Nov. 4, 1891), 511.

40. *MC*, XXXII (March 18, 1896), 21.

41. *MC*, XXXV Oct. 13, 1897), 23.

42. *MC*, XXIV (June 8, 1892), 6.

43. *MC*, XXXII (May 27, 1896), 20.

44. *MC*, XXIV (March 16, 1892), 7.

45. *MC*, XXXIII (Sept. 16, 1896), 16, and XXXVIII (Feb. 22, 1899), 29; JGH, "Musical Adventures of the Season," *Century Magazine*, C (July 1920), 419.

46. *STJ*, I, 6.

47. *MC*, XXXII (May 6, 1896), 20. See also *MC*, XXXIV (April 28, 1897), 22, and XXXVIII (June 21, 1899), 22.

48. *LET*, pp. 276–77.

49. *MC*, XXIV (Feb. 24, 1892), 7.

50. JGH, "Grand Opera in American," *Harper's Bazar*, XXXIII (Sept. 29, 1900), 1358; *World*, Feb. 15, 1920, Metro. Sec., p. 3; *STJ*, II, 61.

51. JGH, *Town Topics*, XXXIX (April 21, 1898), 12; *Times*, Dec. 15, 1918, Sec. 4, p. 4.

52. *MC*, XXXIV (June 16, 1897), 11.

53. *MC*, XXIX (Nov. 14, 1894), 9.

54. *MC*, XXI (Aug. 27, 1890), 211.

55. "Little Annie Rooney" was published in America in 1890 (Edward B. Marks, *They All Sang* [New York: Viking Press, 1934], p. 224).

56. *MC*, XXI (Sept. 17, 1890), 278.

57. Ltr, Becker to ATS, June 11, 1950.

58. Quoted in Philadelphia *Telephone*, June 20, 1891 (scrapbook, Dart).

59. *MC*, XXIV (Jan. 6, 1892), 16.

60. *Tribune*, Oct. 30, 1892, p. 22.

61. Boston *Musical Herald*, XIII, 55.

62. *Music*, II (July 1892), 240, and (Aug. 1892), 332.

63. *MC*, XXIX (Oct. 3, 1894), 10.

64. Lloyd Morris, *Curtain Time: The Story of the American Theater* (New York: Random House, 1953), pp. 271–72.

65. *MC*, XXX (Feb. 13, 1895), 23.

66. Sidney Whipple, *Herald Tribune*, Aug. 26, 1939, p. 5; William M. Reedy, "William Winter's Wordy Woe," *Mirror*, XIX (July 7, 1910), 2.

67. Horace Traubel, ed., *With Walt Whitman in Camden* (New York: Mitchell Kennerley, 1914), III, 431.

68. *STJ*, II, 146–47; *INT*, p. 32.

69. Finck, *My Adventures*, p. 345.

70. Moran, p. 109; *Times*, Oct. 21, 1917, Lit. Sec., p. 418.

71. N.Y. *Dramatic Mirror*, XLIX (March 21, 1903), 14.

72. "The Saunterer," *Town Topics*, XXXV (Jan. 30, 1896), 15; Moran, p. 106.

73. Moran, pp. 106–7; Pollock, p. 93.

74. *Sun*, Feb. 28, 1904, Sec. 3, p. 4.

75. "The Prompter," *REC*, May 14, 1893, p. 14.

76. *Ibid.*, Jan. 28, 1894, p. 24.

77. *Ibid.*, Feb. 18, 1894, p. 30.

78. *MC*, XXIV (Jan. 13, 1892), 8. See "The Prompter," *REC*, Jan. 21, 1894, p. 24.

79. "The Prompter," *REC*, May 6, 1894, p. 24.

80. *MA*, Oct. 27, 1895, p. 5.

81. *REC*, Sept. 24, 1893, p. 22.

82. *STJ*, II, 12. See Madeleine B. Stern, *Purple Passage: The Life of Mrs. Frank Leslie* (Norman, Okla.: University of Oklahoma Press, 1953), p. 155.

83. See, for example, *REC*, March 20, 1892, p. 12, and March 27, 1892, p. 12.

84. *MC*, XXIX (Aug. 15, 1894), 10.

85. *REC*, March 17, 1895, p. 16.

86. *REC*, April 6, 1895, p. 8, and April 9, 1895, p. 8; *MC*, XXX (April 17, 1895), 22; and *REC*, July 1, 1895, p. 5.

87. *Puck*, LXXVI (Nov. 28, 1914), 17 (reprinted in *Unicorns*, pp. 215, 217).

88. *MC*, XXXV (Nov. 17, 1897), iv, and XXXVI (May 25, 1898), 18.

89. *Puck*, LXXVI (Nov. 28, 1914), 17.

90. *INT*, p. 115.

91. *MC*, XXVII (Nov. 8, 1893), 12.

92. *MA*, Sept. 10, 1895, p. 2.

93. *MC*, XXXI (July 17, 1895), 18, and XXXII (April 8, 1896), 25; *REC*, July 18, 1895, p. 5.

94. *MC*, XXX (Jan. 9, 1895), 23.

95. Francis Neilson, interview, Nov. 12, 1951.

96. *LET*, p. 269; *STJ*, II, 67. See the books in the Huneker Collection, NYPL and Dart.

97. *World,* Oct. 10, 1920, Metro. Sec., p. 5.

98. J.-K. Huysmans, *Against the Grain* (New York: Illustrated Editions, 1931), p. 288.

99. *MC,* XXIX (July 11, 1894), 9; also *MC,* XXIX (Aug. 8, 1894), 10.

100. JGH, *MC,* XXXVI (May 4, 1898), 22.

101. JGH, *MC,* XXXIII (Nov. 4, 1896), 21.

102. *MC,* XXIX (July 11, 1894), 9.

103. *STJ,* II, 180.

104. JGH, *REC,* Jan. 3, 1892, p. 16.

105. *Sun,* March 18, 1907, p. 6 (reprinted in *Promenades of an Impressionist,* pp. 262–63).

106. *REC,* March 11, 1894, p. 24.

107. See Milton P. Foster, "The Reception of Max Nordau's Degeneration in England and America," unpubl. diss. (University of Michigan, 1954), pp. 45, 82–90.

108. *MC,* XXXI (July 3, 1895), 18–20. See *MC,* XXXII (Feb. 26, 1896), 23, and (May 6, 1896), 20; XXXVI (March 9, 1898), 23, and (May 18, 1898), 20; *Sun,* May 10, 1903, Sec. 3, p. 4.

109. Oskar Panizza, "Bayreuth und Homosexualität," *Die Gesellschaft Halbmonatschrift für Literatur, Kunst und Sozialpolitik,* erstes quartal, 1895, pp. 88–92 (MSS. of translation in Dart).

110. *Sun,* Nov. 17, 1907, p. 8.

111. *MC,* XXX (Jan. 16, 1895), 25.

112. *Puck,* LXXVIII (Aug. 7, 1915), 10.

113. *MC,* XXIX (Aug. 15, 1894), 10.

114. *MC,* XXIII (Dec. 9, 1891), 709.

115. *MC,* XXXV (Sept. 8, 1897), 20.

116. *Ibid.,* p. 26.

117. *Puck,* LXXVI (Nov. 21, 1914), 20 (reprinted in *Ivory Apes and Peacocks,* p. 28).

118. *MC,* XXV (Oct. 8, 1892), 20.

119. Originally published in the *Fortnightly Review* (N.S., CCXLVIII [Aug. 1887], 170–76), and reprinted in Swinburne's *Studies in Prose and Poetry.*

120. See *MC,* XXXIX (Dec. 6, 1899), 25.

121. John Jay Chapman, *Emerson and Other Essays* (New York: Scribner, 1898), pp. 111–28. See *MC,* XXXVII (Oct. 19, 1898), 22; *Ivory Apes and Peacocks,* p. 31; and *STJ,* II, 241. In his copy of the 1909 edition of Chapman's book, opposite Chapman's reference to Whitman's "inversion of the social instincts" (p. 121), JGH added in the margin: "and sexual" (Huneker Collection, NYPL).

122. JGH, "A Visit to Walt Whitman," *Puck,* LXXVI (Nov. 21, 1914), 20 (reprinted in *Ivory Apes and Peacocks,* p. 31). See *Walt Whitman Fellowship Papers,* Fifth Year (Philadelphia, 1899), pp. 3–6.

123. A word that Swinburne had used in his essay on Whitman (*Studies in Prose and Poetry,* pp. 138–39).

124. *MC*, XXXVII (July 13, 1898), 23.

125. JGH's copy of George Rice Carpenter's *Walt Whitman* (New York: Macmillan, 1909), now owned by Charles E. Feinberg, contains numerous annotations indicating JGH's belief in Whitman's homosexuality.

126. *MC*, XXV (Dec. 21, 1892), 8–9, reprinted in *MC*, XXXIV (April 21, 1897), 20–22; *Mezzotints in Modern Music*, pp. 195–210; *Puck*, LXXVII (June 5, 1915), 11; and *Bedouins*, pp. 94–105.

127. *MC*, XXVII (Nov. 1, 1893), 8; *Critic*, XXII (June 1893), 357. See Dudley R. Hutcherson, "Poe's Reputation in England and America, 1850–1909," *American Literature*, XIV (Nov. 1942), 223–24.

128. *MC*, XXXI (Aug. 21, 1895), 18–19.

129. *MC*, XXVII (July 1, 1893), 10; *MA*, March 11, 1896, p. 4; *MC*, XXXII (March 18, 1896), 22, and (May 13, 1896), 21–22; and Sunday *Advertiser*, May 10, 1896, p. 7. The prediction is in *MC*, XXX (June 19, 1895), 18.

130. *Sun*, Nov. 29, 1903, Sec. 3, p. 4; *Unicorns*, p. 83.

131. *MC*, XXII (April 1, 1891), 304–5, XXX (June 19, 1895), 19, and XXXII (March 11, 1896), 22; *STJ*, II, 171–72, 204.

132. *The Letters of Theodore Roosevelt*, ed. Elting E. Morison (Cambridge, Mass.: Harvard University Press, 1951), I, 390.

133. *MC*, XXXI (Sept. 25, 1895), 18.

CHAPTER SEVEN

1. *World*, Feb. 10, 1921 (Dart).

2. *STJ*, II, 198.

3. Ltr, Mrs. Henry Hadley (who heard this story from Clio) to ATS, Jan. 14, 1954.

4. Francis Neilson, interview, Nov. 12, 1951.

5. "Huneker on Huneker," p. 24. The passage is omitted in the version of the ltr printed in *INT*, pp. 252–54.

6. *STJ*, II, 199.

7. Ltr, EHH to ATS, March 22, 1957.

8. EHH, interview, May 5, 1950.

9. *Times*, April 28, 1895, p. 29, and *Home Journal*, Oct. 2, 1895, p. 1.

10. Gertrude Traubel (daughter of Whitman's friend Horace Traubel) heard this story from her mother, who knew the Hunekers (interview, July 27, 1955). Clio told EHH about the episode (ltr, EHH to ATS, Aug. 19, 1955).

11. *Times*, April 28, 1895, p. 29. For later comments on Clio's work, see an article by her friend (ltr, EHH to ATS, Aug. 8, 1962) Mary Annable Fanton, "Clio Hinton Bracken, Woman Sculptor and Symbolist of the New Art," *Craftsman*, VIII (July 1905), 472–81.

12. AFN, p. 34.

13. "The Shofar Blew at Sunset," *M'lle New York*, I, no. 8 (Nov. 1895).

14. Cable receipts (Dart).

15. Clarke, pp. 227–28.

16. *MC*, XXXIII (July 1, 1896), 18–19.

17. *Ibid.* (July 22, 1896), p. 18.

18. *Ibid.* (July 1, 1896), p. 19.

19. *Ibid.* (July 8, 1896), p. 19. According to their divorce records, Clio and JGH lived together until Aug. 1896.

20. Thirteen ltrs from his father, Senator Henry Cabot Lodge, to JGH are at Dart.

21. *MC*, XXXIII (July 8, 1896), 18–19. Slightly revised versions of the episode appear in *The Pathos of Distance*, pp. 208–18; *World*, Nov. 30, 1919, Metro. Sec., p. 6; and *STJ*, II, 280–89. Wallace Goodrich discussed it in ltrs to ATS, May 31, 1950, and Nov. 20, 1950.

22. *MC*, XXXIII (July 8, 1896), 19, and (Sept. 16, 1896), 16; *STJ*, I, 305–7.

23. *MC*, XXIII (July 1, 1896), 19.

24. *Ibid.* (July 29, 1896), p. 19. Earlier JGH had claimed that he had seen Swinburne only once, in Paris in 1878 or 1879 (*MC*, XXVI [Feb. 15, 1893], 8), but afterward he recalled that the only time had been during the channel crossing (*STJ*, II, 143). Cecil Y. Lang, editor of Swinburne's letters, agrees that "Huneker in all likelihood mistook someone else for Swinburne" (ltr to ATS, Dec. 9, 1959).

25. *MC*, XXXIII (July 29, 1896), 19, and XLV (Aug. 20, 1902), 14.

26. *STJ*, II, 118–19.

27. *MC*, XXXIII (Aug. 5, 1896), 18, and (Aug. 19, 1896), 16.

28. Cushing, pp. 42, 72–73, 201; E. K. Brown, *Willa Cather: A Critical Biography* (New York: Knopf, 1953), pp. 185–86. Mrs. Cushing told me the year of Fremstad's birth (interview, June 9, 1952).

29. Irving Kolodin, *The Metropolitan Opera, 1883–1939* (New York: Oxford University Press, 1940), p. 46.

30. Cushing, p. 118.

31. Ltr, Neilson to ATS, July 17, 1954; ltr, JGH to Krehbiel, July 14, 1918 (Dart).

32. *MC*, XXIII (Nov. 11, 1891), 541.

33. *MC*, XXXIII (Aug. 5, 1896), 19, and (Aug. 12, 1896), 17.

34. *Ibid.* (Aug. 12, 1896), p. 17, and (Aug. 19, 1896), p. 16.

35. *Ibid.* (Aug. 19, 1896), p. 19.

36. They are at Dart. See Cushing, pp. 182–83.

37. *MC*, XXXIII (Aug. 26, 1896), pp. 16–19. The story was reprinted as "Venus or Valkyr?" in *Bedouins*, pp. 225–46.

38. *MC*, XXXIII (Aug. 19, 1896), 19.

39. Cushing, pp. 34, 184–85.

40. See *MC*, XXXIII (Oct. 21, 1896), 22.

41. Ltrs, Olive Fremstad to ATS, June 15, 1950, and June 27, 1950.

42. EHH, interview, May 2, 1950, and ltr, EHH to ATS, Oct. 4, 1956. See *MA*, Jan. 15, 1897, p. 4.

43. The statement by Philip Minoff that Mrs. Carhart "enjoyed, for 30 years, a 'supremely happy' marriage with Carrington E. Carhart" ("Glamour Girl at 87," *Collier's*, CXXIX [May 17, 1952], 48) hardly fits the facts.

44. Sunday *Advertiser*, March 7, 1897, p. 7.

45. Divorce records, New York City, 1899.

46. Mrs. Carhart, interviews, Dec. 28, 1950; May 15, 1952; and Feb. 9, 1956. The account of her relations with JGH, Josephine, and Clio is based on these interviews.

47. A ltr from "Raoul" to Clio, Dec. 24, 1898, is at Dart. EHH identifies him (ltr to ATS, March 16, 1952).

48. Divorce records, New York City, 1899. See *Times*, May 1, 1899, p. 10, and ltr, JGH to John Quinn, Jan. 20, 1917 (Dart).

49. "The Artist and His Wife," *Red Book Magazine*, XI (Sept. 1908), 630 (reprinted in *The Pathos of Distance*, p. 250).

50. Dart.

51. Now owned by Josephine's niece, Mrs. John J. Lonergan of Brooklyn, New York, who allowed me to examine it on June 10, 1956.

52. The following states and cities, which seemed the most likely possibilities, report no record of such a marriage: Connecticut, Delaware, Massachusetts, New Hampshire, New Jersey, New York, Rhode Island, Baltimore, Cincinnati, New York City, and Philadelphia.

53. Ltr, JGH to Israel Zangwill, Dec. 23, 1917 (Scrib). See *LET*, p. 275; *STJ*, II, 4; and AFN, p. 34.

54. *STJ*, II, 201–2; *INT*, p. 12; and *LET*, p. 136.

55. Ltrs, JGH to Frida Ashforth, Dec. 16, 1904 (Dart), and EHH to ATS, May 7, 1957.

56. Ltr, EHH to ATS, Aug. 21, 1956.

57. Mencken's unpublished account of his interview with JGH's sister, held on Aug. 10, 1943 (copy given by Mencken to ATS).

58. *Times*, March 3, 1959, p. 33.

59. Brooklyn *Daily Eagle*, Feb. 11, 1900, p. 28.

60. *Tribune*, May 17, 1900, p. 1; *Sun*, May 18, 1900, p. 6. The information about Bracken is supplied by EHH (ltr to ATS, Oct. 7, 1960).

61. *Town Topics*, LIII (May 24, 1900), 3–4.

62. Ltrs, Mrs. Kasow to ATS, Aug. 8, 1950, and Oct. 26, 1950.

63. Raymond A. Speiser, interview, April 4, 1950.

64. EHH, interview, May 2, 1950.

CHAPTER EIGHT

1. *STJ*, II, 189. The main source for this chapter is *STJ*, II, 189–97.

2. *Herald-Tribune*, June 8, 1925, p. 13; ltr, Office of the Secretary, Princeton University, to ATS, Nov. 12, 1951; George Henry Payne, "Vance Thompson—Poet and Critic," *Forum*, LXXIV (Aug. 1925), 268.

3. See JGH, *MC*, XXXVI (Jan. 26, 1898), iii.

4. Georgiana Carhart, interview, Dec. 28, 1950.

5. Ltr, Rupert Hughes to ATS, Oct. 29, 1950.

6. *REC*, Aug. 1, 1895, p. 5; *MC*, XXXI (Aug. 7, 1895), 18.

7. *MC*, XXXI (Aug. 28, 1895), 20.

8. See *STJ*, II, 124–25.

9. *REC*, Nov. 1, 1891, p. 26; *Times*, Dec. 8, 1918, Sec. 7, p. 9 (reprinted in *Bedouins*, p. 124).

10. Ramsey, p. 226.

11. *Painted Veils*, pp. 101, 104.

12. *M'lle New York*, N.S., II, no. 2.

13. *Painted Veils*, pp. 104–6.

14. JGH (presumably) wrote "1899" on the undated card (autograph book, Mrs. Lonergan). He states that Gourmont translated the story into French and wrote him a *letter* of congratulations when the story appeared in *M'lle New York*, declaring that Huneker's invention was as vivid as Huysmans' (*STJ*, I, 191) ; only the card, however, has turned up. JGH was probably referring to this card when he later remarked that a postcard began his friendship with Gourmont, though he then recalled the date as 1897 ("Remy de Gourmont," *North American Review*, CCV [June 1917], 935).

15. *M'lle New York*, I, no. 8 (Nov. 1895), reprinted in *MC*, XXXV (Sept. 1, 1897), v; *STJ*, I, 170. I have not found this ltr from Zangwill.

16. *STJ*, I, 62; *MC*, XXIX (Aug. 29, 1894), 10; S. Jay Kaufman, "Round the Town," *Globe and Commercial Advertiser*, Feb. 18, 1921, p. 16. A clipping labeled *Hebrew Standard*, April 14, 1899, states that Huneker's grandmother was a Hungarian Jewess (scrapbook, Dart).

17. *M'lle New York*, I, no. 2 (Aug. 23, 1895).

18. *M'lle New York*, I, no. 8 (Nov. 1895). See Thompson, "Israel Among the Nations," *MC*, XXXV (Oct. 27, 1897), vii–ix, and "Was Chopin a Jew?" *ibid.* (Dec. 29, 1897), x.

19. Levin, II, 1077.

20. *MC*, XL (Jan. 3, 1900), 28–29.

21. See Morrissette, pp. 172–74. For poems by Laforgue, see, especially, *M'lle New York*, I, no. 10 (Jan. 1896).

22. *STJ*, II, 191. See JGH, *MC*, XLIII (Aug. 7, 1901), 21.

23. "The Baffled Enthusiast," *M'lle New York*, I, no. 6 (Oct. 1895). The editor's note in the margin is probably JGH's.

24. *STJ*, II, 190.

25. Boston *Herald*, Dec. 1, 1934, pp. 1, 13; Lawrence Gilman, "Introduction," in *Philip Hale's Boston Symphony Programme Notes*, ed. John N. Burk (Garden City, N.Y.: Doubleday, Doran, 1935), xvii–xix; JGH, *MC*, XXVII (July 1, 1893), 11, and (Nov. 29, 1893), 10.

26. See *MC*, XXXV (Oct. 13, 1897), iv.

27. *MC*, XXVII (Nov. 1, 1893), 8; XXV (Oct. 12, 1892), 19; and XXVII (Nov. 8, 1893), 14.

28. Parry, p. 67.

29. Hanighen, p. 477; ltr, Rupert Hughes to ATS, Oct. 29, 1950.
30. Ltr, Ralph S. Thompson (Vance's brother) to ATS, Dec. 29, 1955.
31. For comments by JGH on these two books, see Philadelphia *Press*, April 13, 1918, p. 9, and Sept. 28, 1918, p. 8, and *STJ*, II, 189.
32. *M'lle New York*, II, no. 3 ("last fortnight," 1898).
33. H. L. Mencken, *Newspaper Days* (New York: Knopf, 1941), p. 61.
34. *Philistine*, II (Dec. 1895), 39.
35. Churchill, p. 79.
36. Ltr, JGH to Edward Ziegler, Jan. 6, 1908 (Dart).
37. "Bubble and Squeak," *Lotus*, II (Nov. 1896), 255–57.
38. Springfield *Republican*, p. 13.
39. *MC*, XXXV (Sept. 29, 1897), 22.
40. *MC*, XXXVII, 26.
41. Ltr, Rupert Hughes to ATS, Oct. 29, 1950, and interview, Aug. 31, 1951. See ltr, Hughes to Scribner's, Jan. 21, 1922 (Scrib).
42. *Puck*, LXXV (June 27, 1914), 21; *LET*, p. 174.
43. "Fog," *M'lle New York*, II, no. 4 (1899?). The story first appeared in *MC*, XXXVI (May 25, 1898), 18–19, and was reprinted as "Grindstones" in *Smart Set*, XLI (Nov. 1913), 85–88, and in *Bedouins*, pp. 216–24. See ltr, JGH to Mrs. George Werrenrath, Feb. 15, 1920 (Dart).
44. Author of "Anaesthetics," *M'lle New York*, II, no. 3 ("last fortnight," 1898).
45. Hanighen, p. 479.
46. Morrissette, pp. 174, 177.
47. Smith, p. 270.

CHAPTER NINE

1. The dates given in *STJ*, II, 122, are incorrect.
2. Seitz, pp. 184–85.
3. *Current Literature*, XVIII (Nov. 1895), 378.
4. See Churchill, pp. 54–55.
5. Legal documents (Dart). See *Tribune*, Dec. 12, 1894, p. 4, for an account of the sale of the engravings.
6. Walter Muir Whitehill, "The Vicissitudes of Bacchante in Boston," *New England Quarterly*, XXVII (Dec. 1954), 435–54; Theodore Dreiser, "The Art of MacMonnies and Morgan," *Metropolitan Magazine*, VII (Feb. 1898), 143.
7. *MC*, XXXII (Oct. 21, 1896), 23.
8. *Town Topics*, XXXVII (June 10, 1897), 11.
9. *MA*, April 3, 1896, p. 4; *MC*, XXXV (Sept. 29, 1897), 23; XXXVII (Dec. 14, 1898), 27; and XXXIV (March 17, 1897), 23.
10. *MC*, XL (March 21, 1900), 25, and XXXVII (July 27, 1898), 18. See *MC*, XXXVI (June 8, 1898), 21.
11. *MC*, XXXIV (March 24, 1897), 21.

12. Springfield *Republican,* Sept. 12, 1897, p. 13.

13. *MC,* XXXV (Sept. 22, 1897), 20.

14. *MC,* XXXIII (Oct. 14, 1896), 23.

15. *MC,* XXXVI (Feb. 16, 1898), 23.

16. Sunday *Advertiser,* Jan. 24, 1897, p. 7. See *MC,* XXXII (March 18, 1896), 21–22.

17. *MC,* XXXII (Jan. 22, 1896), 20.

18. *Ibid.* (Jan. 1, 1896), 20; *Sun,* Feb. 15, 1903, Sec. 3, p. 6.

19. *MC,* XXXI (Oct. 30, 1895), 19.

20. *MC,* XXXIII (Oct. 14, 1896), 21–22.

21. *MC,* XXXIV (Feb. 17, 1896), 21.

22. *INT,* p. 56.

23. Elbert Hubbard, *Philistine,* XXIV (Jan. 1907), 47–48; Morris, *Incredible New York,* pp. 256–57; Burton Rascoe, "*Smart Set* History," *The Smart Set Anthology* (New York: Reynal & Hitchcock, 1934), pp. xv–xvi; and *Evening Post,* Jan. 15–19, 23–26, 1906. See Michael Strange, *Who Tells Me True* (New York: Scribner, 1940), p. 67.

24. Lewisohn, pp. 315–16. See *INT,* p. 56.

25. JGH, *MC,* XXXIV (June 20, 1897), 24.

26. Glackens, p. 28.

27. *Forty Songs by Johannes Brahms* (Boston: Oliver Ditson Co., N. Y.: C. H. Ditson & Co., 1903); *Selected Piano Compositions* [*of*] *Johannes Brahms* (Boston: Oliver Ditson Co., N. Y.: C. H. Ditson & Co., 1910).

28. *MC,* XXXV (Aug. 18, 1897), 19, and (Dec. 22, 1897), 22–23.

29. Dec. 27, 1897 (JGH's autograph book, Mrs. Lonergan).

30. *MC,* XXXIII (Nov. 25, 1896), 20.

31. *MC,* XXXII (Jan. 29, 1896), 22; XXXI (July 24, 1895), 18; XXXIX (Dec. 20–27, 1899); XXVIII (June 20, 1894), 8–9; XXXVI (Feb. 23, 1898), 24, and *Town Topics,* XLIII (Jan. 25, 1900), 17; *MC,* XXXVI (Feb. 23, 1898), 24; and *MC,* XXXVI (Feb. 23, 1898), 24, and *Town Topics,* XLIII (Jan. 25, 1900), 17. See also ltrs, JGH to Harry Rowe Shelley, May 11, 1902, and April 9, 1903 (American Academy of Arts and Letters).

32. *MC,* XXXVI (Feb. 23, 1898), 24; *Town Topics,* XLIII (Jan. 25, 1900), 17; and *World,* Jan. 21, 1920, p. 11.

33. *MC,* XXXVIII (Feb. 8, 1899), 28.

34. *MC,* XXXIII (July 29, 1896), 19.

35. Bispham, p. 185. See JGH, *World,* March 21, 1920, Metro. Sec., p. 5.

36. *MC,* XXXIII (Nov. 4, 1896), 21.

37. *Ibid.* (Oct. 14, 1896), 21.

38. *MC,* XXXIV (March 17, 1897), 23.

39. *MC,* XXXII (May 6, 1896), 20; and XXXVII (Nov. 9, 1898), 25.

40. Teddy Bean, *Telegraph,* Dec. 4, 1910.

41. JGH's most substantial criticism of Symons appears in "About Arthur Symons and his New Book," *Lamp,* XXVIII (June 1904), 374–78.

42. See H. W. Boynton, "Significant Books: The Two Pursuits," *Atlantic Monthly,* XCV (June 1905), 841–42; Pollard, pp. 454–55; Marsh, p. 601; and Vincent Starrett, "Carl Van Vechten," *Reedy's Mirror,* XXIX (Jan. 8, 1920), 29.

43. In Havelock Ellis, *The New Spirit* (London: George Bell, 1898). Ellis also edited Ibsen's *The Pillars of Society* (New York: Whitaker, 1888).

44. *MC,* XXXIX (Dec. 6, 1899), 25. See *MC,* XXXV (Aug. 11, 1897), 19, and (Sept. 8, 1897), 20; XXXVII (Dec. 28, 1898), 26–27; *Sun,* Dec. 27, 1903, Sec. 3, p. 4; and *STJ,* II, 243.

45. Havelock Ellis, *Views and Reviews: First Series, 1884–1919* (London: Desmond Harmsworth, 1932), pp. 21, 25, 36.

46. *MC,* XL (Feb. 28, 1900), 30.

47. "Master Artists of the Piano," *Everybody's Magazine,* XVI (April 1907), 560.

48. *MC,* XXXVIII (June 28, 1899), 22–23.

49. *STJ,* II, 151–52. See *MC,* XLIII (Dec. 11, 1901), 26.

50. *MC,* XLI (Dec. 19, 1900), 36.

51. See ATS, "Irish Author and American Critic."

52. Arnold Bennett, *Books and Persons* (New York: George H. Doran, 1917), p. 190.

53. Susan L. Mitchell, *George Moore* (New York: Dodd, 1916), p. 47.

54. *MC,* XXXVI (June 22, 1898), 18–19, and XLIII (July 24, 1901), 21.

55. JGH, review of Moore's *Memoirs of My Dead Life, Times,* Oct. 5, 1906, p. 613.

56. *STJ,* II, 203, 230.

57. ATS, "Irish Author and American Critic," IX, 23.

58. Clark, p. 117.

59. See ATS, "James Huneker's Criticism of American Literature," pp. 70–72.

60. *Sun,* Aug. 29, 1909, p. 6 (reprinted in *Promenades of an Impressionist,* p. 257).

61. *MC,* XXXIII (Sept. 23, 1896), 19.

62. In 1907 Huneker declined an invitation from Garland, pleading the press of work, with this slightly two-edged remark: "I should like to see you in the flesh; I know you so well in print" (ltr, JGH to Garland, March 18, 1907) (University of Southern California).

63. *MC,* XXXIII (Dec. 9, 1896), 20.

64. *Nation,* VII (Oct. 22, 1868), 330–31. See René Wellek, "Henry James's Literary Theory and Criticism," *American Literature,* XXX (Nov. 1958), 298.

65. See *MC,* XXXII (Jan. 22, 1896), 20; (March 18, 1896), 22; and April 8, 1896), 25.

66. *MC,* XXXVII (Sept. 7, 1898), 17.

67. *MC,* XXXIV (June 23, 1897), 24; XXXV (Sept. 29, 1897), 24;

XXXVII (Oct. 19, 1898), 22; and XXXVI (June 8, 1898), 20, respectively.

68. "Raconteur," *MC*, XXXVIII (May 10–17, 1898).

69. "The Literary Show," *Town Topics,* XLI (April 27, 1899), 14.

70. *MC*, XXXIX (July 12, 1899), 20.

71. *MC*, XLI (Dec. 19, 1900), 35.

72. JGH, Philadelphia *Press,* Aug. 2, 1918, p. 8 (the passage is omitted in *STJ*). When the novel was reprinted in 1907, however, Huneker's name appeared in the publisher's advertisement among those who "on the advance copies extend enthusiastic praise" (*Times,* May 25, 1907, Sat. Rev. of Books, p. 339).

73. See Neilson, *My Life in Two Worlds,* I, 94–96, and Waters, p. 83.

74. Ltr, William H. Henderson (the critic's son) to ATS, Jan. 24, 1952.

75. *STJ,* II, 35–36.

76. *MA,* March 10, 1897, p. 4.

77. Isidore Witmark and Isaac Goldberg, *From Ragtime to Jazz* (New York: Lee Furman, 1939), pp. 213–14.

78. Glackens, p. 96; Guy Pène du Bois, *Artists Say the Silliest Things* (New York: American Artists Group; Duell, Sloan and Pearce, 1940), p. 180.

79. Mellquist, p. 134.

80. Seitz, pp. 231–32.

81. Benjamin De Casseres, "O Keg, America," unpubl. MS, p. 6 (William D. Luks). See Kent, pp. 229–30.

82. Glackens, p. 101.

83. *Herald-Tribune,* Oct. 30, 1933, p. 11.

84. See *MC*, XIX (Nov. 20, 1889), 427, and XXXVII (Aug. 24, 1898), 18.

85. *Evening Post,* May 9, 1925, p. 7.

86. Benjamin De Casseres, *Herald Tribune,* Sept. 10, 1933, Sec. 8, p. 10; Duffy, pp. 521ff; Rupert Hughes, *The Real New York* (New York: Smart Set Publishing Co., 1904), pp. 272–73; and Parry, pp. 91ff.

87. Kummer, pp. 57, 63; Beer, *The Mauve Decade,* pp. 154–55; and Clarke, *My Life and Memories,* pp. 257–59.

88. "Flaubert and his *Sentimental Education,*" *Criterion,* XVII (Aug. 13, 1898), 23–24.

89. Reedy's *Mirror,* XI (Feb. 22, 1900), 4.

90. Clarke, p. 261; Kummer, p. 57.

91. Unidentified clipping, labeled Nov. 28, 1897 (scrapbook, Dart).

92. Kummer, pp. 57, 63.

93. Kummer, *passim*; Frank Monaghan, *Dictionary of American Biography,* XV, 48–49; *Sun,* March 4, 1899, p. 9; and Harrison Hale Schaff (attorney for the Pollard estate), interview, Oct. 22, 1950.

94. Kummer, pp. 11–14.

95. Beer, *Stephen Crane,* p. 204.

96. Berryman, pp. 72, 87–88. Berryman got these facts from Beer's copy

of a statement (either written or oral) by Huneker, located in the Beer papers owned by Miss Alice Beer (ltr, Berryman to ATS, Jan. 4, 1952). This document (which I have not seen) is apparently the only evidence indicating that Huneker and Crane were acquainted as early as 1894. Corwin Knapp Linson, the American painter, who was a friend of Crane's in the winter of 1893–94 and saw him occasionally thereafter, does not recall ever having heard Crane mention Huneker, though, to be sure, Linson was in his nineties when queried on the point (ltr, Corwin K. Linson to ATS, July 13, 1958). See Linson, *passim.*

97. Thomas Beer, "Introduction," *The O'Ruddy,* Part I, *Works of Stephen Crane,* ed. Wilson Follett (New York: Knopf, 1926), VII, p. ix. See also Beer, *The Mauve Decade,* p. 152.

98. Beer, *Stephen Crane,* pp. 167–68 (reprinted in Berryman, p. 199, and Stallman and Gilkes, p. 159).

99. See Linson, p. 103; E. R. Hagemann, " 'Correspondents Three' in the Graeco-Turkish War: Some Parodies," *American Literature,* XXX (Nov. 1958), 339ff.

100. *MC,* XXXVII (Aug. 3, 1898), 20. A search, conducted by the Buffalo Public Library, of the Buffalo *Enquirer* for May–July, 1898, failed to uncover the article, though JGH stated (possibly as a playful hoax) that it appeared there.

101. Beer, *Stephen Crane,* p. 207.

102. See Linson, p. 31.

103. *STJ,* II, 128.

104. Stallman and Gilkes, p. 96.

105. *MC,* XXXVII, i. The article is unsigned, but the column was usually written by Thompson.

106. Beer, *Stephen Crane,* p. 244.

107. *MC,* XL (June 13, 1900), 20–21. See Richard Harding Davis, "Our War Correspondents in Cuba and Puerto Rico," *Harper's New Monthly Magazine,* XCVIII (May 1899), 940.

108. *MC,* XLII (April 24, 1901), 42.

109. *INT,* p. 20. The sentence "I waited and saw the sheet catch fire" is omitted from the published ltr but is found in the original (Dart).

110. *STJ,* II, 17–18.

CHAPTER TEN

1. *MC,* XXXIX (Aug. 23, 1899), 17.

2. *Times,* Sat. Rev., April 8, 1899, p. 236. See *Music,* IX (March 1896), 542.

3. *Book Notes,* I (1898), 242.

4. See ltr, JGH to Krehbiel, Feb. 5, 1899 (Dart).

5. Ltr, JGH to Krehbiel, March 14, 1899 (Dart).

6. For reviews by Henderson, Hale, Pollard, and Hughes, see *Times,*

April 8, 1899, p. 236; *Musical Record,* no. 447 (April 1899), pp. 150–51; *Town Topics,* XLI (April 13, 1899), 14–15; and *Criterion,* XX (April 8, 1899), 21–22, respectively.

7. *Nation,* LXVIII (May 4, 1899), 338.

8. Boston *Evening Transcript,* March 29, 1899, p. 10.

9. William Morton Payne, *Dial,* XXVI (May 16, 1900), 340–41.

10. Egbert Swayne, *Music,* XVI (May 1899), 17.

11. *Bookman,* IX (Aug. 1899), 513–14.

12. Undated postcard, JGH's autograph book (Mrs. John J. Lonergan).

13. Ltr, Zangwill to JGH, "Mayday," 1899, in JGH's autograph book (Mrs. Lonergan).

14. Ltr, J. A. Fuller-Maitland to JGH, Dec. 7 [1899], JGH's autograph book (Mrs. Lonergan).

15. *MC,* XXXVI (March 23, 1898), 25.

16. "An American Musical Critic," *Saturday Review,* LXXXVIII (Sept. 2, 1899), 292–94.

17. *MC,* XXXIX (Aug. 9, 1899), 16. See undated clipping, labeled London *Daily News* (scrapbook, Dart).

18. *MC,* XXXIX (Aug. 30, 1899), 21.

19. The review began in XIX (July 24, 1889), and ended on Sept. 25, 1889. See *MC,* XXXVII (Oct. 5, 1898), 18–19 (reprinted in *Mezzotints in Modern Music,* p. 223).

20. *Chopin,* p. 7.

21. *Ibid.,* pp. 19, 49, 51, 61.

22. Elson, p. 322.

23. Ltr, Isidore Philipp to ATS, April 2, 1952.

24. Postcard, Remy de Gourmont to JGH, postmarked May 26, 1900 (JGH's autograph book, Mrs. Lonergan); "R. De Bury," "Les Amours de Chopin et de George Sand," *Mercure de France,* VI (June 1900), 577–91, identified as Gourmont's by JGH (scrapbook, Dart), and reprinted in Gourmont's *Promenades Littéraires: Deuxième Série* (Paris: Mercure de France, 1906), pp. 129–47.

25. The holograph MS. of *Chopin* is at the University of Texas.

26. *MC,* XLIII (Nov. 13, 1901), 23.

27. Ltr, Moore to JGH, July 11, 1902, published in ATS, "Irish Author and American Critic," VIII, 264.

28. Ltr, JGH to Edwin Morse, Scribner's editor, Sept. 6, 1901 (Scrib).

29. JGH, "Parsifal," *Overtones,* pp. 72–73, 93, 103, 104, 106–7.

30. *LET,* p. 7.

31. Neilson, *My Life in Two Worlds,* I, 218–20. See also Neilson, "Miscellany."

32. *MC,* XLIII (Sept. 25, 1901), 6, and (Oct. 2, 1901), 5.

33. *LET,* p. 204.

34. Printed in *Reedy's Mirror,* XI (Dec. 12, 1901), 7–8, and in *MC,* XLIV (Jan. 15, 1902), 20–21.

35. *MC*, XLIII (Dec. 11, 1901), 25.

36. *Ibid.*, p. 26; *STJ*, I, 312–13; and Neilson, *My Life in Two Worlds*, I, 123–24.

37. Neilson, "Miscellany," p. 589.

38. Ltr, JGH to Richard Aldrich, Nov. 10, 1899 (Mrs. Richard Aldrich).

39. Ltr, JGH to Edward Ziegler, Nov. 10, 1899 (Mrs. Lonergan).

40. Ltr, JGH to Edwin W. Morse, Jan. 25, 1900 (St. John's Seminary, Camarillo, Calif.).

41. *MC*, XLIV (March 12, 1902), 25.

42. *LET*, p. 285.

43. *LET*, pp. 162–63.

44. *MC*, XXXIII (Sept. 16, 1896), 16.

45. *Red Book Magazine*, XI (Sept. 1908), 625–40 (reprinted in *The Pathos of Distance*, pp. 245–63.

46. Printed in *MC*, XXXIII (Oct. 7, 1896), 20–22, and (Dec. 30, 1896), 20–22.

47. *MC*, XXXVI (Feb. 2, 1898), 22–23.

48. *Melomaniacs*, p, 231.

49. *Ibid.*, pp. 12, 324.

50. *Ibid.*, p. 119.

51. *Ibid.*, p. 169.

52. *Ibid.*, p. 200.

53. *Ibid.*, p. 346.

54. *Ibid.*, p. 194.

55. *Ibid.*, pp. 103, 122.

56. Ltr, JGH to Joseph Conrad, June 22, 1909, published first in Jean-Aubry, *Letters to Conrad*, and reprinted in ATS, "Joseph Conrad's American Friend," p. 225.

57. *INT*, p. 23.

58. Bernard R. Bowron lists no review in his "Henry B. Fuller: A Critical Study," unpubl. diss. (Harvard, 1948).

59. "Paderewski," *Saturday Review*, CIII (June 29, 1907), 811.

60. Ltr, Symons to JGH, May 2, 1902 (Yale University).

61. Ltr. July 11, 1902, published in ATS, "Irish Author and American Critic," VIII, 264.

62. Ltr, Frank Norris to JGH, March 8, 1902, published in *The Letters of Frank Norris*, ed. Franklin Walker (San Francisco: The Book Club of California, 1956), p. 90; the passage is quoted—but misdated May 8, 1902—in *STJ*, II, 240.

63. Hughes, "James Huneker."

64. Ltr, JGH to Florence Mosher, Jan. 26, 1902 (Clifton Waller Barrett).

65. Ltr, JGH to Harry Thurston Peck, June 28, 1902 (Clifton Waller Barrett).

66. *STJ*, II, 215–16.

67. See *MC*, XLI (Dec. 19, 1900), 36.

68. *MC,* XXXVII (Dec. 21, 1898), 29; *Sun,* March 27, 1904, Sec. 3, p. 4; and *Herald,* Aug. 26, 1906, Sec. 3, p. 8.

69. Samuel L. Clemens, *The Autobiography of Mark Twain,* ed. Charles Neider (New York: Harper, 1959), p. 274.

70. *MC,* XXXVIII (June 28, 1899), 23.

71. *MC,* XLII (Feb. 27, 1901), 25, and (May 8, 1901), 23.

72. *Ibid.* (Jan. 20, 1901), 35, and (April 10, 1901), 23.

73. *Sun,* April 5, 1903, Sec. 3, p. 6, and Sept. 23, 1908, p. 6.

74. *MC,* XLIV (April 30, 1902), 23.

75. *Ibid.* (May 28, 1902), p. 25.

76. *MC,* XLV (Sept. 24, 1902), 20.

CHAPTER ELEVEN

1. H. L. Mencken, "The Library," *American Mercury,* III (Dec. 1924), 505.

2. Mitchell, p. 157; Vance Thompson, "New York Journalism," *MC,* XXXV (Nov. 10, 1897), I; Wilbur F. Fauley, "The Great Newspapers of a Great City," *Book World,* VI (1901), 514–15; "The Literary Show," *Town Topics,* XL (July 21, 1898), 16; and Churchill, p. 15.

3. *Times,* Jan. 24, 1927, p. 16.

4. Mitchell, p. 352.

5. O'Brien, p. 233; Mitchell, p. 214; and *Sun,* Sept. 15, 1909, p. 1.

6. Ltrs, JGH to Edward Ziegler, Nov. 24, 1900, and Feb. 14, 1905 (Dart); *LET,* p. 34.

7. *Sun,* Jan. 18, 1901, p. 7.

8. *MC,* XLIII (Dec. 25, 1901), 23–24. See also "The Caprices of Musical Taste: A Talk by James Huneker," in *Modern Masters of Music: Course II: Booklovers Reading Club Handbook* (Philadelphia: The Booklovers Library, 1901), pp. 81–89. JGH was explaining and defending Strauss in the *MC* during the spring of 1902, beginning in April.

9. *MC,* XXXII (Jan. 8, 1896), 21.

10. *Sun,* Dec. 27, 1900, p. 4.

11. *Sun,* Feb. 5, 1901, p. 7.

12. *The New International Encyclopedia,* 2d ed. (New York: Dodd, Mead and Co., 1924), p. xviii. See ltr, JGH to Harry Thurston Peck, June 28, 1902 (Clifton Waller Barrett). JGH's contributions to the *Encyclopedia* are not identified.

13. Ltr, Blumenberg to Spencer T. Driggs, Jan. 1, 1901 (Dart).

14. *MC,* XXIII (Sept. 30, 1891), 354; XXIV (April 27, 1892), 7; XXXIV (March 24, 1897), 20–21; and XL (Feb. 7, 1900), 29–30.

15. Waters, pp. 143ff.

16. Ltr, Blumenberg to Driggs, Jan. 1, 1901 (Dart). See *STJ,* II, 19, where, however, all reference to Herbert is omitted.

17. *Sun,* Jan. 23, 1901, p. 3. See Waters, pp. 181, 185.

18. *MC,* XLIII (July 17, 1901), 19.

19. Ltrs, Arthur M. Abell to ATS, April 24, 1952, and April 30, 1952.

20. *MC,* XLV (Aug. 20, 1902), 15; (Sept. 3, 1902), 15; (Sept. 10, 1902), 19; (Sept. 17, 1902), 20–21; and (Sept. 24, 1902), 19.

21. *MC,* XLV (Sept. 24, 1902), 28.

22. Liebling, "Variations," p. 21.

23. Ltrs, Arthur M. Abell to ATS, Nov. 29, 1950, and April 16, 1952.

24. Ltr, JGH to Driggs, Oct. 8, 1902 (Dart).

25. Ltr, JGH to Blumenberg, Oct. 8, 1902 (Dart).

26. *MC,* XLV (Oct. 15, 1902), 20.

27. See Ltr, Driggs to JGH, Nov. 25, 1902 (Dart).

28. Ltr, JGH to Ziegler, Dec. 11, 1907 (Dart).

29. Ltr, "Thursday" (1902) (Dart).

30. Leonard Liebling, *MC,* XCIX (Sept. 28, 1929), 27.

31. *STJ,* II, 16. "The Melomaniac's" last column in *Town Topics* appeared on April 10, 1902.

32. Waters, pp. 197ff.

33. *Concert-goer,* Nov. 1, 1902, p. 7.

34. *Sun,* March 22, 1903, Sec. 3, p. 6.

35. *Sun,* Nov. 9, 1902, Sec. 3, p. 6.

36. London *Era,* quoted by JGH in *Sun,* Feb. 20, 1903, p. 5.

37. Binns and Kooken, p. 133.

38. *Sun,* Nov. 22, 1903, Sec. 3, p. 4.

39. *Sun,* April 22, 1903, p. 6, and April 12, 1903, Sec. 3, p. 6.

40. JGH, *Iconoclasts,* pp. 399, 402.

41. JGH, "The Last of the Viking Poets: August Strindberg and his Work," *Harper's Weekly,* LVI (July 27, 1912), 19; *Iconoclasts,* p. 145.

42. *Sun,* March 8, 1903, Sec. 3, p. 6.

43. Ltr, Oct. 11, 1904 (Scrib.). See JGH, *Sun,* Jan. 28, 1912, p. 8.

44. *Sun,* Jan. 11, 1903, Sec. 3, p. 6.

45. *Sun,* Nov. 28, 1902, p. 7.

46. *Sun,* April 5, 1903, Sec. 3, p. 6.

47. *Sun,* Nov. 29, 1903, Sec. 3, p. 4.

48. *Sun,* Feb. 15, 1903, Sec. 3, p. 6.

49. Montrose J. Moses and Virginia Gerson, *Clyde Fitch and his Letters* (Boston: Little, Brown, 1924), pp. 232–33.

50. *Sun,* April 24, 1903, p. 9.

51. *Sun,* Sept. 29, 1903, p. 4.

52. Ltr, JGH to Edward Ziegler, Aug. 26, 1903 (Dart); *LET,* p. 131 (misdated 1912). See Neilson, *My Life in Two Worlds,* I, 223.

53. See Symons, "Notes on Richard Strauss and Beethoven," *Sackbut,* I (March 1921), 397–403, and JGH, "About Arthur Symons and his New Book," *Lamp,* XXVIII (June 1904), 378.

54. *Sun,* July 26, 1903, Sec. 3, p. 5.

55. *STJ*, II, 212. On their meeting, see *Lamp*, XXVIII, 374–75.

56. *LET*, pp. 132–33.

57. Grace Corneau, "Maeterlinck and 'Joyzelle,' " *Critic*, XLIII (July 1903), 114.

58. *STJ*, II, 117–21; *Sun*, June 14, 1903, Sec. 3, p. 6; *Lamp*, XXVII (Jan. 1904), 581–86. I have not had access to a complete file of the *Weekly Critical Review*. The ltrs JGH mentions have not turned up.

59. Ltr, Dec. 12, 1927, published in Upton Sinclair, *My Lifetime in Letters* (Columbia, Mo.: University of Missouri Press, 1960), p. 342. The ltr was written in French; I follow Sinclair's (?) translation.

60. They were running between June 4, 1903 (*LET*, p. 133) and Sept. 3, 1903, and probably afterward.

61. *LET*, p. 133; *STJ*, II, 117.

62. *STJ*, II, 118.

63. *Sun*, July 12, 1903, Sec. 3, p. 4.

64. *LET*, pp. 82–83.

65. *Sun*, July 19, 1903, Sec. 3, p. 5 (reprinted, with slight changes, in *Overtones*, pp. 316–18.

66. *LET*, p. 131.

67. *LET*, pp. 13–15.

68. *Sun*, Aug. 9, 1903, Sec. 3, p. 4.

69. *Sun*, Aug. 30, 1903, Sec. 3, p. 4.

70. Postmarked Aug. 18, 1903 (Clifton Waller Barrett).

71. Ltr, JGH to Edward Ziegler, Aug. 26, 1903 (Dart).

72. *LET*, pp. 42–43 (ltr misdated 1905).

73. *Sun*, Oct. 18, 1903, Sec. 3, p. 4. See JGH, "A Batch of Autumn Plays," *Ainslee's* (Jan. 1904), 149–55.

74. *Sun*, June 16, 1904, p. 9.

75. *Sun*, Nov. 21, 1903, p. 9.

76. Binns and Kooken, p. 141.

77. *Sun*, Oct. 18, 1903, Sec. 3, p. 4.

78. *Sun*, Feb. 7, 1904, Sec. 3, p. 6.

79. *Sun*, Nov. 22, 1903, Sec. 3, p. 4.

80. Joseph Hone, *W. B. Yeats* (New York: Macmillan Co., 1943), pp. 192, 205; ltr, JGH to John Quinn, Dec. 22, 1903 (Quinn Collection, NYPL).

81. *Sun*, Dec. 27, 1903, Sec. 3, p. 4.

82. In ltr to JGH, partially quoted in *STJ*, II, 242–43. I have not traced the original. See ltr, JGH to John Quinn, Dec. 25, 1903 (Quinn Collection, NYPL).

83. ATS, "Irish Author and American Critic," VIII, 265.

84. *Sun*, Dec. 18, 1902, p. 7; Feb. 1, 1903, Sec. 3, p. 6; Feb. 20, 1903, p. 5; April 24, 1903, p. 9; and March 18, 1904, p. 7.

85. *Sun*, March 27, 1904, Sec. 3, p. 4, and June 1, 1904, p. 7.

86. *Sun*, Jan. 31, 1904, Sec. 3, p. 6.

87. Ltr, JGH to Julia Marlowe, Nov. 24, 1909 (Museum of the City of New York). See *Sun*, May 8, 1904, Sec. 3, p. 4.

88. *Metropolitan Magazine*, XIX (Feb. 1904), 732.

89. Ltr, A. B. Walkley to JGH, April 9, 1905 (Dart).

90. *Sun*, April 7, 1904, p. 7.

91. Binns and Kooken, pp. 132–33. He gives no source.

92. Clipping labeled *Baltimore News*, Feb. 16, 1903 (scrapbook, Dart).

93. *World*, Jan. 10, 1904, Metro. Sec., p. 3.

94. JGH, "Looking Backward," *Theatre Magazine*, XI (May 1910), 142–43; *STJ*, II, 146.

95. Undated clipping (scrapbook, Dart).

96. *LET*, p. 23.

97. *Sun*, Nov. 21, 1902, p. 9.

98. *Sun*, Sec. 3, p. 5.

99. See "The Usher," N.Y. *Dramatic Mirror*, LII (Aug. 6, 1904), II; ltrs, JGH to Edward Ziegler, June 12, 1904 (Clifton Waller Barrett), and JGH to Harry Rowe Shelley, Aug. 23, 1904 (American Academy of Arts and Letters); and *STJ*, II, 110–11.

CHAPTER TWELVE

1. Ltr, JGH to Edward Ziegler, Dec. 31, 1903 (Dart).

2. *Sun*, Dec. 25, 1903, p. 2, and Feb. 26, 1904, p. 7.

3. *Sun*, July 23, 1911, Sec. 3, p. 2.

4. *INT*, p. 38.

5. Jordan, p. 205.

6. *LET*, p. 26.

7. *Ibid*.

8. *LET*, p. 28; *STJ*, II, 111.

9. Ltr, Aug. 23, 1904 (American Academy of Arts and Letters).

10. *LET*, p. 33.

11. *LET*, p. 30.

12. JGH, "The Last of the Viking Poets: August Strindberg and his Work," *Harper's Weekly*, LVI (July 27, 1912), 19–20.

13. *STJ*, II, 136.

14. De Casseres, *James Gibbons Huneker*, pp. 34–35.

15. JGH, "Paul Hervieu and His Plays," *Theatre*, V (Feb. 1905), 39–42, and *Iconoclasts*, pp. 231, 219.

16. Viereck, *My Flesh and Blood, passim*.

17. Ltr, Nov. 14, 1904 (Viereck).

18. Ltr, JGH to Viereck, Dec. 1, 1905 (Viereck).

19. Ltr, Viereck to William Marion Reedy, *Mirror*, XX (Oct. 19, 1911), 14. See ltr, JGH to W. D. Moffat, Aug. 8, 1906 (American Academy of Arts and Letters).

20. De Fornaro, p. 74.

21. Ltr, JGH to De Casseres, "Nov. 20," postmarked 1902 (Dart); *INT*, p. 42.

22. *INT*, pp. 35–36.

23. *Sun*, April 10, 1904, Sec. 3, p. 4. See S. Jay Kaufman, "Round the Town," *Globe and Commercial Advertiser*, Feb. 11, 1921, p. 16.

24. *INT*, p. 49 (ltr misdated 1905 for 1903).

25. *INT*, p. 59 (ltr misdated 1906 for 1905).

26. Walter Prichard Eaton, *The American Stage of Today* (Boston: Small, Maynard, 1908), p. 6.

27. *LET*, p. 38.

28. *INT*, p. 98; ltr, JGH to Edwin W. Morse, May 24, 1906 (F. L. Rodgers).

29. *STJ*, II, 214.

30. Ltr, Edwin W. Morse to JGH, May 26, 1906 (F. L. Rodgers).

31. See, for example, *Sun*, Feb. 15, 1903, Sec. 3, p. 6; March 22, 1903, Sec. 3, p. 6; March 29, 1903, Sec. 3, p. 6; Nov. 1, 1903, Sec. 3, p. 4; Feb. 14, 1904, Sec. 3, p. 4; and April 24, 1904, Sec. 3, p. 4. Six ltrs from JGH to Matthews are at Columbia University, and one from Matthews to JGH at Dart.

32. *DeMille*, p. 236.

33. *Outlook*, LXXX(May 13, 1905), 140.

34. *Town Topics*, LIII (April 20, 1905), 17.

35. *Reedy's Mirror*, XV (July 20, 1905), 16–17.

36. *LET*, p. 41.

37. Baltimore *Evening Herald*, May 6, 1905, p. 6.

38. Ltr, May 31, 1905 (H. L. Mencken).

39. *Sun*, April 5, 1903, Sec. 3, p. 6, and Feb. 17, 1904, p. 4.

40. *STJ*, I, 300.

41. *STJ*, I, 300–304. JGH states that he visited Calabria for the *Herald* (*STJ*, II, 112), but I have not been able to find in that newspaper any article by him about the quake.

42. *LET*, p. 45.

43. *STJ*, I, 296–97.

44. *LET*, p. 45.

45. *Herald*, Jan. 14, 1906, Mag. Sec., p. 3. See *Franz Liszt*, pp. 344–52.

46. No prior publication elsewhere has been detected for seven of the stories: "The Purse of Aholibah"; "The Spiral Road"; "Antichrist"; "The Third Kingdom"; "A Sentimental Rebellion"; "An Iron Fan"; and "Nada."

47. *INT*, p. 197.

48. *Visionaries*, p. 10.

49. Ltr, Emma Goldman to JGH, Nov. 23, 1905 (Historical Society of Pennsylvania).

50. *Visionaries*, p. 162.

51. Ltr, JGH to Conrad, June 22, 1909, published in Jean-Aubry and in ATS, "Joseph Conrad's American Friend," p. 225.

52. Ltr, JGH to Brander Matthews, March 30, 1906 (Columbia University).

53. "An Iron Fan," *Visionaries*, p. 284.

54. "Antichrist," *ibid.*, p. 144.

55. "Nada," *ibid.*, p. 328.

56. Ltr, JGH to Matthews, March 30, 1906 (Columbia University).

57. *Visionaries*, pp. 35, 47, 293, 340, 267, 301, and 236, respectively.

58. Ltr, *Scribner's* to ATS, Nov. 15, 1949.

59. *LET*, p. 48.

60. *Bookman*, XXII (Dec. 1905), 360–61.

61. *LET*, p. 46.

62. *LET*, pp. 46–47.

63. Francis Neilson, interview, Nov. 12, 1951.

64. *Sun*, Jan. 3, 1904, Sec. 3, p. 4.

65. *INT*, p. 40.

66. *Herald*, June 24, 1906, Mag. Sec., p. 2 (reprinted in *Unicorns*, pp. 6–17). In ltr to ATS, April 28, 1956, Mrs. Edward MacDowell (aged ninety-eight; she died four months later) categorically denies the picturesque account of JGH's visit to MacDowell found in Elizabeth Jordan's *Three Rousing Cheers*, p. 205.

67. *STJ*, II, 158. Mrs. MacDowell did not recall this incident (ltr to ATS, April 28, 1956), but EHH thinks he may have seen JGH wearing the medal (ltr to ATS, June 3, 1961).

68. *Puck*, LXXVI (Dec. 12, 1914), p. 8.

69. "The Drama of the Month," *Puck*, XXIV (July 1906), 517–18, 520.

70. *Ibid.* (April 1906), p. 122.

71. Pollock, p. 148.

72. *Herald*, July 8, 1906, Sec. 3, p. 6; Sept. 9, 1906, Sec. 3, p. 7; Aug. 1, 1906, Sec. 3, p. 6; Aug. 19, 1906, Sec. 3, p. 8; and July 15, 1906, Sec. 3, p. 7, respectively.

73. *Times*, Oct. 5, 1906, Lit. Sec., p. 614.

74. *Herald*, Aug. 26, 1906, Sec. 3, p. 8.

75. Morris, *Incredible New York*, pp. 226–29.

76. *Herald*, Aug. 5, 1906, Sec. 3, p. 7.

77. "The Drama of the Month," *Metropolitan Magazine*, XXV (Dec. 1906), 380, and (Feb. 1907), 608–9.

78. *Ibid.*, XXII (June 1905), 370, and XXIV (June 1906), 377; ltr, JGH to Florence Mosher, Feb. 8, 1906 (Clifton Waller Barrett).

79. Ltr, Mansfield to JGH, "Thursday" (1907?) (Yale University); *STJ*, II, 236.

80. *INT*, p. 65, and ltr, JGH to Fanny Bloomfield-Zeisler, Oct. 5, 1906 (Mrs. Amelia S. Zeisler).

81. Ltr, JGH to Edwin W. Morse, Nov. 29, 1906 (Scrib).

82. *Herald*, July 29, 1906, Sec. 3, p. 7.

83. *INT*, p. 64.

84. *INT*, pp. 68–70.

CHAPTER THIRTEEN

1. *STJ*, II, 257.

2. "Musical Criticism, Old and New; and Some Notes on the Critics," *MC*, XXVII (Aug. 9, 1893), 19–20 (reprinted from the [London?] *Magazine of Music*).

3. *STJ*, II, 257–58.

4. "The Musical Revolution," *MC* (European) XXIX (Sept. 1894), pp. unnumb.

5. Archibald Henderson, *Bernard Shaw: Playboy and Prophet* (New York: D. Appleton, 1932), pp. 360–61.

6. *REC*, Sept. 23, 1894, p. 16, partially reprinted in *MC*, XXIX (Sept. 26, 1894), 10. I have not located this early Shaw ltr.

7. *REC*, April 28, 1895, p. 14.

8. *MC*, XXXIII (Aug. 12, 1896), 16.

9. *MC*, XXXVIII (Feb. 15, 1899), 28.

10. *MC*, XXXVII (July 13, 1898), 24, and (July 20, 1898), 19.

11. *MC*, XXXVIII (Feb. 15, 1899), 29; XLII (March 6, 1901), 25; and (April 24, 1901), 24.

12. *MC*, XLII (May 15, 1901), 22–23.

13. *Sun*, March 12, 1903, p. 7, and May 17, 1903, Sec. 3, p. 4.

14. *Sun*, Aug. 2, 1903, Sec. 3, p. 5; *LET*, p. 132 (ltr misdated 1912 for 1903).

15. *Sun*, Oct. 25, 1903, Sec. 3, p. 4.

16. *STJ*, II, 268–72. The originals of all the Shaw ltrs quoted in the text are at Chestnut Hill College, Philadelphia, Pa.

17. *Sun*, Dec. 9, 1903, p. 5, and Dec. 13, 1903, Sec. 4, p. 6.

18. *Sun*, Jan. 3, 1904, Sec. 3, p. 4.

19. *STJ*, II, 273–74.

20. *STJ*, II, 268. JGH printed one sentence from this postcard—Shaw's opinion of Strindberg (see *STJ*, II, 267–68)—in "August Strindberg and His Plays," *Theatre*, V (April 1905), 91.

21. "The Truth About Candida," *Metropolitan Magazine*, XX, 632ff. See *STJ*, II, 266, 273, and Arthur H. Nethercott, "The Truth About Candida," *PMLA*, LXIV (Sept. 1949), 639–47.

22. Ltr, JGH to Robert Mackay (Yale University). I have not located Shaw's postcard.

23. Archibald Henderson, *George Bernard Shaw*, pp. 510–11; Mary Shaw, "My 'Immoral' Play," *McClure's Magazine*, XXXVIII (April 1912), 691–92.

24. "George Bernard Shaw," *Success*, VIII, 237–39.

25. *STJ*, II, 255.

26. *Ibid.*, p. 254.

27. "A Study in Self Analysis," *Metropolitan Magazine*, XXIII, 498.

28. Shaw, *The Irrational Knot* (New York: Brentano's, 1918), p. xxi. The novel was first reprinted by Brentano's in September 1905. Archibald

Henderson believes that Huneker took too seriously what Shaw, "indulging, characteristically, in his penchant for colossal humorous extravagance," intended as "good fun with a sting in the tail" (ltr to ATS, March 10, 1957).

29. London *Daily News*, April 26, 1905, p. 4.

30. Ltr, April 9, 1905 (Dart).

31. London *Times*, July 7, 1905, Lit. Supp., p. 218.

32. Ltr, Sir Max Beerbohm to ATS, June 26, 1952.

33. *MC*, XXX (Jan. 30, 1895), 24–25.

34. *MC*, XXXVI (June 15, 1898), 19.

35. "Raconteur," *MC*, XXXIX (Dec. 20–27, 1899), pp. unnumb., and XLIV (March 19, 1902), 23.

36. Riewald, pp. 43–47, 148, 156, 157.

37. Ltr, Sir Max Beerbohm to ATS, June 26, 1952.

38. *Saturday Review*, C (July 29, 1905), 143–44.

39. Riewald, p. 160.

40. "A Cursory Conspectus of G.B.S.," *Saturday Review*, XCII (Nov. 2, 1901), 557.

41. "Mr. Shaw's New Dialogues," *ibid.*, XCVI (Sept. 12, 1903), 329.

42. "Mr. Shaw at his Best," *ibid.*, XCVIII (Nov. 12, 1904), 609.

43. Riewald, pp. 160–61. See "A Letter from Max Beerbohm," in *G.B.S. 90*, S. Winsten, ed. (London: Hutchinson, 1946), p. 56.

44. "Mr. Shaw's Position," *Saturday Review*, C (Dec. 9, 1905), 745–46.

45. Mencken, *Prejudices: Third Series*, p. 77.

46. *Town Topics*, LIV (Sept. 21, 1905), 14.

47. "Chronicle and Comment," *Bookman*, XXII (Sept. 1905), 4.

48. *Outlook*, LXXXI (Nov. 25, 1905), 701, 732.

49. *STJ*, II, 252.

50. *First Editions and Autograph Letters by George Bernard Shaw* (New York: American Art Association, Anderson Galleries, 1933), p. 32.

51. Ltr, Archibald Henderson to ATS, March 10, 1957.

52. Excerpts quoted in *STJ*, II, 257, 259, 264, 272–73.

53. Ltr, JGH to Edward Marsh, July 7, 1905 (Dart); *STJ*, II, 254. Archibald Henderson states (without offering any supporting evidence) that Shaw chose him to edit the drama criticism, but that Brentano's insisted that Huneker do it because he was better known (ltr to ATS, March 10, 1957).

54. *STJ*, II, 275–76. Brentano's had published Shaw's *Cashel Byron's Profession* in 1897 and *The Unsocial Socialist* in 1900 (Archibald Henderson, *George Bernard Shaw*, pp. xv, xviii).

55. Postcard, Shaw to ATS, June 8, 1950.

56. Excerpts quoted in *STJ*, II, 258, 259, 260.

57. *STJ*, II, 259–60.

58. *Metropolitan Magazine*, XXIV, 114, 117.

59. G. B. Shaw, *Dramatic Opinions and Essays*, 2 vols. (New York: Brentano's, 1906), I, xi ff.

60. *Saturday Review,* CIII, 518–19.

61. G. B. Shaw, "The Author's Apology," *Dramatic Opinions and Essays* (London: Archibald Constable, 1907), p. xxiv. The apology, dated 1906, appeared in the 1907, but not in the 1906, edition published by Brentano's.

62. *LET,* p. 97.

63. *Saturday Review,* CVIII, 16–17; ltr, Beerbohm to ATS, June 26, 1952.

64. *Sun,* Jan. 9, 1910, p. 8.

65. "The War of the Sexes," *Metropolitan Magazine,* XXV (Feb. 1907), 609, and "Personalities," *ibid.,* XXVI (April 1907), 80.

66. JGH had the apparently mistaken notion that Beerbohm was Jewish (see *STJ,* I, 313, and ltr, JGH to Edwin W. Morse, April 8, 1909 [F. L. Rodgers], only partially published in *LET,* p. 97). In ltr to ATS, June 26, 1952, Beerbohm states that so far as he knows, the Beerbohms have no Jewish blood.

67. *Sun,* Sept. 6, 1908, p. 7, reprinted in *Puck,* LXXVII (June 12, 1915), 14, 20, and *Unicorns,* pp. 241–48.

68. *Sun,* Jan. 9, 1910, p. 8.

69. William Irvine, *The Universe of G.B.S.* (New York: Whittlesey House, 1949), p. 339.

70. *Sun,* Jan. 7, 1912, p. 8.

71. *Sun,* June, 5, 1911, p. 7.

72. *STJ,* II, 261.

73. Postcard, Shaw to ATS, June 8, 1950. See *Iconoclasts,* p. 243.

74. *Puck,* LXXV (July 11, 1914), 17.

75. *Puck,* LXXVI (Nov. 14, 1914), 8. See *Times,* July 13, 1961, p. 24.

76. *Puck,* LXXVII (Feb. 27, 1915), 11.

77. Ltr, JGH to John Quinn, May 27, 1919 (Dart).

78. Philadelphia *Press,* Oct. 16–19, 21–26, 1918, p. 8.

79. *Ibid.,* Oct. 23, 1918, p. 8 (reprinted in *STJ,* II, 268).

80. *Ibid.,* Oct. 15, 1918, p. 8 (reprinted in *STJ,* II, 251–53).

81. *Ibid.* (reprinted in *STJ,* II, 251).

82. *Ibid.,* Oct., 19, 1918, p. 8 (reprinted in *STJ,* II, 261).

83. *Ibid.,* Oct. 18, 1918, p. 8, and Oct. 22, 1918, p. 8.

84. *Ibid.,* Oct. 19, 1918, p. 8.

85. Ltrs, Shaw to JGH, July 9, 1919, and JGH to Maxwell Perkins of Scribner's, July 23, 1919 (Scrib).

86. Philadelphia *Press,* Oct. 21, 1918, p. 8, and *STJ,* II, 264.

CHAPTER FOURTEEN

1. *LET,* p. 28.

2. See Harry M. Tod, "The Old 'Sun,'" *Reedy's Mirror,* XXV (Aug. 4, 1916), 507, and Rosebault, *When Dana Was* THE SUN, pp. 270ff.

3. *Art News*, IX (Jan. 21, 1911), 4.

4. Rosebault, *When Dana Was* THE SUN, p. 271; O'Brien, pp. 196–98.

5. *Sun*, Nov. 20, 1909, p. 1, and Nov. 22, 1909, p. 8.

6. Ltr, JGH to Dr. Percy Fridenberg, March 21, 1919 (Clifton Waller Barrett).

7. Ltr, Charles FitzGerald to Ira Glackens, Jan. 2, 1956 (Glackens); ltrs, Ira Glackens to ATS, July 15, 1961, and July 24, 1961.

8. Ltr, JGH to William Laffan, Dec. 31, 1908 (Mrs. Edward P. Mitchell); ltr, JGH to Edward Mitchell, Dec. 15, 1906 (Mrs. Edward P. Mitchell).

9. The first art column in the *Sun* that seems to be JGH's is "Around the Galleries," Dec. 17, 1906, p. 9. See *LET*, p. 63, and *INT*, p. 75.

10. *LET*, p. 50 (dated "Wednesday Evening" [Dec. 26]; by internal evidence the year is 1906, though the ltr appears in the 1905 chapter in *LET*).

11. *American Art News*, V, 4.

12. Ltr, March 31, 1907 (Mrs. Edward P. Mitchell).

13. *LET*, p. 60.

14. See Schapiro, p. 225.

15. *Sun*, Oct. 28, 1907, p. 6.

16. *Sun*, Feb. 9, 1908, p. 8.

17. See Mellquist, p. 311.

18. *Puck*, LXXIX (May 13, 1916), 12. See ltr, JGH to Mather, June 1, 1910 (Princeton University).

19. Ltr, Frank Jewett Mather to ATS, Oct. 30, 1951. For comments on Mather, see Van Wyck Brooks, *From the Shadow of the Mountain: My Post-Meridian Years* (New York: Dutton, 1961), p. 104.

20. Baehr, pp. 231–32; *Herald-Tribune*, Oct. 18, 1948, pp. 1, 18.

21. Ltr, JGH to Mitchell, Dec. 15, 1906 (Mrs. Edward P. Mitchell).

22. *LET*, p. 204. See *Unicorns*, p. 101, and *STJ*, II, 164.

23. Rose, p. 251.

24. *Sun*, Nov. 27, 1904, Sec. 3, p. 3 (reprinted in *Promenades of an Impressionist*, pp. 4–5).

25. Sun, Dec. 20, 1906, p. 8; Walter Pach, interview, Nov. 14, 1951.

26. *Sun*, Dec. 20, 1906, p. 8.

27. JGH, *Puck*, LXXIX (March 4, 1916), 12.

28. *LET*, p. 76. See Bulliet, pp. 42ff.

29. *Sun*, Jan. 15, 1907, p. 6; Mellquist, p. 186.

30. *Sun*, Jan. 7, 1908, p. 6.

31. *Sun*, April 10, 1908, p. 6, and Nov. 20, 1910, Sec. 3, p. 4; Mellquist, p. 189.

32. *Sun*, Feb. 27, 1910, Sec. 3, p. 4.

33. See *Camera Work*, No. 22, April 1908, p. 38; No. 27, July 1909, p. 42; No. 29, Jan. 1910, pp. 52–53; No. 30, April 1910, pp. 39–40, 48–49; No. 31, July 1910, pp. 43–44, 49–51; No. 33, Jan. 1911, pp. 47–48; No.

36, Oct. 1911, pp. 47, 53–54; No. 38, April 1912, pp. 42, 45; and No. 45, Jan.–June, 1914, p. 43.

34. Ltr, Feb. 5, 1907 (Mrs. Edward P. Mitchell).

35. *Sun*, March 22, 1907, p. 8. See Mellquist, p. 115.

36. *Sun*, April 5, 1907, p. 8.

37. Ltr, Rockwell Kent to ATS, June 5, 1950. See Kent, p. 148.

38. John Sloan, interview, 1950; *Sun*, April 15, 1907, p. 6.

39. *Sun*, Jan. 21, 1907, p. 6; Jan. 7, 1908, p. 6 (especially) ; and April 7, 1910, p. 6. See Jerome Myers, *Artist in Manhattan* (New York: American Artists Group, 1940), p. 26.

40. The extent of JGH's "cribbing" from art reference books, and of the influence of FitzGerald and Gregg on his art criticism might well bear detailed investigation by an art historian.

41. Brooks, *John Sloan*, pp. 18–21, 74–76; Glackens, p. 89; and Mellquist, pp. 117ff.

42. Glackens, p. 91.

43. Brooks, *John Sloan*, pp. 77, 98.

44. *Sun*, Jan. 21, 1907, p. 6; Feb. 7, 1907, p. 8; March 21, 1907, p. 8; and April 15, 1907, p. 6, respectively.

45. *Sun*, Feb. 9, 1908, p. 8.

46. *Sun*, March 21, 1907, p. 8, and June 20, 1908, p. 6.

47. Brooks, *John Sloan*, p. 80.

48. *Sun*, June 4, 1908, p. 6 (reprinted in *The Pathos of Distance*, pp. 111–21) ; *LET*, p. 87.

49. *Sun*, Nov. 15, 1908, p. 8. See ltr, George Grey Barnard to JGH, Nov. 20, 1908 (Yale University), and Saarinen, p. 353.

50. *Sun*, Dec. 18, 1908, p. 6.

51. *Ibid.*

52. *Sun*, April 7, 1909, p. 6.

53. Mellquist, p. 181.

54. *Sun*, Jan. 16, 1910, p. 8.

55. *Sun*, March 20, 1910, Sec. 3, p. 4. See Holger Cahill, *Max Weber* (New York; Downtown Gallery, 1930), p. 23.

56. Mellquist, p. 195.

57. *Sun*, April 20, 1910, p. 8.

58. Brooks, *John Sloan*, p. 129.

59. *Sun*, April 7, 1910, p. 6.

60. *Sun*, June 26, 1910, Sec. 3. p. 4.

61. Winthrop Sargeant, "Nocturnal Genius," *Life*, XXX (Feb. 26, 1951), 86ff.

62. *LET*, p. 105. See Beer, *Stephen Crane*, p. 207; Weitenkampf, p. 119; and *STJ*, II, 95.

63. *Sun*, July 3, 1910, Sec. 3, p. 4.

64. *Sun*, Oct. 3, 1910, p. 6.

65. *Sun*, Nov. 16, 1910, p. 8. One ltr from La Farge to JGH is in the

collection of the Historical Society of Pennsylvania; JGH's ltrs to La Farge have not been located (ltrs, Rev. John La Farge, S.J., the artist's son, to ATS, Aug. 10, 1954, and Henry A. La Farge, the artist's grandson, to ATS, Oct. 29, 1954). See *STJ*, II, 241–42, and Royal Cortissoz, *John La Farge: A Memoir and a Study* (Boston: Houghton Mifflin, 1911), p. vii.

66. *Sun*, Nov. 6, 1910, Sec. 3, p. 4.

67. *Sun*, Dec. 24, 1910, p. 6.

68. *Sun*, Oct. 25, 1908, p. 8. Borglum's article, "Individuality, Sincerity, and Reverence in American Art," appeared in the *Craftsman*, XV (Oct. 1908), 3–6.

69. *Sun*, May 12, 1909, p. 6.

70. *Tribune*, May 11, 1937, p. 16, and unidentified clipping, Los Angeles Public Library.

71. Middleton, pp. 208–9.

72. *Puck*, LXXVI (Dec. 5, 1914), 8.

73. *Promenades*, p. 283. See *Times*, July 27, 1919, Sec. 4, p. 5.

74. Interview, Dec. 6, 1951.

75. Mellquist, p. 238.

76. Me Tsung Kaung Tang, *William Crary Brownell: Literary Adviser* (Philadelphia: University of Pennsylvania, 1946), *passim*. See John Paul Pritchard, *Return to the Fountains* (Durham, N.C.: Duke University Press, 1942), p. 159.

77. See Mellquist, p. 21.

78. Ltr, June 12, 1914 (Scrib).

79. Brooks, *The Confident Years*, pp. 399–400.

80. Ltr, Brownell to JGH, Feb. 15, 1910 (Scrib).

81. See, for example, William Marion Reedy, *Mirror*, XIX (May 26, 1910), 2.

82. Oscar Cargill, *Intellectual America* (New York: Macmillan, 1941), p. 482.

83. *Times*, Sat. Rev., June 25, 1910, p. 359; *Independent*, LIX (Sept. 1, 1910), 48.

84. Ltr, JGH to Mather, June 1, 1910 (Princeton University). The review appeared in the *Nation*, XC (May 26, 1910), 544, and the *Evening Post*, May 28, 1910, pp. 6–7.

85. Ltr, Oct. 10, 1910 (Dart). Cortissoz' review appeared in the *Tribune*, Oct. 9, 1910, Sec. 2, p. 6.

86. *Sun*, Dec. 10, 1907, p. 8.

87. Ltr, Berenson to JGH, May 16, 1910 (Dart).

88. Ltr, JGH to Florence Mosher, Dec. 22, 1903 (Clifton W. Barrett).

89. Ltr, Berenson to ATS, Oct. 21, 1951.

90. Ltr, May 24, 1910, published in ATS, "Irish Author and American Critic," IX, 33.

91. Ltr, Zuloaga to JGH, July 19, 1913 (Dart).

92. Ltrs, May 25 and 28, 1910 (Quinn Collection, NYPL).

93. Ltr, Augustus John to ATS, July 3, 1952.

94. *Sun*, Dec. 4, 1910, Sec. 3, p. 4.

95. *Sun*, April 2, 1911, Sec. 3, p. 4.

96. Mellquist, pp. 197–98.

97. *Sun*, April 13, 1911, p. 8. See Jo Davidson, *Between Sittings* (New (New York: Crowell, 1956), p. 373.

98. *Metropolitan Magazine*, XXXVII (March, 1913), 30–31, 51–52; *LET*, p. 139.

99. *Times*, Nov. 10, 1912, Sec. 5, p. 12; *LET*, p. 137. I have not found the interview in print.

100. *Times*, Jan. 26, 1913, Sec. 5, p. 14.

101. E. P. Richardson, *Painting in America: The Story of 450 Years* (New York: Crowell, 1956), p. 373.

102. Edward L. Bernays, ed., *An Outline of Careers* (New York: George H. Doran, 1927), opp. p. 55.

103. *LET*, p. 148.

104. Walter Pach, *Queer Thing, Painting* (New York: Harper, 1938), pp. 24, 27, 192–93; Myers, pp. 32–35.

105. Mellquist, pp. 220–21.

106. *Tribune*, Feb. 17, 1913, p. 7. See Cortissoz, *Art and Common Sense* (New York: Scribner, 1913), pp. 152–54.

107. Schapiro, p. 204.

108. *Times*, April 3, 1912, p. 1, and April 4, 1913, p. 8; Pach, p. 193.

109. *Times*, May 11, 1913, Sec. 5, p. 13.

110. "The Melancholy of Masterpieces," *Scribner's Magazine*, LVI (July, 1914), 133ff (reprinted in *Ivory Apes and Peacocks*, pp. 251–52, 256, 258). See *Sun*, Feb. 9, 1908, p. 8.

111. *Puck*, LXXVII (Feb. 20, 1915), 9.

112. Maurice Prendergast, Kenneth Miller, and Luks in "The Seven Arts," *Puck*, LXXV (April 11, 1914) (unnumbered page); Alexander Harrison in *Puck*, LXXV (May 30, 1914), 17; and J. H. Twachtman, Ernest Lawson, William M. Chase, and J. Alden Weir in *Puck*, LXXV (May 23, 1914), 21; LXXVII (March 13, 1915), 17; LXXVIII (Sept. 18, 1915), 10; and LXXVIII (Oct. 30, 1915), 10, respectively.

113. "The Seven Arts," *Puck*, LXXV (April 11, 1914).

114. *Ibid.* (April 18, 1914), p. 9. I could not find the prediction in print.

115. Cover, LXXV (March 21, 1914), and "The Seven Arts," April 25, 1914.

116. *Puck*, LXXVI (Oct. 17, 1914), 17, 20–21.

117. *Puck*, LXXV (May 23, 1914), 16.

118. *Puck*, LXXVII (May 1, 1915), 20.

119. Part of Stieglitz' penciled note about "291" inscribed to JGH and dated March 8, 1915 (Dart).

120. *Puck*, LXXVII (May 1, 1915), 20.

121. *LET*, pp. 185, 206.

122. *Puck*, LXXVIII (Nov. 13, 1915), 10.
123. Review of Bell's *Art* in *Puck*, LXXVII (March 13, 1915), 14.
124. Ltr, William Sergeant Kendall, Director of Yale University School of the Fine Arts, to JGH, July 19, 1915 (Dart). There is no record of any lecture there by JGH (ltr, Dean of the Yale University School of Architecture and Design, to ATS, March 12, 1957).

CHAPTER FIFTEEN

1. *INT*, p. 75.
2. Ltr, Perry to JGH, Jan. 25, 1907 (Dart).
3. *INT*, p. 107.
4. *LET*, p. 83.
5. *INT*, pp. 92–93.
6. EHH, interview, May 2, 1950.
7. *LET*, pp. 75–77.
8. De Casseres, "James Huneker: Steeplejack of Culture," p. 83. Elsewhere, De Casseres wrote that this meeting occurred in 1910 (*Musical America*, XXXII [June 5, 1920], p. 3), but 1908 is probably correct. See note 32 below.
9. De Casseres, *James Gibbons Huneker*, p. 11 (first published in *Musical America*, XXXII [June 5, 1920], 3).
10. Benjamin De Casseres, *Nation*, CXV (Nov. 29, 1922), 582.
11. *INT*, p. 101. See *LET*, pp. 85–86.
12. *LET*, p. 74; ltr, JGH to Laffan, Dec. 31, 1908 (Mrs. Edward P. Mitchell).
13. Edward P. Mitchell, p. 381; ltr, JGH to Alden March, Sept. 16, 1918 (Dart).
14. *LET*, pp. 80–81.
15. Ltr, JGH to Laffan, Dec. 31, 1908 (Mrs. Edward P. Mitchell).
16. *Sun*, Dec. 15, 1907, p. 8.
17. Reprinted in Gourmont, pp. 137ff. (JGH reviewed this book in the *Sun*, June 14, 1909, p. 6.)
18. *INT*, p. 109.
19. Reprinted as an introduction to *The Poems and Prose Poems of Charles Baudelaire* (New York: Brentano's, 1919).
20. George Sylvester Viereck, *Confessions of a Barbarian* (New York: Moffat, Yard, 1910), p. 157.
21. Egan, *Recollections*, p. 124.
22. The extant correspondence between the two men is published in chronological sequence in ATS, "Georg Brandes and James Huneker."
23. *STJ*, II, 214.
24. *Sun*, April 25, 1909, Sec. 3, p. 2.
25. Henry-D. Davray, *Mercure de France*, LXXX (July–Aug., 1909), 369–70.

26. *Times*, April 3, 1909, Lit. Sec., p. 196.

27. Springfield *Republican*, April 25, 1909, p. 27.

28. Ltrs, More to JGH, April 6, 1909, and Oct. 2, 1915 (Dart). See *STJ*, II, 236. The earlier ltr suggests the possibility that More did not write the notice of *Egoists* in the *Evening Post* (April 6, 1909, p. 6) which JGH ascribed to him (*LET*, p. 97).

29. *Mirror*, XIX (April 22, 1909), 6; *Outlook*, XCII (June 19, 1909), 419.

30. *Sun*, Aug. 8, 1908, pp. 6–7.

31. Ltr, April 17, 1909 (Historical Society of Pennsylvania).

32. De Casseres, "James Huneker: Steeplejack of Culture," p. 86. De Casseres must have met JGH by the spring of 1909, when this incident probably occurred.

33. Ltr, William James to JGH, April 26, 1909 (Historical Society of Pennsylvania). JGH's ltr, to which this replied, has apparently not survived.

34. *Sun*, June 7, 1909, p. 4; ltr, William James to JGH, June 15, 1909 (Julius Seelye Bixler, "A Letter from William James," *Colby Library Quarterly*, Series III, No. 7 [Aug., 1952], pp. 101–2); the review Bixler cites herein is incorrectly identified as JGH's.

35. Ltr, April 23, 1909 (Mrs. Richard Beamish).

36. *Harvard Advocate*, LXXXVIII (Oct. 5, 1909), 16.

37. Ltr, T. S Eliot to ATS, Jan. 4, 1952.

38. *Yale Review*, N.S., V (Oct. 1915), 201.

39. Brooks, *The Confident Years*, p. 160.

40. Ltr, Ben Hecht to ATS, Sept. 7, 1953.

41. Ltrs, Floyd Dell, Kenneth Burke, and S. N. Behrman to ATS, Oct. 23, 1951, October 24, 1951, and Nov. 29, 1960, respectively; Malcolm Cowley, *Exile's Return* (New York: Viking Press, 1951), p. 22; and Wilson, "Thoughts on Being Bibliographed," pp. 55–57, respectively.

42. Ltrs, JGH to Edward Marsh, Nov. 24, 1909 (Scrib), and JGH to Julia Marlowe, Nov. 24, 1909 (Museum of the City of New York).

43. Unpubl. passage in ltr, JGH to Edward Ziegler, Dec. 11, 1909 (Dart), publ. partially in *INT*, pp. 121–22.

44. See *LET*, p. 105.

45. Ltr owned by Miss Beatrice Fenton of Philadelphia; it was given to her father, Dr. Thomas H. Fenton, by his close friend John Huneker. See ltr, Algernon Rose to Mrs. Josephine Huneker, Feb. 14, 1921 (Dart).

46. *Telegraph*, Dec. 4, 1910, Sec. 2, p. 1.

47. *Etude*, XXVIII (Dec. 1910), 725–26.

48. Weitenkampf, p. 135.

49. For JGH's adverse criticism of the "Muckrakers," see *Sun*, Sept. 23, 1908, p. 6.

50. Ltr, JGH to Dreiser, June 4, 1911 (University of Pennsylvania), partially published in ATS, "James Huneker's Criticism of American Literature," p. 74. Cf. Forgue, pp. 12, 14.

51. Elias, I, 116, 117; III, 976–77.
52. Ltr, JGH to Dreiser, Nov. 8, 1911 (University of Pennsylvania).
53. Elias, I, 117. A copy of the novel, inscribed to JGH, was sold in 1955 (*American Book Prices Current Index*, 1950–55).
54. Ltr, JGH to Dreiser, May 23, 1914 (University of Pennsylvania). A copy of the book, inscribed to JGH, was sold in 1950 (*American Book Prices Current*, 1950).
55. *Puck*, LXXV (June 27, 1914), 21. See Elias, I, 167.
56. *Puck*, LXXIX (Feb. 12, 1916), 10. JGH's annotated copy of the novel, a copy once mentioned by Christopher Morley ("The Bowling Green: The Folder," *Saturday Review of Literature*, X [Aug. 19, 1933], 55), was sold in 1922 (*American Book Prices Current* [1923]).
57. Brooks, *John Sloan*, pp. 38, 189.
58. Philadelphia *Press*, Aug. 2, 1918, p. 8.
59. Elias, I, 282.
60. *INT*, pp. 150, 152.
61. *LET*, p. 116.
62. *INT*, p. 139.
63. See Philip Hale's review, Boston Sunday *Herald*, Nov. 5, 1911, p. 24.
64. Elson, p. 321. For less favorable comments on the book, see Friedheim, pp. 64, 67, 166–67.
65. *Reedy's Mirror*, XX (Sept. 7, 1911), 8.
66. Harrison Hale Schaff, interview, Oct. 22, 1950.
67. "The Literary Show," *Town Topics*, LXI (April 29, 1909), 19.
68. In his copy of *Their Day in Court*, now in the NYPL, JGH underlined the word "Bierce" in Pollard's statement that "someday, perhaps, a twentieth century Baudelaire may discover Bierce," and wrote "oh!" in the margin (p. 454). For JGH's opinion of Bierce, see *MC*, XXXV (Sept. 29, 1897), 23. See Kummer, p. 39.
69. Pollard, pp. 445ff.
70. "The Literary Show," *Town Topics*, LXIII (April 28, 1910), 17.
71. See ATS, "James Huneker's Criticism of American Literature."
72. See "Raconteur," *MC*, XXXVIII (May 10–17, 1899); XXXIX (Dec. 6, 1899), 26; and XL (May 2, 1900), 21–22.
73. Quoted by Kummer, p. 108.
74. Kummer, pp. 98ff.
75. *Sun*, August 13, 1911, p. 6.
76. ATS, "Irish Author and American Critic," IX, 24.
77. See, for example, *MA*, Nov. 15, 1895, p. 4; *Sunday Advertiser*, Nov. 15, 1896, p. 7; *MC*, XLIII (Oct. 30, 1901), 6; ltr, JGH to Edward P. Mitchell, Feb. 23, 1907 (Mrs. Edward P. Mitchell; *LET*, pp. 190, 270; *Unicorns*, p. 3; *STJ*, I, 120, 134, 278, and II, 12, 249; and *Egoists*, pp. 82, 84.
78. *L'Artiste*, Dec. 14, 1856; quoted in Palache, p. 117.
79. Palache, p. 34.
80. Richardson, p. 23.
81. See "In Defense of Pollard," *Mirror*, XX (Oct. 5, 1911), 14.

82. "A Conflict of Critics," *ibid.* (Sept. 21, 1911), p. 2.
83. *Ibid.* (Oct. 5, 1911), p. 13.
84. "Viereck to the Defense," *ibid.* (Oct. 19, 1911), p. 14.
85. Pollard, *Town Topics,* LVII (June 6, 1907), 14–15; JGH, *North American Review,* CLXXXIV (Jan. 18, 1907), 194.
86. Ltr, JGH to Edward Marsh, Jan. 1, 1912 (Scrib).
87. Ltr, JGH to Viereck, Jan. 1, 1912 (Viereck).
88. Kemler, pp. 48–49.
89. *LET,* pp. 209–10.

CHAPTER SIXTEEN

1. William Marion Reedy, "The New *Sun,*" Mirror, XX (Jan. 25, 1912), 3.
2. *LET,* pp. 140–41. JGH states that he also interviewed Lloyd George for the *World* (*LET,* pp. 142–43), but I do not find the interview there during Sept. 1912–March 1913.
3. The correspondence between JGH and Joseph Conrad, together with a detailed account of their relations, is published in ATS, "Joseph Conrad's American Friend." Conrad's ltrs to JGH are at Dart.
4. *LET,* pp. 140–41.
5. *INT,* pp. 83–84.
6. *Times,* Nov. 24, 1912, Sec. 5, p. 11 (reprinted—without the remark about Garden—in *Ivory Apes and Peacocks,* p. 164.
7. EHH recalls that Garden herself told him that she and JGH were "very good friends" for a short time during the Manhattan Opera period (ATS's interview with EHH, May 2, 1950), but she denies the association in ltrs to ATS, Sept. 10, 1950, and Feb. 19, 1954, and the formal, platonic tone of her extant letters to JGH, none dated before 1919, seems to support her denial.
8. George Jean Nathan, interview, April 6, 1951.
9. See "A New Isolde: Olive Fremstad," *Century Magazine,* LXXVII (Nov. 1908), 143–45.
10. *Times,* Nov. 24, 1912, Sec. 5, p. 11 (reprinted in *Ivory Apes and Peacocks,* p. 166).
11. *Times,* March 2, 1913, Sec. 5, p. 6.
12. Her ltrs to JGH and Mrs. Josephine Huneker are at Dart.
13. *LET,* p. 143.
14. See Arthur M. Abell, "When Heifetz, Aged 11, Stormed Musical Berlin," *MC,* CXLV (May 15, 1952), 6–7; his "Berlin's Golden Age of Music," *MC,* CXLIX (April 15, 1954), 6–8; and his ltr to ATS, Aug. 16, 1952. For a less enthusiastic view of Berlin's music, see JGH, *Times,* June 1, 1913, Sec. 5, p. 12.
15. JGH, *Times,* June 1, 1913, Sec. 5, p. 12.
16. *Ibid.,* June 22, 1913, Sec. 5, p. 12.
17. *LET,* p. 126.
18. *LET,* p. 156. EHH has a copy of the program. See ltr, EHH to ATS,

March 22, 1957; *Book Buyer,* XXXVIII (May 1913), 75; and *STJ,* II, 268.

19. Ltr, JGH to Robert Underwood Johnson, Jan. 28, 1913 (NYPL); *LET,* p. 158.

20. *INT,* p. 173.

21. *Times,* Jan. 19, 1912, Sec. 5, p. 9. See JGH, "A Magician of the Orchestra," *Metropolitan Magazine,* XXXVII (Feb. 1913), 27.

22. *Times,* Feb. 2, 1913, Sec. 5, p. 13, and April 13, 1913, Sec. 5, p. 12 (Schnitzler); Feb. 2, 1913, Sec. 5, p. 13, and March 2, 1913, Sec. 5, p. 6 (Sudermann); and Feb. 2, 1913, Sec. 5, p. 13 (Hauptmann).

23. *Ibid.,* March 2, 1913, Sec. 5, p. 6.

24. *Ibid.,* June 22, 1913, Sec. 5, p. 12.

25. *LET,* p. 153.

26. Remy de Gourmont, *La Culture des Idées* (1900), 18th ed. (Paris: *Mercure de France* [1926], p. ix.

27. *Reedy's Mirror,* XXII (June 6, 1913), 5.

28. *Yale Review,* N.S., II (April 1914), 596.

29. *Bookman* (London), XLIV (Sept. 1913), 270.

30. *LET,* p. 156.

31. First published in *Etude,* XXI (Dec. 1903), 472. Cf. *MC,* XXI (Nov. 5, 1890), 452.

32. *INT,* p. 154.

33. *Old Fogy,* p. 16.

34. *Ibid.,* p. 98.

35. First published as "A Seminary for Music Critics," *MC,* XXXV (Sept. 1, 1897), 18–19. JGH's copy of the book (NYPL) contains further identifications of the characters.

36. *Old Fogy,* p. 99.

37. *Ibid.,* p. 115.

38. Mencken, *Prejudices: Third Series,* p. 71. See Mencken, *Smart Set,* LIII (Dec. 1917), 140.

39. *INT,* p. 153; *Etude,* XXX (Nov. 1912), 769. See reviews in *Sun,* Dec. 13, 1913, p. 10, and *Times,* Feb. 22, 1914, Lit. Sec., p. 84.

40. Ltr, JGH to William C. Brownell, Aug. 23, 1917 (Scrib), and statement from Presser Co., Oct. 1, 1921 (Dart).

41. *Old Fogy,* p. 9.

42. *LET,* p. 154; a passage omitted from the published version of the ltr gives more details about the suit (Dart). The Heine-Liszt material, compiled by Andrew De Ternant, had been reprinted from the London *Magazine of Music* in *MC,* XXIX (Aug. 22, 1894), 16–17; JGH used it verbatim in *Franz Liszt,* pp. 234–41.

43. *LET,* p. 156.

44. *Saturday Review,* CXVI (Dec. 6, 1913), 708–9.

45. *Times,* Jan. 4, 1914, Sec. 5, p. 11.

46. *Gaelic-American,* Jan. 10, 1914, pp. 1, 8.

47. Ltr, JGH to Charles J. Rosebault, June 20, 1913 (Dart).

48. *Times,* March 8, 1914, Sec. 5, p. 7.

49. Ltr, JGH to Willard Huntington Wright, late Aug. 1913 (Yale University).

50. *Times*, Jan. 4, 1914, Sec. 5, p. 11; *INT*, p. 173. Cf. *Times*, Sept. 4, 1913, p. 2, to date JGH's second visit to Dublin.

51. *STJ*, I, 288.

52. Dart.

53. *Melomaniacs*, p. 326.

54. March 16, 1908, p. 4, and July 10, 1910, Sec. 3, p. 2. See *New Cosmopolis*, p. 238.

55. *LET*, p. 121.

56. JGH, "Skulls and Crossbones and Nine-Leaved Clover," *Forum*, LII (July 1914), 1–9, and *Times*, March 8, 1914, Sec. 5, p. 7.

57. *Times*, Jan. 12, 1913, Sec. 5, p. 15.

58. *INT*, p. 172.

59. Ltr, Kappers to Scribner's, Oct. 16, 1921 (Scrib).

60. *New Cosmopolis*, p. 249.

61. *Sun*, Nov. 26, 1916, Sec. 6, p. 8, and March 4, 1917, p. 16, respectively.

62. *Sun*, Oct. 29, 1916, Sec. 6, p. 8 (reprinted in *Unicorns*, p. 156).

63. See Harry Hansen, *World*, Nov. 2, 1929, p. 15.

64. *Sun*, March 18, 1907, p. 6 (reprinted in *Promenades of an Impressionist*, p. 260).

65. Mencken, "Introduction," *Essays by James Huneker*, p. xiii.

66. *LET*, p. 213.

67. See Hoffman, pp. 96, 273.

68. *Ibid.*, pp. 43ff.

69. *Puck*, LXXVI (Nov. 7, 1914), 17.

70. *Ibid.*, LXXX (Aug. 19, 1916), 12 (reprinted in *Unicorns*, pp. 259–60).

71. *Times*, Sept. 28, 1919, Sec. 4, p. 7 (reprinted in *Variations*, p. 39).

72. *INT*, p. 292.

73. See Hoffman, pp. 277–78.

74. *World*, Nov. 16, 1919, Metro. Sec., p. 6.

75. Byrne, pp. 300, 302; ltr, Mrs. Josephine Huneker to Maxwell Perkins, Feb. 25, 1922 (Scrib).

76. *LET*, p. 163, and ltr, Vyvyan Holland to ATS, Aug. 31, 1953.

77. *LET*, p. 164. See JGH, *Times*, June 21, 1914, Sec. 5, p. 11.

78. JGH, Philadelphia *Public Ledger*, Jan. 18, 1914, Mag. Sec., p. 7.

79. *LET*, pp. 165–66.

CHAPTER SEVENTEEN

1. Nathan Straus, Jr., interview, Sept 10, 1952. Straus is the authority—via this interview and correspondence—for all statements about *Puck* not otherwise documented.

2. *Puck*, LXXV (Jan. 14, 1914), inside front cover.

3. *Ibid.* (May 2, 1914), p. 9. JGH had discussed the book in the *Sun*, June 25, 1911, p. 8.

4. *Puck*, LXXV (July 4, 1914), 16, 21.

5. See ATS, "Georg Brandes and James Huneker," p. 35ff.

6. *Puck*, LXXVI (Jan. 2, 1915), 21.

7. *Times*, July 16, 1916, Sec. 5, p. 13 (reprinted in *Unicorns*, pp. 82–95). Howells' ltr—which I have not found—is partially quoted in *STJ*, II, 240. See ltr, JGH to William C. Brownell, Aug. 19, 1916 (Scrib).

8. *Puck*, LXXIX (May 13, 1916), 12.

9. Ltr, Brooks to ATS, Aug. 13, 1954.

10. *Puck*, LXXVII (April 24, 1915), 22.

11. *Puck*, LXXVI (Oct. 10, 1914), 17.

12. *Puck*, LXXVIII (Dec. 11, 1915), 12, 22.

13. *Times*, Oct. 4, 1914, Sec. 4, p. 10.

14. "The Seven Arts," *Puck*, LXXV (April 11, 1914).

15. *Puck*, LXXX (Oct. 28, 1916), 12.

16. Chicago *Tribune*, Oct. 29, 1922, Sec. 7, p. 21.

17. In ltr to Scribner's Nov. 8, 1934, Mrs. Josephine Huneker states that she had a ltr from Straus to JGH in which he quoted Brisbane's remark (Scrib); I have not seen this ltr.

18. Edward Anthony, *O Rare Don Marquis* (New York: Doubleday, 1962), p. 544. See "Suetonius Saltash" (Benjamin De Casseres?), review of *Bedouins*, *Morning Telegraph*, March 14, 1920, Sec. 3, p. 4.

19. *Evening Sun*, June 18, 1915, p. 10.

20. See undated ltr (Nov.? 1916), Straus to JGH (Dart).

21. Ltr, Straus to ATS, June 10, 1952.

22. Saarinen, pp. 206, 232, 236.

23. Ltr, JGH to Quinn, April 14, 1914 (Dart); *LET*, p. 167.

24. Brooks, *John Sloan*, pp. 75–76.

25. See *LET*, pp. 112–13. I could not find the piece in the *Evening Sun*.

26. Hackenburg, pp. 77, 95–96.

27. S. N. Behrman, *The Worcester Account* (New York: Random House, 1954), p. 157; ltr, Behrman to ATS, June 21, 1961.

28. Ernest Seute, former headwaiter at Lüchow's, interview, Jan. 1, 1961.

29. Ltr, Hugo Schemke, longtime waiter at Lüchow's, to ATS, May 30, 1952.

30. Ltr, Sterne to ATS, Nov. 8, 1951.

31. De Casseres, "James Huneker: Steeplejack of Culture," p. 81.

32. *STJ*, I, 1960, and Brister, p. 57.

33. Ltr, JGH to Julia Heinrich, Aug. 15, 1916 (Edith C. Heinrich).

34. *Puck*, LXXVI (Aug. 1, 1914), 8.

35. *Ibid.* (Oct. 3, 1914), 8.

36. *Ibid.* (Oct. 31, 1914), 8.

37. *Ibid.*
38. *MC*, XLIII (Oct. 30, 1901), 5; *Sun*, Dec. 23, 1911, p. 6.
39. Saarinen, p. 218.
40. Ltr, JGH to Quinn, Oct. 29, 1915 (Dart).
41. *Sun*, June 26, 1909, p. 6.
42. Hackenburg, p. 98; date confirmed in ltr, Hackenburg to ATS, Nov. 22, 1951.
43. Ltr, Ralph S. Thompson (Vance's brother) to ATS, Dec. 29, 1955.
44. *Puck*, LXXVIII (Dec. 18, 1915), 12, 22–23.
45. *Times*, July 11, 1915, Sec. 4, p. 14.
46. *Sun*, Dec. 31, 1916, Sec. 6, p. 8.
47. Jim Tully, *A Dozen and One* (Hollywood, Calif.: Murray & Gee, 1943), p. 240.
48. *Puck*, LXXVI (Aug. 29, 1914), 21, and LXXVIII (Oct. 16, 1915), 18.
49. Ltrs, EHH to ATS, Aug. 10, 1954, and Aug. 25, 1954. For Bracken's part in the movement, see Boston *Journal*, May 7, 1912, p. 15.
50. *Puck*, LXXVI (July 25, 1914), 8.
51. Postcard, JGH to Dr. Thomas C. Williams (his physician), July 27, 1911 (Dart); *INT*, pp. 295–96.
52. Entire section based on my correspondence and interviews with "Lydia Barrington," beginning in 1950. The interviews occurred in Oct. 1950, Sept. 1952, and June 1956.
53. *Times*, Aug. 2, Sec. 5, p. 5; Aug. 9, Sec. 5, p. 8; Aug. 30, Sec. 4, p. 9; Sept. 6, Sec. 4, p. 10; Sept. 13, Sec. 4, p. 8; Sept. 27, Sec. 4, p. 5; and Oct. 4, Sec. 4, p. 10.
54. *Times*, March 28, 1915, Lit. Sec., p. 113. See *New Cosmopolis*, p. 40.
55. Holliday, p. 126.
56. W. H. Chesson, Sept. 3, 1915, p. 4, and *Athenaeum*, Nov. 6, 1915, p. 327.
57. *New Republic*, V (Nov. 20, 1915), 22.
58. Ltr, Philip Hale to JGH, Dec. 19, 1915 (Dart).
59. Ltr, JGH to Edward Burlingame, Sept. 30, 1914 (Scrib).
60. See Ramsey, *passim.*
61. See *New Republic*, V (Nov. 20, 1915), Supp., p. 22, and Lawrence Gilman, "The Book of the Month," *North American Review*, CCII (Nov. 1915), 772.
62. Pattee, p. 439.
63. Quinn Collection, NYPL (published in ATS, "Joseph Conrad's American Friend," p. 230).
64. *LET*, p. 196. See *Times*, Oct. 24, 1915, Sec. 4, p. 13.
65. *LET*, pp. 177–78, where Luks's name—supplied in the transcript copy of the ltr (Dart)—is omitted. See ltr, JGH to Charles Mielatz, the etcher, Jan. 26, 1915 (NYPL).

66. *Vanity Fair*, III (Nov. 1914), 54. The caricature, entitled "Our James 1925," is reproduced in the limited (illustrated) edition of *LET*, where it is described as having been "shown at the 'Armory Show' of 1913" (op. p. 156). In *Vanity Fair* it was labeled "from an anticipatory water color portrait," but the portrait was apparently never completed (Luks's ltr to Mrs. Josephine Huneker, postmarked Feb. 22, 1931 [Dart]). Another portrait by Luks of Huneker with Gregg and their friend James Moore was reproduced in *Vanity Fair*, XLI (Jan. 1934), 21.

67. *Times*, May 25, 1919, p. 1. JGH's notebook contains an entry on the accident, but his date is wrong (Dart).

68. *Puck*, LXXIX (Jan. 22, 1916), 12, 24.

69. Neilson, *My Life in Two Worlds*, I, 124.

70. *Metropolitan Magazine*, "Personalities," XXVI (April 1907), 77.

71. JGH, *Times*, Jan. 10, 1919, p. 11.

72. *STJ*, II, 142.

73. *LET*, p. 202.

74. Except where otherwise noted, the following account of the relations between JGH and Nathan is based on my correspondence with Nathan, which began in 1949, and on an interview with him that took place on April 6, 1951. Four ltrs (three of them unpublished) from JGH to him— which were apparently mislaid during Nathan's lifetime—turned up in the Nathan papers bequeathed to Cornell University.

75. Ltr, Nathan Straus to ATS, April 30, 1957. The chronology given in Goldberg, p. 63, is incorrect.

76. Goldberg, p. 59, confirmed by Mencken (ltr, Edgar Kemler to ATS, Oct. 30, 1950).

77. Pamphlet entitled "A Note to Authors," apparently by Mencken and Nathan (Mencken Collection, Pratt Library, Baltimore).

78. Forgue, p. 15.

79. Dart.

80. *Smart Set*, XXVIII (June 1909), 153.

81. *Ibid.*, XLI (Oct. 1913), 153–55.

82. "Grindstones," *ibid.* (Nov. 1913), pp. 85–88, and "Where the Black Mass Was Heard" (Dec. 1913), pp. 63–66. Both stories were reprinted in *Bedouins*, the latter under the title of "The Vision Malefic." Letters concerning these stories, from JGH to Willard Huntington Wright, are at Yale.

83. "His Best Friend," *Smart Set*, XLV (March 1915), 223–25; "Venus or Valkyr?" XLIX (June 1916), 105–12; "Brothers-in-Law," L (Sept. 1916), 251–56; and "A Modern Montsalvat," LI (Feb. 1917), 373–77. "Venus or Valkyr?" and "Brothers-in-Law" were reprinted in *Bedouins*, and "His Best Friend" and "A Modern Montsalvat" in *STJ* under slightly different titles (II, 217–23 and 99–108, respectively).

84. Edgar Kemler's notes of a talk with Mencken on Oct. 3, 1946 (sent to me by Kemler in 1950).

85. Ltr, August Mencken (for his brother) to ATS, June 4, 1952; ltr, JGH to Willard Huntington Wright, July 31, 1913, in which JGH seems to refer to a recent meeting with Wright and Mencken (Yale University). See the necessarily vague statement in Kemler, p. 46. In 1951, when I examined them, JGH's ltrs to Mencken were partly in Mencken's possession and partly in the Enoch Pratt Free Library of Baltimore (inserted in copies of JGH's books presented by Mencken to the library). I have not located Mencken's ltrs to JGH. Statements not otherwise documented are based on my interview with Mencken on Nov. 23, 1951, when, however, his memory was affected by his illness.

86. Apart from his ltr of thanks for the review of *Iconoclasts* (May 31, 1905), the earliest extant ltr of JGH's correspondence with Mencken is dated Nov. 24, 1914 (Mencken).

87. *Puck*, LXXVI (Oct. 3, 1914), 8.

88. Manchester, pp. 65–66.

89. Mencken, "Huneker: A Memory," *Prejudices*, pp. 66–68 (reprinted through the kindness of Alfred A. Knopf, Inc., copyright 1922, 1949).

90. Mencken, "James Huneker," p. 197, and "Introduction," *Essays by James Huneker*, p. xv.

91. *LET*, p. 203.

92. *Puck*, LXXIX (Feb. 12, 1916), 18.

93. "The Prometheus of the Western World," *Smart Set*, XLVI (July 1915), 446.

94. "Professor at the Bat," *ibid.*, L (Nov. 1916), 282.

95. *Century Magazine*, p. 195. See Mencken, *A Book of Prefaces*, p. 183.

96. See *LET*, p. 220.

97. *Sun*, Nov. 5, 1916, Sec. 6, p. 8.

98. "Lydia Barrington," interview. See Isaac Goldberg, *The Man Mencken* (New York: Simon & Schuster, 1925), p. 181; Benjamin De Casseres, *Mencken and Shaw* (New York: Silas Newton, 1930), p. 39; and Brooks, *The Confident Years*, p. 465.

99. See Kemler, p. 123.

100. *LET*, pp. 209–10.

CHAPTER EIGHTEEN

1. Editorial notice, *Puck*, LXXIX (June 10, 1916), 3.

2. Ltr, JGH to John Quinn, Jan. 3, 1917 (Dart).

3. See *Sun*, Aug. 3, 1916, p. 1.

4. *LET*, p. 227.

5. *Scribner's Magazine*, LX, 603–14. It was reprinted as "A Prima Donna's Family" in *STJ*, II, 72–87. See *LET*, p. 222.

6. Ltr, JGH to Edward Marsh, Nov. 7, 1915 (Dart).

7. Ltr, Joseph S. Buhler, Ditrichstein's attorney, to ATS, Sept. 14, 1954. Buhler negotiated the contract.

8. See ltr, JGH to Mitchell, Aug. 4, 1916 (Mrs. Edward P. Mitchell).

9. JGH sailed for Havana on Sept. 2 and returned on Sept. 19 (notebook, Dart). For his impressions of Cuba, see *Times*, Oct. 15, 1916, Sec. 5, pp. 17–18.

10. Both manuscripts are owned by Josephine Huneker's niece, Mrs. John L. Lonergan. A holograph scenario of *All's Fair in Love and Air*, entitled *All's Fair in War*, is at Dart.

11. *Sun*, Aug. 2, 1916, p. 14. See ltr, JGH to Mitchell, Aug. 2, 1916 (Mrs. Edward P. Mitchell), and *LET*, p. 219.

12. Ltr, William McFee to ATS, May 22, 1950.

13. See Gilbert, p. 46; John J. Slocum and Herbert Cahoon, *A Bibliography of James Joyce* (New Haven, Conn.: Yale University Press, 1953), p. 137; and John Quinn, "James Joyce, a New Irish Novelist," *Vanity Fair*, VIII (May 1917), 49, 128.

14. Ltr (Huebsch).

15. *Sun*, Feb. 18, 1917, p. 16.

16. Ltr, JGH to Quinn, May 24, 1917 (Dart). Joyce's ltr to JGH (see *STJ*, II, 247) has not turned up, but Joyce mentions JGH's review in a ltr to Ezra Pound, April 9, 1917 (Gilbert, p. 101).

17. See Alan Parker, *James Joyce: A Bibliography of his Writings, Critical Material and Miscellanea* (Boston: F. W. Faxon, 1948), p. 142.

18. Justin O'Brien, *Portrait of André Gide* (New York: Knopf, 1953), pp. 33–34.

19. Ltr, JGH to Quinn, April 11, 1917 (misdated 1913 on copy at Dart).

20. *INT*, p. 148 (ltr misdated 1912).

21. Philadelphia *Press*, Sept. 9, 1918, p. 8 (reprinted in *STJ*, II, 112).

22. JGH says 1914 (*INT*, p. 313), but the outbreak of war probably delayed it. The translation is dated "1914/1917," and a review appears in the *Deutsche Warschauer Zeitung*, Oct. 19, 1917, fifth page.

23. *INT*, p. 314.

24. Manchester, pp. 88, 91, 102ff; Kemler, pp. 94–95.

25. Ltr, April 17, 1917 (Pratt Library, Baltimore).

26. *LET*, p. 210.

27. Charles Hanson Towne, ed., *For France* (Garden City, N.Y.: Doubleday, Page & Co., 1917), p. x. Others among the contributors were the late Richard Harding Davis, Owen Wister, George Ade, Edwin Markham, Gertrude Atherton, Ida M. Tarbell, Augustus Thomas, Lizette Woodworth Reese, Brander Matthews, Hamlin Garland, Edgar Saltus, John Jay Chapman, Rupert Hughes, John Sloan, William Glackens, Ernest Lawson, and Gutzon Borglum.

28. *Evening Mail*, p. 12. See *INT*, p. 205. Ltrs JGH wrote to Willard Huntington Wright, literary editor of the *Mail*, regarding this article are at Yale.

29. *LET*, p. 232.

30. Manchester, p. 102.

31. Ltr, April 7, 1917 (EHH).

32. Ltr, Zangwill to JGH, Nov. 6, 1917 (Yale University).

33. "Idealism à Rebours," *Nation*, CV (Oct. 11, 1917), 403, identified as More's by Arthur Hazard Dakin, *A Paul Elmer More Miscellany* (Portland, Me.: Anthoensen Press, 1950), p. 170.

34. Mencken, "Critics Wild and Tame," *Smart Set*, LIII (Dec., 1917), 139.

35. Ltr, Dec. 2, 1917 (Mencken; copy at Dart).

36. Stuart P. Sherman, "Beautifying American Literature," *Nation*, CV (Nov. 29, 1917), 593–94.

37. "The Seven Arts," *Puck*, LXXV (April 11, 1914); LXXVII (April 17, 1915), 11; (May 8, 1915), 10; and (April 17, 1915), 20, respectively.

38. *Puck*, LXXV (April 18, 1914), 9.

39. *Puck*, LXXVI (Dec. 12, 1914), 20, and (Jan. 16, 1915), 8, 20.

40. *Times*, July 4, 1915, Sec. 4, p. 14. A German translation of the article appeared in *Der Merker*, VI² (Sept. 1, 1915), 591–98.

41. *Unicorns*, p. 184; Clara Clemens, *My Husband Gabrilowitsch* (New York: Harper, 1938), pp. 127–28; and ltr, Clara Clemens Samossoud to ATS, Dec. 15, 1960. See JGH, "Master Artists of the Piano," *Everybody's Magazine*, XVI (April 1907), 559.

42. *LET*, p. 208.

43. See JGH, *Times*, Nov. 10, 1918, Sec. 4, p. 4.

44. *Town Topics*, XLVII (April 10, 1902), 14; *MC*, XLV (July 2, 1902), 18.

45. Legal documents (Dart).

46. *LET*, p. 224.

47. LXXVI (May 9, 1918), 21; *INT*, p. 219. See ltrs, JGH to Leifels, May 5, 1918, and to Krehbiel, May 29, 1918 (Dart).

48. The Steinway Company has no record of the project, but the original paintings are still at Steinway Hall (ltr, Theodore Steinway to ATS, Feb. 14, 1955). See advertisements (on unnumbered pages) in *Century Magazine*, CI (Nov. 1920–April 1921) and CIII (Nov. 1921–April 1922).

49. *Programme Notes*, Philadelphia Symphony Orchestra, 1917–18, Third Program (Oct. 26–27, 1917), p. 110.

50. Linton Martin, music critic of the Philadelphia *Inquirer*, interview, April 4, 1950.

51. *LET*, p. 233.

52. *INT*, p. 207.

53. *MC*, XXII (April 29, 1891), 413.

54. Mencken, *A Book of Prefaces*, p. 164; Philadelphia *Public Ledger*, Oct. 20, 1917, p. 6.

55. *Puck*, LXXX (Aug. 19, 1916), 12.

56. *MC*, XXXVII (Sept. 14, 1898), 15.

57. *LET*, p. 238.

58. Ltr, JGH to Edward Marsh, Nov. 6, 1914 (Scrib).

59. *STJ*, I, 89.

60. *Puck*, LXXVII (Feb. 6, 1915), 9.

61. See Christopher Morley and T. A. Daly, *The House of Dooner: The Last of the Friendly Inns* (Philadelphia: David McKay, 1928), *passim*.

62. Ltrs, Mrs. Richard Beamish to ATS, June 11, 1950; Sept. 7, 1952; and Nov. 16, 1952.

63. Ltr, Theodocia Walton Bird to ATS, Jan. 25, 1951.

64. Ltr, Glazer to ATS, Aug. 28, 1950.

65. Philadelphia *Press*, March 23, 1918, p. 9. See also *Press*, Nov. 10, 1917, p. 4.

66. "Is There an American Type of Feminine Beauty?" *Everybody's Magazine*, XVII (Aug. 1907), 244.

67. Ltr, Frances Starr to ATS, Sept. 11, 1953. See JGH's review, Philadelphia *Press*, Feb. 28, 1918, p. 9. For an earlier—perhaps his earliest—criticism of Miss Starr as an actress, see *Puck*, LXXVII (April 10, 1915), 14.

68. *LET*, pp. 237, 245. See JGH, *Puck*, LXXVII (March 6, 1915), 9, and *Times*, April 25, 1915, Sec. 5, p. 16.

69. "Grand Opera as the Public Hears It," *Success Magazine*, VIII (March 1905), 152. See *Puck*, LXXX (July 29, 1916), 10.

70. Ltr, Chalmers to ATS, Dec. 24, 1953.

71. Philadelphia *Press*, Dec. 30, 1917, Sec. 4, p. 4 (reprinted in *Bedouins*, pp. 134–43); ltr, Caruso to JGH, Nov. 13, 1920 (Dart).

72. *Times*, March 23, 1919, p. 3.

73. Ltr, Benjamin F. Glazer to ATS, Aug. 28, 1950.

74. *LET*, p. 252. A copy of *STJ*, with the original contract for serial publication laid in, was sold in 1955 (*American Book Prices Current*, 1954–55); it has not turned up.

75. *LET*, p. 253.

76. Ltr, June 17, 1918 (Dart).

77. Philadelphia *Press*, June 23, 1918, p. 10.

78. *LET*, p. 258.

79. Dart.

80. *LET*, pp. 259–60.

81. *INT*, pp. 220, 224, 226, 246; *LET*, pp. 250, 253, 255, 259, 260; ltr, JGH to Alden March, July 30, 1918 (Dart).

82. *INT*, p. 220.

83. Ltr, Neil MacNeil to Luther Ely Smith, quoted by Mrs. David R. Sparks (Chase's niece) in her ltr to ATS, May 26, 1952. MacNeil's ltr was part of an Amherst "Class Letter," a memorial written by Chase's friends. MacNeil confirmed this account of Chase's generosity (interview, May 7, 1952).

84. *LET*, p. 264.

85. *Times*, Oct. 27, 1918, Sec. 8, p. 4.

86. See David Ewen, *Music Comes to America* (New York: Crowell, 1942), pp. 139–40.

87. Irving Kolodin, *The Story of the Metropolitan Opera, 1883–1950* (New York: Knopf, 1953), p. 287.

88. Paolo Gallico, interview, Jan. 3, 1951.

89. Unlabeled clipping, Theater Collection, NYPL.

90. Viereck, "Let Us Remember James Gibbons Huneker," p. 18. See Viereck's *My Flesh and Blood*, p. 298.

91. *Times*, Nov. 16, 1918, p. 11.

92. Ltr, Mme Ponselle to ATS, Oct. 2, 1953.

93. Ltrs, Glazer to ATS, Aug. 28, 1950, and Nov. 24, 1955.

94. *Times*, Nov. 21, 1918, p. 13.

95. *Times*, Dec. 11, 1918, p. 13, and Dec. 12, 1918, p. 13.

96. "The Raconteur," *MC*, XXXVIII (May 10–17, 1899).

97. *Times*, Dec. 22, 1918, p. 17.

98. *Times*, Feb. 21, 1919, p. 11.

99. *Times*, March 16, 1919, p. 20.

100. *MC*, LXXVIII (Feb. 27, 1919), 21.

101. Mrs. Richard Aldrich, interview, April 30, 1950.

102. Ltr, Dr. Sigmund Spaeth to ATS, May 28, 1950.

103. T. R. Ybarra, interview, Nov. 16, 1951.

104. Neil MacNeil, interview, May 7, 1952.

105. MacNeil, same interview.

106. *MC*, LXXVII (Dec. 26, 1918), 10.

107. *Times*, Dec. 15, 1918, p. 4.

108. Mencken, *Prejudices*, p. 81.

109. *INT*, pp. 312–13. See Mencken, *Smart Set*, LXII (Dec. 1920), 141, and "Introduction," *Essays by James Huneker*, p. xix.

110. Richardson, p. 158.

111. H. L. Mencken, *The American Language*, 4th ed. (New York: Knopf, 1947), p. 63.

112. Charles Angoff, *H. L. Mencken: A Portrait from Memory* (New York: Thomas Yoseloff, 1956), pp. 69–70.

113. Kemler, p. 153.

114. *INT*, p. 239.

115. Kemler, p. 153. But see postcard, JGH to Mencken, June 12, 1920 (Dart), and Forgue, p. 161.

116. Nathan, p. 83. Nathan dates the incident and identifies the lady as " 'La Belle Susca,' otherwise Sally Verneux" (undated postcard to ATS, postmarked Nov. 30, 1953).

117. See "The Drama of the Month," *Metropolitan Magazine*, XXV (Nov. 1906), 254.

118. Ltr, James M. Cain to ATS, Sept. 3, 1953.

119. Garden and Biancolli, pp. 25–27.

120. *MC*, XXX (Jan. 23, 1895), 15.

121. Ltrs, Mary Garden to ATS, Sept. 10, 1950, and Feb. 19, 1954; five ltrs, Mary Garden to JGH, none dated before 1919 (Dart) ; *Times*, Feb. 16, 1919, Sec. 4, p. 5.

122. Ltr, JGH to Mrs. Harry Rowe Shelley, Feb. 2, 1919 (American Academy of Arts and Letters).

123. *Times*, March 2, 1919, Sec. 4, p. 4 (reprinted in *Bedouins*, pp. 19–20).

124. *Times*, Feb. 2, 1919, Sec. 4. p. 4.

125. *Times*, Feb. 6, 1919, p. 9.

126. Undated ltr (Dart).

127. George Jean Nathan, *The World of George Jean Nathan*, ed. Charles Angoff (New York: Knopf, 1952), pp. 251–52. Nathan said "sandpaper," but he may have meant sand soap.

128. *Times*, Feb. 16, 1919, Sec. 4, p. 5 (reprinted in *Bedouins*, p. 22).

129. Ltr, JGH to John Quinn, Dec. 26, 1914 (Dart).

130. *Times*, Sec. 4, p. 5.

131. George Jean Nathan, *The Critic and the Drama* (New York: Knopf, 1922), p. 56.

132. Garden and Biancolli, p. 111. See JGH, *World*, Jan. 23, 1921, Metro. Sec., p. 2.

133. See Garden's five ltrs to JGH (Dart). Frances Starr, the star of *Tiger! Tiger!*, recalls that the Hunekers and Garden visited her backstage (ltr to ATS, Sept. 11, 1953).

134. *LET*, pp. 277–78.

135. Interview, Nov. 7, 1950. See Mary Garden, *Musical Observer*, XX (March 1921), 13.

CHAPTER NINETEEN

1. Ltrs in possession of EHH.

2. Ltr, May 18, 1919 (Dart).

3. Ltr, April 27, 1919 (Scrib).

4. Ltr, Scribner's to ATS, No. 15, 1949.

5. Legal documents (Dart).

6. *INT*, p. 249.

7. *Melomaniacs*, p. 238.

8. Ltrs, JGH to Frida Ashforth, March 13, 1905 (Dart), and to Robert MacKay, June 1, 1905 (Boston Public Library).

9. The undated MS is at Dart. "Jet" is mentioned in a list of projects headed "Schedule, 1906" (Dart).

10. *LET*, pp. 145–46.

11. *LET*, p. 188.

12. *LET*, pp. 192, 203; *INT*, p. 198; ltrs, JGH to Mencken, Sept. 2, 1915; Nov. 7, 1916; and April 17, 1917 (Pratt Library, Baltimore).

13. *LET*, p. 283.

14. *INT*, p. 292.

15. *INT*, p. 304.

16. Mencken, *Prejudices*, p. 79.

17. *INT*, p. 294.

18. *INT*, pp. 270–71.

19. Chicago *Daily News*, Dec. 8, 1920, p. 13.

20. Ltr, Jan. 4, 1921 (Burton Rascoe).

21. *Times*, April 14, 1915, p. 13.

22. Interview, Feb. 9, 1956.

23. Saint-Gaudens talked of *hearing* about the party (ltr, Homer Saint-Gaudens, the sculptor's son, to ATS, Feb. 5, 1955).

24. *World*, Oct. 13, 1895, p. 29. See *World*, Oct. 20, 1895, pp. 19, 33.

25. *Town Topics*, XXXIV (Oct. 17, 1895), 9.

26. Churchill, p. 73.

27. See Frederick Townsend Martin, *The Passing of the Idle Rich* (Garden City, N.Y.: Doubleday, Page, 1911), p. 55.

28. Except where otherwise noted, this account of the Holy Rollers is based on interviews with a number of inhabitants of the White Mountain area during August 25–28, 1955, and on correspondence with Jesse A. Barney, Mrs. Charles Davis, Elmer Munson Hunt (director of the New Hampshire Historical Society), Grover C. Loud, Mrs. David Sparks, Shepherd Vogelgesang, and Mrs. Helen J. Young. Especially informative was the interview, on August 28, 1955, with James Elwin Wright, son of the founder of the sect.

29. *Coos County Democrat*, Dec. 30, 1908, p. 1.

30. See JGH, *Herald*, Sept. 9, 1906, Sec. 3, p. 7.

31. Loud, p. 288.

32. Ltr, Loud to ATS, Feb. 15, 1955.

33. *Herald*, Sept. 9, 1906, Sec. 3, p. 7.

34. *STJ*, II, 227.

35. *LET*, p. 307.

36. *Painted Veils*, p. 103. All references to the novel are to Liveright's "Black and Gold Library" edition, first published in 1932.

37. *Forum*, LV (March, 1916), 297–312. See *LET*, p. 187.

38. *Painted Veils*, p. 133.

39. See *STJ*, II, 119.

40. *MC*, XXXIII (Aug. 26, 1896), 16–19. The story was reprinted as "Venus or Valkyr?" in *Smart Set*, XLIX (June 1916), 105–12, and in *Bedouins*, pp, 225–46.

41. *MC*, XXXIII (Oct. 7, 1896), 20–22.

42. Ltrs, JGH to Burton Rascoe, Jan. 4, 1921 (Burton Rascoe), and EHH to ATS, Sept. 21–22, 1953; Aug. 3, 1954; and Nov. 20, 1960.

43. Ltrs, EHH to ATS, March 14, 1952; Sept. 21–22, 1953; April 21, 1957; and May 7, 1957. See *Times*, May 21, 1917, p. 11.

44. Forgue, p. 216.

45. *Painted Veils*, p. 21.

46. *Ibid.*, pp. 186, 263, 274, respectively.

47. *Ibid.*, pp. 131–32; ltr, EHH to ATS, March 14, 1952.

48. Burton Rascoe's identification of her as "a model for Saint-Gaudens . . . immortalized as the Psyche atop the Plaza Fountain" (paperback reprint of *Painted Veils* [New York: Avon, 1953], p. 277) is incorrect, as Rascoe admits in his ltr to me, Jan. 4, 1956, in which he identifies her instead (without furnishing his source) as the model for the Diana placed on the tower of the old Madison Square Garden. Georgiana Carhart recalled that the model for this was her friend Dudie(?) Baird, of whose shaky reputation JGH, she said, was aware (interview, Feb. 9, 1956), but Homer Saint-Gaudens declares that he never heard of Dudie Baird, and is sure that she was not the model for the Diana (ltr to ATS, Feb. 17, 1956).

49. *Painted Veils*, p. 177.

50. *INT*, pp. 310–11.

51. Mencken, *Prejudices*, p. 71.

52. *Painted Veils*, pp. 137–43.

53. *Ibid.*, p. 43.

54. *Ibid.*, p. 239.

55. *Ibid.*, p. 180.

56. *Ibid.*, pp. 182ff.

57. Ltr, JGH to Horace B. Liveright, Dec. 7, 1920 (Dart).

58. Frederick J. Hoffman, *The Modern Novel in America, 1900–1950* (Chicago: Henry Regnery, 1951), p. 117.

59. Carl Van Vechten, *Sacred and Profane Memories* (New York: Knopf, 1932), p. 63.

60. Clark, pp. 117–18.

61. *INT*, p. 258.

62. *INT*, p. 269.

63. *INT*, pp. 256–57.

64. *LET*, p. 285.

65. Forgue, pp. 161–62.

66. Ltr, Nov. 23, 1919 (Dart).

67. See *INT*, pp. 263, 273; ltr, JGH to John Quinn, Feb. 8, 1920 (Dart) and ltrs, Alfred A. Knopf to ATS, Sept. 30, 1953, and Jan. 4, 1954.

68. *Jurgen and the Censors: Report of the Emergency Committee Organized to Protest Against the Suppression of James Branch Cabell's Jurgen* (New York: privately printed for the Emergency Committee [Edward Hale Bierstadt, Barrett H. Clark, Sidney Howard], 1920), pp. 37–38. See *INT*, p. 273.

69. Transcript—the original is missing—of ltr to Quinn, Oct. 22, 1920, with the notation (by the cautious Quinn?) "not sent" in the margin (Dart).

70. *INT*, p. 307.

71. *Evening Post*, Lit. Rev., p. 3. Burke reviewed the book from galleys (ltr, Burke to ATS, June 28, 1954). The University of Buffalo Library has a set of corrected galley proofs of *Painted Veils*.

72. Ltr, Rascoe to Mrs. Josephine Huneker, Oct. 18, 1922 (Dart).

73. Burton Rascoe, "Fanfare," in *H. L. Mencken*, ed. Burton Rascoe (New York: Knopf, 1920), p. 13.

74. Ltr, Rascoe to ATS, May 15, 1954; *LET*, p. 287.

75. Chicago *Daily News*, Dec. 8, 1920, p. 13.

76. Ltrs, Rascoe to ATS, May 20, 1954, and May 30, 1954.

77. *Globe*, p. 8. See Burton Rascoe, *Before I Forget* (Garden City, N.Y.: Doubleday, Doran, 1937), p. 365, and Elias, I, 200.

78. Ltr (Dart).

CHAPTER TWENTY

1. *INT*, p. 253; *LET*, p. 284.

2. *LET*, p. 285. See *World*, Oct. 5, 1919, Edit. Sec., p. 1.

3. James W. Barrett, *The World, The Flesh and Messrs. Pulitzer, passim*, and *Joseph Pulitzer and his World* (New York: Vanguard Press, 1941), *passim*.

4. John L. Heaton, *Cobb of "The World"* (New York: Dutton, 1924), pp. xx, 288.

5. See Barrett, *The World, The Flesh and Messrs. Pulitzer*, p. 82.

6. *World*, Edit. Sec., p. 1.

7. Ltrs, Herbert Bayard Swope to ATS, Aug. 4, 1953, and Sept. 4, 1953.

8. *World*, Dec. 9, 1919, p. 13.

9. *World*, Dec. 5, 1919, p. 15, and April 25, 1920, Metro. Sec., p. 6.

10. *World*, Dec. 10, 1919, p. 13.

11. Ltr, Mrs. Hadley to ATS, Jan. 14, 1954. The incident is dated in JGH's ltr to T. R. Smith, Jan. 26, 1920 (Herbert B. Satcher).

12. Frances Alda, *Men, Women and Tenors* (Boston: Houghton Mifflin Co., 1937), p. 12, and ltr, Mme Alda to ATS, Nov. 29, 1951. I can't find the remark in print.

13. *World*, Feb. 1, 1920, p. 18.

14. *World*, Dec. 21, 1919, Metro. Sec., p. 4.

15. *Evening Post*, Dec. 23, 1919, p. 8.

16. *World*, Dec. 28, 1919, p. 3. See *INT*, p. 263.

17. *World*, March 25, 1920, p. 11.

18. *INT*, p. 260.

19. *Globe*, Feb. 11, 1920, p. 16.

20. Ltr, S. Jay Kaufman to ATS, Dec. 26, 1953.

21. *LET*, p. 281, and ltr, JGH to Charles Scribner, April 30, 1919 (Dart).

22. Ltr, JGH to Maxwell Perkins, Feb. 27, 1920 (Scrib).

23. *World*, Feb. 28, 1920, p. 11.

24. *Times*, March 28, 1920, Lit. Sec., p. 2; *Bookman*, LI (April, 1920), 231–32; *Musical America*, XXXII (June 5, 1920), 3–4; and *Judge*, LXXIX (Aug. 7, 1920), 24.

25. *LET*, p. 290.

26. *Times*, Lit. Sec., March 28, 1920, p. 2.

27. *Smart Set*, LXII (May, 1920), 140. See Mencken's "Introduction," *Essays by James Huneker*, pp. xvi–xvii.

28. *Evening Post*, May 8, 1920, p. 13.

29. Philadelphia *Press*, March 7, 1920, Sec. 2, p. 7.

30. Ltr, Vance Thompson to JGH, June 20, 1920 (Dart).

31. *Tribune*, March 7, 1920, Sec. 7, p. 9.

32. Chicago *Tribune*, March 6, 1920, p. 11.

33. *MC*, XLI (Oct. 24, 1900), 24–25; *Times*, Mag. Sec., Jan. 5, 1919, pp. 6, 14.

34. *Evening Sun*, March 10, 1920, p. 12 (reprinted through the kindness of The New York Sun, Inc.).

35. *World*, Jan. 18, 1920, Metro. Sec., p. 4.

36. Van Vechten, interview, Nov. 10, 1951.

37. Van Vechten, *Peter Whiffle: His Life and Works* (New York: Knopf, 1922), p. 186. See also Van Vechten's *Interpreters and Interpretations* (New York: Knopf, 1917), pp. 303, 306, and *In the Garret* (New York: Knopf, 1920), pp. 29, 39, 163.

38. Ltrs, JGH to Van Vechten, Oct. 3, 1917 (Fisk University) and Dec. 1, 1918 (NYPL). See JGH, *Times*, Aug. 10, 1919, Sec. 4, p. 5, and Aug. 17, 1919, Sec. 4, p. 5, and *Bedouins*, pp. 26–27.

39. *World*, May 2, 1920, Metro. Sec., p. 5; ltr, Morley to ATS, Sept. 2, 1953. Two ltrs from JGH to Morley, both written in 1919, are at Haverford College.

40. *World*, May 9, 1920, Edit. Sec., p. 2.

41. "The Lesson of the Master," *Bookman*, LI, 365, 368.

42. *Times*, May 25, 1919, Sec. 4, p. 5.

43. "Everywhere, Nowhere and Somewhere," *Judge*, LXXIX (Aug. 7, 1920), 24.

44. *INT*, p. 280.

45. *INT*, pp. 281–82.

46. *Times*, May 11, 1919, Sec. 4, p. 5.

47. *World*, Feb. 1, 1920, Metro. Sec., p. 4.

48. Ltr, Harvard Union Library to JGH, Oct. 20, 1920, with notation indicating book was sent to the college (Scrib).

49. Ltr, Saxe to JGH, April 22, 1920 (copy enclosed with ltr, Saxe to ATS, July 3, 1953).

50. Previously JGH had given the same advice to would-be writers (*Sun*, Nov. 16, 1916, p. 14, reprinted in *Unicorns*, p. 123), and he repeated it in the *World*, May 2, 1920, Metro. Sec., p. 5.

51. Ltr, JGH to Saxe, April 25, 1920 (Saxe).
52. *LET*, pp. 296–97.
53. *Extension Magazine*, XV (Sept. 1920), 3–4.
54. Ltr, Kelley to JGH, Dec. 26, 1920 (Dart). See *INT*, p. 320.
55. The book is at Dart.
56. *World*, June 27, 1920, Metro. Sec., p. 5.
57. *World*, Aug. 1, 1920, Metro. Sec., p. 4.
58. *World*, Sept. 19, 1920, Metro. Sec., p. 5.
59. *LET*, p. 297.
60. *INT*, p. 295.
61. *LET*, p. 296.
62. Ltrs, "Lydia Barrington" to ATS, Sept. 27, 1953; early Oct. 1953; and Oct. 28, 1953. There is no other evidence of this Continental trip.
63. *LET*, p. 298.
64. *LET*, p. 299.
65. *Times*, Sept. 12, 1920, Lit. Sec., p. 8.
66. *Times* (London) Lit. Supp., Feb. 3, 1921, p. 73.
67. Ltr, Ellis to JGH, Nov. 18, 1920 (Dart).
68. Published (in the original French) in ATS, "Georg Brandes and James Huneker," p. 46.
69. *Smart Set*, LXI (Feb. 1920), 140, and (March 1920), 138–44.
70. Mencken, *Prejudices*, p. 80.
71. Forgue, p. 200.
72. *Evening Post*, Sept. 25, 1920, Lit. Rev., p. 2. See Forgue, pp. 197, 202.
73. *LET*, pp. 258, 260, and 251–52, respectively.
74. *STJ*, II, 307.
75. *STJ*, I, 168–72; II, 194–95. See *LET*, p. 263.
76. *INT*, pp. 299–300. See *INT*, p. 298, and *LET*, p. 302.
77. *World*, Oct. 10, 1920, Metro. Sec., p. 5.
78. *INT*, p. 303.
79. Ltr, Nov. 5, 1920 (Dart).
80. Pasted on title page, vol. I, of Mencken's copy of *STJ* (Pratt Library, Baltimore).
81. "Chiefly American," *Smart Set*, LXIII (Dec. 1920), 142.
82. *Editor to Author: The Letters of Maxwell E. Perkins*, ed. John Hall Wheelock (New York: Scribner, 1950), p. 26.
83. *LET*, pp. 305–6.
84. *World*, Oct. 3, 1920, Metro. Sec., p. 5.
85. *World*, Nov. 7, 1920, Metro. Sec., p. 9.
86. *World*, Oct. 3, 1920, Metro. Sec., p. 5.
87. *World*, Sept. 12, 1920, Metro. Sec., p. 4.
88. *World*, Oct. 3, 1920, Metro. Sec., p. 5.
89. *Ibid.*
90. *World*, Dec. 5, 1920, Metro. Sec., p. 7.

91. "Musical Adventures of the Season," *Century Magazine,* C (July 1920), 424.
92. *INT*, p. 307.
93. Ltr, Herbert Bayard Swope to ATS, Sept. 4, 1953.
94. *INT*, p. 312. See *INT*, p. 307.
95. *World,* Nov. 23, 1920, p. 13.
96. *INT*, p. 319.
97. *World,* Dec. 19, 1920, Metro. Sec., p. 5.
98. *World,* Nov. 27, 1920, p. 11.
99. *World,* Dec. 24, 1920, p. 11.
100. *LET*, pp. 308–9.
101. *LET*, p. 313.
102. *INT*, p. 320.
103. *World,* Jan. 23, 1921, Metro. Sec., p. 2.
104. Ltr, EHH to ATS, Sept. 21–22, 1953.
105. *World,* Feb. 6, 1921, Metro. Sec., p. 3.
106. See JGH, *Times,* Sept. 21, 1919, Sec. 4, p. 16.
107. According to Mrs. Josephine Huneker (ltr, Mrs. Vera Kasow to ATS, Oct. 4, 1953).
108. *World,* Feb. 6, 1921, p. 19.
109. The note is at Dart.
110. Ltr, EHH to ATS, Sept. 21–22, 1953.
111. Ltr, Mrs. Kasow to ATS, Oct. 4, 1953.
112. *Times,* Feb. 10, 1921, p. 7; *World,* Feb. 10, 1921, p. 11.
113. Ltr, EHH to ATS, Sept. 21–22, 1953.
114. Ltr, Mary W. Cushing to ATS, May 19, 1952.
115. EHH, interview, May 2, 1950; ltrs, EHH to ATS, Sept. 21–22, 1953, and Howard E. Potter (who accompanied Garden to the services) to ATS, Oct. 2, 1953, and (somewhat contradictory) April 22, 1954. Miss Garden, who forgot that she ever corresponded with Huneker or knew Olive Fremstad (her undated annotations to queries in my ltr to her, Feb. 25, 1954, answered shortly thereafter), also failed to recall the funeral episode (interview, Nov. 7, 1950).
116. Georgiana Carhart, interview, Feb. 9, 1956.
117. Ltr, EHH to ATS, Oct. 7, 1960.
118. *World,* Feb. 14, 1921, p. 11, and *Times,* Feb. 14, 1921, p. 9.
119. Ltr, EHH to ATS, Sept. 21–22, 1953.
120. "Dramatic Criticism," *Smart Set,* LXIV (April 1921), 137.

CHAPTER TWENTY-ONE

1. The reprints first appeared in *MC,* LXXXII (Feb. 17, 1921), 23, and ran weekly, starting on March 3, 1921, through March 31. See Leonard Liebling, "Variations," *MC,* LXXXII (Feb. 17, 1921), 21, and LXXXIX (Dec. 11, 1924), 27.
2. See Kazin, *On Native Grounds,* p. 156.

3. *Nation,* CXII (Feb. 23, 1921), 279.

4. Mencken, "James Huneker."

5. *Bulletin of the New York Public Library,* XXV (1921), 367–68. See Sonnenschein.

6. Copy of ltr, Harold G. Rugg, Assistant Librarian, Dartmouth College, to Richard H. Mandel, Dec. 19, 1947, enclosed with ltr, Hazel E. Joslyn, Archivist, Dart, to ATS, July 22, 1954.

7. New York City, Register of Wills. Dart received the material in March 1951 (ltr, Herbert F. West, Secretary, Friends of the Dartmouth Library, to ATS, June 28, 1954). The gift is described in the *Dartmouth College Library News,* March 15, 1951 (No. 10).

8. *World,* Aug. 3, 1921, p. 2.

9. *Times,* Jan. 29, 1922, Book Rev., pp. 7, 31.

10. *Herald,* Dec. 18, 1921, Sec. 7, p. 8 (reprinted, slightly revised, in De Casseres' *James Gibbons Huneker,* pp. 29–36).

11. Ltr, Mencken to Mrs. Josephine Huneker, Feb. 11, 1921 (Dart).

12. Norman T. Byrne, interview, Aug. 30, 1961.

13. Ltr, Alden March to Maxwell Perkins, shortly prior to Aug. 8, 1922 (Scrib).

14. Byrne, pp. 300–303.

15. Ltrs, Mrs. Josephine Huneker to Maxwell Perkins, Feb. 25, 1922 (Scrib), and Perkins to Alden March, Aug. 8, 1922 (Scrib).

16. See ltr, Mrs. Josephine Huneker to Maxwell Perkins, Oct. 21, 1932 (Scrib).

17. See Burton Rascoe's review, *Tribune,* Oct. 15, 1922, Sec. 5, p. 11, and Fanny Butcher's, Chicago *Tribune,* Oct. 29, 1922, Sec. 7, p. 21.

18. See Stanley Edgar Hyman, *The Armed Vision* (New York: Knopf, 1948), p. 20.

19. Wilson, "From Maupassant to Mencken." For other comments by Wilson on JGH, see *The Shock of Recognition,* pp. 1157–58, and "Thoughts on Being Bibliographed."

20. Ltr, Scribner's to Edwin W. Morse, Aug. 18, 1924 (Scrib).

21. Ltr, Mencken to Maxwell Perkins, Jan. 27 (1923?) (Scrib).

22. *Times,* Book Rev., Jan. 4, 1925, p. 3.

23. Ltr, Arthur Pell, Liveright Publishing Corp., to ATS, Aug. 16, 1954.

24. Published in *Musical America,* XXXII (June 5, 1920), 3–4; *Times,* Book Rev., Sept. 12, 1920, p. 8; *Herald,* Dec. 18, 1921, Sec. 7, p. 8; and *Nation,* CXV (Nov. 29, 1922), 582, respectively.

25. De Fornaro, p. 74, confirmed by ltr, Harvard University Alumni Office to ATS, Aug. 21, 1961.

26. De Casseres, *James Gibbons Huneker,* pp. 17, 33–34.

27. De Casseres, "James Huneker: Steeplejack of Culture," pp. 80–87.

28. *INT,* p. 294.

29. Ltrs (copies), Mrs. Josephine Huneker to Lola Lorme, Oct. 6, 1925; Nov. 16, 1925; and Sept. 26, 1926 (Dart).

30. Circular, the Franklin Book Shop of Philadelphia (Liveright Publishing Corp.).

31. Ltr, Arthur Pell to ATS, Sept. 14, 1953.

32. Ltrs, Random House to ATS, Aug. 31, 1953, and Nov. 17, 1961; Arthur Pell, interview, June 5, 1956, and ltr to ATS, Oct. 1961.

33. Ltr, EHH to ATS, Sept. 21–22, 1953. EHH gave me his copy of the radio script.

34. Ltr, Arthur Pell to ATS, June 10, 1954.

35. Unsigned review of *Essays by James Huneker, Times,* Book Rev., Nov. 17, 1929, p. 2.

36. Memo (Scrib).

37. Mencken, *Essays by James Huneker,* p. xxii.

38. *Ibid.,* p. xii; Mencken, *A Book of Prefaces,* p. 164, and *Smart Set,* LXIII (Dec. 1920), 142.

39. Ltr, "Maim" (Mary Huneker Lagen) to "John" (Huneker), "Wed. A.M." (Oct.–Nov., 1929?) (presented to me by Mrs. Richard Beamish, whose husband received it from John Huneker); "R.J.B." (Richard J. Beamish), Philadelphia *Inquirer,* Nov. 9, 1929, p. 14; and G. H. Eckhardt, "The Hunekers of Philadelphia," *Town Crier,* I (May 15, 1930), 15–16. See Josephine's notations on the clipping of Eckhardt's article (Dart).

40. Bulliet, pp. 41–42.

41. Matthiessen, p. 115.

42. Hicks, p. 780.

43. Smith, pp. 271–75, 303–4.

44. Ltr, Scribner's to ATS, Aug. 25, 1954.

45. Ltr, Sagamore Press to ATS, April 30, 1957.

46. Mencken, "Professors at the Bat," *Smart Set,* L (Nov. 1916), 282.

47. Pattee, pp. 436ff.

48. DeMille, pp. 207, 243.

49. Lewisohn, pp. 350, 354.

50. Ltr, Kenneth Fearing to ATS, Dec. 14, 1951.

51. The first of six that I know of. See Sources, Selected Bibliography, p. 369.

52. Ltr, Brother Jason to ATS, Dec. 13, 1960.

53. Black, p. 2.

54. Ltrs, Sister Miriam to ATS, Nov. 3, 1951; Dec. 4, 1951; Jan. 12, 1952 (with Mencken's ltr to her); and Feb. 15, 1954.

55. Mrs. Josephine Huneker, interview, March 20, 1950; EHH, interview, May 2, 1950.

56. Philadelphia, Register of Wills. A printed copy of the will is at Dart.

57. EHH, interview, May 2, 1950, confirmed by Clarence B. Wrigley, attorney for the estate, in interview, April 1950.

58. Helen Noble, *Life With the Met* (New York: Putnam, 1954), p. 5.

59. See *Times,* Oct. 28, 1950, p. 17. Though Josephine wanted them

dropped from a plane, the mixed ashes are still at the Fresh Pond Crematory (ltr, EHH to ATS, Nov. 16, 1953).

60. *Times*, Feb. 13, 1925, p. 17.
61. ATS, "Huneker's Hidden Birthdate."
62. Kolodin, p. 53.
63. Ltr, Kolodin to ATS, March 12, 1956.
64. Brooks, "Huneker in Retrospect," p. 125.
65. Ltr, Irving Kolodin to ATS, March 12, 1956.
66. *Sun*, Nov. 30, 1935, p. 9.

SOURCES

The main sources for this biography are Huneker's autobiography, *Steeplejack* (1920); his published correspondence, especially *Letters of James Gibbons Huneker* (1922) and *Intimate Letters of James Gibbons Huneker* (1924), both edited (somewhat amateurishly) by his widow; his extensive unpublished correspondence, manuscripts, and papers in the possession of various libraries, publishers, private collectors, members of his family, and his friends; notebooks, scrapbooks, legal documents, and miscellaneous materials, particularly those in the Huneker Collection at Dartmouth; church, municipal, and court records; interviews and correspondence with his family and friends; published memoirs of people who knew him; and, of course, Huneker's more personal essays, many of which contain casual (and often contradictory) accounts of incidents in his life. *Old Fogy* (1913) and *Painted Veils* (1920) are, no doubt, partly autobiographical, but I have tried to avoid the pitfalls of mistaking fiction for unadulterated fact.

Perhaps the most regrettable lack in Huneker sources is that of early letters: only three written prior to 1900 have been published, none before 1886, and only a handful of the unpublished letters I have found antedate 1900. Huneker surely wrote far fewer letters in his first thirty years or so, when most of his family and friends lived within easy reach in Philadelphia, than in his last, but one laments the apparent loss of all those he must have sent home during his visit to Paris in 1878–79 and almost all those written to his family and possibly to Lizzie (none to her have seemingly survived) in the period following his move to New York in 1886. One regrets, too, that of all the letters presumably written, somewhat later, to Josephine, Clio, Georgiana Carhart, "Lydia Barrington," and Olive Fremstad, only one very late letter to Clio appears to be extant; Erik Huneker reports that his mother destroyed the rest of her letters from Huneker; Georgiana and "Lydia" have stated that they destroyed theirs; and none was found in the effects of Mme Fremstad, who destroyed the greater part of her personal correspondence shortly before her death. One guesses that Josephine, who saved so many of her husband's papers, felt that the letters to her were too intimate for other eyes, though the couple may have been so seldom apart—except for brief periods, perhaps, during the 1890's—that correspondence was unnecessary.

Steeplejack, at any rate, has necessarily been my chief source for Huneker's early years. (To conserve space, I have not usually given specific references to it in the notes to the early chapters; I have given them later, when other sources are also available.) Like most autobiographies, it is not always helpful or reliable. It is loosely organized, moreover; the exact chronology of certain events is obscured by telescoping. Luckily, however, the first volume, dealing with the period concerning which other sources are scarce, is the fuller, less jumbled, and more personal of the two, despite a significant gap regarding the "dark interval" of 1880–86. How many of the factual errors in the book are as deliberate as the omissions, and how many the result of a failing memory or of hurried writing is not clear. Though I have attempted wherever possible to verify his statements, especially those involving chronology, I have inevitably been forced to lean on them when no other evidence exists.

The bibliography that follows is divided into two parts: a complete chronological list of books by Huneker, and an alphabetical list of other sources that I have found useful. Asterisks in the second list denote books and articles containing letters written by Huneker.

I. CHRONOLOGICAL LIST OF BOOKS BY JAMES GIBBONS HUNEKER

The publisher is Charles Scribner's Sons, New York, unless otherwise specified.

Mezzotints in Modern Music, 1899.
Chopin: The Man and His Music, 1900.
Melomaniacs, 1902.
Overtones, 1904.
Iconoclasts: A Book of Dramatists, 1905.
Visionaries, 1905.
Egoists: A Book of Supermen, 1909.
Promenades of an Impressionist, 1910.
Franz Liszt, 1911.
The Pathos of Distance, 1913.
Old Fogy. Philadelphia: Theodore Presser Co., 1913.
New Cosmopolis, 1915.
Ivory Apes and Peacocks, 1915.
The Development of Piano Music. New York, 1915–16. No publisher listed.
Unicorns, 1917.
The Philharmonic Society of New York. New York, 1917(?). No publisher listed.
The Steinway Collection of Paintings. New York: Steinway Co., 1919.
Bedouins, 1920.
Steeplejack, 2 vols., 1920.
Painted Veils. New York: Boni and Liveright, 1920.
Variations, 1921.
Essays by James Huneker, ed. H. L. Mencken, 1929.

II. SELECTED BIBLIOGRAPHY

Alexander, Calvert. *The Catholic Literary Revival.* Milwaukee, Wis.: Bruce Publishing Co., 1935.

"Author and Critic," Brooklyn *Daily Eagle,* March 27, 1909, p. 5.

Baehr, Henry W. *The New York Tribune Since the Civil War.* New York: Dodd, Mead & Co., 1936.

Barrett, James W. *The World, The Flesh and Messrs. Pulitzer.* New York: Vanguard Press, 1931.

Bean, Teddy. New York *Telegraph,* Dec. 4, 1910, Sec. 2, p. 1.

Beckwith, Natalie Bowen. "Two American Critics: Richard Aldrich and James Gibbons Huneker." Unpublished master's thesis, Brown University, 1955.

Beer, Thomas. *The Mauve Decade.* Garden City, N.Y.: Garden City Publishing Co., 1926.

———. *Stephen Crane: A Study in American Letters.* New York: Alfred A. Knopf, 1923.

Berryman, John. *Stephen Crane.* American Men of Letters Series. New York: William Sloane Associates, 1950.

Beyer, Thomas Percival. "Playboy of American Critics" in *Integrated Life.* Minneapolis, Minn.: University of Minnesota Press, 1948.

Binns, Archie, and Olive Kooken. *Mrs. Fiske and the American Theatre.* New York: Crown Publishers, 1955.

Bispham, David. *A Quaker Singer's Recollections.* New York: Macmillan Co., 1920.

Black, Jason. "James G. Huneker's Critical Technique." Unpublished master's thesis, Catholic University of America, 1927.

Boynton, Percy H. *Some Contemporary Americans.* Chicago: University of Chicago Press, 1924.

Brister, Emma Schubert. *Incidents.* Privately printed, 1936.

Brooks, Van Wyck. *The Confident Years: 1885–1915.* New York: E. P. Dutton & Co., 1952.

———. "Huneker in Retrospect," *High Fidelity Magazine,* X (Dec. 1960), 38–41, 123–25.

———. *John Sloan: A Painter's Life.* New York: E. P. Dutton & Co., 1955.

———. *New England: Indian Summer.* New York: E. P. Dutton & Co., 1940.

———. *Sketches in Criticism.* New York: E. P. Dutton & Co., 1932.

Bulliet, C. J. *Apples and Madonnas: Emotional Expression in Modern Art.* Rev. ed. New York: Covici, Friede, 1930.

*[Burk, Harry R.] "Jim, the Penman: James Gibbons Huneker," *Nucleus,* I (April–May, 1924), 3–12.

Burlingame, Roger. *Of Making Many Books.* New York: Charles Scribner's Sons, 1946.

Byrne, Norman T. "James Gibbons Huneker," *Scribner's Magazine*, LXXI (March 1922), 300–303.

Campbell, John H. *History of the Friendly Sons of St. Patrick and the Hibernian Society for the Relief of Emigrants from Ireland: March 17, 1771–March 17, 1892.* Philadelphia: Hibernian Society, 1892.

Cargill, Oscar. *Intellectual America.* New York: Macmillan Co., 1941.

"Chronicle and Comment," *Bookman*, XXIX (May 1900), 236–37.

Churchill, Allen. *Park Row.* New York: Rinehart & Co., 1958.

Clark, Barrett H. *Intimate Portraits.* New York: Dramatists Play Service, 1951.

Clarke, Joseph I. C. "James Gibbons Huneker," *Journal of the American Irish Historical Society*, XX (1921), 221–28.

———. *My Life and Memories.* New York: Dodd, Mead & Co., 1925.

[Cooke, James Francis.] "The Teacher's Vocabulary," *Etude*, LII (Feb. 1934), 73.

Corbin, John. "Letters of Steeplejack," *New York Times*, Oct. 22, 1922, Sec. 3, pp. 1, 22.

* Cortissoz, Royal, ed. "A Sheaf of James Huneker's Letters," *Scribner's Magazine*, LXXII (Sept. 1922), 306–14.

Cushing, Mary Watkins. *The Rainbow Bridge.* New York: G. P. Putnam's Sons, 1954.

De Casseres, Benjamin. "Foreword," *Intimate Letters of James Gibbons Huneker*, ed. Josephine Huneker. New York: Liveright Publishing Corp., 1936.

———. "Huneker, Knight of the Arts," *Musical America*, XXXII (June 5, 1920), 304.

———. "James Huneker: Steeplejack of Culture," *Popular Biography*, II (May 1930), 80–87.

———. *James Gibbons Huneker.* New York: Joseph Lawren, 1925.

De Crespigny, Claude. "Huneker," *American Speech*, II (Aug. 1927), 451–58.

De Fornaro, Carlo. "Benjamin De Casseres," *Arts & Decoration*, XXII (Jan. 1925), 74, 83.

De Mille, George E. *Literary Criticism in America.* New York: Dial Press, 1931.

Duffy, Richard. "When They Were Twenty One," *Bookman*, XXXVIII (Jan. 1914), 521–31.

Dynner, Audrey Joan. "James Gibbons Huneker: A Study of his Influence on American Literary Taste." Unpublished master's thesis, Ohio State University, 1947.

Egan, Maurice Francis. *Confessions of a Book-Lover.* Garden City, N.Y.: Doubleday, Page & Co., 1923.

———. "Five American Essayists," *Yale Review*, N.S., X (Oct. 1920), 187–88.

———. *Recollections of a Happy Life.* New York: George H. Doran Co., 1924.

Elias, Robert H., ed. *Letters of Theodore Dreiser: A Selection.* 3 vols. Philadelphia: University of Pennsylvania Press, 1959.

[Eliot, T. S.] Review of Huneker's *Egoists, Harvard Advocate,* LXXXVIII (Oct. 5, 1909), 16.

Elson, Louis C. *The History of American Music,* rev. ed. New York: Macmillan Co., 1925.

Fay, Eliot C. "Huneker's Criticism of French Literature," *French Review,* XIV (Dec. 1940), 130–37.

Finck, Henry T. "James Huneker, Virtuoso of the Paragraph, Friend of the Arts," New York *Evening Post,* Feb. 19, 1921, Sec. 1, p. 12.

———. *Musical Laughs.* New York: Funk & Wagnalls, 1924.

———. *My Adventures in the Golden Age of Music.* New York: Funk & Wagnalls, 1926.

———. Review of Huneker's *Letters,* New York *Evening Post,* Oct. 28, 1922, Lit. Rev., p. 147.

Forgue, Guy L., ed. *Letters of H. L. Mencken.* New York: Alfred A. Knopf, 1961.

Friedheim, Arthur. *Life and Liszt: The Recollections of a Concert Pianist,* ed. Theodore L. Bullock. New York: Taplinger Publishing Co., 1961.

Gabriel, Gilbert W. "With Huneker in Europe: Some Names and Quotations from the Critic's Memoirs," New York *Sun,* Feb. 12, 1921, p. 7.

Garden, Mary, and Louis Biancolli. *Mary Garden's Story.* New York: Simon & Schuster, 1951.

Gerson, Robert A. *Music in Philadelphia.* Philadelphia: University of Pennsylvania Press, 1940.

Gilbert, Stuart, ed. *Letters of James Joyce.* New York: Viking Press, 1957.

Gilman, Lawrence. "The Playboy of Criticism," *North American Review,* CCXIII (April 1921), 556–60.

Glackens, Ira. *William Glackens and the Ashcan Group: The Emergence of Realism in American Art.* New York: Crown Publishers, 1957.

Glicksberg, Charles I. *American Literary Criticism, 1900–1950.* New York: Hendricks House, 1951.

Goldberg, Isaac. *The Theatre of George Jean Nathan.* New York: Simon & Schuster, 1926.

Goodrich, Lloyd. *Thomas Eakins: His Life and Work.* New York: Whitney Museum of American Art, 1933.

Gourmont, Remy de. *Promenades Littéraires: Troisième Série.* Paris: Mercure de France, 1909.

Hackenburg, Frederick L. *A Solitary Parade.* New York: Thistle Press, 1929.

Hanighen, Frank C. "Vance Thompson and *M'lle New York,*" *Bookman,* LXXV (Sept. 1932), 472–81.

Henderson, Archibald. *George Bernard Shaw: Man of the Century.* New York: Appleton-Century-Crofts, 1956.

Henderson, William J. "Huneker," *Dictionary of American Biography,* ed. Dumas Malone. New York: Charles Scribner's Sons, 1932, IX, 379–80.

Hicks, Granville. "The Passing of James Huneker," *Nation,* CXXIX (Dec. 25, 1929), 780.

Hind, C. Lewis. *More Authors and I.* New York: Dodd, Mead & Co., 1922.

Hoffman, Frederick J. *Freudianism and the Literary Mind.* Baton Rouge, La.: Louisiana State University Press, 1945.

[Holliday, Robert Cortes.] "Murray Hill's Recollections of James Huneker," *Bookman,* LIII (April 1921), 124–27.

Hughes, Rupert. "James Huneker," *Criterion,* N.S., III (May 1902), 38–39.

* [Huneker, James.] "Huneker on Huneker," *American Mercury,* I (Jan. 1924), 22–26.

* Huneker, Josephine, ed. *Intimate Letters of James Gibbons Huneker.* New York: Boni and Liveright, 1924.

* ———. *Letters of James Gibbons Huneker.* New York: Charles Scribner's Sons, 1922.

* Jean-Aubry, G., ed. *Letters to Conrad.* London: First Editions Club, 1926.

Jordan, Elizabeth. *Three Rousing Cheers.* New York: D. Appleton-Century Co., 1938.

*"J.S." "Huneker Writing Fiction," *More Books: The Bulletin of the Boston Public Library,* XXIII (Feb. 1948), 71.

Kazin, Alfred. "American Fin-de-Siècle," *Saturday Review of Literature,* XXI (Feb. 3, 1940), 3–4, 11.

———. *On Native Grounds.* New York: Reynal & Hitchcock, 1942.

Kemler, Edgar. *The Irreverent Mr. Mencken.* Boston: Little, Brown & Co., 1950.

Kent, Rockwell. *It's Me O Lord.* New York: Dodd, Mead & Co., 1955.

Klein, Herman[n]. *Musicians and Mummers.* London: Cassell and Co., 1925.

Kolodin, Irving. "Huneker's Hundredth," *Saturday Review,* XLIII (Jan. 30, 1960), 53.

Kummer, George. "Percival Pollard: Precursor of the Twenties." Unpublished dissertation, New York University, 1946.

Lawren, Joseph. "James Gibbons Huneker: A Bibliography" in Benjamin De Casseres, *James Gibbons Huneker.* New York: Joseph Lawren, 1925.

Levin, Harry. "The Discovery of Bohemia" in *Literary History of the United States,* ed. Robert E. Spiller *et al.* 3 vols. New York: Macmillan Co., 1948.

Lewisohn, Ludwig. *Expression in America.* New York: Harper & Bros., 1932.

[Liebling, Leonard.] "Variations," *Musical Courier,* LXXXII (Feb. 17, 1921), 21.

Linson, Corwin Knapp. *My Stephen Crane,* ed. Edwin H. Cady. Syracuse, N.Y.: Syracuse University Press, 1958.

Lorme, Lola. "James Huneker," *Münchner Neueste Nachrichten,* June 3–4, 1922, p. 10.

Loud, Grover C. *Evangelized America.* New York: Dial Press, 1928.

Maier, Guy. "The Teacher's Round Table," *Etude, LXIV* (June 1946), 312, 345.

Manchester, William. *Disturber of the Peace: The Life of H. L. Mencken.* New York: Harper & Bros., 1950–51.

Marsh, Edward C. "James Huneker: Individualist," *Forum,* XLI (June 1909), 600–605.

Matthiessen, F. O. "Sherman and Huneker," *New Republic,* LXI (Dec. 18, 1929), 113–15.

Mellquist, Jerome. *The Emergence of an American Art.* New York: Charles Scribner's Sons, 1942.

Meltzer, Charles Henry. "The Huneker of Early Days—Our 'Jim,' " *Musical Advance,* VIII (March 1921) (unnumbered page).

———. "Music," *Weekly Review,* IV (Feb. 23, 1921), 186–87.

Mencken, H. L. *A Book of Prefaces.* New York: Alfred A. Knopf, 1917.

———. "Introduction," *Essays by James Huneker,* ed. H. L. Mencken. New York: Charles Scribner's Sons, 1929.

———. "James Gibbons Huneker," New York *Evening Mail,* July 21, 1917, p. 12.

———. "James Huneker," *Century Magazine,* CII (June 1921), 191–97.

———. *Prejudices: Third Series.* New York: Alfred A. Knopf, 1922.

———. See also Forgue, above.

"Mephisto." "Mephisto's Musings," *Musical America,* XVI (July 20, 1912), 7.

———. *Ibid.,* XXXIII (Feb. 19, 1921), 7.

———. *Ibid.* (Feb. 26, 1921), p. 7.

"M.F." "Huneker Images," *New Republic,* II (April 17, 1915), Supp. 17.

Middleton, George. *These Things Are Mine.* New York: Macmillan Co., 1947.

* Mitchell, Edward P. *Memoirs of an Editor.* New York: Charles Scribner's Sons, 1924.

* Moore, Aubertine Woodward, ed. "Some Hitherto Unpublished Letters of James Gibbons Huneker," *Musical Leader,* XLV (June 7, 1923), 533–34.

Moore, Aubertine Woodward. "Walt Whitman and American Music," *Musical Leader,* LI (May 20, 1926), 5.

Moran, T. S. "New York's Dramatic Critics," *Metropolitan Magazine,* IX (Jan. 1899), 106–7.

Morris, Lloyd R. "The Critic's Cadenza," *Outlook,* CXXVI (Nov. 10, 1920), 469–70.

———. *Incredible New York: High Life and Low Life of the Last Hundred Years.* New York: Random House, 1951.

Morrissette, Bruce A. "Early English and American Critics of French Symbolism," *Studies in Honor of Frederick W. Shipley,* Washington University Studies, N.S., Language and Literature, No. 14. St. Louis: Washington University, 1942.

Moult, Thomas. "James Huneker," *English Review*, XXXII (April 1921), 363–66.

Nathan, George Jean. *The Theatre in the Fifties*. New York: Alfred A. Knopf, 1953.

Neilson, Francis. *My Life in Two Worlds*. 2 vols. Appleton, Wis.: C. C. Nelson Publishing Co., 1952.

[————.] "Miscellany," *Freeman*, II (March 2, 1921), 588–89.

O'Brien, Frank M. *The Story of the Sun*, new ed. New York: C. Appleton, 1928.

O'Connor, William Van. *An Age of Criticism, 1900–1950*. Chicago: Henry Regnery Co., 1952.

Paderewski, Ignace Jan, and Mary Lawton. *The Paderewski Memoirs*. New York: Charles Scribner's Sons, 1938.

Palache, John Garber. *Gautier and the Romantics*. New York: Viking Press, 1926.

Parry, Albert. *Garrets and Pretenders*. New York: Covici, Friede, 1933.

"The Passing of James Gibbons Huneker," *Musical Courier*, LXXXII (Feb. 17, 1921), 23.

Pattee, Fred Lewis. *The New American Literature, 1890–1930*. New York: Century Co., 1930.

[Peck, Harry Thurston?] "Chronicle and Comment," *Bookman*, XI (Aug. 1900), 501.

————. "Literature and Music," *ibid.*, IX (Aug. 1899), 513–14.

* Phelps, William Lyon. *Autobiography with Letters*. New York: Oxford University Press, 1939.

Phillips, Charles. *Paderewski: The Story of a Modern Immortal*. New York: Macmillan Co., 1934.

Pollard, Percival. *Their Day in Court*. New York: Neale, 1909.

Pollock, Channing. *Harvest of My Years*. Indianapolis, Ind.: Bobbs-Merrill Co., 1943.

Portor, Laura Spencer. "On Living Next to James Huneker," *Scribner's Magazine*, LXXI (March 1922), 303–8.

Pritchard, John Paul, and John M. Raines, "James Gibbons Huneker, Critic of the Seven Arts," *American Quarterly*, II (Spring, 1950), 53–61.

Ramsey, Warren. *Jules Laforgue and the Ironic Inheritance*. New York: Oxford University Press, 1953.

Rascoe, Burton. "A Note About Painted Veils," *Painted Veils*. New York: Avon Publications, 1954.

Reedy, William Marion. "A Conflict of Critics," *Reedy's Mirror*, XX (Sept. 21, 1911), 2.

Reining, Janet Bolton. "The Significance of Music Criticism as Exemplified by James Gibbons Huneker." Unpublished master's thesis, University of Southern California, 1938.

Rewald, John. *History of Impressionism*. 2d ed. New York: Museum of Modern Art, 1955.

Richardson, Joanna. *Théophile Gautier: His Life and Times*. London: Max Reinhardt, 1958.

Riewald, J. G. *Sir Max Beerbohm: Man and Writer*. The Hague: Martinus Nijhoff, 1953.

Rigby, George Alfred. "The Literary Criticism of James Huneker." Unpublished master's thesis, University of Southern California, 1939.

Rose, Edgar Smith. "James Gibbons Huneker: Critic of the Seven Arts." Unpublished dissertation, Princeton University, 1955.

Rosebault, Charles J. "Huneker as His Friends Saw Him," *New York Times*, Feb. 20, 1921, Sec. 3, p. 14.

———. *When Dana Was* THE SUN. New York: Robert M. McBride, 1931.

Saarinen, Aline B. *The Proud Possessors*. New York: Random House, 1958.

Sanborn, Pitts. New York *Globe*, Feb. 11, 1921, p. 2.

Sard, Frederick. "James Gibbons Huneker—a Tribute," *Musical Observer*, XX (March 1921), 14.

Schapiro, Meyer. "Rebellion in Art," *America in Crisis*, ed. Daniel Aaron. New York: Alfred A. Knopf, 1952.

Schwab, Arnold T. "The Apprenticeship of a Critic: James Gibbons Huneker (1857–1899)." Unpublished dissertation, Harvard University, 1951.

* ———. "Georg Brandes and James Huneker: A Cosmopolitan Friendship," *Modern Language Forum*, XXXVIII (Sept.–Dec., 1953), 30–49.

———. "Huneker's Hidden Birthdate," *American Literature*, XXIII (Nov. 1951), 351–54.

———. "Irish Author and American Critic: George Moore and James Huneker," *Nineteenth-Century Fiction*, VIII (March 1954), 256–71, and IX (June 1954), 22–37.

———. "James Huneker's Criticism of American Literature," *American Literature*, XXIX (March 1957), 64–78.

* ———. "Joseph Conrad's American Friend: Correspondence with James Huneker," *Modern Philology*, LII (May 1955), 222–32.

Scott-James, R. A. *Modernism and Romance*. London: John Lane, 1908.

Seitz, Don C. *Joseph Pulitzer: His Life and Letters*. New York: Simon & Schuster, 1924.

Smith, Bernard. *Forces in American Criticism*. New York: Harcourt, Brace & Co., 1939.

Sonnenschein, Hugo. New York *Herald-Tribune*, June 15, 1924, Sec. 10–11, pp. 3–4.

Stallman, R. W., and Lillian Gilken, eds. *Stephen Crane: Letters*. New York: New York University Press, 1960.

Swinburne, A. C. *Studies in Prose and Poetry*. London: Chatto and Windus, 1894.

Taffer, Thomas. "A Wandering Capellmeister—His Chronicle: James Huneker," *Musical Record and Review*, No. 493 (Feb. 1903), pp. 3–5.

Van Raalte, Joseph. New York *World*, Jan. 30, 1921, Metro. Sec., p. 1.

Van Roosbroeck, G. L. Review of *Essays by James Huneker*, *Romanic Review*, XXII (Jan.–March, 1931), 62–64.

[Viereck, George Sylvester.] "James Huneker: Super-critic," *Current Literature*, XLVII (July 1909), 57–59.

Viereck, George Sylvester. "Let Us Remember James Gibbons Huneker," *American Monthly*, XVII (March 1925), 18.

——. *My Flesh and Blood*. New York: Horace Liveright, 1931.

Waters, Edward N. *Victor Herbert: A Life in Music*. New York: Macmillan Co., 1955.

Weitenkampf, Frank. *Manhattan Kaleidoscope*. New York: Charles Scribner's Sons, 1947.

Whipple, Sidney. New York *Herald-Tribune*, Aug. 26, 1939, p. 5.

Whittington-Egan, Richard, and Geoffrey Smerdon. *The Quest of the Golden Boy*. London: Unicorn Press, 1960.

Wilson, Edmund. "From Maupassant to Mencken" (review of *Letters of James Gibbons Huneker*), *Vanity Fair*, XIX (Dec. 1922), 26.

Wilson, Edmund, ed. *The Shock of Recognition*. New York: Doubleday & Co., 1943.

Wilson, Edmund. "Thoughts on Being Bibliographed," *Princeton University Library Chronicle*, V (Feb. 1944), 55–57.

INDEX